WITNESS

SYSTEMATIC THEOLOGY

VOLUME 3

JAMES WM. MCCLENDON, JR.
with Nancey Murphy

ABINGDON PRESS
Nashville

WITNESS: SYSTEMATIC THEOLOGY, VOLUME 3

This book is printed on recycled, acid-free, elemental-chlorine–free paper.

Library of Congress Cataloging-in-Publication Data

McClendon, James William.
Systematic theology / James Wm. McClendon, Jr.
3 v. ; 23 cm.
Includes bibliographical references and indexes.
Contents: 1. Ethics—2. Doctrine—3. Witness.
ISBN 0-687-12015-2 (v. 1: alk. paper) — ISBN 0-687-11021-1 (v. 2 : alk. paper) — ISBN 0-687-09823-8 (v. 3 : alk. paper)
1. Theology, Doctrinal. 2. Christian ethics. 3. Christian witness. I. Title.
BT75.2 .M392 1986
241'.046—dc19
85-030627

00 01 02 03 04 05 06 07 08 09—10 9 8 7 6 5 4 3 2 1

MANUFACTURED IN THE UNITED STATES OF AMERICA

WITNESS

SYSTEMATIC THEOLOGY

To all my students,
past, present, and future.

Preface

This is the third and final in a three-volume trilogy, and because its argument is cumulative, readers may wish to begin not here but with Volume I, *Ethics*. If they have done so, continuing through *Doctrine: Systematic Theology,* Volume II, much that may seem to beginners doubtful here will have already been made secure. Yet there is no fixed rule about the order of reading, so a word of present explanation about the entire project may again be in order. This *Systematic Theology* addresses first of all Christians who are neither strictly Catholic nor strictly Protestant (e.g., Lutheran or Reformed), but who fall into a numerous if ill-defined third group. For reasons given in Volume I, I call this third group 'baptists' (note the lowercase *b*), but others prefer other names. In any case, this work is meant to reach out to often overlooked believers, but not to exclude the better-defined others: if rightful Catholics and proper Protestants find these pages helpful, I could not be more pleased.

Theology without foundations? For my seventieth birthday, I was honored with a Festschrift (a volume of essays in honor of the recipient) with that seemingly shaky title. Perhaps *Theology Without Foundations* (Hauerwas, Murphy, and Nation, eds., Abingdon, 1994) was a premature celebration of my achievement, though I was indeed in my seventy-first year, so it may be that my friends thought it's now or never. Yet that book did accurately signal the line of direction of this three-volume series and of all my academic work. Others had supposed that since the trilogy provides no introductory volume, my plan was to produce the foundations of systematic theology last. They charitably thought that like a good house builder I must surely have poured a complete concrete foundation before erecting the rest of the structure, only I had concealed it till the end, meaning to show last what had really come first. That was not so.

Witness is something like Christian missiology (the theory of mission and missions) and something like a theology of culture. The latter term is relatively new to theology, but its task, which is to characterize the world in which witness occurs, is as old as the biblical witness itself: the preached and written and enacted word by which God through chosen messengers—a people, a prophet, a Messiah, an apostle—shows the world to itself so that it may more clearly see its God. This is the age-old task, but its current (and temporary?) name is "theology of culture"—a term explained more fully in chapter 1.

Engaging that task brings this volume to look at some forms of current (American) culture (Part I), then to philosophy since in its philosophy the world (the culture) looks at itself (Part II), and in conclusion back to theology proper (Part III). That theology connects tightly with the two previous volumes (*Ethics and Doctrine*), and with it my project ends.

New readers may be puzzled by the appearance, from time to time, of paragraphs of smaller print like this. These are paragraphs that, while worthy of inclusion, do not directly advance the large-print discussion. They may be skipped by a hasty reader, but I hope there will not be many hasty readers, since the work was written slowly and is, I believe, likely to reward those who read slowly as well.

One more preliminary matter: Single quotes (' ') in this work are used as follows: to designate concepts, for quotes within quotes, and as 'scare quotes.' Double quotes (" ") are used for the mention of terms (such as mention of the term "God") and for all other quotations.

No one does such work unaided, and I have many debts of gratitude. I gave invited lectures or discussions on some of this material at the Claremont School of Theology, at Fuller Theological Seminary (especially to groups meeting in my home), and at Baylor University, and tried some of it out on invited groups in the United Kingdom, especially at the London Mennonite Center; Kings College; University of London; Spurgeons College, London; Regents Park College, Oxford; Bristol Baptist College at the University of Bristol; Offa House in the Diocese of Coventry; and the biblical studies department at the University of Manchester. Thanks to Mark Thiessen Nation, Alan Kreider, and their helpers and associates who arranged these appointments, and to all who were my hosts and listeners in these places.

In the Intermountain West, where I studied the earliest Christian (and pre-Christian) religious cultures, I am especially indebted to Andrew Begaye, Edwin Gaustad, John Kinsolving, Fred Vigil, and

LeRoy Moore. In Waco, Texas, a little group gathered to advise me; I remember especially Barry Harvey, Curtis Freeman, Steve Shoemaker, Mikeal Parsons, Heidi Hornik, and Ralph Wood. In New Orleans, where music was king, I remember especially Michael White, Richard B. Allen, Harry Eskew, and Paul Robertson. Back in Pasadena, I am indebted to the faculty restaurant group who read and discussed several chapters, and especially to Linda Wagener, Glen Stassen, Wilbert Shenk, David Scholer, and Donald Hagner, as well as the rest. From many directions I owe debts to Bill Dyrness, Rob Johnston, Durwood Foster, Diogenes Allen, Rosalee Velloso (Ewell), John Dillenberger, Jane Dillenberger, Michael Goldberg, Julian Hartt, Jonathan Wilson, Terrence Tilley, Steve Jolley, Wallace Matson, Merold Westphal, Mark Lazenby, Beate Eulenhoefer, Brad Kallenberg, Heiko Schulz, and Stanley Hauerwas.

Nancey Murphy expresses gratitude to her readers, John Hedley Brooke and Francisco J. Ayala.

For the title of Volume III I am indebted to my colleague Richard Steele. Most of all I express gratitude to the tireless staff at Abingdon, including my editor, Bob Ratcliff, and his coworkers, to James M. Dunn-Smith (formerly James M. Smith) who read critically every word I wrote, and above all these to my wonderful wife, colleague, friend, and fellow theologian—and in this book co-author—Nancey Murphy.

James Wm. McClendon, Jr.
August 2000

Contents

PROSPECT

A shipload of grain from Egypt, the economic lifeblood of the empire and immediate material sustenance of the population of the capital, is caught in a Mediterranean winter storm. The navigator's considerable astronomical knowhow is useless beneath the clouds. The detachment of soldiers under the centurion Julius is firmly in control, but they have no solutions to suggest except, in the crunch, to kill the prisoners. The captain, exercising his expert vocation, makes the wrong decisions, and the sailors, operating in their sphere of competence, try to escape. The salvation of the travelers (and of the cargo, if he had been heard) was the work of the messianic Jew being taken to the capital in chains for trial. He reads the weather better than the captain and has more authority than the centurion. He did not get on the boat with the intention of directing it, much less of saving its occupants. He did not even choose to get on board. But he was on his mission to Rome, and that made him in dramatic juxtaposition to that other missionary Jew in that other Mediterranean storm—the bearer of an efficacious word of salvation for all his fellows. The story does not report that anyone was converted or that Paul planted a church on Malta. Paul and the anonymous author of the "we-narrative" were enough. The two, present in the name of Christ, sharing the lot of those two hundred seventy-six people who were fortuitously all in the same boat bound for disaster, opened for them all, despite themselves, a new life.

The parable makes its point more strongly than I want to [being vulnerable to a Constantinian misreading?], but still it is the point I want to make. The good news for society. . . with which we have been charged is an alternative; it provides relevant wisdom and enabling vision, precisely because its substance is not its own, not a social ethic for society's sake or for the sake of ethics. The New World that is on its way, and is anticipated in the confessing, baptizing, reconciling, thanks-giving, serving community, is also despite itself the future of the yet unhearing world, for the glory of God. "If anyone be in Christ, the creation is new" [II Cor. 5:17].

John Howard Yoder, "Stone and Morgan Lectures," 1979

CHAPTER ONE

What Is Theology of Culture?

Students of theology understandably want to connect what they learn theologically with the rest of what they know. Theology of culture addresses this need. This does not mean that the theology of culture is a foundation on which the rest of theology is erected. Perhaps disappointing to some, this work offers no non-theological foundation to support theology proper. To understand these volumes, readers are asked to set aside the metaphor, so popular ever since Descartes, of a building, an intellectual structure, in this case the theology itself, resting upon something non-theological that is supposed to be more reliable. Such images are not useful in every case. A voyage has no proper 'foundation,' though it has a port of origin and may happily reach its destination. Marriages have no 'foundation,' either, though the partners' growing trust—in each other, in the goodness of God—may make for their success. I hope that the reader here will progress not like the inspector of a building project, but like a spouse in a happy marriage or like one of the sailors on a prosperous voyage.

Still, good theology wants and deserves connections. Consider the following image: We Christians, in the short time that we have existed, as measured by humankind's longer history—perhaps there have been Christians for about a hundred generations?—have all crossed into an unknown realm, in Jesus' phrase "a kingdom"; we have explored its boundaries, discovered its laws, encountered its majesty, found our true selves by finding it. Now, so many Marco Polos, we return to find our homeland a strange country. Unaware of our journey, it speaks a language we had not heard when abroad. Its ways, seen now through our refocused eyes, are at once familiar and questionable. We wish to tell of our exotic journey and to divide our booty with those at home, but can our offer be understood? The image is in several ways defective, yet it has its point; Christians must take their place anew in the old setting. To find the new standpoint in our earthly homeland calls for a Christian critique of its culture; thus will we see where and how the church must stand to be the church.

Recall that the first volume aimed to show how the church must *live* in order to be a living church—in order, we might now say, to make its voyage prosperous, in order to fulfill its nuptial vow. Its theme was *moral* theology. Then the second volume inquired what the church must *teach* if it is to be not only a faithful but also a truthful church. Its theme was *doctrinal* theology. Thus faith and morals, doctrine and ethics. Now a third question implied in the first two: How is a true and faithful church to take its place in the world? How be the church in the world, a witnessing, faithful, effective servant of the rule of God? To answer requires clear vision of the present age.

In a way, then, this volume is in the tradition of Christian missiology, a study that has two formal aspects: the delineation of the mission field, and the strategy and tactics of the mission to that field. Only at the end, though, will this book come to that second aspect; it will be task enough to survey the world to which we come. As to place, the concentration here will be on the Western world, and particularly upon North America. This is not meant to disparage other places of Christian witness; indeed, others may in the long run be more important; it is only meant to present what I know rather than what I do not. As to time, it is helpful to see with Andrew Walls (1990) that we have reached a certain stage of mission history. When Christianity was entirely Jewish, it must have seemed both to insiders and outsiders a contest between versions of Jewishness—one version that recognized Jesus as the promised Messiah and others that did not. A second stage came when, as the book of Acts relates, Christianity crossed a line into the Hellenistic and Roman world. It was at this second stage that most of the New Testament books were written. The Christians in Antioch and elsewhere who had crossed the threshold must have been conscious of the risk they took: what had been "the hope of Israel" (Luke 24:21) was now backstaged, and "Messiah," though still the name attached to Jesus, became for Gentiles a sort of surname, "Christ." So there were losses at this stage, but gains as well. In the Hellenistic-Roman world Christianity was no longer merely a *Way;* now it became a system of thought among other systems. Indeed, had that not happened, perhaps the Hellenistic-Roman world would never have been penetrated. Walls calls a third stage "barbarian Christianity." Two great crises in world history, the collapse of the Western Roman Empire and the emergence of Arabic Islam as a world power, set the new stage. Christianity survived because it crossed the border from old Rome to the new barbarians and by strenuous effort established a standpoint there. "Once again," Walls writes (1990:18), "Christianity had been saved by its cross-cultural diffusion." The fourth and fifth stages will seem familiar to those with a knowledge of modern European history, the fourth that of (both Catholic and Protestant) reformation, and the fifth, nearly simultaneous, the age of expanding Europe with its voyages of discovery that took Europeans around the globe. Yet even as Europe expanded, Christianity in Europe itself began to wane, and there began at this fifth stage a new cross-cultural transplantation of Christianity to the peoples 'discovered' by the voyaging and militant Europeans. We arrive at a sixth stage, the period in which the center of authentic Christian life can more easily be detected in what were once the frontiers, in Nairobi and Seoul, Buenos Aires and Bombay, than it can in the technologically superior West. These expressions of Christianity, Walls says, are becoming the dominant forms of the faith.

The consequence is that at long last churches in the geopolitically dominant West are awakening to find their homelands mission fields. Yet there is as yet no adequate theological interpretation of this Western mission field. For now the theme is no longer discovering a thought-system, as in stage two, or identifying Christianity with barbarian nations, as in stage three, or reforming Christendom, as in stage four, or elevating the primacy of individual decision, as in stage five. For the West now confronts a new 'post-Christendom' culture that does not yield to these old analyses. Just as first-century Jewish Christians were baffled to think that there might be a non-Jewish but true faith, so it may baffle today's churches to find themselves looking across a time boundary that separates an old, 'modern' age from a new age rising. Examining that time-boundary in theological light is a central theme of this volume.

There are sure to be surprises ahead. A first surprise may be to discover the close connection between the world-missionary experience of the eighteenth and nineteenth centuries and the concurrent rise of the social sciences. Pointing out that parallel will be a first step in this chapter. Thus **Section 1 (§1) shows how the very idea of 'culture' was evolved by European thinkers, overseas missionaries, and social scientists working at apparent odds with one another. Then Section 2 (§2) will examine the work of two social scientists, Peter Berger and**

Robert Bellah, who reveal a theological dimension in even the most scientific understandings of culture. Next, Section 3 (§3) picks out a trajectory of recent theological thought about culture, from Paul Tillich to Julian N. Hartt to John Howard Yoder, a path that taken to its end projects this volume's orientation. Finally, Section 4 (§4) considers some interlocked concepts such as *convictions, imperialism,* and *relativism.*

§1. The Modern Invention of Culture

Christian existence is both individual and social, both a journey of individual selves each uniquely qualified as a follower of Jesus and at the same time a journey together, a communal pilgrimage to realize the world newly disclosed in gospel light. These two, the individual and the social, are inseparable: neither occurs apart from the other. There are no solitary disciples (though of course there are lonely ones), nor is there any Christian peoplehood apart from the opening of each pilgrim's eyes to that one light. This eye-opening journey is in principle within reach of every human creature.

> To the LORD belong the earth and everything in it,
> the world and *all its inhabitants.* (Ps. 24:1, emphasized)

Redeemed peoplehood has always an open membership; none is excluded from it:

> "Come!" say the Spirit and the bride [i.e., the church].
> "Come!" let each hearer reply.
> Let the thirsty come. (Rev. 22:17)

These openings to all humanity define Christian selfhood and Christian peoplehood. Together they establish a policy but create a problem. The policy is evangelism, or more broadly, **witness:** authentic Christian existence is always missionary, possessed only to be imparted to others. Yet the policy can be restated as a problem: How shall present sharers of the journey be related to the human world in which they take their journey? What ties cement the people of the journey to the old, broken peoplehood in which once they did and now in a new way they still do have a part? This question of connections, of witness in the world, underlies this concluding volume. Viewed in evangelical terms, here a theology of evangelism is wanted. In more recent parlance, here a theology of culture is required.

One need not know Christian doctrine to be assured of these very general observations about Christians in the world. Take as a focal instance the change that overtook those who heard the gospel in the pre-Christian societies of Oceania two hundred years ago. In a traditional society there may be little motive to leave one's set place with its duties, whether as a wife, a hunter, a boatbuilder, or a tribal chief. Each is merely a *persona,* a representative part of the whole which is felt as enduring, unchanged, fixed in its time and space. Then via its missionaries the gospel came to this traditional world, and those who responded became storied selves: they entered history; they faced the choice of a new selfhood that might put them at odds with their former roles (Burridge, 1978:15f; cf. *Ethics,* Two). Of course such converts are not, or are not long, alone. Ahead of them is a new fellowship, a new destiny, a whole new world (2 Cor. 5:17 REB or NRSV) to be entered, explored, realized. One becomes in storied self-interpretation a man or woman in Christ, and thus one is literally re-membered, rejoined to a previously unacknowledged human whole. One's word for 'human being' can no longer simply be the word for one's own tribe or people. Meantime, what becomes of the traditional peoplehood amid which the storied self has now come to itself? How is the convert to relate to the traditional world of his or her origin? The broad Christian answer is that each follower of the Way is now commissioned as a witness, in but not of his or her world. Witnessing requires a new sociality, a revised engagement with those still fixed in the culture of origin. Pentecost has recurred; the pentecostal celebrants, sharers of the new that comes in Christ, must explicitly impart that new or be at risk of implicitly denying it (Burridge, 1991:44-48). The believers who appear in the New Testament, engaging their own pre-Christian societies, recognize this risk. "Many are invited," they heard Jesus say, "but few are chosen" (Matt. 22:14). Not all the sown seed springs up to lasting life. Jesus plaintively asks his disciples, as the crisis of the cross nears, "Do you, also, want to leave?" (John 6:67).

Many perplexities face both the missionary from far away and the convert at home among the people of the land. Is the present culture hopelessly corrupt? Or is it itself God's work, a gift to this people that reflects the pied beauty of creation? Or is existing culture partly each, part wholesomely human, part devilishly corrupt? The question presents one of the central tasks of this volume. Answering will require the collective wisdom of missionary and converts, light from holy Scripture with its central christological narrative, unceasing prayer, love, and persistent colloquy. Answering is a task for each generation and for cumulative tradition also; it always requires Holy Spirit in holy church. Nor do the questions vanish when after centuries or millennia the gospel seems domesticated in a culture, shaping it and shaped by it. Theology of culture does not end on the mission field—or rather, that field is all the world (Matt. 13:38), including our own world. Conversions, whether instant or gradual, the creation of storied selves and their discovery of a whole new world, bring up afresh the task of witness in old 'Christian' cultures as they do in new fields. So, too, does that task arise in post-Christendom cultures where the once-central gospel is sidelined as gods change.

Scripture tells of a series of such cross-cultural engagements: Abraham leaves his ancestral home and its culture but arrives in a "promised" land to find already there a culture—one in which shortly his kinsman Lot will narrowly escape destruction (Gen. 12:1–19:29). Israel in Egypt at first gains a powerful hand in the imperial culture (Joseph), but in time Israel is enslaved and cries out to God for (cultural) deliverance. Escaped to the Sinai, Israel is shown a new cultural possibility, one that will require a new land (Exod. 12:37–13:16); in Canaan, that possibility is realized in part by tribal co-existence and kingly rule, but only in part. God's prophets look forward to revision, a fulfillment of the primal promise in their current history and ultimately its fulfillment beyond all conceivable history (Minear, 1946:Part III). In exile and diaspora, JHWH turns Israel's tragedy into a new Jewish possibility: Holy peoplehood (Exod. 19:6*a*) is disclosed as a reality not dependent upon Canaan's land; more than ever Jewish peoplehood in its diaspora grows missionary. In this ripening situation (Scripture calls it "the fullness of time"—Gal. 4:4 KJV) Jesus of Nazareth appears; he acknowledges the earlier peoplehood as authentic, yet by prophetic word and even more by prophetic deed he revises its cultural shape. His resurrection from a shameful (culturally imposed) death empowers his followers to move to the realization of his vision of peoplehood; in that task the new missionaries, none more than Paul, take their 'apostolic' part. In a relatively few centuries these efforts appear to meet with overwhelming success. The world, or more accurately the world that is focused on Rome's Mediterranean *(mare nostrum)*, becomes officially 'Christian,' yet that has disastrous consequences for Jewish people and unhappy ones for Jesus' people as well. When at long last in the Enlightenment the Constantinian arrangements begin to be withdrawn, the outcome is a slow withdrawal of European culture (as by a receding Dover tide) from the gospel itself! Thereby the cultural shape of the world is reconformed, and a new question appears: In this age, what of the heritage of Abraham and Moses, Jesus and Paul? What of the peoplehood they constituted? How is its witness now to engage this present culture?

a. The theological context of modern culture.—"Culture" in its present-day sense is a modern invention. We say the apostle Paul confronted the cultures of his day, but in saying this we project our own thought-world upon him. Biblical writers speak of the mission to all *nations*

(Matt. 28:19f); they tell us God loved the *world* (John 3:16); they describe the site of missionary labor as a *field* to be sown and harvested (Matt. 13:3-43); but the use of "culture" that seems so natural to us today only began in the early nineteenth century. How this happened is relevant to our task. Two historic passages marked the preceding century in Great Britain. One was the *industrial revolution,* which mercilessly excavated and pulverized human resources as steam power mechanized the production, first of cloth in Lancashire mills and a little later of iron and steel in Newcastle and Birmingham. The other eighteenth-century passage was the *evangelical revival* of Christian faith associated with the name of John Wesley (1703–91). Social historians find a connection here: the increase in population, and relocation of persons, families, and entire villages to towns and cities in order to work in the mills, with the entailed harsh devaluing of human life, opened a great door for the Wesleyan gospel: all had sinned and must face judgment, but a new life here and now was available by faith in the grace of Jesus Christ. This was an old Christian message, proclaimed in Britain since Roman days, but in Wesley it passed through a new door to address human need. Evangelical conversions multiplied across Britain, and soon in colonial America (the Great Awakening) as well. A learned man with a deep sense of wholesome religion that would inform all of life, Wesley with his allies organized the Christian lives of followers into discernible stages: infant baptism had admittedly canceled original sin, but this was of little advantage to all who subsequently sinned. Prevenient grace restored the power to accept God's offer of salvation, but conversion was required to secure forgiveness, and even after conversion the tendency to sin lingered: one might by sinning lose salvation and require yet another fresh start, or (in the happier case) converts might progress until they attained Christian *perfection* (or 'perfect love') which freed them from even the disposition to sin (McClendon, 1953:46-58). Thus *holiness* or *perfection* was restored afresh to Christian practice as it had been in primitive times and again in the monastic movement and later still, the Radical Reformation. Still linked with the state church and its liturgies, the Wesleyan evangelicals formed class meetings, little churches within the larger church, to supplement the existing institution. In the lay-led class meetings converts could be disciplined (hence the term "methodism") into progress toward perfection. When, around 1800, the newly formed societies for foreign missions combined several denominations' efforts to dispatch missionaries, their volunteers included men and women strongly shaped by this Wesleyan ideal of holiness.

This corrects a grievous mistake in Christopher Herbert's *Culture and Anomie* (1991:159-70 et pass.). Herbert's thesis is that the labors of nineteenth-century missionaries to the South Pacific produced marvelous ethnographic reports of native cultures, but that these (and those of the cultural anthropologists who succeeded them!) were all flawed by a repressive attitude toward human life generally, and particularly so toward the cultures of the islanders they so diligently studied. The fault, Herbert believes, lies in the "Wesleyan doctrine of original sin" by which he says missionaries construed all cultures (save their own?) devilish. He bases this crippling misunderstanding on a few passages in Wesley's published sermons and their echo in missionary writings. But Herbert shows little sensitivity to Wesleyan (or more generally, to evangelical) rhetoric, and seems quite unaware of the liberating (rather than repressive) effect of the gospel upon its nineteenth-century hearers—a fulfillment of desire rather than its denial.

b. Culture as society's perfection.—The concern for total human well-being that stirred in the Wesleyan revival affected other British Christians as well. John Henry Newman (1801–90) progressed from his own youthful evangelical conversion to become a leader in the Oxford Movement, which sought to re-catholicize the Anglican Church, and then, dissatisfied, he entered the Church of Rome. Newman's enduring concerns transposed those of the evangelicals but did not discard them: each life, captured by Christ, must sense itself part of a greater whole, the church catholic, and must be formed accordingly. In his Roman Catholic stage, though, Newman found the liberty radically to rethink the demand of the Christian message upon society. Lecturing in 1852 on the scope and nature of university education, the scholar-priest groped in vain for a single English term that would describe "simply and generally" society's "intellectual proficiency or *perfection*"—the goal toward which human existence must strive as its proper end (Newman, 1873:93f). This *perfection* is the organizing concept that would come to be called "culture."

It is remarkable that Newman himself did not label this human goal "culture." Nor did Samuel Taylor Coleridge (1772–1834) seize the term, though like Newman he spoke of "the bloom of health" of a civilization "grounded in cultivation." "Culture" finally appeared in Matthew Arnold (1822–88), who in *Culture and Anarchy* (1869) attempted to renew the English vision of a people's *wholeness* (thus introducing "culture" in its full modern sense), promoting an education for workingmen that would offer them the sweetness and light of humanity at its *perfect* best. Only such a quest for national integrity, Arnold believed, could resist the blight of the industrial revolution and its "anarchy." Coleridge and Arnold invoked a class of 'cultured' national leaders, the "clerisy," who could guide society into its own best ways. To the clerisy they assigned the obligation previously borne by the Christian clergy. Finally, the call to culture expressed a concern for the survival of the nation itself. The alternative to such cultural stewardship, as Arnold's title proclaimed, was anarchy. For the advocates of English culture had their eyes firmly fixed not merely on individuals but on "the spirit of the nation" (Raymond Williams, 1958:11).

Yet while Wesley had found the path to perfection in the corporate cultivation of redeemed souls, and Newman in the recovery of a Christian society informed by Catholic universities, Anglicans from Coleridge to Arnold to F. D. Maurice faced a severe difficulty: the education they proposed for the perfection of human existence had no clear content, no organic center. Thus Arnold says that "culture, which is the study of perfection, leads us . . . to conceive of true human perfection as a *harmonious* perfection, developing all sides of our humanity, and as a *general* perfection, developing all parts of our society" (Arnold, 1869:Preface). Yet 'culture' was hardly value-free; all its champions saw it not so much a given to be preserved as a prize to be gained by valiant struggle. Within that struggle lay a great problem: how could a society that increasingly recognized its own historic relativity fulfill the demand of culture if culture meant (as to them it did) *perfection*? (Raymond Williams, 1958:110-30).

The parallel development in Germany had a different origin. Whereas Britain's predicament had arisen with the industrial revolution, intellectual leaders in German-speaking Europe sought a defense for the Germanic way of life (there was as yet no nation named Germany) that could protect it against Napoleon's aggressive and politically more powerful France. Here the role of the British clerisy was to be filled by a *Bildung* (development) inculcated by the rising middle class of bureaucrats in Germany's little states, especially Prussia, and by a new class, the increasingly prominent university professors. This development was to produce *Kultur* in the sense of the *ideal* of learning "as an antithesis to instrumental, institutional training." *Bildung* was thus linked to education, yet not to mere technology but to the ideals of inner growth and integral self-development. As in England, *Kultur* was closely associated with the rise of a nation-state, to be formed around Prussian hegemony. Germans contrasted their *Kultur* with the mere 'civilization' they perceived in France: the latter was only political and social; while 'culture' was refined, ennobling, the realm of spirituality or *Geist* (Masuzawa, 1998:75f).

c. Culture as wholeness.—The deep problem that confronted nineteenth-century thinkers from Edmund Burke to Matthew Arnold was made more perplexing by their realization that existing European (and derivatively, American) society was strongly shaped by its historical relation to the Christian message: this was the involvement that H. Richard Niebuhr, influenced by German theory, later sought to sort out in his *Christ and Culture* (1951). This difficulty was one from which the missionaries were blessedly free, since their fields of labor, India or Africa or Oceania, were almost untouched by Christianity. This difference is highly relevant to the development of our present-day understanding of culture, since these missionaries, turned ethnographers, form a link between the Anglo-German sense of culture as perfection and the later anthropological meaning of a culture as any whole way of life.

As it was understood, English (or German) culture bound a people together by preserving their best aspirations. This cohesive view was not lost on the missionaries who just before 1800 began to enter lands unknown, to learn and inscribe new languages, and to record their findings, all as a necessary prelude to evangelization. The difference was that the missionaries could see, as their European contemporaries might not see, that there was not one culture but many. This was the awareness that would later issue in problematic cultural relativism (§4 below).

No one has brought out more clearly than 'postmodern' literary scholar Christopher Herbert the role of the missionaries as the link between the literary culture-theorists (e.g., Coleridge) and the later cultural anthropologists (e.g., Malinowski). Missionary-ethnographers and anthropologist-ethnographers addressed the same concerns (what constituted the 'whole way of life' that they studied?); they employed the same method (this came to be called 'thick description' or 'close reading' of cultures); and they confronted the same baffling limit (the absence of any neutral standpoint from which to *interpret* the pattern of life that constitutes a given peoplehood). In particular, Christian missionaries like others were troubled by the role of religion in (or as) a culture: Is religion an aspect of culture, or a mere synonym for culture, or is it something that (à la Matthew Arnold) somehow transcends a culture? Finally, to what degree are the modern concepts of culture (and human selfhood) created by modernity rather than merely discovered, so that as modernity wanes, 'culture' in the modern sense will wane with it, producing "a fundamental reconfiguration of the dominant logic of culture" (Masuzawa, 1998:70-75)?

To answer, one must consider the role of Christian missionaries afresh. Not only have they made us aware that the understanding of culture depends on patient, massive, detailed *description* by participant observers. They also showed long ago (and showed by dreadful example, from the viewpoint of later cultural anthropologists) that every interpretation of a culture is just that, an *interpretation*, bringing powerfully into question whether *any* interpretive standpoint can be suitably, totally neutral and non-judgmental.

With regard to the empirical contribution of missionaries to culture studies, the eighteenth- and nineteenth-century missionaries found it impossible to learn native languages well enough to proclaim the Christian gospel without learning as well the whole way of life embodied in a language. Christopher Herbert, despite his bias just noted, provides a fair summary of this missionary project, for example calling attention to missionary William Ellis's report of his years among the Tahitians. Ellis interrupted one of his missionary narratives of a water journey to provide a detailed account of their vessel's construction that "continues for another eighteen pages . . . leading successively into explanation of the various categories of Tahitian canoes and all their many ritual, military, and everyday functions, of the principles governing the names bestowed on them, of canoe manufacturing methods and systems of payment, of the dangers to native mariners from sharks, of their superstitious cults of shark gods, and of other related matters as well." Ellis implies that "every cultural formation such as a canoe or a god must be viewed *as a system* intricately constructed according to an internal logic of its own" (Herbert, 1991:188f). This is exactly the principle of research which the professional cultural anthropologists such as Malinowski and Mead adopted from their missionary predecessors. Culture could no longer be one thing worldwide; the 'complex whole' of European culture theory was forced by such research to bow to unnumbered complex wholes, the one culture replaced by the many.

Yet there was a second, still more controversial inheritance from missionary to anthropologist: the problem of the *standpoint* from which a culture might be interpreted or given *meaning*. Here Herbert's critical theory serves him well, for he shows that just as the missionaries, in their struggle to combine objectivity with their missionary purposes, ran into a profound inner conflict, so did the cultural anthropologists. Herbert contrasts the selfless fieldwork described by Bronislaw Malinowski in his classic work *Argonauts of the Western Pacific* (1921), in which we learn about the complex exchange rituals of the Trobriand Islanders and many another details of island life, with Malinowski's simultaneously kept but only later published *Diary* (1967), in which the islanders whom he has so scientifically and non-judgmentally recorded appear now as "niggers" and "savages"; finally Malinowski quotes Joseph Conrad's Kurtz: "Exterminate the brutes." The enlightened scientist, Herbert comments, "suddenly seems an imposter; the legitimacy of the whole enterprise of empathetic ethnographic study which

Malinowski's work had fostered seemed compromised," for now the morally neutral fieldwork seems to have been "a vehicle and screen for the very different motive of social disaffection," a subtle form of exploitation of the Trobrianders and their kind (Herbert, 1991:154f).

Even apart from such revelations, cultural anthropology has been forced by its own self-searching honesty to reconsider its character and purpose. Where an earlier survey could list some two hundred definitions of anthropology provided by the anthropologists themselves (Kroeber and Kluckhohn, n.d.), it began to be clear that such variety reflected the role of the science itself, which not only provided 'thick description,' but (like the scorned missionaries) brought to this description a "mental chart" or "pattern" or "interpretation" (these terms are the ethnographers' own) in order to assimilate the data into the wanted *meaningful* whole. Yet the patterns were far from value-free; like their other predecessors the English and German culture-theorists, the anthropologists brought to their work what could not be found in it. Thus Clifford Geertz writes:

> To set forth symmetrical crystals of significance, purified of the material complexity in which they were located, and then attribute their existence to autogenous principles of order, universal properties of the human mind, or vast a priori *Weltanschaungen*, is to pretend a science that does not exist and imagine a reality that cannot be found. Cultural analysis is (or should be) guessing at meanings, assessing the guesses, and drawing explanatory conclusions from the better guesses, not discovering the Continent of Meaning and mapping out its bodiless landscape. (Geertz, 1973:20)

§2. Insight from Sociologists of Religion

While those social scientists who labored in exotic mountain kingdoms and remote ocean islands usually called themselves cultural anthropologists, those who labeled themselves sociologists usually sought to apply similar methods to Western society. Apart from the highly specialized views of Karl Marx's followers (views that offer little space for any sort of religion), the most prominent stream of these finds its source in yet another European, Max Weber (1864–1920). Weber's notable followers in the United States include Talcott Parsons and C. Wright Mills as well as those next considered here, American sociologists Peter L. Berger, since 1981 professor at Boston University, and Robert N. Bellah, now retired from his chair in sociology at the University of California, Berkeley, but still active in the religion and society area of the Graduate Theological Union there. The rather exceptional Christian credentials of these two make them worthy of a hearing as we investigate the relations between culture, science, and theology.

a. Berger.—Probably Peter L. Berger (1929–) wrote no book better known than his *Social Construction of Reality* (1966), in which, with his co-author Thomas Luckmann, he made the impressive claim that social reality (whatever in a worldview is construed as 'the real world') is not only the cause of the *outlook* or standpoint of those who inhabit it (thus cultures create outlooks); paradoxically, their social perception of reality is the cause of a people's world or culture *itself* (thus outlooks create cultures). Berger and Luckmann analyze this chicken-and-egg relation in three stages: human beings *externalize* their perceptions, assigning them to the real world; they *objectify* these external projections, which thereby acquire independent reality; they *internalize* anew this external 'reality' that they perceive. These three can easily be found in the appearance of religion among human beings. As Berger described this in a second book, *The Sacred Canopy,* perceptions of the sacred or numinous occur in all primitive societies. These perceptions are 'externalized,' projected upon the skies (thus sky-gods are recognized) and upon persons and natural objects (hence shamans and sacred groves and springs). The externalized sacred objects thereby acquire status as factors in social life (so magic, incantation, and worship arise). One may wonder if this 'social construction of reality' is so sure to occur, but Berger and Luckmann answer that unlike other animals *Homo sapiens* has a native social instability. Not guided by instinct alone as other animals are, man must forever be 'creating' a social world. To be oneself, one must occupy a place in the social order, and to do so there must *be* such an order. To provide it, human beings continually project, objectify, and internalize the order they (humanly) require. Yet when anyone's or any group's grip on this human construct, on the perceived world, totters, say due to the death of one's dear spouse or due to a people's capture, enslavement, and exile, then the order of things can be seriously destabilized. But here religion comes to the rescue: the gods and the realm that they occupy provide a "sacred canopy," protecting ordered human existence from threats to its existence (1967:4-25).

Eventually, though, a new problem may arise: what if some *members* of a society cease to support the sacred order, rebel against its central cultural convictions? In fact, Berger says, this is just what has happened, and happened in biblical history: Abraham and Paul alike abandoned their ancestral social homes in order to obey a call from God. In the heritage made possible by their pioneering action, society or peoplehood was no longer the inevitable outcome of birth in a particular community: "Choice" had become the operative term. Twelve tribes, or one of them, or finally just one individual might elect to follow the God of Abraham—or might not. This leads to the final step: In the modern world the option is no longer merely which god; it may be no god at all. In practice, that last is secular modernity's standard choice. See now what has become of the sacred canopy and of the entire world or reality constructed by our ancestors: it has vanished, for in a world where anyone may choose anything, the social fabric is forever ripped apart. Showing that this is so, Berger rather ruefully writes, has given his book *The Sacred Canopy* the look of an atheist tract! (1967:xvi). Yet this atheistic appearance is misleading, for Berger intends only to describe the development of modernity, not to endorse it. He is a practicing Christian, indeed a rather traditional Lutheran. Thus in subsequent writings (1969, 1979, 1992) he has *defended* his own believing standpoint and provided a *rationale* for Christian belief under modern conditions.

The *defense* of Christian belief in Berger's *Rumor of Angels* (1969) is that just because there is pluralism, making choice necessary, it does not follow that none of the choices is correct. It is still perfectly possible that some choice corresponds to the way things actually are. Sociological relativism makes no truth-claim that rules out the truth of Christian belief; it merely declines to ratify it or any other sort of belief. Though a sociologist, Peter Berger can rightfully choose to be a Christian "*sola fide*," by faith alone—as a Lutheran must. For "once we grasp our own situation in sociological terms, it ceases to impress us as an inexorable fate" (1969:50-81).

b. Bellah.—While Berger seems happy to keep sociology and theology distinct, insisting only that neither denies the validity of the other, Robert N. Bellah (1927–) is more inclined to see them as inseparable: Though religious systems are *objects* for study, he once wrote, the sociologists who study them need also to apprehend themselves as religious *subjects*. So the sociologist of religion "must have a kind of double vision" (Bellah, 1970:256). Bellah means to have such vision. He tells us that though in student years he turned from his childhood Christian faith to Marxism, he recovered from this period of religious doubt by reading Paul Tillich, whose 'symbolic' account of religion eased Bellah's youthful difficulties (Bellah, 1970:xi-xxi). In recent years he has worshiped in an Episcopal parish church. How can this religious loyalty be reconciled with the objectivity demanded of a social scientist? To answer, it helps to review Bellah's theoretical development. His early sociological stance on religion was evolutionary: religion was "a process of increasing differentiation and complexity of organization that endows [it] with greater capacity to adapt to its environment," he wrote in a 1964 article, and religion itself was the "set of symbolic forms and acts that relate man to the ultimate conditions of his existence" (1970:21). By its own evolutionary development, religion is humanity's adaptive response to present circumstances: Why, then, need any objective person spurn anything so characteristically human? So the endless diversity of human religions was explained to Bellah's satisfaction, but that did not satisfy his idealistic hunger for a grand cohesion. What could pull the human world together into a comprehensive (cultural or religious) whole?

At that stage Bellah summoned up (from Rousseau and Cicero) the old concept of a civil religion. As an alternative to the divided and divisive religion of Christian churches, here was an outlook that should unite all. "Civil religion" was not in Bellah's use a form of national self-idolatry, not a substitution of faith in the nation for faith in God, but was an attitude of national humility and reverence, well expressed for Americans by their national holidays and often epitomized in the public religious utterances of the nation's presidents from George Washington to John F. Kennedy. The United States constituted a nation "under God," one whose way of life implied a recognition of "ultimate reality" (Bellah, 1970:168-84). Yet caution implicit in this programmatic piece soon evolved into full-fledged disquiet about the state of religion in America. In 1975 Bellah published *The Broken Covenant: American Civil Religion in Time of Trial,* a jeremiad warning of the perils the civil religion faced whenever it lost the insights of Puritans such as John Winthrop and model republicans such as Thomas Jefferson. Then, climactically, *Habits of the Heart* (Bellah et al., 1985) provided sociological backing for the *Broken Covenant*'s sermon: though America seemed to lose its way, a proper sociological interpretation of the national character disclosed a road to redemption.

Habits's peroration (chapter 11, "Transforming American Culture") pleads for a return to America's biblical and republican heritage. Social commitment has been replaced, it laments, by self-realization, private vacations are more valued than public holidays, poets write chiefly about themselves, individual affluence is rated higher than "moral ecology." In correction, *Habits of the Heart* seeks "to combine social concern with ultimate concern" (the latter is a Tillichian term) in a way that slights the claims of neither (1985:296). "Communities of memory" effectively link some moderns to the past, providing ways of self-understanding and community-understanding that bind past and present together.

Certainly there are more sociologists of religion than Berger and Bellah. R. Stephen Warner claims a "paradigm shift" typified by himself, Rodney Stark, Robert Wuthnow, Nathan Hatch, and others who no longer follow Berger's "European" paradigm by treating "secularization" as the main theme of religion in the U.S.A., but who instead construe religious groups on the model of economic competition in a struggle for mastery in an "open religious market" (Warner, 1993). It may be that workers in this paradigm can gather useful information not available to others. I fear, though, that sharers in Christian peoplehood gain even less self-understanding via a model of free-market economy than via that of a sacred canopy, for the Warner model, unlike that of Berger and Bellah, makes theology irrelevant.

c. The scope and limits of sociology.—What is the harvest of the Weber-Durkheim-Parsons sociological tradition represented by Peter Berger and Robert Bellah? Does either of these, or both taken together, or any new paradigm, show the required path for Christian community vis-à-vis its host culture? If the answer is, Partly, or even, No, this should not be taken to deny the independent value of these studies, far less the value of social science itself. The sociological (or scientific) standpoint they represent is important, not least because it typifies widely shared beliefs about the matters they address. Nevertheless, some cautions are now in order.

First, one must note an important difference in our two examples. Berger as noted is at considerable pains to keep his sociological and his Christian convictions in separate compartments. Values, or at least Christian values or convictions, play for Berger no part in sociology as such. Bellah, on the other hand, is eager to present sociology as a kind of public philosophy which takes a definite convictional stand; for him the sociologists' task, like that of the cultural anthropologists, is to create a sort of philosophical anthropology, which for Bellah will be broadly Christian. At first glance, Bellah seems closer to what I will attempt here: Acknowledge one's standpoint (Christian, in our cases), and take the chances with one's work that this incurs. While that puts one's Christian convictions at risk (for what if the outcome is shabby science or bad theology?), it has the merit of showing readers exactly where a theorist stands. This seems fair. On a second look, though, perhaps Bellah is not so straightforward about what he is doing. We recall that *Habits* found a grand resource for recovering authentic American convictions in "communities of memory." Clearly, some of these are churches. Yet are communities of memory *as such* really what Bellah favors? What if (as suggested in a 1987 review by James M. Smith of *Habits of the Heart*) an articulate and aggressive community devoted to the memory of ideologist Ayn Rand, for whom selfishness was a primary virtue and self-interest the goal of life, puts forward its traditional vision? Would that satisfy Bellah's call for "communities of memory"? Or what if an articulate Ku Klux Klansman argued that his community of memory, with its nostalgic, flag-wrapped patriotism accompanied by rabid racism, stood in the line Bellah admires? Doubtless Bellah would hope neither would, yet *Habits* offers no way to rule them out. Could it be that Bellah's liberal goodwill here obscures the actual convictions he favors and means to promote?

Berger's case is different. In an appendix to *The Sacred Canopy* concerning "Sociological and Theological Perspectives" he insists with vigor that if anyone should believe that theological (or anti-theological) implications are to be sought anywhere in that book's argument, "I can only assure him that he is mistaken" (1967:Appendix II). Of course not all values are in a strict sense theological values, and Berger may only mean that here he is not trying to theologize. Yet a page or two later he writes that the big question is whether "in a world of socio-historical relativity" one can find any standpoint from which to make "cognitively valid statements about religious matters." Indeed that is a big question, and one that I like others must reckon with (see §3 and §4 in this chapter and Part II within). Curiously, though, Berger fails to mention that another big question is whether in such a world as ours one can make "cognitively valid statements" about *sociological* matters. Surely what is sauce for the goose . . . ? Is it sociology when one sees religion as world-maintenance, with God—if there be a God—as the maintainer of the status quo, but theology when one notes a major exception to this view of religion's human role, an exception in which God persistently *overturns* most human religion? Surely, for sociology and theology even to disagree, they have to show up on the same playing field? And they do so frequently, not least in Berger's own work.

Similar points can be made about Bellah's project. Exactly what, for example, is the role of "communities of memory" according to *Habits of the Heart*? Theologically expressed, they mediate salvation to their members, and this insight about the role of the church is an old Christian theme. (Cyprian of Carthage put it this way: *extra ecclesiam nulla salus*—outside the church there is no salvation.) Yet, as I have just argued, the attempt to universalize the old Latin motto so that it says "salvation comes through communities of memory *in general*" is sociologically *and* theologically mistaken; it just isn't so, as Cyprian knew, and as the Ayn Rand and Ku Klux Klan cases show well enough.

These thoughts remind one of the recent work of John Milbank, who has argued that modern social science in general is founded on theological presuppositions that historical Christianity has judged heretical or false. Thus the claim of social science 'discourse' to override Christian theology, 'placing' Christian faith and practice as it pleases, is itself misplaced, since social science typically begs the question by assuming at the outset the contraries of the Christian views it means to override (Milbank, 1990; 1997; see the discussion of Milbank in Murphy and Ellis, 1996:111-14). Thus Milbank proposes in his own way what I have said above, that when they discuss religion, social theory and theology inevitably show up on the same playing field, in position to defeat each other's concrete claims.

Certainly theology needs empirical facts and scientific theoretical insights. The social scientists offer help. Yet they do not accomplish what I must now attempt. My main question is where and how the church must stand to be the witnessing church; that is, what must be the relation between the culture that is the church (and the larger Christian and biblical metaculture the church represents) and those cultures the church indwells, evangelizes, serves? Answering will require all the resources that Christian theology can bring to bear, and not a little help from such as Berger and Bellah as well. Already they have showed us, willy-nilly, that theology is required for the task: they make such ample (and often skillful) use of it, themselves!

§3. A Theological Trajectory

Recent theological discussion of culture has often, perhaps too often, turned on the attractive thesis of H. Richard Niebuhr (1894–1962), who found he could resolve Christian relations with culture into a series of types that stretched from Christ-against-culture to the-Christ-of-culture; among these the favorite, a recurrent rainbow that had appeared here and there through the ages, was Christ-the-transformer-of-culture" (1951:chap. 6). Soon theologians of every stripe decided that this way of transformation, a golden mean among the extremes, was exactly their own.

A spectrum of ideal 'types,' the social scientists' sense of "typology," is usually designed to show real differences, not to achieve unanimous endorsement of one type. The failure of H. R. Niebuhr's typology lay just at this point: it did not genuinely distinguish the real differences among Christian approaches to culture: Few or none recognized themselves in the extreme types—for flagrant example, one he called "Christ against culture"—that Niebuhr subtly disparaged: his instances of counter-cultural Christianity (Tertullian the Roman lawyer and Latin stylist, Leo Tolstoy the Russian landlord, novelist, and prophet, for example) contravened their type, since each of these in one way or another escaped the necessary "againstness" of the type (J. H. Yoder in Stassen et al., 1996:31-90). H. R. Niebuhr's sociological mentors included Max Weber (whom we thus meet again) and Ernst Troeltsch; he wrote his doctoral dissertation on the latter.

Nevertheless, religion-and-culture arrangements do differ. H. R. Niebuhr's failure (still unacknowledged by many of his partisans) to provide a useful way to sort out various theologies of culture does not indicate that the effort is useless, but perhaps that the starting point was incorrect. Given his sociological mentors, it seemed natural to him to treat the world of European culture, perhaps in its modified American version, as the given, the starting point, and then to consider how "Christ" (the living Christian spirit of that culture) might be related to it. Thus "culture" became an empirical given; "Christ" must adjust to it in one of five typical ways (H. R. Niebuhr, 1951:chap. 1). What follows in this volume is a different starting-point, one that must be judged by its own success or failure in displaying the church's role in the world and the world's role for the church. One difference is that the biblical religion that takes shape as church is just as much a given, a fact, a cultural datum as is the culture of Germany or Georgia—or New Haven, Connecticut. The question Niebuhr meant to answer is how an ideal Christ, one "who does not direct attention away from this world to another; but from all worlds, present and future" could connect with a tangible, existing world of "culture" (1951:28). The result was a misconstrual of both sides of the problem. So this book will attempt no smooth Niebuhrian scale of types but will stake out a very different approach.

Consider these facts: Prior to modern times the churches' unity, even in face of much refuting evidence, was often assumed. In modernity's fading light, though, 'the church' has come increasingly to be seen as the reality that it always was: not *one* but many, not always *holy* though frequently counted sacred, not *catholic,* that is, everywhere one, but situated and thus necessarily diverse, not consistently *apostolic* even where stubbornly hierarchical. Such a church (or in Scripture's preferred vocabulary, such a people of God) constituted by diverse Christian peoplehoods, frequently disconnected from its own past, often at odds with itself, rejected on human scales of value yet nevertheless "chosen by God and precious . . . a kingdom of priests, a holy nation, a people . . . to sing the praises of God" (1 Pet. 2:4, 9 NJB)—such a complex people or church or company of God's folk is one (complex) datum of a truly Christian theology of culture. The theologian of culture stands within that empirical reality.

Hunger for a new sense of church to replace failed ones may be the driving force behind the twentieth century's foremost contribution to church history: If the sixteenth century was marked by reform and the nineteenth century by expansion (thus Latourette, 1953:chaps. xxx-lv), was not the twentieth century the time when the Christian movement acknowledged its essential brokenness, dividedness—and displayed enormous ecumenical energy to overcome this failing? One notes the formation during this century of the World Council of [Protestant and Orthodox] Churches (1948), the ecumenical council called Vatican II (1962–65), and parallel though less successful, the World Evangelical Fellowship (1951).

The question addressed in the chapters that follow is not whether American society is being "transformed by Christ" (who is in position to say whether it is or not?). Instead, they ask whether *the church* at some given times and places—in particular congregations, ecclesial bodies, international councils—is or is not itself fitly in step with the gospel of the kingdom. The persistent underlying question is whether a people chosen as God's own is being converted as it seeks to convert others, whether there is mutual *metanoia* (repentance). For the congregation (or denomination, or world fellowship of churches) that ceases in its neglect of the New Testament's gospel to transmit the new in Christ, or ceases to be itself transformed by that newness, cannot truly be the community of word and worship, work and witness commissioned by the Risen One (see *Doctrine,* Six). When that community corrodes, the church descends either into moralism or into pietism—or congeals into rationalism. These first two have been the chief temptations of American Christian existence. Will Christian morality become moralism? Will Christian experience become pietism? (Haroutunian, 1932). The Niebuhrian typology starts at the wrong place to pick these out; it cannot show how moralism and pietism, wherever they fall on his scale, alike miss the point of the gospel.

a. Paul Tillich.—Keeping the preceding cautions in mind, then, here is an alternative strategy for the theology of culture. The departure-point for its trajectory is not H. R. Niebuhr but a German refugee from Nazism, Paul Tillich (1886–1965). Germany's defeat and despair after the Great War of 1914–18 drove many to embrace the religious socialism associated with Hermann Kutter, Leonhard Ragaz, and other radicals (Welch, 1972–85:II, 247-50). (An earlier, American parallel to this Swiss-German movement was the Social Gospel—see Chapter Two §4.) Sharing the standpoint of these religious socialists, in 1919 Tillich delivered in Berlin an address that defined a new (at the very least, a verbally new) conception. This brilliant young Protestant theologian said that the cumulative changes Europe had lately experienced could no longer be accommodated by minor shifts in religious thinking: an entirely new task stood at hand. This was the *theology of culture* (as opposed to church theology). It sought an overlooked or rejected religious dimension in the depths of despairing secularity. For some centuries the West had traded upon its heritage from a monolithic medieval world in which science, art, and culture in general were church-directed; now this time was past. The religious dimension of culture was no longer to be symbolized by the church (which might nevertheless retain a less prominent role); now the religious dimension was to be found in the various autonomous spheres of *secular* society. Thus theology's task was no longer to discover and revise the church's basic convictions; its main work was the discovery of implicit religion lurking in society's crevices (Tillich, 1919).

This 1919 lecture foreshadowed many themes of Tillich's subsequent writing—the end of the Protestant era, religion rather than God as theology's central concern, culture as the form to which religion offered substance, ultimate concern as the essence of religion, expressive art as the clue to culture, and "correlation" with culture (more precisely, with philosophy) as theology's overriding goal (see e.g. Tillich, 1951–63: vol. I, vii; 1957; 1959). The theses of the 1919 lecture were not strictly new: Kant had argued that religion's real concern was expressed in (philosophical) ethics; Schleiermacher had taught that authentic religion sprang from a pre-conceptual awareness *(Gefühl)* that underlay all knowledge, all morality; Hegel had seen cultural values and religion inseparable. Tillich, however, reassembled these nineteenth-century insights into a new synthesis. The old moral certainties represented by natural law and by the more recent thrust of religious socialism were replaced by insights drawn from secular culture.

Tillich brought this strategy with him to the United States of America, a culture that was not recently defeated in war, was not (yet) highly secularized, and had not maintained a state church. In this new setting Tillich nevertheless applied his German lessons, teaching American students to look away from the church in order to discover religious depth. (In this tendency he was joined by second-generation German-Americans Reinhold and H. Richard Niebuhr, whose own weak ecclesiology was grounded in their father's Evangelical and

Reformed Church—the American version of Tillich's Prussian Union church.) There can be no doubt about the influential role that Tillich, despite this backdoor entry, played in American theology. He taught in prestigious places (Columbia University, Union Theological Seminary, Harvard, Chicago) and gave sermons or public lectures almost everywhere. Probably during his later years he was more widely known as a theologian than any other American. By the mid-seventies (ten years after his 1965 death) a survey of textbook use disclosed that his three-volume *Systematic Theology* (1951–63) led all others. Yet the fame left him curiously disconnected from previous American philosophy and theology, and thus from the culture of his new-adopted land. In fact the disconnection and the fame may be connected: The deliberate ambiguity of his style often enabled students and disciples to read their own constructions into his thought.

Nonetheless, there was an impressive continuity in the work Tillich understood as the theology of culture. This ran from 1919 (and before) to his final creative work. With this continuity as our focus, it will be useful to turn back to the beginning, to the crucial 1919 lecture just mentioned, in order to clarify Tillich's achievement. It was not merely despair at the imminent collapse of Germany after defeat in the Great War that had motivated "On the Idea of a Theology of Culture." The entire development of society, he argued, had issued in a terrible duality in modern life: dogma alongside science, community *(Gemeinschaft)* alongside society *(Gesellschaft)*, church alongside state, "all claiming separate spheres for themselves." A cultureless religion confronted a religionless culture. The outcome of this pervasive cultural schism was "a twofold truth as well as . . . a twofold morality and a twofold justice." By the end of World War I, this situation was evidently bankrupt; Tillich said it must be annulled *(aufgehoben)*: The only hope now lay in reconceiving religion: the absolute nothingness of life, values, things in general must (and would!) become the basis of a new, radical Yes. Here was 'dialectical' reasoning, inherited from Hegel: The Yes and the No together (but neither in isolation) pointed the way forward. Confronting the present situation there was a reality (not a being, he said, not a substance, but rather) *"the ultimate and most profound actuality of meaning that convulses everything and builds everything anew"* (1919:24f).

Staked out so early, theology of culture became Tillich's proper claim to fame. His best books were written in its service, and even his last work on world religions (1963) retained many of its themes. In particular, the volumes of *Systematic Theology* bore a "theology of culture" imprint, though this was less than clear to readers who expected from him the 'church theology' Paul Tillich had deliberately set aside. His system's "method of correlation" gave the dominant role to culture, which like Socrates in the Dialogues got to ask all the questions, while theology, like one of Socrates's unlucky interlocutors, could only follow where culture led. Doctrines were thus subordinated to a format that brought with it considerable risk to classic Christian belief. Thus Tillich is too often celebrated for what he did not achieve (a church theology) and too little for what he did.

To make this clear, return to our proposed trajectory. Why is Tillich's theology of culture to be a necessary point of departure, yet a point from which we must necessarily move on? These considerations appear: First, more than any other twentieth-century theologian Tillich is the heir of the preceding century, heir to absolute and romantic idealism (Fichte, Schelling), heir to the Protestant theology of the nineteenth century (Hegel, Schleiermacher, Ritschl, the entire European liberal tradition). But second, he led that theology into the twentieth century under a new corporate logo, as a "theology of correlation." Wherever today theology defines itself as "apologetic," wherever it declares its method to be "correlation," wherever it boldly speaks of itself as "public" theology, there the Tillichian odor lingers. Though the present volumes, lacking such attributes, cannot be counted among these heirs, they must do their work in full awareness of them. This volume in particular must shortly show the differences—in applied theology of culture (applications to religion, to science, to art, for examples), in the relation to philosophy, and in a theological approach—yielded by *departure* from the ground Tillich staked out. On the other hand, third, there can be no question here of completely separating ourselves from this important theological program. In ways seen and unseen, his work will influence what is done here—at least, by showing what it is not; at most, by shaping some of its particulars.

Tillich's account of the religious role of Expressionist art (and he thought all truly worthy art, not merely that of German Expressionism, was 'expressionist') is rejected here (Chapter Four) because of the severe limits of Tillich's early and persistent metaphor ("symbol," he would likely say) of salvation, namely *presence*—participation in Being, or in the abyss of being, or in New Being; the terms vary, but his emphasis is constant. He tells us that as one encounters substance-embodying forms (say an Expressionist painting, or a new German political system, or an updated ethic), these enable one to identify with the power of Being these forms possess. Now salvation as presence or participation (to give it its historical Christian name) is not new: Schleiermacher had exploited it in his day; the Neo-Platonist Christian tradition stands behind both Schleiermacher and Tillich. Yet this dimension sorely needs others to complete it: the dimension of *relation* to God (celebrated in the Protestant doctrine of justification by faith) and the dimension of *following* the Way or following Jesus (made explicit in baptist understanding as taking up the cross). The shorthand account of Tillich's fault is that he excludes narrative from the divine-human encounter—the Great Story of God's saving work and our own storied entry into that heritage play for him no central role. (On this point see *Doctrine*, pp. 109-22.) On the other hand, an example of Tillich's positive influence appears in the following chapter, presenting religion, including Christian religion, as a *cultural* form.

In short, the task of culture-theology, and of Christian theology more generally, is to move forward not backward; it honors the past best by achieving what the past did not. The reasons that theology of culture cannot remain merely Tillichian should become more clear as we follow the trajectory ahead.

b. Julian N. Hartt.—Though as I explained above it is customary to honor one or both of the Niebuhr brothers as the native-born masters of American theology of culture, I propose here to turn instead to the work of a lesser-known American theologian, Julian Norris Hartt (1911–). A generation younger than Paul Tillich, Hartt became closely acquainted with the other's work and saw its value. He admired Tillich's determination to investigate the contents of culture broadly understood (in contrast to those who confined theological work to Scripture and tradition), and he saw that the investigation must indeed lead theology to analyze the world outside the church. Yet at crucial points Hartt contested Tillich's guiding principle, the modern necessity to find authentic religion not in church but in the accompanying (secular) culture, and he questioned Tillich's 'correlation theology' in which culture sets the agenda, raising all the relevant questions, while theology can at best offer answers to these. Nevertheless, Hartt clearly recognized Tillich's concern. Son of a Methodist preacher, committed by his American setting as well as by his Methodist heritage and his own strong convictions to a church that took seriously its evangelistic task, Julian Hartt believed that preaching was authentic only when hearers genuinely understood the message. Yet as the prophets had known long before, the hearers' understanding did not guarantee acceptance—Hartt might have found useful philosopher J. L. Austin's term "uptake." Mere uptake by hearers brings with it no assurance of their *consent* to the gospel. Yet even this laid a heavy demand upon the preacher: if hearers were (minimally) to understand the gospel, if there was to be uptake, the preacher must understand the culture addressed—indeed, must understand it better than it understood itself. As Jonathan Wilson explains, for Hartt

> the church faithfully preaches the kingdom by exposing the lies and illusions of the world in the light of God's redemption in Jesus Christ. In order to do so, theology must use the idiom of its culture. Hartt's theology of culture serves the fulfillment of that mission by continually examining the cultural situation and the place of the church in the light of the revelation of Jesus Christ. (Jonathan Wilson, 1996:80)

Thus Hartt's analysis of culture did not begin as had Tillich's with the discovery of religious depth in the secular world; instead it sought to uncover the illusions and lies with which each human culture perpetually deceives itself.

On one occasion Hartt introduced his analysis of culture by recalling that life's only certainties were death and taxes. This popular saying points to two perpetual determinants of human existence: the demand of nature (whose final word is death) and the demand of sociality (whose toll on each is typified by taxes). Previously Hartt had given this analysis a more formal, philosophical form: there are things we know about being human without which we cannot declare Christ's gospel in any cultural setting. Some of these are *death, love, creativity, anxiety, and guilt:* elements of (Western) human existence Hartt called "ontological essentials" (Hartt, 1967:70). Here every man and woman struggles with these realities to some degree, yet the world distorts the truth about each, and the task of theology of culture is to expose these distortions ("lies and illusions," in a favorite Hartt phrase), and thus liberate dwellers in that culture to hear the gospel. The point is to uncover a true picture of existing culture—a mirror in which the world can recognize itself as world and thus at last be able to hear the gospel addressed to it. For a prime example, Hartt found American culture in his day experiencing a high degree of *anxiety.* This was the age of anxiety, other culture theorists were saying. But diagnosis was not enough: the gospel must uncover the full truth about American anxiety, showing its source and hopefully leading some to redemption by disclosing what God had done for anxious selves in Christ Jesus (1967:xiii-164).

Some will recognize here a style they know from the work of theological ethicist Stanley Hauerwas (1940–). This is no accident; Hartt was Hauerwas's teacher at Yale. In a useful article, Jonathan R. Wilson has set out the main parallels between the work of Hartt and Hauerwas: (1) the emphasis upon *practice* as opposed to system in theology; (2) the requirement for *seeing* things correctly as the heart of Christian theology (cf. Hauerwas's early title *Vision and Virtue*—1974); (3) perhaps most important, the theological use of *narrative,* to be examined below. Wilson finds as well some discontinuities between teacher and student; here I mention only Hartt's lesser and Hauerwas's larger attention to the practical (or moral) life of the *church*—attention focused particularly upon the church as a non-violent community (Jonathan Wilson, 1995; cf. Hauerwas, 1983). The peace theme was not absent in Hartt, though, and with a fresh stress upon church will reappear on the present trajectory in the work of John Howard Yoder, another who influenced Hauerwas. Hartt was an unusually complex workman whose standpoint cannot readily be summarized; a good starting point is the descriptive volume by Jonathan R. Wilson, *Theology as Cultural Critique: The Achievement of Julian Hartt* (1996).

Hartt's own profound *Christian Critique of American Culture* (1967), half a lifetime's work gathered up in a complex four hundred pages and published too quickly without adequate editing, is nonetheless the work that must ultimately be mastered. *Christian Critique* is at first reading mysteriously arranged; it lacks an index; it presents Hartt's genuine profundity with needless obscurity. Yet its veins of theological gold are worth tireless mining. Hartt knew that the Christian church could not make gospel sense of its own life apart from the culture in which it was immersed. In this regard he reversed his senior Yale colleague H. Richard Niebuhr. For Hartt, Niebuhr's pure dichotomy ("Christ" over against "culture") never existed. In its stead Hartt developed a four-sided theological analysis: church, world, kingdom, and gospel were each to be distinguished yet always to be related to one another, and the task was to recognize their mutual involvement, sorting out the contemporary living gospel whose "preachability" would shape the church and inform the world for the sake of the kingdom of God.

> God demands that His church stand out against the world and yet be prepared to sacrifice itself for real human beings in the real world. The church is under a divine obligation to so preach the gospel of Christ's kingdom that the native love of illusion and fear of truth will be understood in their intimate relatedness. This interrelatedness is part of the fabric of everyday. This does not mean that the church should despise everyday as inane or demonic. Rather, everyday is to be offered up to the redemption of Jesus Christ. This offering-up occurs in the faithful praying of the church. That is the beginning and the end; but there is much for the church to do in the middle. (Hartt, 1967:48)

Hartt's quadratic analysis aims to test the adequacy of the gospel as proclaimed. This adequacy is certainly not determined by the church's empirical success or popularity; nor is the church's faithfulness adequately measured by its adherence to the letter of Scripture: a broad fidelity to Scripture is certainly necessary, but not by itself sufficient. A theology's preachability is tested by two criteria: First, *does it lead the church to proclaim a gospel that displays narrative integrity?* In other words, will the church's recital of God's mighty, redemptive deeds, its narrative account of their tension and resolution, disclose the identity of God? Second, *can this preaching of the gospel lead to hearers' commitment?* That is, can it engage a particular cultural situation in such a way that human imagination is rightly stirred and human commitment rightly evoked? (Hartt never forgets, though, that faithful preaching may be unpopular.) If both these conditions obtain, the gospel has proved itself preachable in a given cultural setting (Hartt, 1967:chap. XIV; cf. Wilson, 1996:49-53).

So much has been said about narrative and theology since Hartt's first work on it that it is desirable to recall here what he meant. Hartt's theology of culture has a christological focus. The central Part of *Christian Critique* (1967:pp. 123-346) seeks to establish the identity of Jesus Christ and the sufficiency of his work by an analysis of Scripture's narrative. In proclaiming what Christ proclaimed, the church must not correlate its message (à la Tillich) with modernity, for then modernity becomes the church's god, its idol (p. 133). Hartt assumes as fact what historicism also recognizes: First and foremost Jesus proclaims, "The Kingdom of God is at hand, so repent!" (pp. 129, 167). The kingdom is actual, present, here now as well as here at the end of all things; it contests the world's claim to know itself and be itself with a rival knowledge-claim. Who, then, is this Jesus, according to the gospel of the kingdom? He is one fully and truly human, yet one who does not fall prey to illusion, who is perfectly responsive to the leadings of the Holy Spirit, and (therefore) one who is "the righteousness of the Kingdom of God incarnate" (198). Hartt's Christology is thus formed on a 'revelational' model (on this model, see *Doctrine,* p. 264). His atonement-theology centers on the resurrection of Jesus Christ from the dead: by that resurrection, Christ's death is a saving death: "In him God has done the thing impossible with man: he has reconciled man unto himself" (p. 211). Christ's work is best presented, Hartt thinks, in the Greek-Christian atonement image: Christ is the victor; he has overcome the world (cf. *Doctrine,* Five §1). To say what this image means, Hartt invokes afresh the "ontological essentials": now *death's* power is broken: "the door is opened wide for us to participate in the teleology of God's Kingdom"; now *love's* role is turned from old cultural patterns of idolatry and enmity to participate in God's love, "unalloyed delight" in all that is; now *creativity* is saved from the spurious necessity of making gods for ourselves; now, over against our helpless *anxiety*, we are able to hear Jesus' words, "sufficient unto the day . . ."; now for our *guilt*, "whether we live or whether we die, we are the Lord's. Whether we sin or whether we do not sin, we are the Lord's" (Hartt, 1967:226-29).

So the church's faith is historical, the gospel it must proclaim contains a *true* story, the faith it demands of a faithless world requires *entry* into that story (1967:chap. 8; Hartt in Hauerwas and Jones, eds., 1989:279-319). Hartt's contribution brings the theology of culture well past Tillich. Yet there is more.

c. John Howard Yoder.—The late John Howard Yoder (1927–97) was scion of a family long planted on American soil (his foreparents were early European settlers in Virginia's Shenandoah Valley). He received theological training at Goshen, a Mennonite college in Indiana, and later at the University of Basel under Karl Barth, Oscar Cullmann, and others. Importantly, Yoder's early publications included a close reading of Barth's theology of culture.

For Yoder the measure of his teacher's achievement was Barth's unexpected yet defective "pacifism": More than any European theologian before him, Barth treated the Christian community in distinction from the civil community. For the first time since Constantine, then, a separate Christian stance on the issue of war and peace became theologically necessary (Yoder, 1968; 1994*a*:166f; cf. 1964). I add that a broader approach to Barth's theology of culture requires attention to his comprehensive lectures on nineteenth-century Protestant theology (K. Barth, 1972). In these Barth shows himself a master of interpreting the inherited European culture world and criticizing it (à la Hartt) on the basis of his reading of the gospel.

It has not been customary to consider Yoder (or, for that matter, Barth!) as a theologian of culture, since his constructive social theology, as he himself might have preferred to call it, clearly took a different tack from the correlation theology of Paul Tillich. Yoder's approach first came to wider view in 1972 in *The Politics of Jesus* (2nd ed., 1994*b*). Yet that grew from still earlier studies such as *The Christian Witness to the State* (1964), and the standpoint was developed over several decades, culminating in essay-collections titled *The Priestly Kingdom* (1984), and then a trilogy that included *The Royal Priesthood* (1994*a*), *For the Nations* (1997), and a third volume yet to be published. These titles indicate the thrust of Yoder's work both toward the church and toward the social order. Without renouncing his roots so firm in baptist soil, he increasingly understood himself to be "radically catholic" in outlook. The true or catholic church, congregational in texture, must in its many locations *embody* the gospel, not merely proclaim it. The practices of the Christian community, not limited to though certainly including its preaching, constitute an alternative social ethic—alternative, that is, to the violent ethic of the world that rejects the way of Jesus. This gospel-formed culture provides by its very existence a challenging witness to any host community. When the church is faithful, it offers such a witness to all nations. Doctrinally, Yoder's work was explicitly christocentric (a binding debt to Barth his teacher), yet his theology of culture, while accepting the classic christological dogmas, deepened them to embrace Jesus' "original revolution"—a peaceable revolution, first enculturated on Palestinian soil (1985; cf. 1977, 1994*b*).

What made *The Politics of Jesus* so compelling a book was that while overtly it was about Jesus' ministry in Palestine long ago, it directly challenged contemporary religious ethicists, who in forming their views had neglected the radical Jesus of the Gospels. Nineteenth-century scholarship had been divided on this topic: Protestant liberals such as Adolf Harnack and Albrecht Ritschl had invoked the teaching of Jesus but easily turned it into a bland endorsement of existing social and religious arrangements. Albert Schweitzer, on the other hand, had seen in Jesus an eschatological prophet of no comfort to today's established churches, but thought Jesus' apocalyptic expectation of the end of the age made him morally irrelevant. For neither side had Jesus' radicality (his demand for self-sacrificial peacemaking and discipleship) become the norm. Following this lead, Christian ethicists had pushed aside the aims and example of the human Jesus. Yet *Jesus in his original first-century Palestinian setting* was for Yoder the overwhelming first fact of the theology of culture. Consequently one had to question some current readings of Jesus. These made him only a dispenser of wisdom sayings, or a heavenly figure whose goal was to sacrifice his life for human sin, or a near-helpless figure in a world over which he had no control (this in supposed contrast to the 'responsible' posture of today's ethical leaders) (1994*b*:4-8). Over against all such misreadings, Yoder pointed out that what here we are calling culture-theology, far from being a twentieth-century invention, was as original as Jesus' life and ministry. No sort of Christian theology could be right apart from a return to this origin. Jesus had been a revolutionary figure whose revolution was social and enduring, demanding communal obedience by his followers in every fresh generation.

Later Yoder wrote that this message, while at one time or another it had been nearly approached by mainstream figures in American social ethics such as

H. R. Niebuhr and John Bennett, never came to fruition in their work. An exception, he noted appreciatively, was Julian N. Hartt, who had articulated a powerful witness in his *Christian Critique of American Culture.* In retrospect, Hartt's *Christian Critique* and Yoder's *Politics* indeed seem to have been on the same track; perhaps Yoder made the track more plain; certainly he eventually made its destination more clear (Yoder, 1984:88-91; 202, note 11).

The theological argument that underlay *The Politics of Jesus* was thus a complex one. There was a biblical stratum, well-based in current scholarship, that focused on the revolutionary appearance and action of Jesus of Nazareth. As a Reformation historian Yoder found yet another focus in the sixteenth-century repetition of the original drama: various sorts of reform in Renaissance Europe had recalled the original revolution and were thus relevant to its reinterpretation today. And the options that had confronted Jesus appeared once again in the modern world. Again today the way of Jesus confronted the 'powers'; again the old temptation, the easy path of violence, sought to capture the followers of the Lamb. Each of these foci requires exposition.

i. The original revolution.—The earthly, fully human Jesus was paradigm and foundation for Yoder's culture-theology. According to *Politics,* the designated Messiah, Jesus, faced four persistent temptations, each well represented in the culture of occupied Palestine (these representations were the Zealot crusade, the 'realistic' Sadducean and Herodian arrangements with Rome, the Essene withdrawal, and the segregated, 'uninvolved' Pharisees—see Yoder, 1977:18-26), yet among these it was finally the Zealot alternative that chiefly tempted Jesus, as still it does today's Christians: This was "the temptation to exercise social responsibility, in the interest of justified revolution, through the use of available violent methods." Launching a cultural revolution that consistently refused this central temptation led directly to Jesus' death. The original meaning of the cross was not found in later images and metaphors such as the heavenly sacrifice or the exemplary penitence of the God-man. Instead, his crucifixion was "the price of his social nonconformity, . . . the social reality of representing in an unwilling world the Order to come" (1994*b*:96f). Yoder locates this central theme first in Luke's Gospel (1994*b*:chap. 2), but then traces it through the remainder of the New Testament, especially through Paul's epistles and the Apocalypse of John. Paul's theology, Yoder urges us to see, was not simply that of Augustine or Luther written beforehand; Paul's focus is rather on a new kind of righteousness that he had discovered in Messiah Jesus (1994*b*:chap. 11). For Yoder the hermeneutic center of the book of Revelation lies not in its sequences of seals, trumpets, bowls, and horsemen; these gain their meaning from chapters four and five, where the one who can open the sealed scroll, that is, provide creation with its true significance, namely the Lion, turns out to be the sacrificed Lamb, the same crucified Jesus who was central to the Gospels and Paul (Rev. 5:6-10; cf. 1 Cor. 2:2). Jesus, far from being a culture-denying sectarian, is constantly engaged in the cultural ferment of his time, though never pressed into its molds, and Yoder means to follow Jesus.

Seeing Jesus in his cultural setting meant taking first-century Judaism into fresh account. This involved the investigation of relations between the church and post-70 rabbinic Judaism. While liberal Catholic scholarship maintained that the eventual Jewish-Christian schism was already present in the New Testament, conceding that this was a bad thing, and while some Protestant scholars held that orthodox Christianity was only an illegitimate offspring of its Hebraic heritage (Paul van Buren?), Yoder sought a third way of interpreting the division (*Doctrine,* Eight §2). Perhaps the baptist concept of 'restitution,' that is, the constant looping back to correct the present Christian course by reference to beginnings, might give a clue for current Christian-Jewish relations: might not here also a happier footing be achieved by the recovery of the actual past? Synagogue Judaism, arising in Babylon not Palestine, had taken shape in a counter-cultural setting. For a few crucial decades the original paths of counter-cultural Christianity and counter-cultural Judaism had run in tense parallel; when that relation ended with Constantine, Christianity fell into self-diminishing conduct from which it still suffered, but for Yoder recovery was now possible. Part of the task was to recover the 'Jewishness' of earliest Christianity; another part was noting how today's free churches (our baptists) retained 'Jewish' elements in their life as other Christians did not (for example, both were aware of their minority status always); still another part was examining the shift in vision or standpoint that the free church critique of 'Christendom' made possible for today's Jews and Christians (Yoder, 1997-chap. 3).

ii. Reformation and history.—Hence Jesus' relation to culture was paradigmatic for Christians. Again and again through Christian history the paradigm is repeated, producing variations on its theme. A variation of singular interest was the Radical Reformation, the so-called 'Anabaptist' movement of the sixteenth century. Since these reformers had survived in small numbers to the present, one strand being Yoder's own Mennonite Church, it was easy to misunderstand his presentation of radical reform as only a denominational polemic: "Be like us." But this was never his point (1984:5-8). For him the radical reformation was simply a historical test case, distant enough to permit some perspective yet with valuable parallels in the present. We are not to archaize ourselves, either into the sixteenth century or the first; nevertheless, 'Anabaptism' provides a key way for theology to think about history and thus about culture as it journeys through time. In an essay, "Anabaptism and History," Yoder challenged any alternative to his view of Christian history to a contest: "only the mental structure of restitutionism," he argued, "can be at once Christian and serious about history." This did not mean that only Mennonites and the like could be good church historians. It meant that the reclaiming of Jesus' vision anywhere anytime would require a sense of the church's present *kairos* ("opportune time," a term Tillich had earlier found useful); historians must see church history as a stream always fed by its Messianic source, and accordingly their work must press "beyond historiography to contemporary issues of the mission, structure, and unity of the church," a demand some historians might feel they could not consistently meet (1984:130).

iii. A whole new world.—We come here to the deep basis of Yoder's theology of culture. A shift in vision is required! He never tired of repeating certain recent translations of 2 Corinthians 5:17, which reads (in the Revised English Bible), "For anyone united to Christ, there is a new creation: the old order has gone; a new order [John Yoder sometimes capitalized it, 'New Order'] has already begun." He contrasts this to the way *The Living Bible* puts the same verse: "When someone becomes a Christian he is a brand new person *inside*"! In the theology of culture, these two versions represent the wide gulf between seeing the difference converted individuals can make in a sinful world (a difference not to be scorned, but not the Apostle's point) and the discovery anyone united to Christ must make, that he or she has entered a whole new world, which as it happens is the real world (1994*b:*185, 221-23). Here we see Yoder's realized eschatology: the old aeon lingers, but is replaced by the new; the corrupt powers of the lingering past are challenged by the warfare of the Lamb, the power of the way of Jesus (Berkhof, trans. Yoder, 1962; cf. *Ethics:*173-77). Yoder, as had Hartt, insists on the cognitive truth of the gospel: the unfolding New Order is earth's true history. Far from any stereotypical religious apoliticism, Yoder from the beginning of his career to the end urged an *alternative concept of politics,* based upon realistic perception of the New Order being born. For example: "In the politics of rebellious mankind every concession is defeat, [while] on the other hand, truth is patient . . . can accept risks . . . can distinguish essentials from nonessentials and accept delay or defeat" (1997:229). For Yoder the quiet history that was witnessed in Scripture's story was the real history, while the history of emperors and attack weapons, violence and deceit was itself deceived and stood in urgent need of the church's witness.

* * * * *

Many others have made and continue to make valuable contributions to a Christian theology of culture. This section has traced an overlooked but enormously important line of direction: from Tillich to Hartt to Yoder. Were not such summaries misleadingly concise, I might risk saying that while Tillich focused upon culture itself as the bearer of meaning, Hartt shifted the focus to the gospel addressed to that culture, and Yoder refocused upon the gospel-embodying practices of the church. These theologians offer a continuity that brings us to the present—where all their gains may be retrieved. I have spoken of this combination as a trajectory; consider it now as a three-stranded cord in which the whole is stronger than any of its contributing parts. This is the cord I mean to extend if I can. The present line will acknowledge God's positive command expressed in the long narrative of the Jews as it climaxes in Jesus and as it is echoed in the church's enculturated (i.e., new-culture-based and old-culture-remaking) witness. In transmitting this Great Story, the church must be alert to openings, hungers, hidden religious depths within the contemporary environing culture (thus Tillich). Even more must it become aware by the light of that long narrative of the illusions and self-deceit of the culture-world, so that its preaching enables the world rightly to see itself (thus Hartt). This strategy demands afresh that the church practice the gospel it preaches. The church must be not only the preacher but also the present instance of the gospel of Jesus Christ (thus Yoder).

§4. Relativity's Riddles

Some preliminary questions have yet to be addressed. At this point readers of this chapter are merely returning navigators, exploring a coastline they feel they know, yet lacking assurance of just where they are along its shore, far less whether there are inlets permitting successful landings. Does previous exploration (the 'trajectory') provide a usable chart of these waters? Are the prior soundings accurate? Further explanation of where we are now and what lies ahead is surely in order. In particular, the concepts of 'culture' and 'convictions' which have already been used demand further clarification. If author and readers are to remain in the same boat for the chapters to come, some of these matters require at least preliminary discussion.

a. Which culture?—Now that we know more of its history, what should anyone make of the term "culture" in this book? To some, the word still has a snooty ring: The cultured are assumed to know the 'right' way to hold a teacup and what to say at the opera, while others do not. To more scientific-minded folk, a culture is something such as *E. coli* bacteria that grows (is 'cultured') in a petri dish. Clearly neither of these is the intended use here. Following the anthropologists, I mean by a culture the set of meaningful practices, dominant attitudes, and characteristic ways of doing things that typify a community (or a society or a civilization). To say it more briefly, its culture gives significance to what a group of people do. Basketball is just as likely to display the sense of one particular culture as basketwork or *basso* arias do others. None of these activities in themselves is in any elevated sense 'cultural.' Yet any and all may provide clues, as may country music or gospel singing—or high society! (Geertz, 1973:chap. 1). In the coming chapters it will prove helpful, in examining Western and (particularly) American culture, to say something about its religion and science and art as well as something about its philosophy and theology. Why these are good choices must come out along the way. But especially in light of this chapter, no one should mistake theology of culture for an attempt to promote 'culture' in an elitist or snobbish sense.

This brings up *cultural relativism,* which (to put it crudely) says that whatever we know and respect and delight in, the convictions we hold dear and the goals we pursue, are all *relative* to the culture we inhabit, so that what is worthy or justifiable or true or meaningful varies from culture to culture. The worry is real enough: if relativism is true in general, even belief (or disbelief) in God must be a relative belief, and this is a difficult position for Christians or for any sort of convinced believers since it seems to cut all beliefs that matter down to the status of cultural props, mere furniture of the culture at hand and thus with no standing to analyze that culture theologically or in any other deep way. In that case the theology of culture would be balked before it began. If the theologian, like everyone else, can only speak from and within some particular culture (which at first glance seems an obvious truth—think of Tillich's needed reorientation on coming to the United States), or if Christian 'culture' is just as liable to the limits of relativity as any other sort (again obvious, at least to most), then theology of culture is a viciously circular enterprise. No matter who undertakes it, the present game never gets off the ground.

There are some needless worries here as well as some that will require more attention as we go. A first step is to clear away the needless ones. Sarah Coakley, in "Theology and Cultural Relativism: What Is the Problem?" (1979), starting from her speciality in the thought of Ernst Troeltsch, provides help. She divides recent relativism proposals into some main types and then shows that some of these are not properly worrisome relativisms at all, but only the acknowledgment of various kinds of harmless relatedness. An example of the latter, drawn from social science, is its demand that "social or historical or religious phenomena be studied at least in the first instance *in their own terms*" (p. 226). (Polynesian *tabu,* for instance, is to be treated *as tabu,* not as something already known and classified in the West.) Coakley then argues that while *of course* all truths appear in some context or other and thus have to do with something besides themselves, and while *of course* knowledge develops, grows, so that what was known at one time is relative to that time and not necessarily to an earlier or later one, and while *of course* what is true in one place (it's raining) may not be true in another so that its truth is relative to its place—none of these truisms adds up to relativism of the sort that challenges religious convictions.

Does any sort of relativism do so? Yes, "relativism proper," as Coakley calls it, when it expresses theories about what can possibly be true, that is, theories of knowledge, claims that "proposition *p* is actually 'true' (not, note, merely thought true) relative to, or in virtue of, framework *f*" (p. 227). Outside that culture-framework (so goes the claim) *p* proposes no truth. Now even this thesis may be held in so weak a form that it is itself harmless, reducing to one or more of the truisms just noted (e.g., that everything has its context, without which it cannot be understood). Alternatively, though, this thesis may be intended in so strong a form that it becomes internally incoherent, fails to make sense even of itself. An example of the latter failure is to hold that the division between cultures is so sharp that communication cannot possibly take place between one's own and another culture: In a term Coakley appropriates for her special use, their cultural frameworks are deemed 'incommensurable.' Yet if this is the case, Coakley says, "presumably we [in one of these frameworks] would not know that the alien framework existed." The Kwakiutl might be utterly and forever incapable of recognizing the existence of the Sioux culture—or vice versa. If such a state of affairs is inconceivable, it is in Coakley's view "a dead duck." For another instance of emptiness, she says that a framework may be supposed so lacking in reference to whatever is outside the framework (perhaps the way the world is?) that 'outside' is held irrelevant to life inside, and again trans-framework communication must fail. Coakley finds this another dead duck, since so strong a framework limitation must give up any claim to correspondence (or reference?) as an aspect of truth. Or (a third case of an extreme) if the culture-framework is supposed actually to *determine* whatever is said or done inside the frame, then culture has become an iron grid, and those inside it are at best robots or automata, not human beings—dead duck number three. Yet between the weak truisms and the incoherent 'dead ducks' lies a real truth, and this intermediate reality of relativism is what Coakley believes needs to be discussed: What is the nature of actual "frameworks"? What work is done in the discussion by "true" (a term she carefully keeps in scare quotes in her definition of relativism)? Finally, how does all this bear upon the theological task?

I agree with Coakley's analysis as far as it goes, so that my own approach to the discussable sort of relativism will appear only briefly here but at greater length throughout the volume. There is one knock-down argument against any strong or hard cultural relativism that readers should be aware of at the outset: all such claims are self-contradictory. This can be made clear by asking just where the relativist means to stand when making his relativist-claim. In other words, is the relativist saying, "All claims are cultural-context-dependent, *including* this one"? Or is he saying, "All claims are cultural-context-dependent *except for* this one"? If the former, the relativist seems to confess that he doesn't really know about other cultures, after all. Who says he does, or even that his rule applies in their cases? Not he. Yet if the latter is meant, the supposed culture barrier is already broken in this important case (since the speaker claims that this one exceptional truth applies across the board), but if it is broken in even one case, the game is really up: relativism's universal sway is admittedly broken. For such reasons James M. Smith and I found in writing *Convictions* that we had to abandon both what we there called hard relativism (Coakley's dead ducks) and soft relativism (her truisms) to shape our understanding of the problem. We turned instead to a view of culture-relatedness we called *perspectivism,* which "regards convictional conflict as expected, but not inevitable, fundamental but not ultimate, enduring but not inherently ineradicable" (*CONV.*, p. 9).

b. Whose convictions?—If 'perspectivism' is true, does that mean that the world is just as impossible a place for Christians, or as useless a place for the theology of culture or any other sort of Christian theology, as it might have been if the hard or 'dead duck' kind of relativism had been the right view? No, for as we said in *Convictions,* perspectivism acknowledges

> common elements among differing sets of convictions [differing cultures], but to discover and use them in resolving conflict requires measures that cannot be limited along convictional lines. Persons or communities with different convictions will experience, think, and speak about their worlds differently, and these differences will not necessarily be the result of mistakes or character flaws. But neither are [the differences] walls or electronic scramblers, making communication, understanding, or even persuasion among worlds impossible. (*CONV.,* p. 9)

So here is a cautiously optimistic view about what some call cultural relativism, the way matters stand among cultures estranged from one another, sometimes even fatally opposed to one another by their tortoise-shell boundaries, and perhaps by those same boundaries separated from the rest of reality as well. To take the most obvious and (for us) most relevant case, Christian culture of the sort that Julian Hartt and John Yoder favor will take the divine Trinity (Hartt) or the lordship of Jesus Christ (Yoder) as givens that all their thinking must factor in if it is to be reasonable and true, while the 'scientific' (or 'economic') versions of modern Western culture will differ from these at the very root: For these versions, something else takes the place of the biblical God. The 'something else' may present more than one form. For a Ruth Benedict or a Clifford Geertz it may be the claim that any convergence of human life, any culture, has to be found 'meaningful,' or found to display a meaningful 'pattern,' since that discovery is what makes human life worthwhile. For capitalism after Adam Smith, the idolatrous belief (or less judgmentally, the unspoken presumption) is that when exchange of goods and services goes unregulated by government, some 'hidden hand' sees to it that the resultant commerce benefits all, so that non-regulation of the economy is a necessary good. In still another 'scientific' version of the world there is the parallel belief (or idolatrous assumption?) that unhindered scientific investigation will on the whole or normally make for the good of those who support it, if not for everyone. Now these varied primary assumptions, Christian, capitalist, scientific, and so forth, are not on their face mutually contradictory—many even see two or more of them as mutually supportive. Yet history suggests that a culture (such as early Christianity) built around the lordship of Jesus Christ will be quite different from a culture built around the hidden rules of capitalism or one built around the even-better-hidden rules of modern science (on the latter, see further Chapter Three).

I call the enduring, basic beliefs that typify cultures their *convictions.* As the first volume of this work laid it down, convictions are persistent beliefs of such a sort

> that if X (a person or a community) has a conviction, it will not be easily relinquished, and it cannot be relinquished without making X a significantly different person (or community) than before. (*Ethics,* p. 23, following *CONV.*, chap. 1, §1)

Without some such notion as "conviction" (no one term for this is in universal use) it is difficult even to explain what theology as a discipline or 'science' *(Geisteswissenschaft)* is all about: in a vague and general way, theology is about God, or better, God-and-creation. Yet in a more exact sense (again quoting *Ethics*), theology is

> the discovery, understanding, and transformation of the convictions of a convictional community, including the discovery and critical revision of their relation to one another *and to whatever else there is.* (p. 23)

The last phrase, "and to whatever else there is," proclaims that a conviction-oriented approach to theology is not doomed to be a relativistic 'dead duck.'

Working with such a notion as 'convictions' (or one of its cousins such as 'presuppositions,' 'incorrigible assumptions,' 'metaphysical beliefs'—no single term for this widely recognized phenomenon is in common use), it is possible to pry cultural relativity in its healthiest sense (our 'perspectivism') away from cultural imperialism (the view that one's own culture has it all right all the time, culturally speaking, so that other cultures had better fall in line) and also pry it away from despairing cultural *apartheid* (the view that one's culture really has nothing to do with some other or others, and vice versa, so that everyone's best hope is to stay segregated). Perspectivism makes room for rival truth-claims and other rival value-claims. Indeed, it assumes there will be such rivalry. It also recognizes the ways in which variant cultures encounter one another, clash, combine, persuade, and are persuaded, with the possibility that new cultural forms may inherit and appropriate the old ones. We have already seen possibilities of this sort in the foregoing section (§3): Tillich's discovery of 'meaning' in the depths of secular phenomena, Hartt's 'ontological essentials' that may be found across cultural dividing lines (death, love, creativity, anxiety, and guilt, or more briefly, death and taxes), Yoder's theme of a recurrent 'original revolution' associated with the prophets and Jesus—all imply cross-cultural journeys human beings have actually taken and may take again. In *Convictions*, Smith and I show that such journeys, encounters, quests, and the like are possible roads to *justified sets of convictions:* that is, those who undertake such passages have reason to hope that the outcome will not only be intraculturally satisfying, but will appear reasonable across cultural boundary lines as well (*CONV.* chaps. 4–6). In a broad sense, we have defined the rules mission must follow if there is to be any mission.

* * * * *

Here, then, is a theological trajectory to continue, an inlet worth exploring as reconnaissance for redemptive mission. As servant of the gospel of God (Mark 1:14), Christian theology will find the divine footprints already pressed down into the cultural shores. Here Paul Tillich's instinct was sound. Creation, as Paul the Apostle saw it, "groans as if in the pangs of childbirth" (Rom. 8:22). In light of the glory coming, even creation's agony is a sign of hope. The world aches as it does without for the most part knowing the source of its pain, since the world distorts and thus despises and rejects the divine glory. This rejection is the painful focus of the story of Jesus that repeats the tale of the Suffering Servant—despised and rejected (Isa. 53:3). As Julian Hartt knows well, this is the deep truth of any theology of culture faithful to the story: God by his Servant redeems the world from its self-deceit, illusions, lies. Thus part of the task is to recognize the cultural sin which mars (though it can never efface) divine creation. The footprints of God along the shore lead to an execution site. It is a cross. Theology of culture finds that cross and its neighboring grave—but it finds them empty. He is risen. The resurrection is a signal of hope calling culture on to its full redemption. John Yoder's vision of God's redeemed people, a gathering community, culture remade by grace, is a form of this realized apocalyptic: for him the last things are present possessions of the children of God. The church constitutes a culture of hope in a world that cannot live without some hope. The three Parts ahead will investigate **(Part I) some concrete expressions of contemporary culture—religion, science, art—then (Part II) the message of philosophy as underlying cultural indicator, and finally (Part III) theology itself confronted with the task of making sense of all these**

in line with Christian convictions. In brief (too brief) a form, this theology must confess that *God is the God of culture as well as of nature; therefore culture's hope like nature's destiny lies in the gospel of God's grace (Rom. 8:21-23).* Only when that brief claim is unfolded in the following chapters will we be in position to say more clearly what culture can be.

PART I

CULTURAL VISTAS

Religion as ultimate concern is the meaning-giving substance of culture, and culture is the totality of forms in which the basic concern of religion expresses itself. In abbreviation: religion is the substance of culture, culture is the form of religion.

Paul Tillich

The God met in physics as the divine wellspring from which matter-energy bubbles up . . . is in biology the suffering and resurrecting power that redeems life out of chaos. . . . The secret of life is seen now to lie not so much in the heredity molecules, not so much in natural selection and the survival of the fittest, not so much in life's informational, cybernetic learning. The secret of life is that it is a passion play. Things perish in tragedy. The religions knew that full well, before biology arose to reconfirm it.

Holmes Rolston

The illusions of art are able, as hardly anything else is, to expose the illusory character of the normal, the conventional world. I believe that the suspicions of art and artist so deeply engrained in plain, sensible people in our age express clearly an anxiety for the conventional world. They might well be suspicious. . . . The real threat is authentic art itself because in it we see what love of truth can lead to as transformation and transvaluation of the given world.

Julian N. Hartt

Introduction to Part I

Jesus, according to Mark 4, offered the parable of Sower and Seed:

> As he taught he said: "Listen! A sower went out to sow. And it happened that as he sowed, some of the seed fell along the footpath; and the birds came and ate it up. Some fell on rocky ground, where it had little soil, and it sprouted quickly because it had no depth of earth; but when the sun rose it was scorched, and as it had no root it withered away. Some fell among thistles; and the thistles grew up and choked the corn, and it produced no crop. And some of the seed fell into good soil, where it came up and grew, and produced a crop; and the yield was thirtyfold, sixtyfold, even a hundredfold." He added, "If you have ears to hear, then hear." (Mark 4:2*b*-9)

This is primary Christian teaching. Already, according to Mark, Jesus has been going about "proclaiming the gospel of God: 'The time has arrived; the kingdom of God is upon you. Repent, and believe the gospel'" (1:15). In chapter 6 Jesus will authorize the Twelve to go and make the same proclamation, demanding of their hearers the reorientation that this good news entailed (6:7-13). These events are the (Marcan) context of this parable. Planting seed, Jesus says, is a risky business; it may have more than one outcome; one must consider the soil.

Many have interpreted the parable of sower and seed by applying it to individuals or to classes of people (among the earliest who did this were the inspired Evangelists themselves: Mark, Matthew, and Luke). In a recent interpretation in this spirit by two New Testament scholars, the seeds that fall by the way stand for this Gospel's hard-hearted religious authorities; the seeds that spring up only to wither in "rocky" ground represent the disciples in Mark's story, notably Peter (the "Rock"; a pun here?); the seeds on good soil correspond to the minor characters in Mark's Gospel: the woman who anoints Jesus, the centurion, beggar Bartimaeus (Rhoads and Michie, 1982:119, 128, 135). Such interpreters progress from parable-as-metaphor to parable-as-allegory; in the latter, each part of the parable has a historical referent.

These 'explanations' of the parable of sower and seed by the Evangelists (Mark 4:14-20; Matt. 13:18-23, cf. 36-43; Luke 8:11-15) are *allegories;* in them the broad metaphors of the parable (sower, seed, hard path, etc.) are assigned to corresponding historical figures. An allegory explains a parable by giving its parts references that specify (but thus narrow) the parable's meaning. Due to flagrant excesses in its use in ancient and medieval times, allegory fell into disrepute; in particular, Jesus' parables were until recently ruled ineligible for allegorical readings (and so much the worse for Matthew, Mark, and Luke!). Yet this twentieth-century rule, prescribed from Jülicher to Dodd to Jeremias, has itself been challenged (Parsons, 1988): Rhoads and Michie (as noted) find the rule fails to respect the narrative coherence of Mark; Ched Myers finds it fails to recognize the intense, immediate relation of Jesus' proclamation to the "socio-historical site" in which an astounding harvest (thirty, sixty, a hundredfold as opposed to the ordinary sevenfold) symbolizes the astounding release promised poor farmers who will hear the good news and enter the kingdom (Myers, 1988:174-76). Guided by these examples, I offer my own 'cultural' exegesis of the sower and the soils. Explaining a related parable, Matthew's Jesus declares that "the sower . . . is the Son of Man" and *"the field is the world"* (Matt. 13:37f)—just the interpretive key I propose.

Here is my reading: The parable of sower and seed advises apostolic messengers—whether the Twelve or today's missionary church—to attend to the cultural soils that lie beneath their witnessing feet: look at the soil, Jesus says, look at the cultural setting, the world in which you minister, if you would understand the fruitfulness of your labor or its failure. According to all the Synoptic Gospels, Jesus next quotes Isaiah 6: "They may look and look, but see nothing; they may listen and listen, but understand nothing; otherwise they might turn to God and be forgiven" (thus Mark 4:12). For forgiveness is not a harvest to be expected in hard-soil cultures.

The grim fate foretold for Isaiah's preaching in his own ancient culture repeats a common theme in the biblical narrative: foremost in the prophets; notably in the fate of Jesus (e.g., Luke 13:34-36); again in the mixed reception later Christian missionaries meet (cf. Acts 28:26f). The overall lesson is never merely that a certain culture is hopeless (Isaiah

6 itself closes with the assurance that "holy seed" will survive even the felling of a great culture-tree); it is that cultures differ significantly in their reception of the word of God. Some cultures have audiophile ears that yet can hear nothing; they have twenty-twenty vision and yet must carry white canes. Thus Paul Tillich's hope to find religious depth outside the German church of his day in a desperately secular culture, and Julian Hartt's warning that theology must expose the "lies and illusions" that blind the world to the gospel, and John Yoder's demand that the church acknowledge itself to be located in a *kainē ktisis* (a new creation) that redeems the old—each expressing the apostolic optimism that God does not forget the world but remains the source of its good news, even where that requires bringing life out of death. This present Part embodies afresh that biblical hope. It asks, not in general but in three particular areas, religion, science, art, *what must a contemporary culture be in order to lie fallow to the gospel of Jesus Christ?* And beyond that: *What is to be the standpoint of the church facing low-yield cultures?* To use a gardener's term, can the church be the church by *amending* the cultural soil? Must a church abandon a familiar cultural path that shows itself congenitally sterile? When are thistles too dense for the gospel? In such ways the parable of the sower stirs the imagination that seeks a theology of culture.

Soil is not the only image of culture in Scripture. The apostle Paul speaks metaphorically of one particular culture, that of Jewish law, as "a slave to look after us, to lead us to Christ" (Gal. 3:24 NJB). His imagery assumes his Galatian readers' familiarity, not indeed with Jewish law (about which he thinks they are sadly misguided), but with the Hellenistic culture of their day. There a wealthy Greek or Roman father could commit his offspring to the care of a slave, a *paidagogos* or *epitropos* with the role of guardian or tutor (Gal. 4:2), or more accurately, of disciplinarian. This servant's task was to make sure the privileged child of the family studied his lessons, got to school on time, and paid attention to the teacher. (That Paul used this image of the law as humble *paidagogos* rather than the more prestigious *didaskolos,* teacher, just fits the rhetoric of Galatians.) Even so, the analogy is inescapable: Jewish law is a kind of educator, while Hellenism, we can infer, provides a different *paidea.* Moreover, these two are the only possible cases then and now: a culture either stands in the heritage of Abraham and Moses, or it does not; culture is either biblical or it is pagan. Neither of these cultural educators, from Paul's perspective, is adequate apart from the gospel; the question is whether the *paidogogos* leads students on to the true *didaskolos,* to the Teacher whom Paul follows.

Culture as educator (or education as the core element in culture) continued to captivate writers during the Christian era. Gotthold Ephraim Lessing (1729–81), the father of the German Enlightenment, published a play, "Nathan the Wise," and an essay, "The Education of the Human Race," in which evolving culture was not a farm for the cultivation of true religion (its role in the parable of the sower) or a mere "slave to look after us" as in Paul's Galatian Letter. For Lessing, culture-education was the thing itself, the substance of true religion, since the entire "moral and religious development of human life is at one and the same time a natural and a divine activity, in which mankind moves (is led) toward the fullness of truth" (Welch, 1972–85:I:51). Lessing was a rationalist; he believed that the various religions each conveyed part of the truth, but that it was the educational task of a civilization to sift each, retaining what was true and discarding the rest. For him, religion served culture, not vice versa.

Two centuries after Lessing, Paul Tillich inherited this Enlightenment tradition. Thus it is not surprising that he often returned to the strong link between education, culture, and religion. In an essay (1959:146-58) Tillich set out three aims of education: these are (1) teaching the skills required for members of the culture (education as technique-acquisition such as learning to read, to compute, to research), (2) inducting the next generation into the culture (education as social initiation—a kind of extended ceremony), and (3) conveying the humanistic ideal. For Tillich, this third aim entailed the development of all human potentialities, a goal he associated with the early Renaissance religious experience—"the presence of the infinite in everything finite" (1959:147). Insightful this account of the roles of education may be, yet like Jewish law and Gentile *paidea* it remains subject to Paul's warnings to the Galatians: it must not substitute for the gospel.

To express Tillich's comprehensive triad in my own language, and in a different order: **Human culture is (1) humanity reaching out to whatever lies beyond humanity, to the gods and their gifts; at its best this is humanity's response to the holiness and goodness and presence of God; thus Chapter Two, Religion as Culture. Culture is (2) that form of life in which a people acquires and extends the skills required to cope with nature and enjoy its goods—at its best, we call such cultural knowledge science; thus Chapter Three, Science and Society. Finally, culture is (3) the persistence of beliefs and practices across the generations, each new generation being initiated, socialized into the ways of the tribe, into the traditions represented by its art; thus Chapter Four, Art: Cultural Telltale or indicator.** To each sphere, we will hear the gospel speak both a Yes and a No. The church's

Spirit-ordered task is to discern that Yes and No so that earth may again lie fallow for gospel seed to grow.

In emphasizing the cultural shape of religion and the religious dimension of culture, this Part maintains the *theological* aim of this book. It does not look at religion or science or art from the standpoint of culture (whatever that might mean) or from the standpoint of any 'scientific' culture-theorist such as Marx, Freud, Durkheim, or Malinowski. These have their value, but it cannot be emphasized often enough that each of them has a standpoint just as Christian theology does. Working from the present standpoint—that of Christian theology, and in particular the theology of these three volumes—entails no need to devalue others' work, but it asks what can be said about religion and culture from this (theological) standpoint.

CHAPTER TWO

Religion as Culture

For the purposes of this chapter, religion is treated as a complex set of cultural phenomena, so that it will not be appropriate to favor or disfavor religion as such—neither to baptize all religion nor to demonize it. Instead, the task will be to consider in particular cases those religious convictions and practices that constitute it a revealing cultural phenomenon, doing this in order to gain a vantage point for the gospel critique of the culture it embodies (see *Doctrine,* Ten §1*a*). Although my special interest here is religion in America, there can be no chance in a brief chapter of doing justice to all varieties of religious practice. I mean only to choose some instances of American cultural formation, showing in each case their underlying convictions and goals, noting the practices that most clearly express and embody these, and then in each case trying to discover the good news of Jesus Christ that those convictions and practices evoke or that they require. Thus though the task seems at the outset descriptive, it moves toward normative judgments. In this chapter, then, I will consider **(§1) an American Indian culture of the Southwest, the Navajo culture; (§2) the religious dimension of the American Revolution of 1776–83; (§3) religion as it appeared in the revivals of the first third of the nineteenth century with their aftermath; and finally (§4) the Social Gospel viewed not primarily in its theology but in its practice.** This is not a chronological arrangement: the earliest instance, the Navajo culture, is alive and flourishing today as is revivalist Evangelicalism, while the American Revolution and the Social Gospel appear to have ended somewhere in the past. Yet the arrangement displays something of the almost limitless religious variety of America of which these are at best samples.

I am particularly sorry to pass over American Judaism in this chapter, both because of its intrinsic interest and because of its relevance to Christian theology. (On Judaism see *Doctrine,* Eight §2.) Also omitted are such recent arrivals in America as the immigrant Asian Buddhist phenomena of the Pacific Coast and elsewhere, along with the ever-repeated phenomena of 'new religions.' Yet this chapter is not meant as a survey but only as the illustration of a method. Others can (and in some cases already have) pursued this method in these other cases.

§1. Navajo Culture as Religion

Due to its dynamic history, its mutually significant encounters with other Original American cultures in the Southwest and with the Spanish and the English-speaking Americans, and because of its adaptive vitality through all this, there can hardly be any culture on the North American continent of greater interest than the Navajo. The self-styled *Dine'éh* (which means simply "the People") have lived in the high desert and mountain country, now mainly south and east of today's Four Corners intersection of Utah, Colorado, New Mexico, and Arizona, for perhaps four hundred fifty to a thousand years by historians' reckoning, though much longer—indeed, for all time—by their own mythical account. They came down (the historian's version) from the north where they had been hunter-gatherers; they came trading and marauding, violently seizing for themselves the food, the cattle, and the women and children of previous inhabitants. In time they learned from their victims to become a pastoral and sometimes a horticultural people, herding livestock where there was less water and growing row crops where there was a little more. In part these skills of survival were learned from the Pueblo and Spanish women the Navajo had taken in raids (Karl Luckert in Brugge and Frisbie, 1982:187-97). The Navajo learned much else from their predecessors in the region, including ritual practices of a religious sort, but they never imitated others' concentration of dwellings in pueblo villages or towns. Instead, they scattered widely across the land in clan and family groups, each nuclear family sheltering in tent-like hogans, huts made of wood or earth as material came to hand, with a smoke hole in the roof and a doorway facing east. The east doorway layout turned each lonely hogan's back to the prevailing westerly winds and the fierce afternoon sun of the region. Its single door facing the rising sun, each hogan served a ritual function as well. Goods were sought and ills averted or healed by ceremonies there that invoked the supernatural Holy People, promising them gifts, ceremonies that employed sympathetic magic to remove troubling spirits or physical pains, and (perhaps most interesting to us) ceremonies that re-identified the participants gathered in the hogan with the forces that governed nature and human life (Louise Lamphere, ER 10:337-40).

It was while living in this fashion that the Navajo with other native peoples of the Southwest witnessed the arrival of the Spanish-Mexican conquerors, *arrivistes* hardly more recent than themselves; later both would feel the impact of the English-speaking Americans, who in the nineteenth century came from the northeast and amid much blood and tears overcame the Spanish as well as the Navajo and the other inhabitants of the land. The Spanish were important to the Navajo because they brought European skills such as working with precious stones and silver and building with sun-dried brick, and as well because they and their Anglo successors brought versions of Catholic and Protestant Christianity. The newcomers offered, sometimes they imposed, these versions upon the Navajo when they could. There were certainly other impositions: In mid–nineteenth century, the Navajo in New Mexico Territory fought prolonged wars against the United States. They were devastated by these wars; in time their survivors were rounded up and deported from their high country homeland to a 'reservation' in east-central New Mexico (the Long Walk, 1864–68); there many of them perished from hunger and hopelessness. Yet after many years this sad story had a happy ending. In time, Washington authorities were persuaded to restore the Navajo to their traditional country. There this adaptable people acquired new skills of survival, indeed, skills of flourishing. Once again there were the hogans, the crop lands (some of them now irrigated in sophisticated fashion), the herds of livestock (mostly small as befits a dry country); also now there were industries, power plants, factories to assemble electronic goods alongside the old Navajo and Mexican handiwork arts in jewelry and clothing. The Navajo population became the largest of any American Indian people, and at last report it was growing; the Navajo reservation surrounding Four Corners, wrung from a reluctant federal government, is the size of New England, the largest of any Indian reservation in the country. To be sure, there is much poverty: Navajo children in distressing numbers are undernourished, and Navajo culture sometimes fails to relieve its people's needs, though the same could be said of the culture of New York City or Los Angeles. On the whole, the Navajo's story is to this point a positive one.

Every adaptation has its price. A power plant produces unwanted smog even in the arid Southwest. Efforts to reduce smog by burning low-sulfur coal may lead to local strip mining that entails the displacement of inhabitants of the area to be mined—on land 'owned' in the traditional way by the entire people and controlled by the tribal Council. Thus lifelong inhabitants of Black Mesa at this writing find themselves permanently displaced. Outsiders (an Anglo coal company and Anglo ecological activists) insert their own opposed weights into the resultant controversy. Balancing these complex human needs and costs places heavy demands on Window Rock leaders not previously equipped with the required moral skills. The need is for convictions and practices that will enable the Navajo to continue their flexible survival as a people (Jaimes, 1992; Brugge, 1994).

a. Navajo convictions and practices.—What are the convictions and practices that have shaped this surprisingly effective culture on North American soil? Compared with other peoples the traditional Navajo were not much concerned about an afterlife; their beliefs in this regard were comparable to those reflected in the Old Testament. Their prevailing concern was rather with this present life and the rituals and myths that maintained it. Present well-being (long life, good health) was closely related to the presiding concept of harmony or beauty *(hózhó)*, whose opposite is imbalance, disharmony, ugliness *(hóchó)* (Lamphere, ER 10:337). Navajo hogans are traditionally located on sites that take advantage of the striking beauty of the natural scenery of the Southwest. Navajo family life emphasizes getting along with other family members, even at the expense of individual dispositions or needs (Kluckhohn and Leighton, 1962:chap. 3). Navajo ranching and farming of necessity emphasize cooperation with fellow laborers, with the elements, the seasons, and the traditional terrain bounded by its four sacred mountains.

These elemental convictions were grammatically linked with accounts of creation and human origins—or to speak more exactly, accounts of the origins of the People. From the four directions represented by the four sacred mountains came winds that directed the natural phenomena and the mysterious Holy People as well as the *Dine'éh*. The wind was both outer and inner: "each Navajo also has a 'wind within one' that enters at birth and guides the individual." This belief provided at once an explanation of the force that guides natural phenomena (plants, animals, seasons, volcanoes) and the force that shapes individual human life. And there was better reason to see why harmony, *hózhó,* was appropriate: human beings were not merely part of nature; they were each inspirited by the very power that shaped nature. Moreover, these natural-supernatural connections had an interior relation to the origin stories of the People that bound the ritual practices, the wind, and all nature into one beautiful whole. The emergence stories recalled a layered series of 'worlds'; each had given rise to the one above it, until the Fifth World (the present land of the Navajo) appeared. In the chain of originating events,

> First Man, First Woman, and other Holy People set in place the "inner forms" of natural phenomena (earth, sky, the sacred mountains, plants, and animals), creating the present world. It was into this world that Changing Woman was born; she was impregnated by the sun and gave birth to twin sons, [hunters and warriors] who killed various monsters that had been endangering the Holy People. Using the medicine bundle [brought from previous underworlds], Changing Woman created maize. She also created the Earth-Surface people, or the Navajo, from epidermal waste rubbed from her skin. (Lamphere, ER 10:337)

So (to paraphrase here an older Book of Origins) the People were created in her image, skin of her skin, part and parcel of their original. The mythic concept of Changing Woman connected earth and sky. The old cultural way of dealing with the evils that beset human flesh employed rituals designed to restore the original harmony between man, world, and the supernatural Holy People. For example, a much-used sing or chant, Lifeway, treated injuries resulting from accidents. In it the victim was painted red, the color of blood, symbolizing a return to life and health. Evilway rituals, in contrast, exorcised ghosts and overcame ugly and harmful aspects of Navajo life (10:338).

This touches upon a darker side of Navajo existence: witches and ghosts. It was deemed possible for an individual to become a witch. Witches had supernatural powers, and were a threat to the beauty *(hózhó)* of life; indeed, a threat to life itself. For death was a feared, dreaded, almost unspeakable aspect of the People's existence. The only conception of an afterlife was that a ghost escaped the body of the deceased only to linger nearby, working harm on any who came near. Prescribed forms for the disposal of the dead human body aimed at deceiving this evil ghost and rendering it harmless. For the People by their own reckoning lived in a world that combined great promise, the promise of beauty here and now, with great dread, the fear of supernatural powers that threatened their lives and made death a thing feared rather than accepted in hope (Laura Thompson, *Enc. Brit.* 13:335-39).

Here a correction is in order: the account of 'traditional' Navajo existence just furnished is twice flawed. Its presentation of the ritual and convictional aspects of Navajo culture, its "religion," if we choose that term, is related in past tense, for its point has been to present the People as they existed in the Southwest before interaction with the Spanish and later the Anglo Americans. Yet the data come mainly from twentieth-century anthropological accounts—research done long after Spanish and English-speaking influence had entered the picture. So the account is only a reconstruction, and second, it is a reconstruction that assumes a continuous stability in Navajo religious and cultural life. Yet the evidence itself shows that this is not so. The 'timelessness' associated by some writers with primal religious practices is the timelessness of a still camera that takes its exposures at the moment the anthropologist arrives on the scene—or worse, it is a reconstruction based upon that still photo (Luckert in Brugge and Frisbie, 1982:187-89). If this double flaw in the preceding report is kept in mind, perhaps it can still be of some service.

b. Enter Franciscans and Protestants.—European impact upon the Southwest began late in the sixteenth century, about a hundred years after Columbus's ships first reached the West Indies. These voyages were part of a worldwide quest for empire and colonization and evangelization (the three were never separated) by the rival Iberian kingdoms of Spain and Portugal. The Spanish made landings on the coasts of the Gulf of Mexico, but their political center was Mexico City. There diligent missionaries, mostly Franciscan, worked from the beginning to bring the defeated Aztec peoples to accept both Spanish rule and Roman Catholic allegiance—both with evident if limited success. The Southwest (present New Mexico and Arizona including the Navajo reservations) was considered by Spaniards to lie on their frontier, boundary regions deserving only marginal attention. Nevertheless, competition with the French to the north and east coupled with a sense of divine right embodied in papal decrees led Spanish colonists, soldiers, and missionaries to press on through El Paso del Norte (site of later El Paso, Texas) and thence northwestward into New Mexico in the 1500s.

The principal missionaries here were Franciscans, who already by the early 1600s had established schools and churches in many places. Their missionary method closely coupled church and school: where children could be enlisted as little missionaries, their families might follow them into the arms of Christ. This missiology was devised by the pioneering strategy of a learned Franciscan friar, Bernard de Sahagun, whose monumental studies set the Spanish understanding of New World culture. In brief, the observation that Mexican pagan religion featured human sacrifice so horrified the Franciscans that they resolved to make no syncretic compromise with existing religious practices: New World inhabitants must be weaned away from their present beliefs and accept a completely new, Spanish-Christian way of life (De Vaulx, 1961:66-69).

By this late medieval time, European Catholics were wedded to a version of Christianity fixed upon seven sacraments, of which the utmost in holiness was the eucharist or mass. Baptism, penance, and marriage were freely administered by the Franciscans in New Spain whenever possible; confirmation and extreme unction only with great caution, while the eucharist (with the holy orders that administered it) was withheld almost completely from Original Americans until the anticipated time when new generations would be fully separated from the old Mexican culture (De Vaulx, 1961:66-69). This was the strategy, then, that came with the Franciscans to the Navajo borderlands in New Mexico and persisted with the Anglo missionaries who followed. It was notably successful among the Hopi and Eastern Pueblo peoples; it was far less successful among the scattered Apache and Navajo. The reason is not far to seek: how could children living in isolated hogans dispersed across hundreds, perhaps thousands of sections of land be recruited to attend school and learn the Franciscan way? Though beginning in the 1860s, Presbyterian, Christian Reformed, Methodist, and other missionary efforts were launched among the Navajo; these missions were tied to the United States government policy of 'civilizing' the Indians. Though often served by faithful missionaries, these Constantinian enterprises, far from the spirit of the American Constitution's First Amendment, and farther still from Jesus' example and commission ("render unto Caesar"), showed only small results (M. Warner, 1970:209-12; Spicer, 1962:436-38; see further Warner, 1977). As Kluckhohn and Leighton point out in their standard anthropological survey, the

> imagery and the excitements and fears accompanying [Navajo ceremonies] were stored away in the unconscious long before the youngsters [in mission schools, whether Catholic or Protestant] could reason or objectify what they saw. All this conditioned them fundamentally, so that subsequent Christian imagery could not supplant or alter it. Anything which affected them from white culture in later years was a veneer which readily cracked when they had occasion to reëxperience their own tribal religious emotions. (1962:137)

One reads such a judgment with a vivid awareness that the absolute separation between the European and Mexican cultures laid down four centuries earlier by Father Sahagun was still the goal of both Catholic and Protestant missionaries—and, as this quotation shows, it was the standard for twentieth-century anthropological thinking as well: Cultures must not mingle! In contrast, the dominant truth about the Navajo seems to be not only that they were and are a people capable of clinging to their inherited convictions and practices, but that they can make remarkable adjustments to new circumstances, new possibilities. As anthropologists Kluckhohn and Leighton themselves say a few pages later, "The Navajos are distinguished among American Indians by the alacrity, if not the ease, with which they have adjusted to the impact of white culture while still retaining many native traits and preserving the framework of their own cultural organization" (1962:171).

c. A gospel response.—Recall now that the gospel of Jesus Christ comes in story form: it speaks of a God who has time for us (Karl Barth), a God who is not only Creator but also comes as Redeemer and stays as Reconciling Spirit. When this storied gospel comes to Navajos today it finds not a storyless people but one with two stories already. There is the Enlightenment story of the Navajos as one tribe linked by similar language to the Apache and to other groups in the West—a people descended from migrant hunter-gatherers who came across the straits from Siberia. That story has its truth. However, it acknowledges no distinct role for Navajos. They are for it only one Indian tribe among many. In line with that Enlightenment story Navajo lands are administered by the United States through its Bureau of Indian Affairs, an even-handed if unfeeling administration of all the conquered peoples under its power. Second, there is the somewhat older story of the Navajos, descended from the skin of Changing Woman, guided by their mystic unity with First Man and First Woman, constituting in themselves the People—unique, alone, with their holy aim of beauty and their unnerving fear of witches and ghosts. Both of these stories are intersected by the still older gospel story. Its business is not to deny these, the scientific Enlightenment story and the legendary-mythical Navajo one. Its business is to affirm them where they are true, to correct them where they are *harmfully* wrong, and to complete them by showing the relation between these stories and an inclusive story of all the earth. For the gospel announces that God has never left creation alone, but has spoken in "many and varied ways" (Heb. 1:1). By that same account, "in the first bright glimmers of opportunity God sent—himself, incognito, without splendor and fanfare, the Maker amid the things made, the fundamental Web as if a single fiber, the Ground of Adventure risking everything in this adventure" (*Ethics*, Five §3*b*,

p. 147). When this story of the saving Son intersects the story of these children of the sun and sharers of one humanity, it generates—already this has become a reality for some of the *Dine'éh*—a new story fulfilling the old, as Navajos while remaining Navajos discover themselves in the new that comes in Christ.

The main theological question, it seems to me, is not how clearly the old patterns of Navajo practice have been abandoned and the new adopted (this was Sahagun's sixteenth-century question); it rather asks what the gospel has to say both to the old that persists and to the new that has come. For the gospel of the new that comes in Jesus Christ can only exclaim with an amen to the Navajo sense of the wholeness of life and the beauty *(hózhó)* it evinces. Would that Europeans and Anglo Americans had perceived such a wholeness sooner and more clearly! Here Navajo 'religion' (or better, their religiousness) has much to teach the Christian missionaries and witnesses who come near it. On the other hand, the gospel must proclaim good tidings (see e.g. Ps. 23:4; 1 John 4:18; 1 Thess. 3:13f), a word of great good cheer to Navajo people who, for whatever reason, are hounded by fear of witches and dread of ghosts. One recalls that Europeans prior to the Enlightenment, though nominally or even actually Christians, often evinced similar fears. However, where did the Enlightenment itself come from? Was it not a Christian cultural phenomenon, and one that allowed the mainly baptist and Protestant Christians who first enjoyed it to escape those dark fears forever? (see Chapter Five within). Thus, to repeat, the gospel is not a simple no or yes to Navajo 'religion' but declares a simultaneous yes and no.

However, that yes and no are not addressed only to earlier Navajo and other Original American religious expressions; they are God's judging and redeeming word also to the Catholic and Protestant forms of Christian cultural existence that in due time appeared in *Dinetah,* Navajoland. My understanding of that yes and no has already appeared in *Volumes I* and *II.* There the questions, what the church must do and must teach to be authentic, faithful church, have been asked and by my lights answered. What is said there applies here as well. The Franciscan missionaries with their misleading attachment to the cult of saints (mainly European saints, be it noticed) and with their exceedingly narrow eucharistic practice should have heard both a no and a yes from the Good News. Likewise (and not a whit less) the other Christian missionaries to the Navajo, mainly Reformed and baptist, will find in these volumes a no and a yes to their own preaching and their schools for Indians. For their projects, too, stand under gospel judgment—as does this present book. For example, a particular task of

Christian mission in coming days is to widen its witness from concern with individuals (a concern certainly in order) to an appreciative concern for Navajo social structure with its assets and its new problems, notably with its attempts to cope with a changing social and economic order that involves coal mining and power plants as well as hand crafts and agriculture.

§2. The Religious American Revolution (1776–83)

Readers who approached the religious stance of the Navajo with calm disinterest may find such detachment more difficult in this section. For the Revolution of 1776–83 with its aftermath lays claim to the self-understanding of many readers. For citizens of the United States in particular (and in some degree others as well) the Declaration of Independence, the colonists' war of liberation from Britain, the formation of a new 'federal' (i.e., a 'covenanted') government with its written Constitution, along with the lives of heroic leaders such as George Washington—all are formative for many readers' identity. American schoolchildren sing "My country, 'tis of thee / Sweet land of liberty / Of thee I sing." They are indoctrinated in school and home to treat this Revolution as their own: by it their own freedom (from what is claimed to have been virtual slavery to the British) has been obtained. Yet all this is understood as *political* verity: how can it be religion as well? Is not religion just what the Founders separated from public polity? Is not that separation the very creed of the democracy—a nation baptized in the fire of *war,* confirmed in civil *strife:* "One nation, under God, with liberty and justice for all"? Religion, on this view, was relegated to its proper, private place by a new nation. Indeed? The truth is that this section does not address alien myths and legends, but the very myths and legends that are constitutive for my primary reading audience. It will be best to expose these tales step-by-step, peeling away the layers that conceal the religion of the republic, as well as gospel religion, from schoolchildren's innocent gaze—and their teachers' gaze, as well.

a. The Americans were not anti-religious.—A first step toward understanding is to *desecularize* the account of American beginnings. The colonial churches north and south, far from being preoccupied with private concerns alone, were thickly involved in fomenting and guiding the Revolution, except in the case of the few, mainly Anglican, who took the British side—or the even fewer, mainly baptist, who refused to endorse war or take up arms. The patriots who led the Revolution were almost to a man religious by ordinary standards, and their religion was nearly indistinguishable from their politics, unseparated by the wall or line the First Amendment seemed later to require. American clergymen were the pacesetters of public opinion; while the clergy preached revolution, the soldiers and politicians urged religion as the instrument of a common cause. The pioneer Baptist leaders Isaac Backus and John Leland, hoping for religious liberty via revolution, were among these clerical leaders, and their flocks in the main followed. The revolutionaries knew they must have a "black regiment" of clergy and churches on their side if they were to prevail.

All this seems flatly to contradict the story of American beginnings that recent generations of American students have learned. They have heard nothing of religion in early American history. This is no accident: earlier in the twentieth century, historians intentionally secularized American history by privatizing the role of colonial religion. Of course, these historians meant to be truthful. By their day, Christian religion in the United States had truly become for the most part private. These mid-twentieth-century historians (like their predecessors) explained the character of their own time by projecting it upon the American past. More recent historical study, however, has again revised this secular account of revolutionary America by inspecting the facts afresh.

The revision is twofold. From one side, historians such as Alan Heimert (1966), Patricia Bononi (1986), and Harry Stout (1986) have shown how the American pulpit traversed the ground from traditional Puritan jeremiads (calls for public repentance) to the fiery fighting sermons of 1776–83. From the other, political side, historians such as Sidney E. Mead (1963) and Edwin S. Gaustad (1987, 1996*a*) have shown that the new nation's founders (especially Pennsylvania's Benjamin Franklin, Virginia's George Washington, Thomas Jefferson, and James Madison, and Massachusetts' John Adams) led in shaping a "religion of the Republic" (Mead's term), a civil religion. None of these founders was an orthodox Christian, yet each professed religious views with a Christian flavoring that formed his own career and significantly guided the Revolution. The upshot is that the American Revolution was penetrated by some sort of religiousness from beginning to end. As Yale historian Harry Stout writes: "When understood *in its own time,* the American Revolution was first and foremost *a religious event*" (1996:13, emphasis added; see further Jerald Brauer, 1976; Nathan Hatch, 1977, 1989; Mark Noll, 1977; Ruth Bloch, 1985).

Even earlier, American literary historian Perry Miller (1905–63) had uncovered the colonial period's religious substratum. His (1961) essay, "From Covenant to Revival," demonstrated that the Revolution had a richer theological basis than was displayed in the official political documents of its day. The theology of the revolution was not adequately disclosed in the Declaration of Independence, for example, with its appeal to "Nature's God." The Declaration, and the war itself, were consequences of the covenant theology inherited by the revolutionary preachers from their seventeenth-century forebears. Americans' secret strength was not merely their belief in "rights" that "all men" reckoned reasonable; beneath these rights lay something more holy, namely the colonists' responsibility to keep covenant with God and thus, only thus, to be set free (Miller in Smith and Jamison, eds., 1961:322-68).

Miller and after him the 'religious' historians made a final but crucial point: the colonial preachers had found America's plight foreshadowed in biblical Israel. This was *typology:* the faltering kingdom of the Jews was a type or preview of the colonists' situation in the New World. Jehovah's promises to Israel were to be made good in an 'antitypical,' that is, a fulfilling narrative, the anticipated history of thirteen converging colony-states. Since the Old Testament had called royal rule into question (cf. 1 Samuel 8), the colonists were likewise destined to have no king over them. Behind the new social compact lay the conviction that America was the new Israel, *Israel redivivus,* afflicted by foreign government, crying out to God for release not from Egyptian but from British slavery.

Alongside the churches were the religious politicians: *Benjamin Franklin* (1706–90), Philadelphia printer, moralist, and opinion shaper, thought it best to speak well of all the churches and their messages, though he agreed fully with none of them. Franklin is best categorized theologically as a Deist: God is earth's original Creator and final Judge, but moral duties in the interim are to be discovered in Reason and Nature (terms capitalized by these leaders), not in Scripture. *George Washington* (1732–99) was a lifelong Anglican communicant, but many even of the clergy in that church professed the intellectual Deism of the day. To the end of his days Washington remained aloof from the "person and ministry" of Jesus. *John Adams* (1735–1826) was an heir of New England Puritanism, but he had followed many others of that persuasion into the more recent Unitarianism. Believing strongly in the sovereignty of God and in his own finitude, Adams simply anticipated a "future state" in which free men would receive their just reward. *Thomas Jefferson* (1743–1826) talked and wrote constantly about religion, and he read the New Testament for an hour daily (in the original Greek, but with the miracles expunged). Like Franklin, Washington, and Adams, Jefferson tied his political philosophy to his deistic religion, to Nature and to Nature's God. His chief religious concern was religious liberty. That was the concern of *James Madison* (1751–1836) as well. He was a main sponsor of Virginia's Statute for Establishing Religious Freedom (written by Jefferson) and of the later First Amendment to the Constitution with its two-clause guarantee of freedom from governmental interference in religion. Unlike Jefferson, though, Madison in his maturity had nothing more to say about religion; historian Edwin Gaustad once told me religious liberty was Madison's *only* religious conviction (see Gaustad, 1996*b*).

Historians' judgments, like those of theologians, are subject to revision in every generation. It is possible at this stage, though, to summarize what historians have lately been telling us about religion and the American political and military revolution. The secular historians had a point—there was indeed a 'secular' change in these former colonies from the state-church arrangements of England (though this was not a complete change—state churches persisted in several former colonies; e.g., in Massachusetts, until 1833). Yet the change was not that the new nation had ceased to be religious. Its leaders saw a vital link between their new religion and the new politics. Meantime the churches, or most of them, saw a link as well, basing their patriotism upon their inherited covenant theology. On both accounts, then, the Americans remained, as a later Supreme Court justice would write, a religious people. By a logic present readers may find obscure, preachers found it possible, indeed necessary, to warn colonists that the obedience God required of covenant-keepers included resistance to that tyrant of tyrants, George III. Thus Perry Miller could paraphrase the jeremiads of the revolutionary period:

> [W]e have sinned, therefore we are afflicted by the tyranny of a corrupt Britain; we must repent and reform, in order to win the irresistible aid of Providence; once we have wholeheartedly performed this act, we shall be able to exert our freedom by expelling the [royal] violators of the compact; when we succeed we shall enter upon a prosperity and temporal happiness beyond anything the world has hitherto seen. (1961:346)

Such a covenantal theology not only underwrote rebellion against England but also undergirded the developing federal or covenanted politics that was forming the nation. The politicians found it prudent to express their political appeals in terms reminiscent of John Locke's purely secular social compact. But their appeals were effective because they reached the ears of a populace convinced of "original sin and the need of grace" (Miller, 1961:342). Thus covenant theology not only called the colonists to arms; it also drew them together in what Abraham Lincoln would later call "a more perfect union."

b. A gospel critique of Revolutionary religion.—As with the Southwestern Navajo episode in American culture history, it is proper here to reflect upon the gospel's no and yes to America's Revolution. Positively, one can be grateful that the Founders and their Christian followers were aware that religion could not be relegated to a private sphere. Such a reading of their First Amendment is in stark contradiction to the role religion had played in their Revolution in the first place. They correctly proclaimed the gospel as good news to the nations, that is, as a gospel to people collectively as well as to individuals, one by one (cf. Matt. 28:19). So far, so good. Yet negatively, the Founders misperceived the gospel. In particular the colonial Christian use of typology committed a fateful error: it applied Old Testament types or models to present Christian circumstances *without allowing for the central typical role of Jesus Christ.* Roger Williams (1603?–1683), himself no stranger to biblical typology and no mean politician, either, had warned more than a century before the Revolution that Christ alone was the end, the goal or terminus of all the Old Testament types or foreshadowings of the New. In Christ, who was prophet, priest, and king (here, particularly king), every type had been fulfilled. Thus colonial Christians could not, must not read their own situation as a replay of the Hebrew monarchy without asking how this replay was transformed by the pivotal role of Jesus of Nazareth. Williams's warnings all forgotten or ignored, eighteenth-century American Christians made exactly that mistake.

Of special interest here is the revolutionary role of pioneer American Baptist Isaac Backus (1724–1806). A New England Congregationalist, Backus's ecclesiology had gradually evolved from Congregational separatism to a church in which both believers and infant baptism were tolerated and finally into the formation of a strict (separatist) Baptist church (1756). By 1776 he had shepherded such a church for twenty years; in its pulpit he became one of the insurrectionist preachers described above. Significantly, in his defense of the Baptist view in contentious New England, Backus had evoked the name of Roger Williams; indeed it is chiefly through Backus that later generations of Americans heard of Williams. Yet at one crucial point, Backus fell silent. He never repeated Williams's explicit warning against a typology that applied the Old Testament's kings, wars, and violent deliverers to colonial America without reckoning the difference made by the coming of Jesus Christ. Yet (in the *Bloody Tenent,* a volume Backus frequently cites) Williams had written,

> Those former types of the land, of the people, of their worships, were types and figures of spiritual land, spiritual people, and spiritual worship *under Christ.* [So they must] have their *spiritual* antitypes, and so consequently not civil but spiritual governors and rulers—lest the very essential nature of types, figures and shadows be overthrown. (Williams, 1644:353)

Only when Christ was seen as Roger Williams saw him, one who had transformed history into a new mode, can Christian typology avoid the terrible mistake of "compelling a whole nation or kingdom to be the antitype of Israel." Backus the revolutionary seems simply not to have noticed Williams's warning. It is far from obvious that Roger Williams like Backus would have sponsored a military revolution—Williams who struggled to make peace with his Narragansett and other Indian neighbors, Williams who gave years of his life to securing a *royal* charter for Rhode Island. Yet the silence of Backus is not corrected by his chief twentieth-century interpreters, Thomas B. Maston (1962), William G. McLoughlin (1967), and Stanley Grenz (1983), none of whom tells us that here Backus stood not on the side of Roger Williams but on the side of his persecuting New England opponents.

The outcome of this christologically defective use of typology by the revolutionaries was that they lacked the *norm of peace* with which the gospel equips Bible readers. Jesus' determinative role has been explored in the previous volumes: Jesus the preacher of the gospel of peace took the way of the cross as a deliberate alternative to the ways of violence (*Ethics,* Eleven §1; *Doctrine,* Five §3*b;* Yoder, 1994*b*). What soon followed, though, was a centuries-long Constantinian compromise. In it the political gain of the cross of Christ was sacrificed to the politics of empire—a sacrifice ratified by the great Augustine of Hippo. Still later, Constantinianism was exported to the New World by colonists from each of the leading European powers. Regrettably, the American Revolution *did not escape* from this ancient but perverse heritage regarding church and state.

There were, as mentioned above, European Christians who rejected the Constantinian way. Such (small-b) baptist colonists in America as Quakers (from 1656), various groups of Mennonites (from 1683), and Brethren (from 1719) recognized that obedience to Christ demanded nonviolence; in particular it demanded the rejection of the old Constantinian warfare ethos. To these believers, Christ was the founder and sovereign of a new peaceable kingdom to which all owed first allegiance. *No Cross, No Crown,* the title of a book by the Quaker founder of Pennsylvania, William Penn (1644–1718), expressed the basic idea succinctly. In the Revolutionary War these disciples of the Way tended the wounded on both sides, buried the dead, counseled the perplexed, and prayed for peace on earth. Yet their standpoint remained an oddity among colonial Christians. For those who had more recently adopted the radical way, including numerous Baptists, a different story prevailed. Though there were prophetic voices among these as well (for noteworthy example, John Allen, an English Baptist preacher who reminded white colonists that the real slaves in America were not themselves but their African captives), Baptists in the main were driven by the winds of war. As we have seen, some, like Isaac Backus, became strong revolutionary advocates.

American nationhood was indeed founded on a religious basis—yet when this religion took the shape of nationhood it swiftly lost sight of the gospel at its root. In one way the agitation of the late twentieth century's religious right wing for a 'Christian America' is true to American history: the revolutionary beginnings of this country were indeed strongly religious. Yet these advocates of religious patriotism overlook not only the complex variety of colonial religiousness—from Deism to Dunkards, from Moravians to Roman Catholics. They also lack any gospel critique of American beginnings. Correspondingly, they fail to hear the gospel's prophetic challenge to their own nationalist pride. Christians of biblical heritage are never required to ratify the past; it stands, like the present, in the hands of God. Would this be a better land, by gospel light, if there had been no American Revolution? Such a question, though, defies the myth of violent American beginnings. And what would the alternative have been? Does the Canadian experience suggest an alternative worth considering? (On the myth of redemptive violence see further Walter Wink, *Engaging the Powers*, 1992.)

Two related consequences of this 'religious' Revolution will occupy us again in what follows. By painting the British oppressor in more and more gory depravity, the preachers subtly committed themselves to the view that America was by contrast a pure society. When in course of time the British yoke was decisively cast off (an outcome keen military observers might have predicted, but one which the pulpits attributed to God's delight in the revolutionary cause), the ideological lesson seemed inescapable: Here was a people delivered by God to make a new beginning, a collective Adam, as it were, created to occupy a new Eden (cf. Chapter Four, §2). Hence the past no longer mattered; all that mattered was Adam's invincible future. Yale College President Ezra Stiles preached in 1783 before the Connecticut General Assembly a sermon titled "The United States Elevated to Glory and Honor?":

> This will be a great, a very great nation, nearly equal to half Europe. . . . [B]efore the millennium the English settlements in America may become more numerous millions than that greatest dominion on earth, the Chinese Empire. (in Thornton, 1970:440)

By the success of the Revolution, Americans were translated into a lasting state of lyrical innocence; their cause having prevailed, it was clearly the British, not they, who were disobedient to God's covenant. Yet with that transfiguration of self-esteem there came a new disquiet. Were the people of the newly united American states now beyond all need of pastoral reproof? Need there now be no more jeremiads? Is the diminished church attendance and church membership of the revolutionary period (1775–1800) not evidence of a new lapse of faith to which lyrical innocence is a blindly sinful response? Is not an even more widespread disobedience revealed by the godless French Revolution (1789–99)? Perhaps no one of these questions adequately formulates the state of mind of the early federal period in the United States, yet their drift is clear enough: the outcome of the Revolution was a new American *anxiety.* As Perry Miller writes,

> a chill strikes the exulting heart. If this [American success] be so, are we not, under the Providence of God, on leaving the exciting scenes both of war and spiritual conflict, now headed for a monotonous, an uninteresting prosperity, the flatness of universal virtue? (1961:349)

Two remedies offered themselves to this nameless anxiety; we will shortly see more of each. Anxious American Christians looked to the future and envisioned American virtue spread around the globe, culminating in Christ's triumphant return. This post-millennial vision (to give its technical theological name) projected a territorial growth of the kingdom of virtue: Americans were destined to build a worldwide Rule of God. The long issue of this vision would be called the Social Gospel. The other remedy for anxiety looked not outside and beyond but into individual American Christian hearts: Christians of all denominations yearned for, nay, they demanded—a revival.

§3. The Evangelical Revival, 1800–1835

Revival means many things to many people, from its etymological sense ("coming to life again") to its more recent reference to a stylized series of religious meetings following a well-known format, trading upon emotion and easily caricatured. For early-nineteenth-century Americans, however, the revivals, taken together, constituted an extended event that swept the country after the Revolution and prior to the Civil War (more exact dates may be arbitrary). Revival took on different forms in different regions: in the West, whose far reach at the century's beginning was remote Kentucky, or in New England, where a Second Awakening echoed with a difference the Great Awakening of the 1740s, or in the South, where the revival was given special poignancy by its involvement with race relations. Common features, however, characterized revival in all these regions: a fresh vitality for church members converted from a nominal to a heartfelt Christianity, but also the conversion of newcomers to the faith and the establishing of new churches and new denominations shaped by the revival spirit. The new alignments included new groupings of Presbyterians and Baptists, the beginnings of the Campbellite restorationist movement, and (perhaps most striking of all) an enduring orientation for American Methodism. For a nation with a novel political arrangement under a federal Constitution that dissolved old privileges of hierarchy and rank and left the ordering of public life undetermined, the revivals of this period were without parallel in social significance and in theological consequences.

To take this view requires that we not limit revival to a single sort of phenomenon such as the Cane Ridge, Kentucky, camp meeting of 1801, or to a single doctrinal change such as the softening of determinist Calvinism, or to a single psychological motif such as the healing of pervasive anxiety or low self-esteem. The revivals were all this and more. Recent historians have noted that one of the first echoes of the earlier Great Awakening occurred among German Americans strongly influenced by European Anabaptism and eighteenth-century Pietism. The Mennonite evangelist Martin Boehm, for example, brought evangelistic passion to his native Pennsylvania and created links between Christians of his heritage and those of Reformed and Methodist persuasion.

Martin Boehm (1725–1812) had been chosen by lot as preacher of a Mennonite congregation, but was deeply troubled by his unworthiness for that role. In about 1758 his self-doubt was overcome in a powerful conversion. Thereafter he began to preach with new power. Three years later, in Virginia, he encountered the Great Awakening heritage of George Whitefield and took it home with him. In 1767 Boehm was preaching for revival in Isaac Long's barn (in present Lancaster County). In attendance was the pietistic German Reformed preacher, Philip William Otterbein (1726–1813). After Mennonite Boehm had related his conversion, Otterbein embraced him, exclaiming, *Wir sind Brüder!* (we are brothers!). From this meeting grew the United Brethren in Christ, formed by German speakers of assorted backgrounds and focused on conversion and revival. Their strand of church life, after several intervening mergers, came together with Methodists to create The United Methodist

Church. A prescient twist in this story is that Boehm was excommunicated from his Mennonite fellowship because his revivalism had grown too close to other denominations of Christians. So it came about that the preacher for Martin Boehm's Lancaster County funeral was his good friend, American Methodist founder Francis Asbury (J. O'Malley, DCA 1011f; Don Yoder, ME I:378).

a. Revival on the frontier.—Better known than the German churches' revivals are those encouraged by Presbyterian, Baptist, and Methodist leaders on the frontier. Perhaps these are remembered so well because of the extraordinary phenomena they evoked. As English-speaking Americans pressed west in search of new land and new opportunities, much that had made their lives human was left behind. Though they labeled the Indian inhabitants of the forest "savages," there was as good or better reason to have called these pioneers the savages. As an English traveler to the region scornfully reported,

> They depend more on hunting than agriculture, and of course are exposed to all the varieties of climate in the open air. Their cabins are not better than Indian wigwams. They have frequent meetings for the purpose of gambling, fighting, and drinking. They make bets to the amount of all they possess. They fight for the most trifling provocations . . . tearing, kicking, scratching, biting, gouging each others eyes out by a dexterous use of a thumb and finger, and doing their utmost to kill each other, even when rolling over one another on the ground. (Fortescue Cuming, quoted in Ahlstrom, 1972:430)

This account, historian Sydney Ahlstrom suggests, is fueled by British animus; still it is not merely a fabricated tale. In coming West these Americans had deserted their schools and their churches and whatever civilizing effect their near neighbors had provided. At best only one in ten of these pioneers crossing the Alleghenies in 1800 was a church member; yet even the nine-tenths left behind what had been their strongest social and spiritual institution, the church. Now, however, a wonderful thing happened. Into the wilderness came the missionaries—men whose lives were staked on the gospel truth. Ordained evangelical Presbyterians and Baptist farmer-preachers and Methodist circuit riders came west with the pioneers. They journeyed from isolated farmhouse to farmhouse, reading the Bible to illiterates, urging people to pray, reminding them that God was a missionary, too, having come in the life of Jesus of Nazareth to bring salvation. It was impossible for such pioneers, living on widely separated farms, to have a gathered church, so the preachers proposed a new plan. In the summer, when the crops were laid by, every family could pack its wagon with camping gear, hitch up a team, and come across country to an appointed meeting for revival. Come they did, all ages; the urgent preachers came, too. In response to hot gospel preaching, many pioneers trembled in awareness of their sins. With the imminence of salvation, sin was recognized for what it was—an affront to God's gracious offer of redemption full and free. So revival came to the frontier. There were baptisms; the Lord's Table was set and served in meetinghouses or in the open air; families went home refreshed and in many a case transformed; churches were organized; community reappeared. Reports estimate attendance as high as twenty thousand for the remarkable Cane Ridge meetings (Weisberger, 1958:31; Conkin, 1990:88).

Much, I think too much, has been made of the unusual physical phenomena, from crying to uncontrollable barks and jerks, displayed by converts in these wilderness revivals. Two points should be kept in mind here. One is that these were people whom an English visitor could characterize (or caricature) as just noted—in short, they were rough, crude men and women; no wonder that their religion, if they were to recognize its reality, must have taken a stark shape. The other point is that the raw behavior did not last, vanishing in a few years, while the heartfelt faith with its signs and acts of reconciling love did endure, to be repeated often in coming generations.

b. Revival in the North.—Back on the eastern seaboard matters were different. Here we recognize a division South and North—a division that would have fateful consequences in a few decades. Of the two, Northern revivalism presents a better-known story, and one that had profound consequences for American culture. A primary task faced by New England divines in the new nineteenth century was the revision of inherited Calvinism so that prospective converts could be confronted with an inescapable demand: God has provided the means of your salvation; if you are still lost, it is your own fault, not divine destiny. This logic set predestination on the back burner, while it elevated the human will into a determinative position. Yale professor Nathaniel W. Taylor (1786–1858) dismissed Christian doctrine's heavy burden of original sin: Sin, he said, was "in the sinning," so that it was the sinner's own fault, not that of humanity's most remote ancestor. Thus revival preachers in the Congregational tradition could demand decision of their hearers without the handicap of an outgrown theology. Lyman Beecher (1775–1863) carried the Taylor gospel into prominent New England pulpits, combining revivalism with social reform (one successful reformist campaign opposed dueling), and ended his days in the West as president of Lane Theological Seminary in Cincinnati. Such work resulted in pervasive revival in the North, a giant fruit being the manifold American Protestant foreign mission enterprise. The dramatic 1806 origin of this mission lay in a "Haystack Prayer Meeting" of Williams College divinity students shaped by the revival spirit. Among those who were there committed to mission was Adoniram Judson (1788–1850), whose later ministry extended the revivals of 1800–1835 to distant Burma. The same impulse sent Protestant missionaries to Navajo-land.

A further extension of the Northern revival occurred through the life work of Charles Grandison Finney (1792–1875). Growing up in Oneida and Jefferson Counties in western New York, Finney was a skeptical small-town lawyer until his striking conversion in 1821. (Encountered on the street that signal day, Finney rebuffed a client's demand for legal representation: "Deacon B______, I have a retainer from the Lord Jesus Christ to plead his cause, and I cannot plead yours"—Finney, 1876:24.) Before long Finney was conducting protracted meetings from town to town in western New York and even beyond in quest of revival. In their course, he developed what were for the time spectacular "new measures." The revivals came, not as a "Surprising Work of God" (thus Jonathan Edwards), but in exact response to these measures, which Finney said were available to any church at any time. Not laid down in divine writ, they were to be discovered afresh in each new age of the church. While providential circumstances might signal the need for revival, revivals came when Christians united to pray for them, when they pointed out sins and sought the conversion of sinners explicitly named, and when these efforts persisted until the awakening came. Thus Finney could say to skeptical churches, "You see why you have not a revival. It is only because you do not want one" (Finney, 1868:34). Finney went on to preach in New York City and New England, and to serve as professor and president of newly founded Oberlin College, where he was also a noted abolitionist. During his day Oberlin became the first coeducational college in the nation, granting a degree to a woman in 1850 (Ahlstrom, 1972:459-61, 643). Well beyond the present account, Finney's successors included nationally known evangelists Dwight L. Moody, Billy Sunday, and Billy Graham.

c. Revival in the South.—The South was not typified by the vast camp meetings of the frontier or by the theological revisionism of New England. Instead, most evangelism proceeded locally at a steady pace, less frequently interspersed with general gatherings. Records indicate that the chief Anglo beneficiaries of the revival spirit were rising middle- and lower-class folk who joined the South's young evangelical churches—Presbyterian, Baptist, and the rapidly rising Methodist, with a number of groups calling themselves simply "Christian." In congregations of all these names, the common doctrinal theme was derived from Scripture: The universality of sin demanded conversion of each hearer. Preachers inclined toward Reformed orthodoxy might present this in terms of the original sin of Adam; others were content to urge sin's ubiquity—*all have sinned* and are therefore lost, doomed, at risk of eternal punishment. The gospel's objective remedy for this plight was the redeeming work of God in Christ, yet for those who persisted in unbelief, redemption simply did not apply (the Calvinist view) or was of no avail (the Arminian view). Extreme Calvinism even inferred a quietist conclusion: the sinful human will was truly helpless; God would grant faith to those whom he would, and until that should happen, nothing more was to be done. Evangelicals of every stripe, though, were united in reaching a different conclusion: God was (almost certainly) already active on your behalf, but you had to cooperate by a single crucial act of *faith.* Such faith was converting; it entailed the confession of sinfulness and the profession of trust in Christ's redemption. In obedience, the converted were baptized (here revivalists were divided between those who acknowledged infant baptism as meeting this demand and those who did not); in any case converts were expected to seek church membership and accept the disciplined life of church members (Ahlstrom, 1972:chap. 27; Mathews, 1977:1-80).

Here, however, a profound complication arose for the Southern revival. Blacks, having arrived from Africa in bondage, were still held as slaves. Yet these Southerners, too, were participants in the revival as preachers wooed them to Christian faith and invited them into the life of the church. Church membership, especially as Baptists, Methodists, and many other revivalists understood it, entailed equality, which was hardly consistent with slave status. (Equality brought the churches into conflict with patriarchal family structure as well—see Heyrman, 1997.) This racial problem brought an enormous tension into Southern culture. Northern states had already ended slavery, and though as W. E. B. DuBois discovered later, even in New England legal liberty did not end the problem of color and equality, it did modify it. Meantime the South was increasingly confronted by two absolute yet conflicting demands: that of the culture, which insisted that slavery was a necessary and permanent arrangement for African Americans as a class, and that of the Christian gospel, which proclaimed that to be converted was to enter a realm of equality for all, a kingdom beyond caste. In the formative days of the revival (1800–1835) this tension was in part resolved as converted whites manumitted their slaves and converted blacks sought and occasionally found freedom. Blacks and whites attended the same meetings, heard sermons by preachers of both races, took part in common church discipline, and shared in song and rejoicing at a common gospel mutually embraced (Boles, 1985, 1994:chaps. 1–2 and p. 114). To be sure, blacks and whites heard the same gospel somewhat differently. As just noted, whites most susceptible to the evangelical message were upwardly mobile though often without wealth or status; they heard the gospel declare that though "disallowed indeed of men," their lives were nonetheless "chosen of God, and precious" (1 Pet. 2:4 KJV; Mathews, 1977:chap. 1). Black slaves heard the message from a still lower rung on the ladder of respectability: they perceived the gospel, sealed with baptism in Jesus' name, as elevating them from the rank of non-persons to become each a child of God—a status still outwardly denied them by slavery. These blacks could sing, with eschatological hope, "The trumpet sounds within-a my soul" (Mathews, 1977:chaps. 1 and 5; Boles, 1997). Black Christians' hope was destined to grow until it issued, via a terrible swift sword, in emancipation. Whites, too, enjoyed a new status as converts, but in time that status came to separate the church from the world in a new Southern class system. After about 1831 white Christians, Presbyterian, Methodist, and Baptist came increasingly to ape the social Constantinianism—the church as the chaplain of the wider society—that their revivalist forebears had so passionately rejected (Mathews, 1977:246). In the longer run, then, the gospel lost and the slave culture won; in church as elsewhere the South gradually acquired a color line not even the gospel of Jesus Christ could be permitted to cross.

Black Christianity in America grew from two roots. On the one hand there were the traditional religious practices brought from Africa by these unwilling immigrants. They had a fertile sense of the power and presence of the departed dead, expressed in a practice of conjure that laid claim to the spirit world and related it to things visible. This was realized in meetings, often kept secret from white masters, that included dancing, drumming, and singing presided over by holy men of spiritual power (Raboteau, 1978:chap. 1; Theophus Smith, 1994:Part I; cf. also W. E. B. DuBois cited in *Ethics,* p. 83). The other root of the black church grew in New World soil: it was the participation of blacks in church life shaped by the colonists' immigrant Christianity. At first this new religion must have seemed inaccessible to Africans, but in time the quickening revivalism of the South, especially its demand for heartfelt conversion, grew close enough to the other, African root to open the doors of new life and new hope to blacks as well as whites. Thus the two roots of the black church were intertwined: It turned out that African Americans, thanks in part to their African spiritual heritage, could hear the gospel preached, be convinced of sin, and by faith turn from it to embrace the Christian Savior. Thereby they acquired in their own eyes a new status as children of God, though this was implicitly denied by their status as slaves. The immediate consequence was that evangelical Christianity in the South in this period was (not integrated, but) fully biracial: both races contributing substantially to the cultural shape of Southern evangelical Christianity.

d. A gospel critique of the revivals.—It may seem strange to find a *gospel* critique of these confessedly evangelical movements, but such a critique is just as surely needed here as in the Navajo Southwest or in Revolutionary rhetoric. The gospel critique of the revival centers on the Christian integrity of these intense and earnest efforts. The main focus here has been on the South, where an important distinction appears: in the first third of the century, promise of new life was extended to whites and blacks alike, so that the growing curse of slavery was softened though regrettably not ended. After that, economic and political pressure led white-controlled Southern churches to retract this revolutionary promise: slavery, they now assured themselves, was after all accepted in both Old and New Testaments and functioned in the best interests of an African race they considered "child-like." Meantime the North, itself no stranger to racial discrimination and prejudice, enjoyed a revivalism that after Finney's day was increasingly interior and privatized so that the race and gender issues that had stirred Finney, if they were any longer perceived, were relegated to the realm of public law: had not a Civil War, sealed in new constitutional amendments, settled the race issue for good? Did not still another amendment grant women the vote? Thus Northern and Southern Christians found themselves on different tracks until after mid twentieth century, when a Civil Rights movement bred in the African American church in the South (!) would summon blacks and whites both South and North to their forgotten common destiny (see McClendon, 1990:chap. 2) and when a feminist movement inside the churches promised to reverse an even older betrayal of the inclusive gospel.

§4. The Social Gospel

The Social Gospel has suffered a bad reputation: it is often billed as naive, or theologically heretical, or (worse than these) hopelessly out-of-date. Readers may accordingly be inclined to pass very quickly over this section. Yet its business is to reveal this movement in American Christianity, the Social Gospel, for what it really was—a cultural expression of the gospel of Jesus Christ—another episode in which religion expressed itself in culture, or culture was disclosed as religious. As fresh gospel criticism is brought to bear upon that episode, it will be relatively easy to account for and assess the prejudice that still weighs against it, and to ask how much the Social Gospel heritage remains, giving distinctive flavor to Christianity in America today.

It would certainly be misleading to treat the Social Gospel as primarily a political movement, a kind of socialism whose present-day counterpart might be left-wing Democratic politics. One can be a political party member without joining a church, but churchlessness was never an option for the sharers of the Social Gospel. In its day political movements with conscious Christian connections certainly did exist. Europe had various movements and parties designated both as socialist and as Christian. Christian socialism was also the slogan of prominent British Christians—John Ruskin, Frederick D. Maurice, and Charles Kingsley among them—whose sphere of operation was the British national culture. The message of these Christians, like that of the Europeans, was frequently independent of their churches. This was not true of the Social Gospelers, who consistently spoke to and through the churches they served.

It is even more important to distinguish the Social Gospel from a theological stance which appeared about the same time and is characterized by Sydney Ahlstrom as a "group of more radical theologians, men who took scientific method, scholarly discipline, empirical fact, and prevailing forms of contemporary philosophy as their point of departure." This was Protestant Modernism. It saw "religion as a human phenomenon, the Bible as one great religious document among others, and the Christian faith as one major religio-ethical tradition among others." From this standpoint Modernists "sought to salvage what they could of traditional belief"—which was very little, in many cases (Ahlstrom, 1972:782f). As the new century progressed, Modernists at the University of Chicago Divinity School included principally its dean, Shailer Mathews, New Testament scholar Shirley Jackson Case, and philosopher Henry Nelson Wieman. The latter two were not known as Social Gospelers, while the majority in the Social Gospel movement were not greatly interested in Modernist theological concerns, for they were doers rather than thinkers, and as thinkers they were more prophets than theologians. As we will see, many Social Gospelers remained close to the traditional biblical roots.

a. The Social Gospel as a popular religious movement.—Rather than with theological schools or political parties, the Social Gospel belongs with such historic episodes in the Christian church as the reform of monasticism (Benedict), the revival of overseas missions (Francis Xavier, William Carey), and the evangelical drive to abolish slavery

(William Wilberforce). In varying degrees such movements spoke and acted not only through the church but in and upon it; they sought to change the world but only by changing the church in the world. In this volume's terms, each addressed the environing culture by addressing the culture that was the church. Similarly, it is significant that in its day the Social Gospel was better known for its hymns and sermons than for its embrace of theological or political views (later this was to change). Many of the hundreds of hymns it generated still appear in Christian hymnals a century later. Perhaps the best known of these, Katherine Lee Bates's "America the Beautiful" (1893), is sung beyond churchly settings as well, though some of the singers never sense the irony in its patriotism: "God mend thine every flaw" (so there are flaws in America); "May God thy gold refine / Till all success be nobleness" (so American commerce is sometimes ignoble), and most telling, an eschatological hope, a millennial dream foretells "thine alabaster cities gleam / undimmed by human tears" (so America's tear-filled cities are still the subject of holy promise). "America the Beautiful," a patriotic hymn in tune with the Social Gospel, deplored human misery. Another well-known example is Social Gospel leader Washington Gladden's hymn of self-dedication:

> O Master, let me walk with thee
> In lowly paths of service free;
> Tell me thy secret; help me bear
> The strain of toil, the fret of care.

Toil and care are the lot of working people; the hymn makes clear that Christians who care about the worker's plight will share it as their Master did. Though the Social Gospel movement slowed after the First World War, its hymnic energy continued, for example in British playwright and poet Clifford Bax:

> Turn back, O man, forswear thy foolish ways.
> Old now is earth, and none may count her days;
> Yet thou, her child, whose head is crowned with flame;
> Still wilt not hear thine inner God proclaim:
> "Turn back, O man, forswear thy foolish ways."

Bax's hymn expressed a hope that had survived the Great War, calling Christians to forsake the mindless militarism and empire-building of the war-makers in order to embrace the promised unity of the human race: "Earth shall be fair and all her people one" (see Bailey, 1950:473f).

Many other such hymns survive. As Stanley Hauerwas has abrasively pointed out, the Social Gospel had its hymns, while its proud successor in the spotlight of Christian ethics, Reinhold Niebuhr's Christian Realism, had none.

This entire Section is strongly dependent on an extended, unpublished essay by Stanley Hauerwas on Walter Rauschenbusch and the Social Gospel, which may some day be published.

The need to which the Social Gospel responded was rooted in economic and social changes in America after the Civil War. While the South nursed its deep war wounds and struggled with Reconstruction, Northern industry accelerated. Its growth drew young workers from the farms to the cities and attracted millions of European immigrants. Soon Northern cities were crowded with laboring families living in wretched tenements yet lacking a public voice. Thus Henry F. May writes that although in 1876 "Protestantism presented a massive, almost unbroken front in its defense of the social status quo, two decades later social criticism had penetrated deeply into each major church." And again, "the immediate cause of this important change lay neither in theological innovation nor in the world 'climate of opinion' but in the resistless intrusion of social crisis, and particularly in a series of large-scale, violent labor conflicts" (May, 1949:91). These troubles provided the external demand for a Social Gospel, but there was an internal cause as well. *The driving moral and social interest of the nineteenth-century revivalists* had long before opened springs of mercy that flowed naturally to heal the sorrows and evils of industrial America. As Timothy Smith powerfully argues in his revisionist account of the period, "[T]he quest for [Wesleyan or holiness] perfection joined with compassion for poor and needy sinners and a rebirth of millennial expectation to make popular Protestantism a mighty social force" even before the Civil War, thus providing "an evangelical explanation of the origins of the social gospel" (Timothy Smith, 1957:149). While distinguished historians May and Smith differ on the social awareness of nineteenth-century churches, their arguments converge: a hurting nation required a good physician, and thanks to perfectionist revivalism and millennial optimism it found one in the Social Gospel.

Sensitive readers may notice that the Social Gospelers (mostly Northerners) paid little or no attention to the persistent American dilemma, racism. Having seen an end to slavery, white Christians in the North too often lapsed into self-righteousness about race: they ignored what they supposed was no longer their problem. Meanwhile, white Southern Christians, maintaining racial inequality at home, experienced daily guilt which they sought to expunge with tired arguments, now defending not slavery but its successor, second-class citizenship for African Americans. In these circumstances, succor finally came not from the Social Gospel in the North or from most Southern white churches but from the black church in the South. More than any other, the African American church was the institution that gave birth to the Civil Rights movement of the 1950s and 1960s (see McClendon, 1990: chap. 2).

In the industrial North, leaders such as Congregational ministers Washington Gladden (1836–1918), Charles Monroe Sheldon (1857–1946) and Josiah Strong (1847–1916), Baptist preacher and church historian Walter Rauschenbusch (1861–1918), and university economist Richard T. Ely (1854–1943) were able by their speeches, books, and sermons to gather sentiment for a social Christianity in an increasingly individualist age. Like the others, Gladden seized upon the glancing, dancing image of the kingdom of God: the kingdom was no far off hereafter but the actual present world of people and things viewed in its capacity to express the intent of God in Christ (Gladden, "The Church and the Kingdom" in Handy, ed., 1966:102-18). Though it was not yet finally saved, the world was daily *being* saved because the kingdom was at work in it, pervading it as electricity pervaded physical nature. The church, Gladden said, existed to serve such a kingdom. The church was not itself the kingdom but a God-provided agent for the kingdom's coming. Like a brain in a body, the church's sole task was to direct society toward kingdom ends. Thus its functions—worship, prayer, teaching, and the human unity that each of these requires—are foretastes and enablers of the same worship, prayer, and so forth, in society at large. The care of the sick and the poor had once been functions of the church; they have since become functions of society, and the process must continue until "the kingdom of God is represented by a regenerated and sanctified society" (p. 114). Consequently, Gladden's hearers were confronted with a demand: They must be transformed to become obedient to the law of the kingdom: For example, "[I]n all our bargains and dealings, instead of getting as much as we can, to give as much as we can. . . . [T]he whole attitude of life is changed; and life, instead of being a discipline of greed, becomes an opportunity of ministry" (p. 115). So there were two foci of Social Gospel preaching: it was the proclamation of good news to a needy and yet hopeful world, and it was simultaneously an old-fashioned evangelistic summons to be converted one by one to serve that need. Gladden preached this gospel throughout a long ministry in Columbus, Ohio. Add to his message the moral energy of Josiah Strong, whose powerful book, *Our Country* (1885), advocated a selfless patriotism (colored, admittedly, by "intimations of Anglo-Saxon racism"—Ahlstrom, 1972:798). Strong's book sold close to 200,000 copies. Add as well the prophetic soul of Walter Rauschenbusch, and a picture emerges of a movement that would shape Protestant Christianity for decades. In America the new era was expected to be, as a periodical of the day called it (thus naming itself), "The Christian Century."

b. The soul of the Social Gospel.—An earlier volume has already provided a sketch of Walter Rauschenbusch, not only the prophetic soul but also the scholarly theologian of this movement (*Doctrine,* One §3*d*). For him as for other Social Gospelers, Christianity had two defining poles: there was the recovery from the past (fortified by the new liberal biblical scholarship) of a prophetic Jesus and his socially conscious Jewish ministry. At the other pole were present-day Christians, who were summoned to embody that ministry afresh in their own lives ("O Master, let *me* walk with thee"), confronting American social evils just as Jesus had done—confronting and overcoming them. Here is a version of the biblical reading strategy called the prophetic or baptist vision: for it the Gospel account of Jesus is not merely a record of a bygone day; it has become a script to be enacted afresh by Jesus' followers here and now. "This is that" (Acts 2:16 KJV). Rauschenbusch was providing a fresh stanza for a very old song.

At both these poles surprises await today's reader of Rauschenbusch's writings. The biblical pole is conveniently set out in his *Social Principles of Jesus* (1916), a little book Rauschenbusch was commissioned to write as a study guide for college youth in Sunday school or other gatherings. It begins by listing "the axiomatic social convictions of Jesus." These are just three in number: the sacredness or utter value of each human life, the solidarity of the human family, and the principle that the strong must stand up for the weak: in words that foreshadowed Liberation Theology, "standing with the people." Discovering these axioms in the four Gospels occupies the first section of *Social Principles.* They give rise to "the social ideal" of Jesus, which (as it was for Gladden and other Social Gospelers) is the kingdom of God with its values, tasks, and standards. All this is based on the ministry of Jesus as depicted in the Gospels. The remainder of *Social Principles* recounts the opponents Jesus faced and the nonviolent methods ("conquest by conflict") with which he overcame them, yet in each chapter student readers are provided with questions that address the other, present pole: how are these principles to be realized today? With exquisite delicacy Rauschenbusch refrains from dictating conclusions; his student readers are left to discuss each principle in Scripture light and devise proper applications. Of course if they chose they could consult two large Rauschenbusch books already in print: *Christianity and the Social Crisis* (1907) and *Christianizing the Social Order* (1912). In these, he had explored in greater detail the biblical pole presented in the student book, and had also proposed applications (in the 1907 book) that became questions to students (in the 1912 book). The present social order, he had said, is "in acute contradiction to the Christian conceptions of justice and brotherhood" (1912:viii). In journalistic style, *Christianity and the Social Crisis* set out to show how this was so, while *Christianizing the Social Order* laid out a program of remedy, showing what would count as "christianizing" society. In brief, society must "institutionalize the Christian convictions of the worth of manhood and the solidarity of mankind"—two of Jesus' three axioms according to the *Social Principles*. These analyses displayed the surprisingly radical character of Rauschenbusch's own convictions. For example, since gigantic accumulation of wealth in the hands of a few was a consequence of capitalism, there must be a new economic and social order in which property is *socialized:*

> If a farmer who has a spring on his land near the road should set up a trough on the road and allow the public the use of the water, he would socialize the spring and be a public benefactor. If a man closed up a vacant lot and refused the boys permission to play ball on it, he would desocialize it. (1912:419)

Rauschenbusch did not call for the abolition of private property. He wanted rather a restitution of society's ancient rights "even in the most purely private property" (1912:426). Clearly, though, that called for sweeping changes in popular thinking, and such changes must happen first at church.

The Social Gospel argued its case at many levels. Charles M. Sheldon, a Topeka, Kansas, pastor, devoted himself to writing heartwarming novels that depicted the Social Gospel's demands upon ordinary Christians. The most famous of these, *In His Steps* (1890?), tells how a pastor raised with his congregation the challenging question, "What would Jesus do?" That is, if Jesus were in my situation, how would he meet it? The novel depicts an entire town transformed by considering the question; some readers of this and Sheldon's other novels were in real life transformed. Here, again, the prophetic or baptist vision was at work in the Social Gospel. It is significant that a sequel to *In His Steps* was titled *Jesus Is Here!* (1914).

While John Augustine Ryan (1869–1945) was not directly associated with the Social Gospel, this account would be incomplete without noting his parallel role in American church life. Educated for the Catholic priesthood in Minnesota, Father Ryan went on to study moral theology at Catholic University in Washington, D.C., where he absorbed the papal social encyclicals that from the time of Leo XIII (Rerum Novarum, 1891) had shaped European Catholic social teaching. The general character of these authoritative pastoral letters (which continue to the present time) was to steer a course between socialism on one side and capitalism on the other, drawing where they could on natural law, a 'law' theorists might deduce from physical nature and from custom in human affairs. In 1920 Ryan became the director of the social action department of the new National Catholic Welfare Council, the first body formally to unite Roman Catholic bishops in the United States. In 1919 this council of bishops published a profound and startling document, "Social Reconstruction"; its drafter was the persistent John A. Ryan. This "Bishop's Program," as it came to be called, was regarded with horror by many conservative Catholics, but it endured as the first document by the American Catholic hierarchy advocating progressive social action. It applied viewpoints advocated in Ryan's doctoral thesis, *A Living Wage* (1906) and his *Distributive Justice* (1916). One can see the parallels here with Rauschenbusch and other Protestant Social Gospelers, even though the climate of religious controversy at the time prohibited either side from acknowledging their common goals. Ryan later became an advisor to President Franklin D. Roosevelt's New Deal in its early years (Broderick, 1963). This political program sought to bring social responsibility into national law, aiding and protecting the poor and workers, regulating high-flying financial schemes, and establishing social security for the ill and elderly. In response to the claim that the Social Gospel and the Bishop's Program both failed, it is sometimes said that their actual outcome was the New Deal.

c. Reaction and critique.—To understand the Social Gospel today, it is necessary to recall the fierce opposition it evoked. In part this came from fundamentalism, that new form of American culture. Preoccupied with doctrine, it perceived the Social Gospel as liberal heresy, and so opposed it. This blunder was eventually spotted by neo-evangelical Carl F. Henry, champion of an orthodoxy become more catholic in its sweep, but by the time Henry's corrective, *The Uneasy Conscience of Modern Fundamentalism* (1947), had appeared, the damage had been done: many conservative Christians had dismissed as heresy the Social Gospel with its earnest prayers and hymns. The harm done the Social Gospel by organized fundamentalism was small, however, compared with that inflicted by Reinhold Niebuhr and his followers. It would be a separate task to find all the reasons for Niebuhr's reaction, but I think most of all he abhorred the conversionist Wesleyan and holiness doctrine of salvation that underlay the Social Gospel. The way of Jesus was for Niebuhr an "*impossible* ideal," and this impossibility made the Social Gospel an exercise in futility (1935). Given such underlying disagreement about the nature of salvation, it was not likely that Reinhold Niebuhr would have given the Social Gospel favorable billing. Finally, the Social Gospel always had to face what Sydney Ahlstrom calls the villain in the plot: the public ethic Americans (perversely) gleaned from their Puritan past, America's basic contempt for poverty. On this moralistic worldview, "those who begged and did not work either were being or ought to be punished for their sins" (1972:789). In more current terms, social Darwinism (see Chapter Three) defeated the Social Gospel in America.

In critical retrospect, the Social Gospel should have made more evident the solid Christian doctrine that underlay its claims. It had good reason to remind its opponents that the New Testament writers had identified Jesus with God Most High and had confessed that the Spirit among Christians was God's own Spirit. Only if this identification and this confession remained true, only if Jesus had a right to be absolute Lord (cf. *Doctrine,* Part II, Intro.), were the Gospelers justified in demanding that *we* should be like Jesus. New Testament orthodoxy was in their favor, and they should have said so, much more clearly than they did. Social Gospel ecclesiology betrayed a similar defect: If Christianity is essentially a social religion, if it is a culture, then that culture will appear in the Spirit-gifted church if it appears at all (Hartt, 1967:chap. 13). If they believed this, Social Gospelers did not say it emphatically enough. More attention to the doctrine of the church and its powerful signs as presented in the epistles to the Hebrews and Ephesians might have corrected their merely instrumental ecclesiology (cf. *Doctrine,* Nine). Pressing their holy warfare into the very territory of greedy capitalism, they too often left their own base camp, the Christian congregation, undefended. (In this they were followed by the Niebuhrians who came after them, whose eyes like theirs were on the world, not the church.) Finally, the Constantinian bugles of nationhood deafened the Social Gospel to some of its own claims. Revivalist predecessors had had little reason to wave national flags; for them Christian culture focused on a molten encounter between Jesus and lost souls. Social Gospelers, though, attempted to make all society the crucible of that divine-human encounter, and in the effort such leaders as Josiah Strong *(Our Country)* gave unguarded support to America's ideology of Manifest Destiny. Indeed, no one in the era found a good way to address the nation's needs without an unseemly waving of the nation's flag.

* * * * *

The proposal to treat religion as culture or vice versa was alarming if it denied the transcendent or holy nature of religion, regarded it as merely of the earth, earthly. No such reductionism was intended, for the true gospel appears on earth or not at all; even when sung by angels it proclaims not only glory to God in the highest, but also "on earth, peace" (Luke 2:14). Gospel religion partakes of transcendence in order to announce God's immanence; it heralds faith *on earth* (cf. Luke 18:8). Religion and culture belong together indivisibly. If we use his old Greek categories, Paul Tillich was right when he claimed that religion is the substance of culture, culture is the form of religion (Tillich, 1959:42). He was wrong, though, to assume in nineteenth-century fashion that at any given time and place there will be only one religion, only one culture. It has steadily become more clear that in his day as now there were many cultures, many religions, many 'gods' (1 Cor. 8:5). This chapter has recalled some episodes that display the varieties of American culture. To become aware of this rich variety is to look with new wonder and respect on the history of this country, and all the more upon that of other countries. Yet these are *not* presented here as links in a single, Hegelian dialectic of development. Each episode displays for us its proper qualities, its own dignity and shame, its loss and gain for the Rule of God (see *Doctrine,* Part I, Intro.). Navajos and Revolutionaries, revivalists and Social Gospelers have each showed us something of the way the gospel of Jesus Christ can take cultural form. None of these forms has been devoid of religion. (If against all odds some cultural form devoid of religion were to appear, we would doubtless revise the sense and reference of the word "religion" in order to include it, too.) Yet none of these episodes so fully discloses the gospel, even in its time and place, as to become a standard measure, a measure given for good and all in Jesus Christ. If these samples are representative, there is instead an ongoing need in every religious culture, every cultural religion, for the correction of ethics and doctrine that seeks once again to set Christ at the center (*Doctrine,* Six).

CHAPTER THREE

Science and Society

by Nancey Murphy

It is often said that the only force comparable to science in the shaping of Western society is Christianity. Certainly, no account of Christianity and culture, therefore, can omit consideration of this powerful practice (see *Ethics,* Six §1*b*). Science has contributed dramatically and directly to the contemporary Western worldview; equally important have been the indirect effects of science brought about by technological revolutions. The church and its theology have been deeply affected by science through theologians' acceptance of scientific developments; it is ironic that they have been shaped even more, perhaps, by theologians' attempts to insulate themselves from scientific influences.

There are two popular understandings of the relation between theology (or Christianity, or religion generally) and science. One is the conflict account, promoted by John W. Draper and Andrew Dickson White in the nineteenth century and still promulgated enthusiastically by the news media. The other account, sometimes called the "two worlds" view, holds that science and religion are so different that they cannot properly interact, either for good or for ill. Both of these models are inadequate, and perhaps the actual relations between religion and science are too complex to be captured under a general theory. Furthermore, there is no conviction-free ground from which to assess the (actual or ideal) relations between these two convictional enterprises (cf. *CONV.:* chap. 5).

Some accounts of the relations between science and Christianity suffer from failure to recognize a three-way interaction among science, religion, and the rest of culture. Correcting this defect obviously requires attention to all three, and this will be attempted here. *So this chapter is an attempt to bring more gospel light to bear, not so much on the content or theories of science itself, but on the full truth of science's role in our society—exposing to view its alliances for good or for ill with other spheres of culture.* Modern biology will be our case study. Our goal will not be, as for so many, to relate evolutionary biology either positively or negatively to the doctrine of creation, but to examine the complex interaction linking Darwinian theory, Christianity, and reigning social ethics. As is well known, ethical views have been (and continue to be) derived from evolutionary biology. What is not equally well appreciated is the extent to which Darwin's account of natural processes was itself a product of the economic and ethical theories of his own day. Our claim will be that the baptist concept of "the gospel of all creatures" (a motto from sixteenth-century radical reformer Hans Hut—see *Doctrine,* Two §3*b*.ii) raises suspicions, from a theological standpoint, of a view of nature dominated by images such as "struggle for existence" and "survival of the fittest." This in turn allows for critical reflection on alliances between evolutionary theory and social policy that depend on such a dismal characterization of nature itself.

So this chapter will embody the standpoint of the larger work in which it is incorporated: all intellectual work is done from a convictional location—even natural science (*Ethics,* One §1*a;* cf. *CONV.:* chap. 5). It will also illustrate Paul Feyerabend's claim that such convictional plurality is not all bad (Feyerabend, 1975): from this minority (baptist, pacifist) perspective, facts show up that from the dominant perspective have hitherto gone unnoticed.

So far we have suggested a gospel critique of science and its worldly alliances. This critique needs to be balanced by keeping in mind the general point that as a means of searching for truth, science is one way to fulfill a divine mandate. So we shall close this chapter by reflecting on one of the many ways in which scientific developments have called Christians back to a more authentic understanding of their own teachings: developments in biology have reminded us that we human beings are fully a part of the natural world.

The present chapter, then, **(§1) criticizes both conflictual and isolationist accounts of the relations between Christianity and science; (§2) examines the influence of economics and social policy on Darwin's theory of biological evolution; and on that basis (§3) questions the negative images of both nature and God that Darwinism has been taken to sponsor; and, finally (§4) recounts ways in which**

biology has reestablished the unity of humankind with its natural family, to the betterment of our theological grasp of God's relation to nature.

§1. Warfare or Isolationism?

Many Christians at the conservative end of the theological spectrum are convinced that science is an enemy, and here they most often have in mind evolutionary biology. Many scientists, too, believe that there is an underlying conflict between scientific and religious mentalities. Here they have in mind not only Christian reactions to Darwin but the Catholic Church's silencing of Galileo. Yet, often as these views appear in public discourse, those who hold them are in the minority, both of Christians and of scientists. Even to use the categories "Christians" versus "scientists" as though they were mutually exclusive is misleading, since at least 40 percent of scientists believe in a personal God who answers prayers (Larson and Witham, 1997) and many are professing Christians. So where does the idea of the warfare between science and Christianity come from?

a. The warfare myth.—Historians point out that the terms of the debate over religion and science were set in the nineteenth century by John W. Draper (1811–82) and Andrew Dickson White (1832–1918). Draper taught chemistry and physiology at New York University, but later in life turned to writing history. Invited in the early 1870s to contribute a volume to a science series, he wrote his *History of the Conflict Between Religion and Science* (1875). The book's purpose was to recount the clash of two powers, the human intellect versus traditional faith; its emotive force was an extended and vituperative attack on the Roman Catholic Church. David Lindberg and Ronald Numbers write:

> Aroused by recent proclamations from Rome declaring papal infallibility and elevating "revealed doctrine" above the "human sciences," Draper welcomed the opportunity to excoriate the Catholic church for its alleged long-standing opposition to science. Although the title of his book suggested an exploration of the relations between *religion* and science, Draper's quarrel was almost exclusively with Roman Catholicism, which, ever since seizing political power in the fourth century, had displayed "a bitter, a mortal animosity," toward science. The Vatican's persecution of scientists and other dissidents, he charged in language

> calculated to arouse emotion, had left its hands "steeped in blood." (Lindberg and Numbers, eds., 1986:1)

Draper's narrative of ferocious theologians hounding the pioneers of science "with a Bible in one hand and a fiery faggot in the other" attracted wide readership. "Draper modestly predicted that his book would be only 'the preface, or forerunner, of a body of literature, which the events and wants of our times will call forth.' In this instance his sense of the future proved more accurate than his knowledge of the past: scarcely a year passed during the later nineteenth century that did not witness the appearance of a new work echoing—or attacking—Draper's views" (Lindberg and Numbers, eds., 1986:1f).

The most influential study to follow Draper's was Andrew Dickson White's *History of the Warfare of Science with Theology in Christendom* (1896). White, president of Cornell University, began writing on science and religion as part of a larger effort to discredit religious critics envious of the funds given to the university for science and critical of its secularism (Lindberg and Numbers, eds., 1986:2). This was one instance of a widespread conflict based on scientists' felt need to emancipate themselves from what they perceived as clerical interference in and domination of education (Desmond, 1989:1; Miller, 1965:272).

White's military rhetoric ("warfare") continued to influence perceptions well into the twentieth century. However, important countermovements began to appear early in the twentieth century. Alfred North Whitehead became convinced that Christianity had encouraged science through its assumption that God's creation must behave in an orderly way (Whitehead, 1925). Robert K. Merton argued that Puritan values contributed to the rise of modern science (1938). Most important was the fact that starting about 1955 a number of historians of science (A. Hunter Dupree, Charles C. Gillespie, Paul H. Kocher, Giorgio de Santillana, Gertrude Himmelfarb, Martin Rudwick, Richard S. Westfall, Robert M. Young, Margaret C. Jacob, and others) simply found the history to be more varied and complex than the warfare metaphor suggested. It was helpfully pointed out that it is one thing to have disagreement between scientific theory and religious doctrine, and quite another to have individual scientists attacking Christianity, since a scientist might oppose religion for a variety of reasons having nothing to do with science (Chadwick, 1975). The 'sides' of the conflict over Darwinism could not rightly be designated as science versus religion since scientists themselves were divided over Darwin's theories, while a large proportion of theologians had quickly come to terms with

Darwin (Moore, 1979). In fact, the Darwinian controversy was as much as anything else a conflict over the nature of science. What was at stake was the question whether science should incorporate theological sources or whether it should attend solely to natural, secondary causes and empirical evidence (Gillespie, 1979). Another related factor for change was the shift in prestige from theology and the clergy to science and scientists (Turner, 1978). Finally, contemporary historians emphasize that the effects of social circumstances and interests on the content of scientific knowledge must be taken into account (e.g., Jacob, 1976; Rudwick, 1981).

One of the most effective attacks on the warfare model—we might now call it the warfare *myth*—has been a collection of essays edited by David Lindberg and Ronald Numbers (*God and Nature,* 1986), from whose introduction the foregoing account of the shift in historiography has been drawn. These essays patiently examine the history afresh, from the early days of Christianity up through the twentieth century. For example, Robert S. Westman's essay shows that the "Galileo affair" was not so much a conflict between science and faith as an intramural dispute within Catholicism over the proper principles of *biblical* interpretation—a dispute won by the conservatives at Galileo's expense (Westman, in Lindberg and Numbers, eds., 1986:98-103).

More recently there has been John Hedley Brooke's *Science and Religion: Some Historical Perspectives,* in which he concludes that the debate had been too complex and many-sided ever to be seen as a war between religion and science:

> Serious scholarship in the history of science has revealed so extraordinarily rich and complex a relationship between science and religion in the past that general theses are difficult to sustain. The real lesson turns out to be the complexity. Members of the Christian churches have not all been obscurantists; many scientists of stature have professed a religious faith, even if their theology was sometimes suspect. Conflicts allegedly between science and religion may turn out to be between rival scientific interests, or conversely between rival theological factions. Issues of political power, social prestige, and intellectual authority have repeatedly been at stake. And the histories written by protagonists have reflected their own preoccupations. (Brooke, 1991:5)

So the warfare myth lies thoroughly discredited for being not only a partial account, but also an *interested,* that is, self-serving, point of view.

b. Isolationism and its effects on theology.—An equally extreme account of the relation between Christianity and science grew from a thorough reinterpretation of the nature of theology. This has its roots in the work of the great Enlightenment philosopher Immanuel Kant (1724–1804). One can summarize two goals of Kant's philosophy as follows: to save Newtonian physics from David Hume's skepticism, and to save religion and human freedom from the determinism of Newtonian science. He accomplished the latter goal by making an absolute distinction between the phenomenal world (the world as it appears to the senses) and the noumenal world (things as they are in themselves). Human selves are noumena, not phenomena, and causal determinism applies only in the phenomenal realm.

What is important for our purposes was Kant's assignment of religion to the noumenal sphere, and his insistence that arguments transgressing the boundary between the noumenal and phenomenal were absolutely illegitimate. Thus, there could be no arguments for God's existence based on the existence or order of the natural world, and this was a great loss to eighteenth-century natural theology. But many took this loss to be well compensated by the fact that, on this account, science could not possibly contradict religious belief. Christian theologians at the liberal end of the spectrum, and then their neo-orthodox rivals, have in one way or another followed Kant in isolating their theologies from science.

Friedrich Schleiermacher (1768–1834), the 'father' of modern liberal theology, distinguished religion from both knowing (science) and doing (morality). Rather, religion is a kind of feeling or awareness, and Christian doctrines are "accounts of the Christian religious affections set forth in speech" (CF §15; see *Doctrine,* p. 26f). Since what doctrines are *about,* in the first instance, is Christian experience, scientific developments are for Schleiermacher irrelevant. For example, the doctrine of creation expresses the Christian's awareness of the absolute dependence of all finite being upon God. As such, it is entirely independent of any possible information about the origin of the universe, a topic which is to be handed over entirely to science. "[T]he controversy over the temporal or eternal creation of the world . . . has no bearing on the content of the feeling of absolute dependence, and it is therefore a matter of indifference how it is decided" (CF p. 155, see further §§40f). Karl Barth (1886–1968), most influential of the neo-orthodox theologians, rejected Schleiermacher's particular form of anthropocentrism, but he had his own reasons for insulating theology from science: an impassable epistemological gulf separated the Word of God from the results of any sort of human inquiry (see e.g. CD III/2 §43). Rudolf Bultmann

(1884–1976) best of all exemplifies our claim that the move to isolate theology from the results of science has its own dramatic effects on the content of theology. Bultmann, a theologian and New Testament scholar, argued that the gospel needed to be demythologized for modern readers lest they be distracted from its main point by the supernatural trappings of the New Testament writings: angels, demons, miracles, heaven and hell. The essence of the gospel has to do with the transformation of human existence by faith here and now. Why must modern readers reject these "mythological elements"? Because *they are incredible in light of the modern scientific worldview:* nature is an object entirely governed by its relentless cause-and-effect laws (Bultmann, 1958; cf. *Doctrine,* 151; and below, 4*b*). So the irony, from the present theological perspective, is that attempts such as Bultmann's to argue for a conception of theology that made it immune from scientific criticism resulted in the evacuation of so much of its content.

Notice that acceptance or rejection of this second way of understanding the relation between theology and science (namely, their mutual irrelevance) is not to be based on historical evidence, as was the rejection of the warfare model. Rather, it depends on arguments that go to the very heart of Christian theology itself. What is Christianity basically all about? Is it about religious experience; about existential orientation? Yes, to both of these. But much more. It is, as displayed in two previous volumes, about the story of God and God's people, embedded in the history of the world and the history of the universe. Any account of God's doings that leaves out God's *active* concern for the natural world is too narrow (*Doctrine,* Four).

The tendency of modern theologians to anthropocentrize Christian teaching, to focus on the human apart from the natural world—and Barth did this as much as the liberals (CD III/2)—depends for its cogency on one or another sort of dualism, an assumption about human nature that has plagued much of modern thought. Cartesian mind-body dualism became Kant's noumenal-phenomenal distinction. This set the stage for the distinction between nature and culture, between the natural sciences and the human sciences. All of these divisions are at odds with both biblical teaching (*Ethics,* Three) and with what current science tells us about the relations of ourselves to nature (see the last section of this chapter).

Finally, we point out that science and theology can be insulated from one another *only if one or both are insulated from the rest of culture!* We turn now to an examination of the interactions among evolutionary biology, recent Western culture, and the gospel.

§2. Economics, Darwin, and Social Policy

This section explores some of the complex interrelationships among Darwinian theory, economic and political theories of Darwin's day, and natural theology. It is common to consider the effect of evolutionary biology on both theology and social theories. More recent history concentrates as well on the effect of both natural theology and economic theory, especially the economic theory of Thomas Malthus, on Darwin's thought.

a. Darwin's revolution.—To perceive what was central to Darwin's 1850s and 1860s 'revolution' it is useful to note how many of his ideas were *not* new. The long age of the earth was already widely accepted, due largely to developments in geology. The idea that species can be transformed into one another was proposed in ancient times and was lent credence in Darwin's day by the fossil evidence of continuous change through geological ages. The idea that life could arise from inorganic matter was widespread in the Middle Ages (Dobzhansky et al., 1977:9-12). It had even been proposed earlier that the human species must have evolved from other life-forms under the governance of natural laws. In short, by the end of the eighteenth century and the beginning of the nineteenth, speculation on organic evolution, though not commonplace or widely accepted, was no longer particularly novel (Ruse, 1979:4f). Two earlier evolutionists were Darwin's grandfather, Erasmus Darwin, and Jean Baptiste de Lamarck (1744–1829). Darwin had formulated his theory by 1844 but he only went to press in 1859, spurred by the discovery that Alfred Russel Wallace had arrived at nearly the same conclusions. Darwin wrote in a letter to Lord Baden-Powell in 1860:

> No educated person, not even the most ignorant, could suppose that I meant to arrogate to myself the origination of the doctrine that species had not been independently created. The only novelty in my work is the attempt to explain *how* species became modified, & to a certain extent how the theory of descent explains certain large classes of facts, & in these respects I received no assistance from my predecessors. (quoted in Young, 1985:81)

Charles Robert Darwin (1809–82) was born in Shrewsbury, England, the son of a successful physician. The younger Darwin, following his father, enrolled in medical studies at the University of Edinburgh, but finding medicine not to his liking he transferred to Christ's College, Cambridge, to study for the

Church of England ministry. In the course of his studies, though, he had pursued an interest in natural history (geology and biology). Before taking a post in the church he accepted an offer to travel on HMS *Beagle,* bound for the coasts of South America. The *Beagle* left England in December of 1831 and returned in October 1836. On the voyage Darwin made extensive trips ashore, and it was on these occasions that he had opportunity to observe the adaptation of species to their environments. During the two years after his return Darwin began to piece together his hypotheses. His reading of Malthus (also an Anglican clergyman) in September 1838, enabled him to formulate his theory of natural selection. Darwin married in 1839. In the 1840s he became ill and moved to the country, where he continued to write for the rest of his life, publishing *Origin of Species* in 1859 and, twelve years after, *The Descent of Man* (1871), which dealt explicitly with human evolution.

Darwin's chief contribution, then, was to postulate a viable mechanism for evolutionary change. Lamarck's theory had been based on what is now seen as a flawed account of the means of heredity. Lamarck believed that living organisms adapted themselves to their environments and that these adaptive changes could be passed along to their offspring. Darwin's own theory is encapsulated in the title of his book, *On the Origin of Species by Means of Natural Selection, or The Preservation of Favoured Races in the Struggle for Life* (1859). The mechanism Darwin identified was selective preservation of randomly occurring variations among members of a species. The theory depended in part on an analogy between natural selection and the intentional selection breeders make in improving domestic livestock. Breeders make use of naturally occurring variations among individuals of a species and create population changes by breeding only those individuals that display the desired characteristics. A fresh source of evidence for Darwin was his observations made on the *Beagle,* showing significant differences between populations in isolated geographical regions. He was also influenced by the fossil evidence recorded by his day in Charles Lyell's *Principles of Geology* (1830–33), and by evidence from comparative anatomy and embryology. So there was ample evidence of variation within populations, of change, and of continuity among species. The question was simply what *caused* the change, if it was not the intentional selection of a breeder. The answer was natural selection by means of the survival of the fittest.

Our interest here is not so much in the scientific evidence for Darwin's theory as in the sources of his language: "natural selection," "struggle for existence," and "survival of the fittest." A large role was played by Darwin's reading of Thomas R. Malthus, *An Essay on the Principle of Population* (1798). But an important context for this reading was the natural theology Darwin had studied at Cambridge in preparation for the ministry.

"Natural theology" refers to the attempt to construct a doctrine of God without appeal to faith or special revelation, but based solely on reason or experience. The ancient philosopher Plato is sometimes credited with being the first natural theologian. Christian theologians have held various attitudes toward natural theology. One view is that it provides a partial but valuable account of God, which revelation completes (e.g., Thomas Aquinas). Others have seen it as peripheral (e.g., Martin Luther); and some have rejected it outright (e.g., Karl Barth). Natural theology was respected by many in Darwin's day—indeed, it was seen as essential by intellectuals who had taken seriously claims that undercut the authority of Scripture (historical criticism, the plurality of religions) yet wanted to maintain some sort of religious belief.

William Paley's *Natural Theology* (1802) was at that time still a standard work. Paley argued that, just as a watch evidently must have a maker, so must there have been a Maker for biological organisms. He compiled massive amounts of data regarding the adaptation of organisms to their environments and the fitness of their organs to serve biological purposes. Paley was particularly interested in the bones and muscles of animals and the equivalent parts of insects because their fitting together and effective operation best conformed to the analogy with mechanical design. He also gave great attention to the eye, claiming that the remarkable combination of its parts and their adaptation to function as an instrument of sight was alone sufficient to convince one of the existence of the divine intelligence that created it. Paley also drew conclusions about the character of the Creator. God's goodness was shown both by the fact that most biological contrivances are beneficial and by the fact that animals have been designed to feel pleasure.

This optimistic view of the benignity of God and nature contrasted sharply with one that had appeared only a few years earlier in Malthus's *Essay* (1798). In it, Malthus had proposed his principle of population: If unchecked, population will increase geometrically but food supply can increase only arithmetically at best. Struggle, competition, and starvation are the natural result. The first edition was written against currently popular utopian views regarding the infinite perfectibility of the human race, transcending, through the use of reason, the limits of organic nature. Such writings had "affronted Malthus's sense of reality" (Young, 1985:25). Against them Malthus had brought about in nineteenth-century readers an essential change in perspective, placing humankind squarely within nature once and for all.

Malthus was an Anglican clergyman who wrote, as Paley did, within the received eighteenth-century heritage of natural theology. His book, therefore, was a (pessimistic) statement on the place of humankind in nature, but also a statement on the *divinely appointed* role of struggle, strife, and inequality. His work was a theodicy of sorts, justifying suffering and death as the *natural* outcome of the tendency toward overpopulation, but also as the result of divine providence, in that evil produces exertion, exertion produces mind, and mind produces progress. Because humans are by nature sinful, inert, sluggish, and averse to labor, "[h]ad population and food increased in the same ratio, it is probable that man might never have emerged from the savage state" (Malthus, 1798:358). The one 'happy' note in Malthus's views was that sexual restraint, if exercised, could provide an antidote to human overpopulation.

So Darwin set out on the *Beagle* expecting to find (Paleyan) evidence of the adaptation of organisms to their environments, and he was not disappointed. But was divine design required to account for this adaptation? No. Adaptations could be accounted for as the result of two factors: variation and selective rates of reproduction. The selection would be the natural outcome of Malthusian population pressure: Animals breed without "the moral restraint, which in some small degree checks the increase in mankind." Therefore, "the pressure [for biological change] is always ready . . . a thousand wedges are being forced into the economy of nature. . . ." "The final cause of all this wedging, must be to sort out proper structure, and adapt it to change" (Darwin's notes, quoted in Young, 1985:41f).

This newfound ability to account for biological facts in terms of laws of nature would have been no challenge, in itself, to Christian theology. In the wake of Newton's physics (*Principia,* 1687), many educated Christians had long since concluded that a God who governs by natural law, not by 'meddling,' is a grander God. There was already in the 1820s and 1830s, exemplified by Oxbridge geologists such as Adam Sedgwick and William Whewell, an alternative natural theology based on models of progressive creation. What Darwin, influenced by Malthus, produced was a new perspective on the 'moral character' of nature—a worldview changed from harmony to a scene of struggle and discord (Ospovat, 1981:60). *Malthus's theory of riotous population growth, now bolstered by Darwin's authority, buttressed as it was by research, came to dominate the perception of the mood of nature and society, and has done so up to the present* (Young, 1985:192). The image of Paley's "myriads of happy beings" was replaced by Alfred, Lord Tennyson's image of "nature red in tooth and claw." Darwin's popularizer Thomas Henry Huxley wrote that "[f]rom the point of view of the moralist, the animal world is on about the same level as a gladiator's show" (quoted in

Himmelfarb, 1959:401, 404f). Huxley went on to draw theological conclusions, condemning Christians for worshiping what was plainly unworthy of worship: a God who had created evil, including evil humanity itself. "I know no study which is so unutterably saddening as that of the evolution of humanity," he said. Humankind had acquired its leading position within nature by virtue of success in the struggle for existence, and had excelled over the ape and the tiger in just those qualities that are commonly associated with these animals—cunning, ruthlessness, and ferocity. Pain and grief, crime and sin, remain to remind humans of their amoral origins (Himmelfarb, 1959:405).

Another of Darwin's contemporaries, George Romanes, vacillated between theism and skepticism. Would a merciful God have instigated such a tortuous, wasteful, bloodstained scheme? Romanes drew a poignant contrast between the personality of the deity as inferred from evolutionary biology and the qualities of love, mercy, and justice as proclaimed in religion. The two sets of qualities, he wrote with a sense of despair, were almost exact opposites (Brooke, 1991:316).

b. Darwin's loaded language.—What accounts for the powerful cultural ramifications of Darwin's scientific achievements? The answer is that Darwin had drawn the language of his theory from his cultural context. Not surprisingly, the resulting perception of nature was particularly effective in reinforcing cultural movements from which the language had originally been drawn. Darwin's readers were primed to find in his account of nature a one-sided picture—to read his often ambiguous language in a particular manner. In psychologists' terms, the cultural context provided a mental set, likely to influence their readings. It is also important to ask if this same culturally induced expectation influenced nineteenth-century scientists' own perceptions of nature, leading to readiness to perceive conflict rather than cooperation, suffering rather than symbiosis. We turn to this issue below (§3*a*). There are three crucial phrases in Darwin's account: "struggle for existence," "survival of the fittest," and "natural selection." The first two of these connote conflict. Struggle in nature was not merely against the conditions of the organism's environment, but also against other individuals of the species and against members of other species. Darwin only introduced the phrase "survival of the fittest" in later editions of the *Origin*. Fitness referred to comparative rates of reproduction—by Darwin's definition, the most fit are the ones that leave behind the most offspring—and *he,* at least, was careful to avoid attaching any other *values* to the term. But "fitness" was unlikely to be read as the neutral, technical term Darwin intended when it was paired with the conflictual image of struggle and also when associated in the minds of his readers with issues of government or private support for the "lower classes." The unused or uncontrolled elements in metaphors such as "struggle for existence" took on a life of their own (Beer, 1983:9).

If the Malthusian context of Darwin's revolution predisposed him and his followers to perceive a natural world "red in tooth and claw," so the Paleyan context predisposed his readers to attribute this terrible state of affairs to God. "Natural selection" is the most important term in Darwin's theory. It is a figure of speech, pairing terms whose literal meanings are mutually contradictory. The tension in the metaphor lies in its depiction of selection in nature as if it were by choice; 'selection' presupposes a selector—a conscious agent doing the choosing. Yet, as early as the seventeenth century, the canons of scientific method had banned purposes, intentions, and anthropomorphic expressions from descriptions of nature. Nevertheless, anthropomorphic and voluntarist descriptions of natural selection occur throughout Darwin's writings. It is not the anthropomorphism, however, that raises theological difficulties. Rather it is the attribution of selective power to nature *combined with* the tendency to speak of *Nature* with a capital 'N.' Darwin attempted to dismiss these readings:

> It has been said that I speak of natural selection as an active power or Deity; but who objects to an author speaking of the attraction of gravity as ruling the movements of the planets? Every one knows what is meant and is implied by such metaphorical expressions; and they are almost necessary for brevity. So again it is difficult to avoid personifying the word Nature; but I mean by Nature, only the aggregate action and product of many natural laws, and by laws the sequence of events as ascertained by us. With a little familiarity such superficial objections will be forgotten. (Darwin, 1872:59)

Darwin's last sentence turned out to be wrong, and this was for very good reasons. While freeing himself from belief in static, designed adaptations, which as a divinity student he had once found so appealing in Paley's writings, Darwin had retained the *rhetoric* of design (Young, 1985:97).

The power of metaphors based on science to change a worldview is widely recognized. Newtonian physics provided the seventeenth-century with the clockwork image of the universe, and the eighteenth-century Deists' image of God the Clockmaker lasted through the writings of Paley. In evolutionary biology, metaphors are not excess baggage that can be left behind; as we have seen above, the metaphor of natural selection and the image of the struggle for existence are part and parcel of Darwin's explanation of the mechanism of evolutionary change. Metaphors provide insight, they encourage us to see one system or aspect of reality in terms of another and thus highlight factors we might not otherwise have noticed. In addition they carry a wealth of connotative meaning. So in his choice of metaphors we have at least a partial account of the power of Darwin's scientific theory to induce a new cultural mood regarding nature, society, and God.

If Malthus, Paley, Darwin, Lyell, Wallace, and others were part of a single debate (Young, 1985:24; Beer, 1983:6f), it should come as no surprise that Darwin's science was cited as the source of a view of human society most commonly labeled "social Darwinism." Malthus's own work was in the tradition of Adam Smith's *laissez-faire* economics. Smith had participated in a movement to extend the concept of design through natural law from the natural world to the social order. In *The Wealth of Nations* (1776) he had argued that the pursuit of self-interest will contribute to the general welfare because it is as if a "hidden hand" is providentially at work. Smith's contemporaries already used such views of providential ordering of society for the purposes of theodicy—at one stroke both justifying God's providence and excusing human misery. Soame Jenyns had even argued that crime had an important social function (Milbank, 1990:38).

The difference between pre-Malthusian political-economic views and those after is the loss of optimism. The limits placed on economic growth by the capacity for food production meant that the growing population of urban poor was seen in terms of surplus mouths to feed rather than as an economically beneficial surplus of labor. Thus Malthus and his followers argued that relief to the poor should be restricted, since it only put off the death of those who could not support themselves. Malthus argued that a law should be passed such that no child born from any marriage taking place more than a year after the law was passed should be entitled to parish assistance (Young, 1985:38), thus making Christian charity illegal! After Malthus it was not uncommon for theologians to take up the cause. Thomas Chalmers, Professor of Divinity at the University of Edinburgh, emphasized the necessity of moral restraint (especially sexual restraint) if the poor were to avoid the miseries to which the principle of population would lead. The necessary connection between moral weakness and misery was a reflection of the very character of God:

> It is not the lesson of conscience, that God would, under the mere impulse of parental fondness for the creatures whom He had made, let down the high state and sovereignty which belong to him; or that He would forbear the infliction of the penalty, because of any soft or timid shrinking from the pain it would give the objects of His displeasure. . . . [W]hen one looks to the disease and the agony of spirit, and above all the hideous and unsparing death, with its painful struggles and gloomy forebodings, which are spread universally over the face of the earth—we cannot but imagine of the God who presides over such an economy, that He is not a being who will falter from the imposition of any severity, which might serve the objects of a high administration. (Chalmers, 1833:292f)

This was 'social Darwinism' a generation *before Origin of Species*! What role, then, did Darwin's own work play in the development of social Darwinism? Historian of science Robert Young argues that whereas the justification for the hierarchical division of labor in society had earlier been justified on the combined bases of divine ordinance and human efficiency in the writings of Adam Smith, Paley, and Malthus, in the course of the nineteenth century it acquired a new basis. Now the basis of social stratification among rich and poor is no longer to be justified as God's will and wisdom. In the new scheme,

> the so-called physiological division of labor provides a scientific guarantee of the rightness of the property and work relations of industrial society. . . . The famous controversy in the nineteenth century between science and theology was very heated indeed, and scholars have concentrated on this level of analysis. However, at another level, the protagonists in the debate were in fundamental agreement. They were fighting over the best ways of rationalizing the same set of assumptions about the existing order. An explicitly theological theodicy was being challenged by a secular one based on biological conceptions and the fundamental assumption of the uniformity of nature. (Young, 1985:191)

It is important to note that while Darwin's work was used to support laissez-faire economics and politics, with their justifications for the pursuit of self-interest and the disproportionate accumulation of wealth in the hands of the few, it was also used at the same time to argue for the whole gamut of social programs—including the opposites or contraries of laissez-faire, both liberalism and socialism.

The ability of Darwin's theory to lend itself to a multiplicity of causes was due in part to tensions in his exposition that could be resolved in different directions (Greene, 1981:96). His account of human kinship with animals carried a humbling, egalitarian message, while the emphasis on development tended to promote a hierarchical view with "European man" at the apex. While his theory placed value on biological diversity, it also accorded value to compliance in the sense that an organism had to conform to the demands of its environment. There was optimism in that natural selection invariably worked for the good of the species, but also pessimism in that nature was inevitably riven with struggle and strife (Brooke, 1991:289). The position that is most commonly designated as social Darwinism was justified by exploiting the optimism in Darwin's exposition as regards the prosperous, while it used the pessimistic strand to justify the suffering of the "unfit." It is striking that political liberals were among the first to use Darwin as a justification of their policies. They attacked the remaining areas of social and political privilege of the British aristocracy on the grounds that awarding status for reasons of birth rather than achievement protected the idle and unproductive, and thus interfered with the evolutionary process. Walter Bagehot defended liberal democracy by emphasizing cultural rather than individual selection (Bagehot, 1869). The Darwinian theme of variation shows up in the emphasis on social variation—that is, modifications in forms of government, institutions, morality—and only societies with intellectual freedom would give rise to these variations. This emphasis on variation, however, is in tension with the theme of compliance, which shows up in Bagehot's theory that the society most coherent in its customs would be superior (Jones, 1980:42; Himmelfarb, 1959:428).

Socialism has been called yet a third form of social Darwinism. Darwin's theory appealed to Marx and Engels because Darwin had abandoned traditional theological conceptions of teleology and had transformed the history of life into one of the interplay of unconscious forces. This notion of unconscious forces in biology fit nicely with Marxist views of the unconscious forces of history. However, Engels criticized the conclusion of earlier social Darwinists, that poverty was an inevitable consequence of the struggle for existence, by pointing out the circularity involved in projecting Malthusian principles onto nature and then reversing the projection from nature to history (Brooke, 1991:293).

The eugenics movement was a program put forward by Darwin's cousin, Francis Galton, to raise the physical and mental level of the race. This program was based on two propositions: first, that desirable human qualities were unequally distributed throughout the race and, second, that those who had the desirable qualities could be encouraged to multiply faster than the others. Galton claimed that eugenics was practical Darwinism. However, his theory was in sharp conceptual tension with Darwin's: for eugenicists, the problem as they perceived it was that the "unfit" (the poor, especially) were leaving the most progeny; yet in Darwin's own theory the most "fit" are exactly those who leave the most progeny.

The fact that Darwinism has shown itself equally useful for supporting opposing social programs suggests that arguments for any one such program should be regarded with suspicion. Indeed, while ethics must take account of the facts of biology, no attempt to *derive* ethics from biology alone can hope to succeed (cf. *Ethics,* Three). Apart from an account of what human life (and the rest of life) is *for*—its *telos*—we have no interpreter's key to decipher the meaning of nature. For an account of nature's *telos,* we must turn to theology (*Doctrine,* Two; Murphy and Ellis, 1996; Murphy, 1997:chaps. 9–10).

§3. Critical Questions

The foregoing account of the entanglements of evolutionary biology, social policy debates, and natural theology raises a variety of questions. Some might inquire whether the exposure of the ideological rootage of Darwin's language should cast doubt on the credibility of his theory. A crude version of the sociology of knowledge would answer Yes. However, more sophisticated understandings of the relations between scientific theories and the social matrices out of which they emerge lead to a refusal to oppose truth and social utility. Early work in the sociology of scientific knowledge supposed that it is necessary to distinguish on epistemological grounds between true and false theories; between rational and irrational inferences. Causal ("external") explanations were needed to explain irrationality and the tenacity of false beliefs, but logic, rationality, and truth served as their own ("internal") explanations.

It is now recognized, though, that all scientific knowledge is underdetermined. We see this in the case of sensory perception. Perceptions do not lead directly to belief; rather they impinge on a mind already stocked with beliefs and interact with those beliefs to form new beliefs (Bloor, 1976:31). Philosophers of science have made it clear that no amount of evidence ever amounts to proof of a scientific theory. There are usually competing theories in any field, each with a good amount of confirming evidence to its credit and a handful of persistent anomalies to its discredit. Even when one theory is clearly ahead in the contest it can never be known in advance that the loser will not someday be turned around by a genius with a brilliant insight, or that some undreamed-of theory might not be proposed in its place (Murphy, 1990). So attention to so-called internal factors (empirical evidence, consistency, scope) is never a complete answer to the questions of why a scientific theory has been accepted, and especially why it became the accepted theory when it did. Thus, sociological accounts are complementary to 'internalist' accounts, not rivals.

Because all science—good science as well as bad—is in this measure underdetermined and partial, the falsification of Darwinian theory is not entailed by the recognition that its origins and transformations were the result not so much of interaction *between* the scientist and nature as *among* the scientist, nature, and socially constructed conceptions of nature. Nature exists independently of human consciousness, but an exclusively contemplative relation to nature is out of the question. "It is in our practical behavior—encountering, suffering, struggling, laboring, and cooperating—that we come to know ourselves, one another, and things" (Young, 1985:241). So while recognition of the social conditioning of Darwin's theory is no reason to reject it, recognition of the negative mood of the cultural milieu in which Darwin worked calls for a degree of suspicion. We need to ask the following questions: (a) To what degree does the conflictual language in which Darwin expressed his theory prejudice or distort scientists' observations of nature itself? and (b) What corrections are needed in the presumed theological implications of evolutionary biology?

a. Good-natured nature?—The image of nature "red in tooth and claw" was not an adequate account of Darwin's own perceptions. Besides the "battle of life" of one organism against another, Darwin recognized additional, non-conflictual elements in the mechanisms driving the evolutionary process. One was "sexual selection," which refers to competition within the species for mates. This sometimes involves conflict, such as between male elk, but it sometimes involves only differences in appearance, such as tail displays of male peacocks. The Russian naturalist and anarchist Petr Kropotkin recognized that in Darwin's *Descent of Man* (1871) the term "struggle for existence" was used broadly to include the evolution of social and moral faculties as well as the everyday battle for survival against the environment. He set out to elaborate these insights in depth, and came to view sociality, rather than life-and-death struggle between individuals, as typifying the animal world (Heyer, 1982:156).

Textbook accounts of evolution have long been expressed in much less loaded language than were the theories of Darwin and Wallace. Natural selection is defined simply as the differential reproduction of alternative genetic variants, that is, as higher rates of reproduction for individuals with certain useful characteristics. Commenting on the uses of Darwin's theory to justify war, aggression, classism, and unrestrained economic competition, the great synthesizer of evolutionary and genetic theory, Theodosius Dobzhansky, with his co-authors, points out that in nature the struggle for life does not necessarily take the form of combat between individuals. Among higher animals combat is often ritualized and victory may be achieved without inflicting physical harm. Plants "struggle" against aridity not by sucking water from one another but by developing devices to protect against water loss. Thus, "[i]t is no paradox to say that under many circumstances the most effective 'struggle' for life is mutual help and cooperation" (Dobzhansky et al., 1977:98). This line of scientific thought on the ingrained morality of animals was appropriated in *Volume I* to argue against the association of human bodies with the "beastly" beasts (*Ethics*, 91ff).

In fact, "altruism" among animals has become an important topic of research. "Altruism" here means any behavior that puts the individual at risk or disadvantage but favors the survival of other members of its species, such as a bird's warning call when predators approach. This is not altruism in a moral sense, of course, but it is a far cry from the old image of intraspecific conflict.

A recent book by ethologist Frans de Waal, titled *Good Natured* (1996), nicely illustrates current reactions against images of nature that overemphasize conflict. De Waal points out that

> [i]n biology, the very same principle of natural selection that mercilessly plays off life forms and individuals against one another has led to symbiosis and mutualism among different organisms, to sensitivity of one individual to the needs of another, and to joint action toward a common goal. We are facing the profound paradox that genetic self-advancement at the expense of others—which is the basic thrust of evolution—has given rise to remarkable capacities for caring and sympathy. (1996:5)

De Waal is convinced that Malthusian influences have biased scientists' perceptions of animal behavior. In the minds of many, he says, "natural selection" has become synonymous with open, unrestrained competition. This raises the question of how such a harsh principle could ever explain the concern for others and the benevolence that humans display. Thus, there has developed the subdiscipline of sociobiology—the study of animal (and human) behavior in an evolutionary perspective. The core explanation of altruistic behavior is "kin selection." It is hypothesized that behavior patterns favoring the survival of kin, even at cost to the individual, could have been selected since the survival of kin results in the survival of close approximations to the individual's genes. So, for example, if an individual animal possesses a gene that predisposes it to bring food to its offspring, this will contribute to the survival of the offspring, who are likely to carry the same gene, and, as a result, that gene will spread. So sociobiologists such as Richard Dawkins find themselves explaining apparently altruistic behavior as a result of the operation of "selfish genes." De Waal sees this paradox (selfish altruism) as the result of an unfortunate refusal to countenance genuine sympathy and care in the natural world; he attributes it to the influence of Thomas Malthus and his principle of population (see §2 above).

Even the language used by most ethologists to describe animal behavior is negatively biased. De Waal notes,

> [A]s a corollary to the belief in a natural world red in tooth and claw, there remains tremendous resistance, both inside and outside biology, to a terminology acknowledging beauty in the beast. . . . The current scientific literature routinely depicts animals as suckers, grudgers, and cheaters, who act spitefully, greedily, and murderously.

Yet, if animals show tolerance or altruism, these terms are placed in quotation marks lest their author be judged hopelessly romantic or naive! Alternatively, positive inclinations are given negative labels, such as when preferential treatment for kin is not called love for kin, but nepotism (1996:18).

One must be careful not to go to the other extreme of providing romantic characterizations of animals. De Waal shows due caution in asking whether terms used to describe desirable human traits can legitimately be applied to similar traits in animals—for example, whether animals should be described as displaying "sympathy," or merely "caring behavior." His wealth of descriptions of animal behavior, drawn from his own and others' observations, includes a series of increasingly complex abilities that go into caring behavior. The most basic is mutual attachment, which occurs among pack animals, such as wolves, and sea mammals, such as dolphins and whales, who will beach themselves collectively out of reluctance to leave a disoriented group mate. He reports a striking example of attachment observed in a dwarf mongoose colony.

> A British ethologist, Anne Rasa, followed the final days of a low-ranking adult male dying of chronic kidney disease. The male lived in a captive group consisting of a pair and its offspring. Two adjustments took place. First, the sick male was allowed to eat much earlier in the rank order than previously. . . . Second, the rest of the group changed from sleeping on elevated objects, such as boxes, to sleeping on the floor once the sick male had lost the ability to climb onto the boxes. They stayed in contact with him, grooming him much more than usual. After the male's death, the group slept with the cadaver until its decay made removal necessary. (de Waal, 1996:80)

Another element involved in caring behavior is emotional contagion—vicarious arousal by the emotions of others. Human babies display this trait—crying at the sound of another's cries—and so do a variety of animals. When infant rhesus monkeys scream, other infants rush to them to make physical contact. The example of the mongoose illustrates yet another element of caring behavior: learned adjustment to others' disabilities. A further example is the case of Azalea, a rhesus monkey born with a condition comparable to Down syndrome in humans. She was slow to learn climbing and jumping and also slow in social development. Her troop adjusted to her handicaps; for example, an elder sister carried her long beyond the age for such sisterly care, often pulled her out of physical entanglements, and defended her against attacks by other monkeys (1996:49).

Finally, de Waal gives examples of caring behavior among higher primates. Chimpanzees excel at "so-called *consolation.*" For example, after a fight, bystanders hug and touch the combatants, pat them on the back, and groom them. It is interesting that their attentions focus more on the losers than the winners. If such behavior does not occur quickly enough, loser chimpanzees resort to a repertoire of gestures—pouting, whimpering, begging with outstretched hands—so that the others will provide the needed calming contact. In some cases animals act as if they recognize what their caring means to the other. Consider another of de Waal's observations:

> The Arnhem chimpanzees spend the winters indoors. Each morning, after cleaning the hall and before releasing the colony, the

> keeper hoses out all the rubber tires in the enclosure and hangs them one by one on a horizontal log extending from the climbing frame. One day Krom was interested in a tire in which the water had been retained. Unfortunately, this particular tire was at the end of the row, with six or more heavy tires hanging in front of it. Krom pulled and pulled at the one she wanted but could not move it off the log. . . . Krom worked in vain on this problem for over ten minutes, ignored by everyone except Otto Adang, my successor in Arnhem, and Jakie, a seven-year-old male chimpanzee to whom Krom used to be the "aunt" (a caretaker other than the mother) when he was younger. Immediately after Krom gave up and walked away from the scene Jakie approached. Without hesitation he pushed the tires off the log one by one, as any sensible chimpanzee would. . . . When he reached the last tire, he carefully removed it so that no water was lost and carried the tire straight to his aunt, where he placed it upright in front of her. (1996:83)

So is nature better captured in Paley's "myriads of happy beings" or in Tennyson's "red in tooth and claw"? Obviously *both* are natural, and the picture is complex: the same animals that comfort one another and share food also cooperate in hunting and killing prey. De Waal points out that animals that share food tend to do it when the foodstuff is highly valued, prone to decay, too much for individual consumption, procured by skill or strength, and most effectively procured through collaboration—in short, the food most likely to be shared is meat killed in a hunt. He speculates that this tendency, shaped among social animals by evolutionary necessity, creates a predisposition among humans for sharing. Although a natural tendency among animals to share food is not equivalent to human generosity, human morals cannot be entirely independent of our evolutionary past:

> Of our own design are neither the tools of morality nor the basic needs and desires that form the substance with which it works. Natural tendencies may not amount to moral imperatives, but they do figure in our decision-making. Thus, while some [human] moral rules reinforce species-typical predispositions and others suppress them, none blithely ignore them. (de Waal, 1996:39; cf. *Ethics*, Three)

This point aptly illustrates de Waal's "profound paradox," noted above, that genetic self-advancement at the expense of others has given rise to remarkable capacities for caring and sympathy. He concludes:

> If carnivory was indeed the catalyst for the evolution of sharing, it is hard to escape the conclusion that human morality is steeped in animal blood. When we give money to begging strangers, ship food to starving people, or vote for measures that benefit the poor, we follow impulses shaped since the time our ancestors began to cluster around meat possessors. (de Waal, 1996:146)

b. A baptist theology of nature.—If both Paley's and Tennyson's accounts of the biological world have turned out to be simplistic, perhaps the account of God associated with each is equally simplistic—both Paley's benevolent designer and Chalmers's sovereign God who will not "falter from the imposition of any severity, which might serve the objects of a high administration" (1833:292f). In this section we pursue an image of God more complex yet conceivably more Christian than either of these alternatives. The hope is that it is consistent with, even if not entailed by, the more complex and balanced accounts of nature presented by recent biologists such as de Waal. To show this it may be helpful to recall yet once more the summary of Christian narrative first introduced in *Ethics.*

> The Christian story in its primal form tells of a God who . . . is the very Ground of Adventure, the Weaver of society's Web, the Holy Source of nature in its concreteness—the one and only God, who, when time began, began to be God for a world that in its orderly constitution finally came by his will and choice to include also—ourselves. We human beings, having our natural frame and basis [in the evolutionary process], with our own (it seemed our own) penchant for community, and (it seemed) our own hankerings after adventure, found ourselves, before long, in trouble. Our very adventurousness led us astray; our drive to cohesion fostered monstrous imperial alternatives to the adventure and sociality of the Way God had intended, while our continuity with nature became an excuse to despise ourselves and whatever was the cause of us. We sin. In his loving concern, God set among us, by every means infinite wisdom could propose, the foundations of a new human society; in his patience he sent messengers to recall the people of his Way to their way; in the first bright glimmers of opportunity he sent—himself, incognito, without splendor and fanfare, the Maker amid the things made, the fundamental Web as if a single fiber, the Ground of Adventure risking everything in this adventure. His purpose—sheer love; his means—pure faith; his promise—unquenchable hope. In that

> love he lived a life of love; by that faith he died a faithful death; from that death he rose to fructify hope for the people of his Way, newly gathered, newly equipped. (*Ethics*, 147)

Risk, adventure, and suffering unto death are ineliminable parts of the story, not only the divine risk and suffering on behalf of humankind, but that risk and suffering as the intended model for all human faithfulness. In baptist thought the suffering of Christians is seen not so often as punishment for sin but as costly participation with Christ in the likely consequences of obedience to God in the midst of a sinful world. Anabaptist leader Hans Hut proclaimed "the Gospel of Christ crucified, how He suffered for our sake and was obedient to the Father even unto death. In the same way we should walk after Christ, suffering for His sake all that is laid upon us, even unto death." It is interesting to note that several Anabaptist writers extended this account of human suffering to include "the gospel of all creatures." Hut himself taught that the suffering of animals and the destruction of other living things conforms to the pattern of redemption through suffering, and in its own way preaches the gospel of Christ crucified (Armour, 1966:78-82).

Chapter Four of *Doctrine* described creation itself as travail. The theme of God's own struggle in creation is found in Old Testament and New, from Isaiah's likening creation to a woman giving birth (Isa. 42:5, 14) to the claim that the suffering Messiah is the very one through whom all things came into being. Paul in Romans asserts that the Christian's sufferings are but a part of the groaning of the whole created universe in all its parts (Rom. 8:22), and all of this is associated with the labor of God to bring forth something "we do not yet see" (Rom. 8:25; cf. *Doctrine*, 160-76).

Philosopher of religion Holmes Rolston has developed similar insights with particular reference to the suffering inherent in the evolutionary process. Rolston emphasizes our continuity with the rest of the biological world and at the same time reconciles the suffering in nature with a Christian concept of God. In both the life Christians are called to live as followers of Jesus and in the biological realm there is an analogy with the self-sacrificing character of God. The key to his interpretation of nature is his recognition that God identifies less with the predator than with the prey. We quote his beautiful prose at length.

> The Earth is a divine creation and scene of providence. The whole natural history is somehow contained in God, God's doing, and that includes even suffering, which, if it is difficult to say simply

that it is immediately from God, is not ultimately outside of God's plan and redemptive control. God absorbs suffering and transforms it into goodness. . . . [N]ature is . . . cruciform. The world is not a paradise of hedonistic ease, but a theater where life is learned and earned by labor, a drama where even the evils drive us to make sense of things. Life is advanced not only by thought and action, but by suffering, not only by logic but by pathos. . . . This pathetic element in nature is seen in faith to be at the deepest logical level the pathos in God. God is not in a simple way the Benevolent Architect, but is rather the Suffering Redeemer. The whole of the earthen metabolism needs to be understood as having this character. The God met in physics as the divine wellspring from which matter-energy bubbles up . . . is in biology the suffering and resurrecting power that redeems life out of chaos. . . .

The secret of life is seen now to lie not so much in the heredity molecules, not so much in natural selection and the survival of the fittest, not so much in life's informational, cybernetic learning. The secret of life is that it is a passion play. Things perish in tragedy. The religions knew that full well, before biology arose to reconfirm it. But things perish with a passing over in which the sacrificed individual also flows in the river of life. Each of the suffering creatures is delivered over as an innocent sacrificed to preserve a line, a blood sacrifice perishing that others may live. We have a kind of "slaughter of the innocents," a non-moral, naturalistic harbinger of the slaughter of the innocents at the birth of the Christ, all perhaps vignettes hinting of the innocent lamb slain from the foundation of the world. They share the labor of the divinity. In their lives, beautiful, tragic, and perpetually incomplete, they speak for God; they prophesy as they participate in the divine pathos. All have "borne our griefs and carried our sorrows."

The abundant life that Jesus exemplifies and offers to his disciples is that of a sacrificial suffering through to something higher. There is something divine about the power to suffer through to something higher. The Spirit of God is the genius that makes alive, that redeems life from its evils. The cruciform creation is, in the end, deiform, godly, just because of this element of struggle, not in spite of it. There is a great divine "yes" hidden behind and within every "no" of crushing nature. God, who is the lure toward rationality and sentience in the upcurrents of the biological pyramid, is also the compassionate lure in, with, and under all purchasing of life at the cost of sacrifice. God rescues from suffer-

> ing, but the Judeo-Christian faith never teaches that God eschews suffering in the achievement of the divine purposes. To the contrary, seen in the paradigm of the cross, God too suffers, not less than his creatures, in order to gain for his creatures a more abundant life. (Rolston, 1994:218-20)

So here in the writings of Hut, McClendon, and Rolston is an account of the moral character of a God who participates with creatures in a world where suffering is inevitable, and who brings good out of evil in all imaginable ways—even creating the capacity for sharing in the midst of "carnivory." A central thesis of this chapter is that biology is not only a potential shaper of theology, but in fact has been shaped by the alliance between the (misguided) natural theology of Darwin's day and Malthusian justifications for the suffering of the poor. We propose an alternative view of God and of God's relation to those who suffer, a view that more nearly reflects the gospel of Jesus Christ than does Chalmers's (merely) sovereign God. Happily, it can be shown, as well, to better reflect the character of the biological world as it has come to be known in our own day. If Rolston's account of God was shaped by biologists' accounts of nature, it is not far-fetched to say that some current biologists' views of nature have been shaped by theology as well—de Waal's critique of sociobiology is in a section whose title is "Calvinist Sociobiology," and he speculates that the dark mood in which nature has been perceived since Darwin's day goes back not only to Malthus but, before him, to (certain Dutch) Calvinist doctrines of original sin (1996:17).

§4. Embodied Selfhood

In *Ethics* it was suggested that one reason why the biblical standpoint has become difficult to grasp in our day is that while the *embodied* character of human life was assumed by the biblical writers it has lost its self-evidence in intervening centuries. A long history of dualism in Christian thought has often allowed Christians to leave out of account the drives, needs, capacities—and delights—of organic existence; in extreme cases the body has been seen as the enemy of the spirit. This alienation from our own embodied selfhood has been accompanied by a denigration of the organic and natural world of which we are a part. Our latter-day difficulty was described this way: "we simply do not believe that the God we know will have to do with *things.* Yet this biblical materialism is the very fiber of which the first strand of ethics is formed" (*Ethics,* 91). This section will review some of the ways in which developments in biology point contemporary Christians back to an appreciation of the body and of the materialism of the Bible.

a. Darwin and dualism.—Already in Darwin's day the theory of evolution raised the possibility that humanity and all its works, including society and culture, could be explained in purely biological terms. If so, free will and responsibility seemed to be in jeopardy. To protect the dignity of humans, many then relied on the mind-body (or body-soul) dualism that had been employed since the rise of modern physics to exempt human freedom and intelligence from the blind determination of natural laws. It became a common strategy among Christians to reconcile theological and biological accounts of human nature by granting that the human *body* may well have evolved from animals, but to insist that human distinctiveness is a function of the *soul,* specially created by God.

The origin of the modern concept of the soul is complex. It was common fifty years ago to count body-soul dualism as *the* Greek view and to distinguish it from the physicalist and holist view of the Bible (or at least the Hebrew Bible). Later Christian accounts of human nature were certainly influenced by a variety of Greek philosophical views. It is fair to say that a modified Platonic account of body and soul predominated from Augustine's day until the high Middle Ages, when the reintroduction of Aristotelian thought provided a much different competitor. Aristotelians saw the soul as the immanent form of the body (hylomorphism), and since the soul is the life principle, animals and plants as well as humans must have their own appropriate sorts of souls. Modern views of body and soul owe as much to René Descartes as to Plato. Early modern physics involved the rejection of Aristotelian hylomorphism in favor of a view of matter more closely akin to Democritus's atomism. Galileo and his followers developed from this atomist conception of matter a purely mechanical view of the natural world. Descartes accepted this picture of nature: animals, he believed, were automata, and so were human bodies. In addition, though, to account for human freedom and intellect, he devised an account of soul or mind that was closer to Plato's account than Aristotle's. (Note that while 'mind' and 'soul' have different connotations today, the terms can be used interchangeably with regard to Descartes's views.) Descartes defined the mind as "thinking substance." Along with this very significant shift in conceptions of the relation of mind and matter, Descartes's account also represents a shift regarding the human attributes or capacities that were attributed to soul and body. For Thomas Aquinas, the human soul accounts for the rational faculties of intellect and will, but also for sensation, emotion, and appetites. Descartes considered sensations and passions to be "emotions of the soul," yet he believed them to be caused by the body. Since Descartes, then, accounts of mind have focused on the cognitive capacities, while emotions have been judged an interference in the intellectual life.

It may have been reasonable in Darwin's day to imagine that there was some point in evolutionary history when the first human body was conceived and that God began at that point to create human souls. That is, humans were said to have evolved from apes, and it made sense to assume that humans had souls but (post Descartes) apes did not. (However, this image cannot be pressed too far: was this first human infant borne by a soulless ape?) Current accounts of the evolution of humans make this notion of 'soul insertion' even less plausible. Paleontology now traces human origins to an extinct common ancestor of both humans and apes, a creature that lived 5 to 7 million years ago. Between then and now there have been a variety of hominid species. The first known hominid, *Ardipithecus ramidus,* lived 4.4 MYA (million years ago), but it is not clear whether it is in the direct line of descent to modern humans. Those known to be our ancestors include *Australopithecus anamensis, Australopithecus afarensis, Homo habilis,* and *Homo erectus.* Other hominids not in the direct line of descent to *Homo sapiens* (modern humans) include *Australopithecus africanus, Paranthropus aethiopicus, Paranthropus boisei,* and *Paranthropus robustus.* Between 3 and 1 MYA, three or four hominid species lived contemporaneously in the African continent. More recently, *Homo neanderthalis,* a subspecies with brains as large as ours, lived contemporaneously (approximately 100,000 to 40,000 years ago) with our own subspecies (Francisco Ayala in Brown et al., 1998:33f). The burial practices and cave drawings of Neanderthals are often taken to show religious awareness. So did all hominids have souls, or only those in the direct line of descent of *Homo sapiens*? What about the Neanderthals? Or was it only modern humans? The very oddity of these questions may lead to a suspicion that evolution and dualism are odd bedfellows.

b. Neuroscience.—It is said that Darwin completed the Copernican revolution, bringing living things within the purview of the natural sciences (Ayala, in Russell et al., eds., 1998). If this is the case, then one might add that contemporary neuroscience is now completing the Darwinian revolution, bringing the mind within the purview of biology. *In short, all of the human capacities once attributed to the immaterial mind or soul are now yielding to the insights of neurobiology.* The development of new brain-imaging techniques, along with new techniques for computer modeling of cognitive processes, made the 1990s the "decade of the brain."

One of the most elaborate and perceptive accounts of the functions of the soul was that of Thomas Aquinas (ST 1.79-89). He followed Aristotle in recognizing three levels of functioning: that which we share with both animals and plants, that which we share with only the animals, and that which is distinctive of humans. The faculties attributed to the lowest aspect of the soul—nutrition, growth, and reproduction—have long fallen within the sphere of biological explanation.

A number of the faculties we share with animals have also been understood biologically for some time: locomotion and sense perception. In addition to the five external senses, Thomas postulated four "interior senses." One of these is the *phantasia* or sensory imagination. It is now possible to study visual imagination using PET scans (positron emission tomography), which shows the level of activity in various regions of the brain by recording the amount of blood flow. These scans show that during an exercise in visual imagination the visual cortex is active, but not to the same extent as when the visual object is actually present. Another of Thomas's interior senses was the *sensus communis,* the capacity to collate the inputs from the various external senses in order to associate them with the same object. This is now studied by neuroscientists as the "binding problem." The third of Thomas's interior senses was the *vis aestimativa,* the ability to judge something as friendly or unfriendly, useful or useless. One instance of this faculty in humans is the ability to recognize others' emotions. Although it has not been possible to determine the exact regions of the brain involved, some victims of strokes or tumors do lose this capacity. The fourth of Thomas's interior senses is the *vis memorativa,* the ability to conserve memories of friend or foe, of what has given pleasure and what has caused injury. Neuroscientists now distinguish at least a dozen memory systems, and brain structures have been associated with many of them. The sort of memory Thomas refers to here is an aspect of episodic memory, and it has been shown that such memories cannot be formed without the part of the brain called the hippocampus. We also share with animals the *sensitive appetite,* that is, the ability to be attracted to the objects of sensation, such as food or potential mates. Neuroscience has made contributions here, as well, for instance in beginning to understand the role of neurotransmitters (the chemicals that conduct electrical impulses in the brain) in producing feelings of hunger or satiation. The emotions, according to Thomas, are a product of both the *vis aestimativa* and the sensory appetite. Emotions, too, are now known to be mediated by physical processes, with the involvement of neurotransmitters.

Among Thomas's faculties distinctive of humans (the "rational" faculties), two were the active and passive intellects. The *passive intellect* is yet another sort of memory, closely resembling what current neuroscientists call declarative memory, and this has been found to be dependent on the medial temporal lobe of the brain. *Active intellect* is responsible for abstracting concepts from sensory experience and for reasoning and judging. These latter capacities are less well understood in neurobiological terms. However, they all involve the use of language, and language use and acquisition are an important area of current study. Two regions of the brain, Wernicke's area and Broca's area, have long been known to be involved in language. Language memory involves a variety of regions; selective damage due to strokes or tumors shows that access to common nouns, proper names, verbs, and even color terms depends on separate regions. Furthermore, syntactic and semantic capacities depend on different regions of the brain.

The third of Thomas's rational faculties was the will. He defined it as the capacity to be attracted to goods of a non-sensory sort. Along with intellect, this is the seat of moral capacities. Furthermore, since God is the ultimate good, the will also accounts for the capacity to be attracted to God. Neuroscience now contributes to our understanding of both morality and religious experience. Antonio Damasio has studied the neural processes that go into practical reasoning, that is, the ability to make both moral and prudential judgments. In his book, *Descartes' Error* (1994), he reviews the familiar case of a nineteenth-century railway worker, Phineas Gage, whose brain was pierced by a metal rod. Gage recovered physically and his cognitive functions (attention, perception, memory, reasoning, language) were all intact. Yet he suffered a dramatic character change after the accident. The doctor who treated him noted that he had become "fitful, irreverent, indulging at times in the grossest profanity which was not previously his custom, manifesting but little deference for his fellows, impatient of restraint or advice when it conflicts with his desires, at times pertinaciously obstinate, yet capricious and vacillating, devising many plans of future operation, which are no sooner arranged than they are abandoned" (quoted by Damasio, 1994:8). Damasio's wife, Hanna, was able to calculate from the damage to Gage's skull exactly which parts of the brain would have been destroyed in the accident—selected areas of his prefrontal cortices. Damasio concludes from this and other similar cases that this area of the brain is "concerned specifically with unique human properties, among them the ability to anticipate the future and plan accordingly within a complex social environment; the sense of responsibility toward the self and others; and the ability to orchestrate one's survival deliberately, at the command of one's free will" (1994:10). In short, what Thomas described as the "appetite for the good" appears to depend directly on localizable brain functions. A number of neuroscientists have begun to study more directly the role of the brain in religious experience. For example, patients with temporal lobe epilepsy often develop strong interests in religion, and this has led to speculation that the temporal lobes are involved in certain sorts of normal religious experiences as well (Russell et al., 1999).

What are we to make of all this? It is important to note that no such accumulation of data can ever amount to a proof that there is no nonmaterial mind or soul in addition to the body. But if we recall that the soul was originally introduced into Western thought not from Hebraic Scripture but as an *explanation* for capacities that appeared not to be explainable in biological terms, then we can certainly say that for scientific purposes the hypothesis is no longer necessary.

A second caution is in order. It would be easy at this point to fall into the reductionist's error of claiming that 'morality' or 'religious experience' is *nothing but* a brain process. However, the fact that acting according to an ethical principle requires the participation of brain circuitry, Damasio points out, does not cheapen the ethical principle. The edifice of ethics does not collapse (1994:xiv). Furthermore,

> [t]o discover that a particular feeling [including any feeling involved in responding to God] depends on activity in a number of specific brain systems interacting with a number of body organs does not diminish the status of that feeling as a human phenomenon. Neither anguish nor the elation that love or art can bring about are devalued by understanding some of the myriad biological processes that make them what they are. Precisely the opposite should be true: Our sense of wonder should increase before the intricate mechanisms that make such magic possible. (1994:xvi)

The point, then, of our survey of scientific findings bearing on human nature, both from evolutionary biology and current neuroscience, is to see the way they point Western Christians back to what is now widely recognized as a more biblical view of the human race—one that recognizes that, as with the other animals, God formed humans from the dust of the ground (Brown et al., 1998). In English we lose the Hebrew pun in calling the first human *adam* because he is formed from *adamah,* dust or ground (Gen. 2:7). We can recapture the imagery if we think of ourselves as *humans,* made from *humus.* In the Genesis stories of creation the only clear difference between the human animal and the others is this: this creature is *addressed* by the creator (cf. Karl Barth, CD III/1 §41.2). And again, "[o]ur life as Christians *is* our life as organic constituents of the crust of this planet" (*Ethics*, p. 89).

One might ask why this recognition of our physicality is important from a gospel perspective. One reason has been spelled out at length in *Ethics:* no account of Christian morality that neglects our embodied selfhood can do justice to gospel ethics. A second reason is spelled out in *Doctrine:* it is impossible to do justice to God's relation to the natural world without an appreciation of humans' role in nature. The whole of modern theology has suffered from an anthropocentrizing tendency. Whereas earlier generations had perceived a 'living' universe in which spirit and matter were closely intertwined, not only in plants and animals, but in stars, mountains, and rivers, the scientists of the seventeenth century, as we have seen, adopted a mechanical model of the universe. This not only created problems for theologians in understanding human nature, but also affected their accounts of the role of God in nature. As it were, they extracted physics from its theological home and setting. Conforming to received science, many modern theologians relegated nature to the realm of the secular. According to Rudolf Bultmann, nature is an object, entirely governed by natural laws; the religious value of the doctrine of creation is strictly limited, since the authentic dependence and freedom that humans can feel must face not nature, but God only. Ironically, while the architects of this anthropocentric doctrine of creation believed they were protecting faith from alien elements, the unhappy outcome was the banishing of God from nature (*Doctrine,* 151).

Yet, after Darwin, this separation of humankind from its organic family can legitimately be maintained only by associating our distinctive humanness with something other than the body, and, as shown above, it is becoming increasingly difficult to conceive of what this other element might be. All of the functions originally assigned to the immaterial soul or mind are now clearly bodily functions. And this conclusion is not to be lamented: only when humans are seen as part and parcel of nature, can communion with God be seen as the *telos* of the whole evolutionary (and cosmic) process, and nature's trials be taken up into divine reconciliation. "Creation," *the whole of it,* "has a goal, and that goal lies in God" (*Doctrine,* 149). Jesuit theologian Edward Oakes speaks of humans as the "priests of the universe." Humans' ability "to offer thanks to God recapitulates and makes conscious the praise the universe already makes for its own being, as the Psalmist implicitly (Psalm 148), and Paul explicitly (Rom. 8:18-27), recognized" (1998).

Praise the LORD from the heavens;
praise him in the heights above. . . .
Praise him, sun and moon;
praise him, all you shining stars;. . .
Praise the LORD from the earth . . .
all mountains and hills;
all fruit trees and cedars;
wild animals and all cattle,
creeping creatures and winged birds.
Let kings and all commoners,
princes and rulers over the whole earth,
youths and girls,
old and young together,
let them praise the name of the LORD . . .
Praise the LORD. (Psalm 148)

* * * * *

Science is what this present work calls a "powerful practice" (*Ethics,* Six §1*b*). It is a socially established cooperative human activity with its own appropriate goals and standards of excellence. Science at its best not only aims at its own internal goods but also fulfills a divine mandate to seek truth. The human creature is special in God's creation because it alone is addressed by the Creator and is thus able to know, albeit "in a glass, darkly," the character of that Creator. Scientists from Kepler to contemporary physicist Paul Davies have understood science as a means of discovering the mind of God (Davies, 1992). Yet social practices, as is the case with all human activity, are capable of falling short of the glory of God. Science is not immune from the impulses that distort human goods of every sort. We have seen how self-interested attempts to justify rather than combat poverty influenced Darwin's culture and Darwin's science as well. But we have also seen how scientific practice itself can work to correct such distortions. Thus, no simple account of science in conflict with Christianity is appropriate—or even possible. But neither can theology be insulated from science, or science from theology. Sometimes science calls theology to account, as in its potential criticisms of theology distorted by the related tendencies toward dualism and anthropomorphism. Sometimes theology raises critical questions for science, as we have done here in seeking the source of Darwinism's negative view of nature. Always the gospel must call the whole of human culture to account when it loses sight of the lordship of Christ in the social realm.

CHAPTER FOUR

Art: Cultural Telltale

To find what art is, what counts as art, is as difficult as finding general agreement about religion or politics. Yet however slippery the task, without an account of art something vital is missing in a Christian theology of culture. Though this gap cannot be properly closed by the present brief chapter, the matter is too important merely to be ignored. Part of the trouble here is that while acknowledged art objects—pictures, poems, songs—are as old as culture itself, being already in human prehistory intertwined with primitive religion by means of incantatory drawings, sacred myths, and ritual music, today's concept of 'art' is quite modern. Ironically, the *philosophes* of the Enlightenment sought to avert this modernization, arguing that art and craft must not be separated. Yet in the wake of their work such a separation did nonetheless occur: the educated artists who produced 'real' art were distinguished from mere artisans who made 'useful' products. Of course, aesthetic problems had been discussed by philosophers from Plato onward—must art imitate nature? educate? entertain? what defines beauty and sublimity?—but modernity progressively separated art from the rest of life and in that sense created art in its own likeness. A related development pointed out by French man-of-affairs and intellectual André Malraux in his *Voices of Silence* (1974:13f) was the extraction of art from life by the establishment of art museums, something that had not existed in premodern times. A certain portrait was no longer an emblem of a human being as he appeared in his time or place; it had become part of an exhibition of *artistic* merit, hung alongside comparable portraits by other artists in a museum or gallery. Similarly, historical and biblical scenes ceased to situate public buildings and churches by recalling their past; these paintings had now become 'art' even when not removed to a museum. A similar fate overtook music as it was transferred from worship and social festivities to concert halls where serious listeners gathered not to worship or to have a party but to listen (in respectful silence) and 'appreciate.' Even music played or sung during church services became a performance and was openly applauded! If this fate has not yet overtaken literature, there is nonetheless a tendency in that direction: scholars speak of a 'canon' of literature as if its items were somehow detached from all other discourse. Art thus functions as a cultural telltale, a weather vane, in this case signaling modernity's fractured self-awareness.

Let it be said in resistance to all this that this chapter accepts no final separation of art from life or politics or society or the practices of religion; its intention is rather to locate art exactly in such settings as far as possible and explicitly to ask about the relation of art to the gospel there. To the extent that this stance and goal challenge current aesthetic theory and current museum practice, the challenge is deliberate.

Such a declaration creates an extra burden: if we are to question modernity's art-theory (and sometimes, as will be seen, its art as well) then what shall we say art is? In an earlier work, *Convictions (CONV.),* James Smith and I appropriated philosopher John L. Austin's account of linguistic communication. Speaking was understood as a kind of *action,* so that 'speech acts' (oral or written) were in a class with other purposeful acts (as varied as cooking an egg, wedding a mate, building a boat), activities undertaken by someone using recognizable means to achieve some goal or gain some point. For both speech and other cases, *achieving the goal* is the primary thrust of such action—the cooked egg, the wed mate, the issued word. In the case of speech acts, that goal is always, broadly put, to say something to someone. This primary thrust or *primary force* (for Austin, "illocutionary force") could in most cases be further specified: in speaking, one is ordering or consenting, advising or protesting, estimating or proposing, and so forth among a wide but not limitless range of possibilities. (Thus 'stating,' a common philosophers' fudge that tries to avoid these specifics, is properly moved to the sidelines and benched in most speech action, being permitted on the floor only for certain special plays—*CONV.*, 53-56.) This *doing* something, Austin made clear, is the conventional role of language; other roles turn upon it. For in connection with this *conventional* or *primary* or *illocutionary dimension,* other dimensions typically appear: Human utterance rarely or never avoids a *psychological or affective dimension.* This includes the speaker's (or writer's) intentions and, in happy communication, some of the hearer's (or reader's) intentions as well. Hearers, for example, *intend* to understand what is being said—in short, they pay attention. And again there will be in most if not all speech a *referential dimension*—most speech action either represents or in some way *refers* to the world: If what I say is neither about nor even has reference to anything at all, real or imaginary, present, past, or future, then my utterance is vulnerable to criticism or may simply be disallowed on this account—I am judged to have said nothing. (Asking, doubtfully, what someone is talking *about* is an example of such disallowing.) These three dimensions (primary, affective, referential) are all normally present in human acts of speaking, and the incautious diminishing of any one of them is likely to issue in defective speech (as Austin liked to say, in unhappy speech acts), as when someone infelicitously says, "Please pass the butter," when there *is* no butter there to be passed (see further *CONV.*:chap. 3; Austin, 1975).

Now it would impoverish both works of art and the distinctiveness of language to suppose that art can be reduced to speech or communication. Frank Lloyd Wright's Falling Water, as built, is not a 'statement' except in a metaphorical use of that word, though in one sense of the term the imperious architect doubtless submitted more than one statement to his wealthy client. Nevertheless, the Austinian account of language as action as we summarized it in *Convictions* also provides an adaptable grid for understanding the role of art in human life. Artists, like ordinary language-speakers, have to employ certain *conventions* in their work: In one culture certain stick-like marks scratched into soft rock stand for or count as a human being; in our own very different culture, the brush-strokes of paint on canvas that constitute *Whistler's Mother* do the same. In both cases the artist has used existing conventions in order to create something (more broadly, to do something, to act). In art as in language the conventions change, but if they change so quickly or totally that sense can no longer be made of them, there is no action; would-be art that employs indecipherable 'conventions' is only marks on surfaces or a scrabble of words or a cacophony of sounds. Again, in art as in language whatever is said or done is furnished with certain *affects* including the artist's and the viewer's (or listener's or reader's) intentions; of art we say (in an admittedly circular way) that these are 'aesthetic' intentions—the circularity may even arouse in some a naughty metaphysical urge. And again in art as in language there is *reference* to the perceived creation or its Creator, but *here is a big difference: art also refers to a new world, a world that is created by the artistic action itself.* Artists may stretch or may minimize any of these three dimensions: modernist painting, literature, and music, for example, intentionally play havoc with conventions (art's first dimension) and do so, perhaps, in order to reveal more closely the artist's creative intentions (part of its second dimension), and both these raise complex questions about reference (its third dimension). Music is a case in point. Certainly not all music is program music, depicting some scene or other. Yet music continually refers to other music, and at the root of such a chain of reference lie the represented sounds of nature—for example, the natural harmonics of a plucked string or the rhythmic and melodious sounds of brook and forest, as well as primal human sighs and cries. So music at one terminus refers to the perceived world of nature, and at the other terminus music's artistic action creates a world—a new world—for us.

In a chapter on art, Julian Hartt corrects a Tillichian theme: art indeed uses symbols (conventions?) "to show forth reality not otherwise discoverable" (1967:355). Any real art does this, he says, not just 'realistic' art. Yet art's necessary illusions serve to expose the illusory character of the experienced world: "love of truth can lead to a transformation and transvaluation of the given world" (1967:362). True artistic creativity is grounded in the real world, but from that start the artist creates a world anew (1967:364f). Hence follows my claim about the *double* reference of any work of art. Artists of necessity refer to the given world, yet to be art their work must imply (refer to) a whole new world of unrealized possibility.

So here we have a rough definition of art—it is human *action* that makes fit *reference* to the perceived world and to the new 'world' created by the action of the art; it 'artistically' employs *conventions* with appropriate 'aesthetic' affects, and it thereby expresses (and may evoke) the affects, the *feelings,* of both artist and audience. Though that definition is circular, it is not empty or claimless: It emphasizes that art is human action, and it pays attention, like many another definition, to tradition ('convention'), to creativity ('intention,' etc.), and to what there is or might be ('reference'). The artist employs the available conventions in order to act, showing forth or disclosing something, and that something (the art product itself) makes demands upon the artist's and viewer's feelings and also comments upon the given world. The chapter's question, then, is this: what has one culture's art, so understood, to do with the gospel? If this is what art is, where will the church *stand* with respect to it in order to *be* the church?

My limited scope is art in America; here I will attend in uneven fashion to three main fields of art, visual, verbal, musical—arts of display and sign and sound. My thesis follows an insight gleaned from art critic Robert Hughes, who has pointed out that visual art in the United

States from its colonial beginnings to the present has migrated to one of two poles: either American art is robustly empirical, attempting to present its subject matter "just as it is," or it has gravitated to the opposite pole, seeking in Tillichian fashion to show beyond its subject matter the spiritual, the transcendent, the sublime (Hughes, 1997:pass.). Grant Wood's *American Gothic* is empirical without admixture; Mark Rothko's final dark abstracts are spiritual or they are nothing.

I think Hughes's assessment is correct, and it leads to another: *Both poles, singly or even joined together, miss the central point of the gospel of Jesus Christ,* "the Word become flesh" (John 1:14), for the reality the gospel recounts is neither unearthly nor time-and-space bound, neither gnostic (concerned to escape this world) nor positivist (concerned only with scientific facts and phenomena), nor is the gospel a layered amalgam of the two (just as in the classical doctrine of the Incarnation the divine and human do not exist in some hybridized state). Instead, it transmutes these two, flesh and spirit, into a distinct biblical whole ("God with us"), a reality best understood as *the hypostatic union of God's* story *with our own* (see *Doctrine,* Six §3). This central frame becomes explicit as narrated gospel; it has shaped Christian art wherever that has appeared; yet American art with a few exceptions has missed it. This miss is most evident in American visual art, not only painting and sculpture but architecture and film. At this writing the center is still notably absent from American literary art as well, though with important exceptions: in fact most American literature repeats the split; either it pursues transcendent truth (Ralph Waldo Emerson comes to mind) or it portrays an empirical world that effectively filters out transcendence (Ernest Hemingway is a case among many), or it tries to amalgamate these, yet lacks the vital narrative bond that gives form to the world of the gospel. There are significant exceptions in our literature, though, and I must indicate some of them. Finally, music in America has either been European-influenced so that it cannot properly be assessed apart from that dominance (so I will bypass it here), or it is rooted in jazz and blues, uniquely American musical forms and perhaps the only uniquely American art music. In this case, happily, the story of art-and-gospel changes. Jazz, which even from its African American origins showed itself capable of transcending ethnicity, is a riotous musical overthrow of American art's primary temptation. Mirroring the gospel's heaven-come-to-earth reality, its transcendence within (rather than beyond) the earthy, its insouciance in face of suffering, jazz with blues provides a fit cultural companion to the gospel, signaling the presence of arable gospel soil.

This present thesis concerning art and gospel religion constitutes a rejection of the best-known recent work on 'religious art' in America, represented by two important exhibits in the 1970s organized by Jane Dillenberger, aided by her husband of that time, John Dillenberger (Dillenberger and Taylor, 1972; Dillenberger and Dillenberger, 1977). The many paintings selected for these exhibits were said to display "religious art" or were expressions of the "religious impulse" (thus Jane Dillenberger) or "the modalities of imagination and spirit" (thus John Dillenberger). More concretely, Joshua C. Taylor of the Smithsonian Institution writes that "religious art" is (1) art whose subject matter is associated with a sect or with religious literature (e.g., the Bible). Or (2) it is art that displays a certain aesthetic formulation—Taylor mentions the long survival of classical aesthetic taste among those holding theological concerns. Alternatively, (3) religious art is art that invests nature with transcendent significance, as in paintings of the Hudson River School. For my part I would include all this and more: We should grant that *all* art, if it is indeed art, is in some sense 'religious.' But as Taylor concedes, "'religious art,' then, is basically meaningless" as a descriptive term; Taylor even says it is "a false and misleading" category (Dillenberger and Taylor, 1972:10f). Nonetheless, we are deeply indebted to both of the Dillenbergers for their rich recovery of many forgotten or neglected American artists and their works.

Accordingly, this chapter has four sections: **(§1) a preliminary look at visual art in America that will illustrate this artistic schism; (§2) a brief look at the same polarity in American literature, noting some important exceptions to the schism; (§3) a section on jazz, showing how in it the schism is overcome; and (§4) a brief reflection on art and Christian peoplehood in the American setting.** In this closing reflection we may see that 'Christian art' (that is, art openly related to the gospel and in service for the church—the church's music or its sermons, for two obvious examples) can *flourish* only in an environing culture that supplies suitable conventions, motifs, and referents. Concretely, Christian music is heard only when the culture offers suitable musical conventions, Christian writing flourishes only in a literary world open to gospel themes, Christian visual art appears only in a world in which the gospel truth can make itself visible. This outcome implies a churchly demand upon a culture, but even more a Macedonian call from the environing culture to the witnessing church.

§1. The Schism in American Visual Art

The division between empirical and spiritual American art has deep roots in American history. Admittedly these are not American art's deepest roots: the Indian and Spanish cultures of the old Southwest, for example, reflect a different grasp upon the world. Both Navajo sand-painting, still practiced today, and the vivid art of New Mexican pueblo churches reflect spiritualities deeply seated in earthy reality (on Navajo and Spanish culture see Chapter Two §1). Yet English colonists arriving on the East Coast imported a different tradition. Iconoclastic European Calvinism had shunned representation in religious art as idolatry. New England's seventeenth-century churches (still visible in the extant Hingham, Massachusetts, meetinghouse) housed Christian spiritual exercises—hymns, sermons, prayers—but their box-like form was not meant to express their spiritual contents. This same Puritan caution spilled over into English colonial painting, which limited itself to portraits meant to preserve a cherished or honored visage or to still-life paintings meant to please by showing fruit, tablecloths, and glassware as if real. The great European Christian iconographic heritage (biblical events, heavenly visions, saints, angels) was deliberately forsaken. As best they could, artists painted their world as they saw it; they laid no explicit claim to another world of reference.

This Puritan point of view was inherited by a long line of American painters who cared nothing for Puritan faith and morals. Raphaelle Peale and Thomas Eakins, John James Audubon and Winslow Homer, Mary Cassatt and Edward Hopper, George Bellows and Grant Wood, Roy Lichtenstein and Andrew Wyeth (names chosen at random) lived in different times, occupied different cultural spaces, and had strikingly different artistic aims, yet they had this pervasive common intent—to enable their viewers to see the existing world 'as it really is': art's second reference must closely resemble its first. So powerful is this tendency in American art that for most Americans any work of art that neglects it, any that falls short of pictorial representation in empirical fidelity to perceived reality, simply fails as art. This is distinctively American: other cultures from ancient Greece to the present have painted and sculptured 'realistically' (a term whose use certainly requires some caution), but for a long time in America, empirical art exhausted the category of artistry so thoroughly that the advent of photography with its own sort of 'realism' led many to wonder whether any role was left for paint on canvas.

a. The transcendental impulse.—Nevertheless, in due course an overtly religious American art arose. Or, to speak more carefully, more than one sort of art appeared that looked beyond the given empirical world to create its second reference and express its aspirations. For this 'transcendental' art was not all of a piece; profound theological differences were at work.

i. The Hudson River School.—To understand the setting of the Hudson River School (1825–75), recall that the nineteenth century brought cascading changes to American life. The rise of industry and the accompanying accumulation of wealth by owners and managers enabled artists to sell expansive canvases to grace the homes of the newly rich. Continued expansion on the frontier gave Americans a renewed sense of their impressive virgin wilderness, filled with awesome natural beauty but also with great economic promise. The relaxing of the old Puritan religious ties meant that Americans such as Ralph Waldo Emerson (see *Doctrine*, pp. 302-6) felt liberated to explore a religion of nature unfettered by the old religion of book and story, law and gospel. All this contributed to the rise of artists who met all these conditions. They were America's first transcendental school. Most of them had studied in Europe, and some were aware of the writing of Irish philosopher Edmund Burke, who in an essay had celebrated the *sublime,* a phenomenon of nature and culture not identical with beauty yet of compelling artistic interest. All of them discovered that Europe's romantic nineteenth-century aesthetic could be replicated in the wild American landscape: the wilderness was as rich in possibilities as the Roman Campagna, perhaps richer. The wilderness was a sacred precinct whose awesome beauty must be treasured (foreshadowing later ecology and preservation movements). The pioneer Hudson River artist was Thomas Cole (1801–48). An English immigrant, Cole found that such scenes as *Falls of the Kaaterskill* in Upstate New York (ironically, a painting now owned by the Gulf States Paper Company) and *The Oxbow,* showing a bend in the Connecticut River seen from a mountain near Northampton, Massachusetts, could profitably be sold to rich New Yorkers. In doing so, he and his peers created a style of painting that was no longer merely empirical. Others in the Hudson River School included Thomas Doughty, Albert Bierstadt, a German immigrant famous for his paintings of the mountain West, Asher Durand, Samuel F. B. Morse (of telegraph fame), and Cole's lone pupil, Frederick Edwin Church (1826–1900).

In 1828 Cole painted *The Garden of Eden,* now in Fort Worth's Amon Carter Museum. It displays his desire to enhance his landscape realism with appeals to the ideal and references to holy Scripture. A foreground framed with palm and hardwood trees depicts the beauty of created nature. Beyond, a meadow is dotted with grazing animals. On an overlooking bluff stand Adam and Eve, innocent in their nakedness but diminutive in size as if to emphasize the enveloping grandeur of the scene. In the far distance a lake, a waterfall, and craggy peaks wrapped in mist dissolve into aerial perspective evoking the sublime, the artist's sense of awesome nature. Many critics believe Cole meant to represent America as a new Eden where unspoiled nature could return humankind to a state of innocence. Here, then, was work so far unequaled in grandeur of subject, executed with technical competence, yet pointed in a nostalgic direction—back to Eden rather than forward to the kingdom of God.

The 'new Eden' theme was repeated by other artists, notably Church. One such repetition, Church's 1849 oil on canvas (another Amon Carter holding) is titled *New England Landscape (Evening After a Storm).* The beauty and power of the scene, depicted more clearly than by Cole's sometimes murky paint, present in the foreground a lake fed by a waterfall. The waterfall powers a mill, and beyond it low rounded mountains, separated by wooded valleys, recede into the distance. The haze at the horizon conveys a sense of infinite distance. All together, mill (emblem of human industry), distant mountains, sky with cloud colors reflected in the lake form a harmonious whole achieved not by exact imitation of any actual scene but by transporting elements of actuality into a contrived painterly harmony. Church was celebrated for this and other like achievements; he was America's first famous visual artist. Yet this work (and Church's masterly paintings of the Andes, conceived while on expedition but actually painted at home) was the opening note in an artistic rendering of Manifest Destiny—the divine vocation of the United States to rule the New World and (as the idea grew) the rest of the world as well. So understood, Church and his fellow artists sadly perverted the Genesis creation narrative: they revised the story of an earth created by God for purposes best unfolded in the prophets and in Jesus of Nazareth into a story of Eden revisited by a new Adam, the pioneering American, whose industrial mills (and by extension, whose territorial conquests) perfect God's plan.

Were there any doubt about the aim of the Hudson River School to celebrate America as the very site of the sublime, it is resolved by the work of another member of the school, Albert Bierstadt (1830–1902). Bierstadt accompanied a surveying expedition from Fort Laramie to the Rocky Mountains, traveled through Wind River and Shoshone country, and then returned to his New York studio to paint "huge landscapes" that purported to show the West "as it really is," but which in fact presented a transmogrified scenery that used factual detail only to idealize the view—an unstable mix, as even art critic of the time James Jarves could see (Hughes, 1997:195). Bierstadt's venture in Manifest Destiny art achieves its effects by the *amalgamation* of transcendence and empiricism, an achievement still remote from an art that can support Christian existence.

Hudson River transcendental art never replicates the created world; it cannot even pretend to do so, since all art employs conventions in order to act artistically—to paint, to speak, to sing—engaging in its action particular aesthetic affects and in the same action referring in some way to the world. So this art does not form a doublet of reality as given, and it could not have done so. The theological point to note, however, is that it was equally unable to "climb up to heaven" (cf. Rom. 10:6); that is, its grasp for the transcendent was doomed to fail because it began with human existence unable to transcend itself—a theological point Reinhold Niebuhr would underscore for a later generation (R. Niebuhr, 1941–43, vol. 1).

ii. Edward Hicks.—Yet there was another sort of American 'transcendental' or spiritual painting, contemporaneous with these yet unrelated to Emerson and the transcendentalists, that constituted an exception to the empirical-transcendental split. Philadelphia carriage-maker, artist, and itinerant preacher Edward Hicks (1780–1849), who according to art critic Robert Hughes was "the only artist who lived and died a Quaker" (1997:38), belonged to the Hicksite branch of the Society of Friends but supported himself by working as a 'mechanic,' that is, a skilled artisan. He is best known for his *Peaceable Kingdom* paintings, often reproduced; for a quarter-century Hicks himself painted numerous versions. In the 1834 version that hangs in the National Gallery in Washington one sees in the near foreground an infant petting a sleeping leopard while her young Quaker baby-sitter watches. Both children are drawn in the awkward style of an American folk artist. Beyond them, sheltered by verdant forest, a variety of beasts stand as if posed for their portraits. Some are grazing animals, sheep, goats, cattle; others, lions, bears, leopards, a wolf, are animals of prey. Yet all assemble peaceably, since

> [t]hen the wolf will live with the lamb,
> and the leopard lie down with the kid;
> the calf and the young lion will feed together,
> with a little child to tend them. . . .
> There will be neither hurt nor harm in all my holy mountain;
> for the land will be filled with the knowledge of the LORD,
> as the waters cover the sea. (Isa. 11:6-9)

Hicks's peaceable kingdom, like Isaiah's, reigns over humankind as well: in the painting's far distance a group of colonists led by William Penn conclude a treaty with Indians in feather headdress. Beyond all these, the Delaware River placidly flows between its hills. The millennium has come. Hicks's painting does not bespeak spiritual reality by projecting a luminous glow upon creation as did the transcendentalists: children, beasts, men, and nature itself are simply what they are. Yet the rearrangement of human and animal relations depicts the transformation of earth already enjoyed between early Quaker colonists and Original Americans. Transformed relations constitute a transformed world. According to an 1837 sermon by Hicks, the grazing animals symbolize the good in human nature; the feral beasts, man's evil nature. In the peaceable kingdom, evil itself is redeemed; the savage creatures "eat straw like the ox" (Ford, 1985:134f). The artist's (and many viewers') intent, the explicit dual reference to nature and redeemed nature, and the artistic conventions unite to capture a holy vision. *Peaceable Kingdom* is thus a compelling work. Symbolic animals apart, in Hicks's painting the baptist vision controls everything: *this is that* (Penn's colony, the painting declares, has fulfilled Isaiah's prophecy in part), and *then is now* (the harmony of end time is partly realized in William Penn's leadership). There is thus a profound contrast within transcendental art: on the one hand we have Church's Edenic empire, the fiction of an innocent New World with its American Adam; on the other, Hicks's promise of a peaceable kingdom, realized, if only in part, by Quaker treaties with Original Americans and fulfilled, if only in anticipation, by divine, eschatological transformation of existing nature.

b. The dominant, empirical mode.—Yet empirical painting, not transcendentalism, has been the strength of American style. Empiricists do not wrap creation in a holy gauze, nor do they announce Edens past or millennia coming. They only say, "Here it is." Or do they?

i. Eakins.—A first example here is Thomas Eakins (1844–1916), who according to Robert Hughes "gathers the strands of empirical vision" for his own generation. "No American artist ever worked harder to make the human clay palpable" (Hughes, 1997:287). Eakins was born and raised in Philadelphia, studied art in France and Spain, and returned for a lifetime of practicing and teaching art in his home city. He aimed to incorporate the traditional skills of old European and new American art in order to capture in his work the facts, the facts, the facts.

A painting that illustrates Eakins's fine achievement is *The Swimming Hole* (c. 1883–85), now hanging in the Amon Carter Museum. Nude boys and men scramble over a large rock that overhangs the water; in the water are two swimmers (Eakins himself and his English setter, Harry); a boy is caught in mid-dive; others clamber on the rocks or recline, sunning. Water, sunlit rock, dark background foliage, and distant meadow are presented with exquisite skill, as are the swimmers. Surely this is realistic representation at its very height! Yet further thought corrects this impression. To begin, how likely is it that so many swimmers can be caught in so picturesque an instant? One has only to attempt to photograph such a tableau at the nearest public swimming pool to realize how difficult it is to capture. And in fact Eakins himself, who regularly used photography in his work, had in this case made preparatory photographs of naked boys grouped along just such a rock—had posed them for the pose (illustration, Hughes, 1997:296-98). Yet in the painting he has rearranged the scene to achieve an artistic effect, following not photography but iconographic models as old as Michelangelo and as recent as Poussin. Far from capturing a candid glimpse of actuality, Eakins has revised a classic genre. Moreover, there is a distinct erotic flavor in the painting—the pronounced buttocks of the standing boy and the broad pectorals of the reclining man make an impact recalling the *Apollo Belvedere.* Yet Eakins's erotic achievement makes no prurient appeal—he seems simply to say, This is the way things are. Even Eakins's sole 'religious' work, the *Crucifixion,* now in the Philadelphia Museum of Art, seems to repeat this factuality: as John Dillenberger writes of the painting, "[I]t was done without reference to any religious body or beliefs." For Eakins, as it happens, was an agnostic (Dillenberger and Taylor, 1972:56f).

In fact there is no such thing as an artist's simply 'seeing it as it is' or merely 'painting reality.' The impressionists, admittedly, attempted this, but the outcome of their movement was to refute the belief. The art historian E. H. Gombrich has made this point most plainly. In *Art and Illusion* (1961:pass.) he establishes the proposition assumed at this chapter's beginning: the act of artistic creation necessarily employs conventions whose association with the world in which we dwell is, to say it briefly, conventional. Eakins's magnificent achievement in *Swimming Hole* and a hundred other works is a construction, and one which invites a corresponding effort on the part of the viewer, for seeing is act as surely as painting is.

ii. Bellows and Wood.—George Bellows (1882–1925), a Midwest-born New York artist whom Robert Hughes classifies with the painters of "the gritty cities," attempted the empirical approach upon human subjects. Most memorable are his paintings of the club prizefights that flourished in his era despite the law. Bellows captured these in vivid oils. Like Eakins, though, his work falls short of the humanity it seeks to depict because it fails any narrative test: in *Stag at Sharkey's* and *Both Members of This Club* (both from 1909) the emphasis is upon vulgarity and violence; possibly these paintings constitute a moral cry of protest, but they do not even cause us to ask (as does, for example, a Rembrandt portrait), Who are these people? Where did they come from, how did they get here, where are they going?

Grant Wood (1892–1942), part of whose work stands in the same empirical succession, is best known to the general public for his *American Gothic* (1930), now in Chicago's Art Institute. Its portrayal of an older man and younger woman wearing the clothes of an earlier period and standing in front of a house with a Gothic-arched upstairs window is so open to subjective interpretation as to have become the vehicle of many caricatures. Looked at for itself, however, the remarkable thing about this double portrait is that, like an empty frame, of itself it evokes no story at all. Are the pair religious? She wears a pagan goddess brooch; there is no other religious emblem. Are they virtuous or wicked? Who is to say? They look out at us in anonymity. Wood in this and other paintings has redeployed the empirical conventions without transcending in any direction the empirical ground bass of American art.

What the factuality of Eakins, Bellows, and Wood cannot do is what the far less skilled Edward Hicks could do—evoke a story embraced by a cultural master story that can unite earthly fact with heavenly transcendence. Swimming out-of-doors is action, but it does not (yet) tell any story or require the viewer to supply one any more than *Stag at Sharkey's* does. The viewer *may* supply a story—or not. Yet in Hicks the narrative shape of his art-culture enables the Christian gospel to grasp it. To qualify here, a painting need not represent the Great Narrative of Christian faith from Abraham to Jesus to today, and it certainly need not be moralistic (*pace* Tolstoy, there need be no 'moral' in an authentic work of art), yet it must somehow establish a connection with that Great Story if it is to furnish cultural soil for Christian faith. Rembrandt's paintings, even of 'secular' subjects, do this; so (as we have seen) does the technically untrained Hicks. Eakins, Bellows, and Wood do not, and we are thereby the losers. Wood, like Eakins, painted truthfully, and Bellows (by one reckoning) painted moralistically as well, while there is undeniable artistic power in the work of each. Yet truth, beauty, and goodness (those classical values) cannot by themselves turn empirical art into what it is not, cannot enable it to provide deep soil for Christian seed to grow.

In this category American painter Edward Hopper (1882–1967), like preceding empiricists, painted 'realistically,' but more than any of them his work reflects a deep and lonely individualism. Hopper paints a world in which each of us is alone; no human connections are visible. In the 1942 *Nighthawks* (in Chicago's Art Institute), a cafe throws light upon the dark street, showing it empty. At the counter a man and a woman sit together. Neither seems to speak, nor does the attendant or another customer. Here is a setting, but (as in all Hopper's work) there is no story. "I never tried," he wrote, "to do the American scene. . . . I always wanted to do myself" (in Hughes, 1997:423). This inwardness links him to the later modernists, otherwise so different.

iii. Curry, the exception.—Empirical art did produce some exceptions to the schism. While no transcendence troubled Grant Wood's (or fellow American Regional artist Thomas Hart Benton's) canvases, another of their number, John Steuart Curry (1897–1946), provides a rare instance of American visual art overcoming its own schism by linking itself to the Great Story. Curry received training as a 'Russian realist' in Europe between the wars, but his character formation came from the Scottish Presbyterianism of his Kansas parents, who taught and practiced a strict biblicism. While studying at Chicago's Art Institute Curry met students from Moody Bible Institute and struggled to read the Bible in light of their dispensational premillennialism. As he returned to paint in Kansas, though, his attention was drawn not to these city fundamentalists or to his staid Presbyterian parents but to livelier baptist, holiness, and pentecostal religious ways. For much of his life Curry attended their revival services, sharing in worship he was learning to paint (Gambone, 1989:23-33). As John Dillenberger insightfully writes, Curry's works "cannot be fully appreciated if one does not understand the impact which his own spiritual perceptions had upon his life" (Dillenberger and Dillenberger, 1977:18).

At home in Kansas, Curry painted this church life, sensitive to its country style and to its profundity. In doing so, he conveyed not only the empirical immediacy of baptism, prayer meetings, preaching, and community meals, but also the holiness of the faith they expressed. His most powerful resolution of America's artistic schism came, though, in paintings to which he gave biblical titles but American settings: *Flight into Egypt* (a heat-stricken Midwest family with their donkey-drawn wagon), *Mississippi Noah* (a black family trapped on a floating rooftop in a flood on the river), *Prodigal Son* (a farm youth shoveling cobs to waiting swine). Consider *Sanctuary,* a 1935 oil now in the Pennsylvania Academy of the Fine Arts: In Scripture, the sanctuary is God's holy place; it is the tent of meeting or the temple, and in every case a place of refuge. On Curry's canvas, floodwaters cover the plain. Yet assorted animals—cattle, horses, pigs, and what look to be a family of skunks—have found high ground and huddle harmlessly together, safe from the flood. Thus Curry offers a painter's "this is that," a biblical theme reenacted in the animal kingdom here and now. Not accidentally, the arrangement reminds a viewer of Edward Hicks's *Peaceable Kingdom* theme—a peace enforced in this case by earthly disaster, yet captured by a painter alert to eschatological passages in Scripture. Curry ranks after the ablest twentieth-century painters, but he shows a way they might have taken.

*c. **Modernist art.***—Enough has been said now to make the understanding of 'modernist' art possible. (The mere term "modern" is here no longer precise, since artistic 'modernism' seems to abandon the standards of earlier modern work.) Yet such American modernists as O'Keeffe, Motherwell, Warhol, Lichtenstein, Rothko, and Stella only did in their generation what earlier American artists had. For visual art, the shift of generations came in 1913, when New York's Armory Show of European art shed startling new light upon the contemporary artistic task. (One widely noticed entry in the show was *Nude Descending a Staircase* by French artist Marcel Duchamp—its cubist vision of space seemed to most viewers to deny any relation between the painting and its title.) Shifting conventions, revised intentions, and a new sense of art's responsibility to nature and culture converged to produce new generations of American artists who would sometimes overshadow corresponding modernist European work.

It should be possible, then, to analyze every variety of 'modern' art in terms already developed in this chapter, in this way distinguishing it from mere quackery while relating it to the artistic past as well as to its contemporary culture. Yet some selection must be made for these paragraphs, and I single out Georgia O'Keeffe (1887–1986), an artist whose work is readily accessible. Her modernist work over a long period of creativity constitutes an *amalgam* of empirical and transcendental modes without at any point touching the vital third stream of this chapter's quest.

Born to a farm family near Madison, Wisconsin, O'Keeffe studied at Chicago's Art Institute for a season and briefly at Columbia University in New York. Yet the great influence in her life (influence that ran both ways) was artist and art dealer Alfred Stieglitz (1864–1946), her lover and from 1924 her husband, an *avant-garde* photographer who famously sponsored new work of quality. Under his influence O'Keeffe shifted her subjects from the Texas plains where she had taught for a time to New York skyscrapers treated in the modernist fashion. Yet the great impulse in her work came from the scenery of northern New Mexico, a region through which she had traveled in 1917 and which she visited in the summers of 1929 and 1930. In 1945 she purchased with a friend an adobe in Abiquiu, New Mexico, near Taos, and lived there until her death. Having already invented "the American sublime" in West Texas, in New Mexico she would continue painting "in touch with the vibrations of the cosmos" (Hughes, 1997:391-93).

It may be misleading, though, to speak of O'Keeffe as painting either 'landscape' or 'city buildings,' for she looked at these and painted what she would. A work of her second summer in New Mexico, *Ranchos Church—Taos (Ranch Church—Grey Sky),* 1930 (one of eight such paintings, this one in the Amon Carter Museum), illustrates the point. In the perceptive words of Sarah Cash, the painting's "sculptural, almost abstract shapes appear to grow out of the ground and seem to assume the characteristics of the area's mountains" so that O'Keeffe's "exaggeration of the structure's curves and of the slope of the earth upon which it sits, as well as the nearly monochromatic palette which unites the ground with the church, further likens the structure to a natural formation" (Cash, 1992:54). Yet if one visits its site and stands where O'Keeffe must have set up her easel, it is difficult to associate the actual shape of the surviving adobe parish church, Francis of Assisi, with the succulent painted shape. Most striking, perhaps, is that while the actual church is unmistakably a church, O'Keeffe's rendering gives no clear signal that it is. It is instead, as Cash suggests, a part of nature. The earth (O'Keeffe seems to say) is one whole; its colors, its shapes, its texture one continuous substantial presence, and that presence is of infinite value; it is in itself sublime.

This impression of O'Keeffe's work may be corrected in part by her flower paintings. These are blossoms and plants painted many times life size, painted as they might appear to a bee. So here the first impression is not of sublimity but of an overwhelming factuality. (Much has been made of the blossom shapes that seem to imitate female genitalia, flowery lips beseeching penetration.) Broadly, O'Keeffe's work represented in the O'Keeffe museum in Santa Fe presents an amalgam of spiritual and empirical style. It is impressive work. Yet like her predecessors and successors in these fractured traditions, she incurs the criticism addressed to each: Of the "American sublime," one notes afresh the inability of this gnostic spirituality to achieve its patent goal. Until the spiritual reach of visual art answers the prior descent of Spirit, until, that is, it takes its place in the story of God's way with all the earth, a story fully divine as it enters into the full human enterprise of suffering and death, its spirituality, like its factuality, remains incomplete. Yet this incompleteness remains the dominant story of American visual art.

Less accessible but worthy of notice here are the modernist works of the *abstract expressionists.* These painters meant to revolt against the entire history of Western art and culture. They attempted this by turning first to primitive art (as had the Europeans Matisse and Gauguin); then, influenced by surrealism, they sought to express the primordial depths of human nature. As John Dillenberger writes, "[A] concern for the mysterious dignity of humanity, not degradation or fantasy, was their controlling passion" (1986:158). Among the abstract expressionists, Mark Rothko (1903–70) led the way to a new 'transcendentalism.' By giving up virtually all reference to the existing world and rejecting all existing conventions (eliminating all drawing, all figures), Rothko sought to express spiritual truth not of this world. Thus arose "the essential Rothko form: a series of stratified blocks—or rather, oblong blurs—of color, some deep and others thin bars, stacked up on the canvas" (Hughes, 1997:490). One is reminded of the 'negative theology' of the mystics. Using these means, the paintings in the Rothko Chapel in Houston are successfully mysterious, yet their transcendence, unlike that of the gospel story, is purchased at the expense of any immanence whatsoever.

My thesis about art's schism is less than convincing unless it can show concrete alternatives. Yet in American modernism, noteworthy exceptions to the rule are hard to find. (Comparison with recent Christian art in other cultures is of course instructive.) Happily, some exceptions appear even here. One is the work of African American painter Jacob Lawrence (1917–2000). During the Depression of 1929–39, many American artists embraced Social Realism, the artistic expression of Marxist ideology. Though his concerns were in part the same as theirs, Lawrence's vision was different. Robert Hughes reckons that the series of sixty paintings titled *The Great Migration* that Lawrence produced during this time may be "the most powerful American work of art produced under the auspices of social commitment in the 1930s and 40s." The Great Migration was the exodus of countless Negroes from the poor, racist South into the (relative) freedom of the Northern states. As Hughes writes, "It went largely uncommemorated . . . Lawrence simply picked up the subject and made it his own" (1997:454). The works, painted in tempera on small pieces of construction hardboard and now widely scattered, display in stages worthy of the book of Exodus the oppression, persecution, misery, escape, new misery in the North, and lasting achievement of a people bound to be free. In this series, the references to the Great Story of Christian redemption are subtle. At least, as David Driskell writes, Lawrence's paintings "present to us a segment of reality which ties our own lives to history" (1976:182). Consider, though, Panel Number 10 of the Migration series, *They Were Very Poor,* now in New York's Museum of Modern Art. A black male and female sit at a bare table. Poorly dressed, they have between them only a single plate and a single mug, each with its spoon. On the blue wall behind, an unused kettle hangs. The pair sit with heads bowed nearly to the horizontal. Hughes's interpretation is that they are staring hungrily at the empty dishes. Another reading seems obvious, however, to one at home in Southern culture. These sufferers bow their heads in prayer, perhaps asking for more, but certainly pausing in gratitude for their scanty meal. The angle of their arms suggests they are holding hands as they pray. There is solidarity in this painting, not only the solidarity of Lawrence's remarkable modernist construction, but of the couple's communion with the unseen Companion they address, and with one another. Here, within modernist style (Lawrence's links are to Cubism and to Matisse among Europeans, and in North America to his teachers at the Harlem Art Center and to Arthur Dove and Diego Rivera), there appears a striking exception to the schism in American art.

Critics note the "primitivism" of Lawrence's painting, which in his case deliberately reaches back to Africanisms as do the sophisticated primitivisms of Matisse. Lawrence was no more a folk artist than were Matisse or Gauguin, however, and his violations of Western perspective are deliberate. Yet the parallel is evident, as appears in the work of a purely primitive folk artist, African American painter Clementine Hunter (1886–1988) of Melrose Plantation on Cane River near Natchitoches, Louisiana. Hunter's work reflects the resilient spirit and deep inner joy of Lawrence's, though perhaps without his social protest. Certainly it deserves classification in the third stream of American art, neither soaring gnostic nor flat empiricist but participating richly in the Great Story of biblical culture in America. Her *Funeral* and *Wedding* (both c. 1955), in the collection of Jack and Anne Brittain of Natchitoches, capture the joy and sorrow of black Americans who did not enter the Great Migration but remained in the South; utterly unsentimental, these folk paintings proclaim in vivid color the deep spirituality of an artist and a people aware of the depth and height of human life while fully engaged by its narrative reality (see further James Wilson, 1990).

Much is omitted in this whirlwind passage over four centuries of visual art on this continent. In particular, sculpture and (my own favorite) architecture are passed by in silence, as is immensely popular cinema. The present book aims to leave plenty of work for others; my hope is that what stands here offers help for those who must figure out how to go on.

§2. Sailing Against the Wind: American Literature

What the painter can at best shadow forth, the writer has words to declare. If the artistry that represents American culture is to display in culture an answer to the Great Story of Christian faith—if art is ever to reflect not merely life but the true light "which lighteth every man that cometh into the world" (John 1:9 KJV)—art's better opportunity would seem to be not paint but narrative text. This is because the Great Story of the divine-human encounter *is a story*. It presents the coherent, intelligible action of its central character, God. God *spoke* to Abraham, *liberated* Israel, *sent* the prophets, *became* flesh, *raised* Jesus from the dead, *poured out* the Spirit on the church. Art as action is privileged to answer that divine action with its own action, and narrative literature seems to provide full opportunity for such action, Scripture itself furnishing the aboriginal model. Yet in America, land where faith has flourished and in a degree flourishes still, literature has fallen well short of its promise. The American novel, where opportunity might have abounded, repeats our art's polarization (empirical versus transcendental), with most work clustering at the empirical pole. For confirmation pick up at random almost any American novel. Nevertheless, there are more than a few exceptions, and this section moves to concentrate on them. To this end, I will focus here on only one theme, but a recurrent one, *redemption* or its absence in American literature of distinction.

a. The empirical broad reach: Cooper.—James Cooper (1789–1851), who later added the middle name Fenimore, was America's first distinguished novelist. He grew up in rural and small-town New York just after its colonial days; his father was a successful landowner. Restless at school and expelled from Yale College, Cooper went to sea. His first writing, and in a sense all of his writings, drew on his experience of boundless ocean. In time, Cooper's interest turned to the frontier, that sea on land, and he produced the Leatherstocking novels, a series centered on the character and adventures of a single but many-named heroic figure. These books interpreted the ever-extending West for Americans of the federal period; readers found in them a prototypical American, found in a sense themselves.

One of these novels, *The Last of the Mohicans* (1826, in Cooper,

1985:467-878), is at surface the swaggering, violence-racked tale of two sisters of Scots parentage who during the colonial war between the English and French (1757) seek to reach the British outpost on Lake Champlain commanded by their officer father. They are escorted by a junior officer returning to his post in that command, by a comically displaced sacred chorister, and eventually by the Hunter, or Hawk-eye, or Long Rifle, properly Nathaniel (Natty) Bumppo, who along with his Indian cohort (father and son) serve as scouts for the British force. The Mohican son, Uncas, heir to chiefship of his tribe, is destined to perish. In due course this mixed group of six are attacked, and all but the elder Mohican and his companion Hawk-eye are captured by Iroquois, Indians allied with Montcalm's French invaders. The tides of battle turn and turn again. In time the British, withdrawing from Lake Champlain under a truce after their defeat, are raided by treacherous Iroquois, and the women are captured once more. Fierce wilderness battles follow as the Scout and his helpers attempt to liberate them anew. At tale's end, one daughter has been murdered, as has the gallant younger Mohican. The surviving colonials return to their accustomed roles, but Bumppo vanishes into his wilderness.

Last of the Mohicans has enough cruelty and carnage to satisfy any age's demand for 'adult' realism. The reality Cooper evokes remains as surely earthbound as did the dominant American visual art of the era. There is in the novel no vault toward the sublime: Cooper's wilderness never becomes that of Thomas Cole or Frederick Church. He places 'religious' utterances in the mouths of several of his characters including the Scout, but their diverse opinions about this life and the next provide no affirmation of a Great Story that might sustain westering America as did the actual frontier revival preachers of Cooper's era. There is in the novel no sublime, no transcendence to lure these venturers of the New World onward. Flat empiricism reigns.

In an exchange with Hawk-eye, the Scottish psalm-singer (named David Gamut, perhaps to honor his biblical namesake and his musical scales) offers Hawk-eye a predestinarian doctrinal interpretation of their recent perils: "He that is to be saved will be saved, and he that is to be damned will be damned!" Caressing his long rifle in a manner that foreshadows the behavior of subsequent generations of American males, the Scout replies that Gamut's is only "the belief of knaves." Events, Hawk-eye grants, certainly take their determinate course, and this may to some degree be anticipated by keen observation. In that sense outcomes are "fore-ordained." But this fatalism wears no spiritual aureole. Challenged to prove his point from "the Book," Hawk-eye appeals instead to the only book he reads, the wilderness, the book of nature. It posits a God, to be sure, but allows no further "subtleties of doctrine" (603-5).

Cooper's hero rejects his Christian heritage to embrace a rough deism consistent with his sturdy, empirical habit of mind.

Distinguishing from its plot the *action* of *The Last of the Mohicans,* what the novel as a whole *does* (thus R. W. B. Lewis, 1955:99-111), allows assessment of James Fenimore Cooper's artistic achievement. Hawk-eye's undoubted loyalty to his 'side' in the war with France, his emotional adherence to his fellow whites versus Indians, his straightforward engagement with the novel's other actors in its prolonged adventure—all these are finally trumped by the novel's action, which is the hero's persistent *disengagement.* In his reflection and in his spoken avowals, Hawk-eye dissociates himself from his European past, from the nearer institutional life of the colonists, and from his Original American companions and enemies in order to be simply self-governed. When David Gamut urges forgiveness, not vengeance, if he is killed by the Indians, the Scout replies:

> "There is a principle in that," he said, "different from the law of the woods! and yet it is fair and noble to reflect upon." Then, heaving a heavy sigh, probably among the last he ever drew in pining for the condition he had so long abandoned, he added— "It is what I would wish to practyse myself, as one without a cross of blood, though it is not always easy to deal with an Indian." (p. 788)

This detachment is Bumppo's from the novel's earliest chapters; he does not change. Notably gifted as a marksman (thus Hawk-eye), independent of the cultures he temporarily appropriates, wearing for example Indian moccasins and camouflaged hunting shirt yet carrying the Western hunter's long rifle, his rule is always experiential: "It can't be denied, . . . for I have been there" (p. 503).

Hence redemption, that central Christian occasion in which the unmade self meets its final Deliverer and is in the meeting remade, has no place in *The Last of the Mohicans* either in overt or in symbolic form. I think it has no place anywhere in Cooper's fiction. Redemption is never sought, never given as grace, since (according to Cooper's genius) it is never in order. R. W. B. Lewis makes Cooper's Natty Bumppo the prototypical American Adam, an unfallen Adam, though one who does not walk with JHWH God in the garden in the cool of the day. This Adam's scepter is his long rifle; by it he is self-created, self-preserved. Certainly, then, he is as he frequently says of himself "a man without a cross (of blood)," that is, a human being without even the emblem of Jesus Christ's redemption. Hawk-eye is puzzled by, is assaulted by, is even in some degree shaped by society, but his eye is on the horizon, the mountainous wilderness confronting the colonists and beyond it the limitless prairie. These boundless vistas constitute (as Thomas Cole was proclaiming about this time in paint) the American Adam's New Eden. Yet for Cooper even that metaphor comes too near to the Great Story's transcendence to be right. Cooper's hero endures no fatal fall either in person or as vicar for his American descendants; he stands always apart. For "in America, experience in that social sense has not always been so easily come by"; instead, the hero typically takes his start "outside society" (Lewis, 1955:101).

This course is that of American fiction to the present, whether in Twain, James, Fitzgerald, Hemingway, or Bellow. Ever recurring, it has shaped American culture as well. Nevertheless, not all voyagers have taken an empirical heading.

b. The romantic gybe: Whitman.—The work of Walt Whitman (1819–92), called the quintessential American poet, might illuminate either side of the divide that cleaves the national literature. In fact, his verse does both, yet does so not by resolving them into a third that embodies both yet goes beyond them—such a resolution was beyond his wide reach—but only by creating a thinly layered *amalgam* of the empirical and transcendental modes. This reflected an existing amalgam within nineteenth-century culture, yet it avoided almost as if by divination the available Great Story that could have carried Whitman's impressive achievement beyond itself.

His achievement and its ultimate inadequacy are both rooted in Whitman's life. He was born in West Hills, New York, one of eight surviving children of a housebuilder who, like Walt's mother, came of old Long Island stock. Four of Walt's seven siblings were mentally unstable; Walt himself, having become a schoolteacher, was removed from his place (and tarred and feathered, by one account) for alleged sexual abuse of male students (Reynolds, 1995:8-29; 68-80). Yet he overcame these unpromising beginnings, worked on Long Island and in Manhattan and Brooklyn as a newspaperman, took an active part in local and national politics, and through the years wrote stories, a novel, and the gathering notebooks that became *Leaves of Grass*. In 1855 its first edition, a preface and twelve long poems, appeared (Whitman, 1982:1-146). It was hailed by Emerson and honored abroad as authentic American poetry, though it made slow headway among Whitman's audience of choice, the American public, who preferred Longfellow or Whittier. Over Whitman's remaining life (he was just short of thirty-six when *Leaves of Grass* appeared) he produced successive editions, revising and adding other work so that the definitive edition of 1891–92 was nearly four times as long as the original (Whitman, 1982:147-672). Meantime, he pursued his political loyalties (early on a Free Soil Democrat; later, a great admirer of Lincoln and his chief elegist), traveled as far as Texas and California and once to England, served as an unpaid nurse of Civil War wounded, Yankee and Rebel, worked at assorted literary tasks, published more verse, much of it ("Children of Adam," "Calamus," "Drum-Taps," etc.) eventually folded into *Leaves of Grass,* and labored to create a rough, rascal image of himself ("Tho' always unmarried I have had six children"). From his fifties Whitman was frequently ill, but he persisted in his work. Suffering but stoical, he died of natural causes in his Camden, New Jersey, home, surrounded by friends and admirers. His life almost spanned his nation's first century; his work embodied much of it.

This reminder of his life is indispensable because as much as he could make it so, it was one with his poetry. The original *Leaves of Grass* may be read in its entirety as a single, lingering look in the mirror. Especially the opening poem later named "Song of Myself" treats self-knowledge as the road to all knowledge.

> I celebrate myself
> And what I assume you shall assume,
> For every atom belonging to me as good belongs to you. (p. 27)

Arguably "Song of Myself" contains everything Whitman believed and proclaimed. It takes up about half the original volume. This primary "leaf," as Whitman called them, provides much physical self-description ("Stout as a horse, affectionate, haughty, electrical . . . / Not an inch . . . is vile"—28f). Yet at once Whitman affirms his soul as the equal of his body: "I believe in you my soul" (p. 30). This dual selfhood, soul with body, is not confined; it stretches from a leaf of grass to the stars, it embraces all time and all space, comprises the living and also the dead. In particular it encompasses America, its cities, slums, slaves, its workers, men, women, its vast out-of-doors (which he romanticized as Cooper never would have), its multiple races and diverse cultures, its patriotic history and majestic future: "I am the poet of commonsense and of the demonstrable and of immortality / . . . I do not decline to be the poet of wickedness also" (p. 48). The poem's frequent catalogs of people and tasks (pavingman, Yankee girl, squaw, drover, fare-collector, and every such occupation and state of life) allow nothing to elude the wide reach of the narrator's "I":

And these one and all tend inward to me, and I tend outward to them,
And such as it is to be of these more or less I am. (p. 42)

Who, then, can such a narrator be? In one sense, it cannot be Walt Whitman, who is, after all, limited by the laws of time and space as the narrator seems not to be. Then is it not God whose words Whitman utters? It is God, but not the God of Abraham, Isaac, and Jacob, not the God who declares "I will be what I will be" (Exod. 3:14), not the God of the prophets, not the Father of Jesus Christ. No, the God of "Song of Myself" is a panentheist God (though that term was not used in Whitman's day), one who was in all things yet not quite, as pantheism stipulated, identical with all things. On the other hand, though, the "I" is indeed Walt Whitman, or the persona he offers us—loafing on the grass, pansexual, "stout as a horse," but no god. The poem thereby sets us a problem of identity, yet the solution is at hand. Whitman believes in the soul, in "you my soul" (p. 30), and a soul not just identical with his body—that would be materialism, which he flatly rejects (Reynolds, 1995:236f). Yet all souls are part and parcel of God. So there is a dualism in the cosmos, its elements separated by a line similar to that drawn by Whitman's contemporary, theologian Horace Bushnell, between nature and supernature. The line goes right through each human being, separating soul or spirit from body (cf. Bushnell, 1965:129ff). Both are essential to cosmic reality. God and soul are identified with the supernatural (though "transcendence" is more nearly Whitman's term—see Reynolds, 1995:333f), while bodies are part of nature. Body and soul cleave; they kiss; they are intimate lovers, soul and body, God and world.

I believe in you my soul, the other I am must not abase itself to you,
And you must not be abased to the other. (p. 30)

Empiricism and transcendence are amalgamated; experience and vision converge. Their lacing cord runs through Whitman's verse and through his life.

Then what of redemption, that central Christian tenet—what of the great redemption achieved once for all at Golgotha and the empty tomb, and what of its counterpart, the answering redemption of this woman's, that man's actual life? It seems most accurate to say not that Whitman denies these, or that like Cooper his account of life finds no place for them, though those sayings might be true; rather Whitman provides an alternative redemption that is achieved by a return to Adamic innocence. Not a race estranged from God, restored in Christ, finally redeemed by grace to live by faith; but only a race that retains a perennial capacity to go back to Eden, a capacity evoked by the poet on behalf of all. This comes clearest, perhaps, in a later section of *Leaves of Grass,* "Children of Adam":

> I, chanter of Adamic songs,
> Through the new garden the West, the great cities calling,
> Deliriate, . . . offering myself.

That is, the poet, though he must seem to skeptics delirious, now in Adam's name summons all who live in the new Eden, America, to accept a new birth into Adamic (yet highly erotic) innocence:

> Bathing myself, bathing my songs in Sex,
> Offspring of my loins. (p. 264)

Whitman has nothing to say against the Christian gospel; for that matter, he has nothing to say against any point of view. "Do I contradict myself? / Very well then I contradict myself, / (I am large, I contain multitudes)" (p. 246). This may be dauntingly incoherent (I find it so); nevertheless, it is incontestably Walt Whitman. Toward the end of his life his self-identification with deity became even more striking; he thought his verse might replace the Bible; he was a medium for spirits; he was a messiah for hurting and distressed humanity. No wonder he sensed no need of a Messiah from Nazareth; he was himself the messiah of the children of Adam, and this was increasingly confirmed by his admiring audience: "[B]y far the most common response to his poetry expressed in letters he received was that he was a healer and soul rescuer" (Reynolds, 1995:277f).

c. The redemptive tack: Melville and Percy.—Make no mistake about it, what we demand of our serious fiction is truth. A novel's world may seem strange, even repellent. Consider the opening scene of Hawthorne's *Scarlet Letter* (1850). To read on past its grim jailhouse, its ghastly gallows, its nasty lynch-crowd, and its demeaning punishment requires some persistence. If we do continue, it may be because we trust a story from that alien world to bring us back to our own, showing us as in a distant mirror some truth about ourselves. (Escape fiction has a different function; its facticity is set to lure us by degrees into a world comfortably remote from everyday.) My complaint is not that

Cooper is realistic or Whitman romantic: they may happily be so if only in the end they bring us to our own truth, show us in their own ways our humanity. Rather the complaint is that for all their empiricism and romance they have not reached this goal. The claim here, whose truth each of us will judge, is that this partial failure, persisting in American literature, reflects a breach irreparable between empirical and transcendental poles. This breach in American art closes only as art engages the Great Story of redemption.

A full account of American redemptive writers would include Nathaniel Hawthorne (1804–64), for Hawthorne addresses redemption and says some enduringly true things about it. Briefly, *The Scarlet Letter* (1850) tells anew of fallen Eve and Adam expelled from Eden. The guilty pair (in this version lovers whose sin has scandalized Puritan Boston) suffer, and in her suffering, Eve (Hester Prynne) matures, while suffering Adam (Arthur Dimmesdale) sickens and dies. Hawthorne claims redeeming happiness for neither, nor any for judgmental Puritan society. The novel's fidelity is to the biblical realities of guilt and loss. Hawthorne comes closer to redemption in *The Marble Faun* (1860), whose British title, significantly, is *Transformation.* Its setting is Hawthorne's nineteenth-century Rome; the characters are four friends residing there; the plot unfolds from the crime of two of them, Donatello and Miriam, who have impulsively killed a sinister enemy. Donatello, at the outset a happy animal, is stunned into moral awareness by his guilt and slowly gains the wisdom of repentance; in the end he confesses and goes to prison, while the others experience less striking changes. Theologically, *The Marble Faun* celebrates the *felix culpa,* Augustine's theme of guilt that is blessed since it brings redemption in its train. Yet the redemption Hawthorne allows his protagonists, whether Hester Prynne or Donatello, is never more than sad earthly knowledge of evil's cost.

i. Melville.—In his lifetime novelist and poet Herman Melville (1819–91) earned but slight credit for engaging the redemptive theme. A genuine if erratic Christian believer, Melville confronted the realities of his century—the omnicompetence of science, humanity's recurrent inhumanity technically enhanced—and his own faith in God besieged by doubt. He sought to make sense of all that for himself and his readers. Born to aristocratic New York merchant families who could trace ancestry to seventeenth-century Holland on his mother's side (Gansevoort) and to thirteenth-century Scotland on his father's, Melville was handsome, with magnificent bearing and physique. If destined for prominence, he had a discouraging start: His father failed at business, "went mad," and died when Herman was twelve; he recalled his mother as "haughty," and hated her. At sixteen he left school and by seventeen had gone to sea. Yet this rough beginning was the making of his career. He sailed on merchant ships and whaling ships, reading all the while, jumped ship, adventured in the Marquesas, was captured by cannibals, took up with a lovely Polynesian girl, escaped to Tahiti, and then enlisted as able seaman aboard the U.S. Frigate *United States,* which in a year's voyage took him around Cape Horn from Hawaii to Boston, ending four years of nautical adventure. Now twenty-five and a renowned traveler, he needed money and began to write novels based on his adventures (*Typee, Omoo, Redburn,* and others). So far he stood in the empirical line with Cooper and company. Then *Moby-Dick* (1851) appeared. On its surface it was one more adventure, the tale of a long whaling voyage. Yet Melville had come right onto a new course: *Moby-Dick*'s rich symbolism, its intense though usually implicit theologizing, and its vivid construction of characters took a new tack in American literature. It failed as a publication in this country; in England it did only a little better, for what it attempted was beyond the grasp of most readers including most critics. Melville's career slumped; despairing, he took a long trip to Palestine (1856) in search of better spiritual health; he wrote more novels of lesser quality; he composed a very long narrative poem (*Clarel,* 1876) based on his own struggles with God. None of it measured up to *Moby-Dick.* He died in New York City, virtually forgotten, in 1891. On his desk were the pages of *Billy Budd,* a novella not published until 1924.

By then, however, a new generation had rediscovered Melville; he had grappled with the central issues of his time, and later experts have judged him one of two or three chief American novelists. It was a renaissance he did not live to enjoy, but which in present estimate is richly appropriate, for Melville is superbly a theologian's novelist. His difficulty was that his beliefs did not match the orthodoxy of the day. Even today he is often wrongly tagged an atheist, a skeptic, an infidel.

Correcting that mistake requires further investigation. R. W. B. Lewis understands *Moby-Dick* as yet another delineation of the innocent American Adam, free of tribe and tradition, who encounters the common world. Such a figure, Ishmael, is the novel's narrator (for Bible readers his name recalls that son of Abraham who was cut off from the line of God's promise—Genesis 21). Melville's Ishmael, an unfallen Adam, requires no redemption; at the end he alone survives the voyage of the *Pequod.* Yet he is more nearly Greek chorus, an observer chanting the tale of the disastrous voyage to its end, than an Adam confronting a dewy new world. The *Pequod*'s tragedy itself represents the whole fallen world; it is a ship vainly sailing to destroy an evil that will destroy its "god-bullied hull":

> . . . all their enchanted eyes intent upon the whale, which from side to side strangely vibrating his predestinating head, sent a broad band of overspreading semicircular foam before him as he rushed. Retribution, swift vengeance, eternal malice. (1951:1405f)

Is *Moby-Dick* then a novel not of Adam but of the last Adam, Christ, who according to Paul is "a life-giving spirit" (R. W. B. Lewis, 1955:145; 1 Cor. 15:45)? Is 'redeemer' the authentic role of Ahab, "a man cut away from the stake," stricken Ahab "with a crucifixion in his face" (Melville, 1851:925)? Ahab destined to vanquish the world's monster evil but destroyed in the attempt? Ahab a (failed) Christ-figure (cf. Lewis, 1955:109, 145f)? Hardly even that, for Ahab means to destroy evil by evil's own means—exactly what his everlasting original everlastingly refused (Matt. 4:8-10). No, Ahab is himself a victim—his character perverted, his neck fatally wrapped by the line of the harpoon he has thrown at the whale—so twice a victim of the evil he fights. Christ-figures, if authentic, are lambs, not Furies, yet victorious lambs, not mere victims. *(Vicit agnus noster.)* In any case, *Moby-Dick* departs from the standard American mode of flat empiricism (Cooper), nor is it a dualistic amalgam of empirical moments interlayered with transcendental (Whitman). It is more. A deep story pervades *Moby-Dick* that echoes and in some measure answers the Great Story that is the true story of every life truly lived. Though in *Moby-Dick* redemption is only wanted, never fulfilled, its very want is a gospel plea:

> Pass me not, O gentle Savior, hear my humble cry:
> While on others thou art calling, do not pass me by.
> (Fanny J. Crosby)

The surface of chapter 86, "The Tail," is devoted to a natural-history discourse on whales' tails. Yet beneath that the theme is (malignant) power, the power of the sperm whale's great horizontal after-flipper, as much as twenty feet wide, which can dispatch a whaleboat or a swimmer with a toss. As if meditating on this, Melville continues:

> Dissect him how I may, then, I go but skin deep; I know him not, and never will. But if I know not even the tail of this whale, how understand his head? Much more, how comprehend his face, when face he has none? Thou shalt see my back parts, my tail, he seems to say, but my face shall not be seen. But I cannot completely make out his back parts; and hint what he will about his face, I say again he has no face. (1851:1198)

Thus the chapter ends. Yet by now the literate reader thinking of whales' tails or of abstract power must address instead the abysmal hiddenness of God (see Exod. 33:18-23). Here is the melancholy struggle of Melville with God's elusiveness, to be spelled out at length in Clarel. Stan Goodman writes of that narrative poem that "'this hunt without one clew' . . . takes place within the context of a central biblical metaphor and idea of the Hebrew Bible: the hiddenness and silence of God." Consequently, Melville's is a "protest theism" (1993:8). Clarel's 150 cantos are meant to parallel the 150 chapters of Psalms so that often they cry out as the psalmist does against God. Such protest cannot be addressed to a God who is not GOD (cf. Steuer and McClendon, 1981). For Melville, God is (elusively) there, but what about redemption?

The cold early reception of *Moby-Dick* has been reversed by later critical judgment; now some acclaim it as America's epic novel, to be compared with Dante's *Divine Comedy.* Yet if that is so, the parallel must be with the first part of the *Commedia,* the *Inferno,* for it is the hell of human existence under the sun, unredeemed earth's desperation, that *Moby-Dick*'s darkness discloses.

Melville's *Billy Budd, Sailor* (1924) passes beyond this strategy. In this tale of a youthful sailor who meets harsh and unjust punishment in the British navy, Budd is an Adamic innocent, not sinless yet without guile, a crewman who implicitly trusts his superiors. One of them, the satanic master-at-arms, Claggart, hates Billy without cause and accuses him of mutiny. Billy's stammer undoes him: unable to protest the false charge, he lashes out with a fist—and strikes Claggart dead. Now the ship's captain has to choose between the demand of morality (by which Billy is plainly innocent) and the demand of martial law (which requires hanging for such a deed). Fearful of mutiny, Captain Vere opts for punishment, and Billy Budd, loyal to his captain to the end, is hanged from the yardarm at dawn, the ship's surgeon supervising the hanging and the chaplain reading the service for burial at sea. Here, Melville suggests, is no Ahab but a Christ-figure indeed: Billy Budd was hanged to save the order of the (naval) world. The narrative emphasizes the beneficial outcome: After the hanging, discipline is indeed maintained (there is a murmur in the crew, but the boatswain's pipe quickly quells it); the sailors thereafter cling to Billy Budd's memory: some of them treasure chips of the spar from which he hung as if "a piece of the Cross"; one shipmate even composes a memorial ballad. So Budd is not a fallen Adam redeemed but an innocent redeemer whose scapegoat death preserves, 'saves,' a harsh society perpetually threatened by its own chaos. Thus Billy Budd 'crucified' became (in R. W. B. Lewis's phrase) "the apotheosis of Adam." Here are Melville's key lines:

> The hull, deliberately recovering from the periodic roll to leeward, was just regaining an even keel when the last signal, a preconcerted dumb one, was given. At the same moment it chanced that a vapory fleece hanging low in the East was shot through with a soft glory as of the fleece of the Lamb of God seen in mystical vision, and simultaneously therewith, watched by the wedged mass of upturned faces, Billy ascended; and, ascending, took the full rose of the dawn. (p. 1427)

Thus Melville transcends his earlier "protest theism." An innocent, suffering savior, a dawn of redemption, justice begotten of human injustice, all fulfilling in a degree what the gospel requires of an art: the Great Story is answered in earthly story. Two flaws mar the achievement. First, the society that is 'redeemed' by Budd's death remains one whose *ultima ratio* is war: As Vere says to the court martial he has convened, "We proceed under the law of the Mutiny Act. . . . that Act resembles in spirit the thing from which it derives—War" (p. 1416). Budd's punishment, a legal injustice, preserves an unjust world, but not from its injustice, not from its war. Second, the character of Budd is only that of the Adamic innocent. Yet it was not innocence that made the work of Jesus Christ redemptive; it was *faithfulness*—his full faithfulness to his Father's purpose (*Doctrine,* 237, 273). Of course Melville's innocent sailor does not, cannot represent such faithfulness, yet without it, an innocent death is at most a scapegoat killing, not a redeeming sacrifice (*Doctrine,* 232f). Finally, these two flaws cohere, for a faithless society can be transformed only by the work of a faithful Redeemer.

ii. Percy.—It may seem that there is little connection between the preceding succession and Walker Percy (1916–90), whose chosen literary antecedents were the European existentialists (Sartre, Camus, and behind them Kierkegaard), yet Percy addresses the same concerns as the novelists of the American Adam in the same way and even goes beyond them to present not only Adam innocent and then fallen, but in the end Adam, by courtesy of Eve, happily redeemed.

Percy was born in Birmingham, Alabama, and save for some years in medical school in New York spent his life in the South (see Percy, ed. Lawson and Kramer, 1985, for details). His father, Leroy, had committed suicide when Walker was twelve, and the surviving family were taken in by Leroy's cousin, William Alexander Percy. Soon after, Walker's mother was killed in a possibly suicidal accident. The children were thus left to the care of their "Uncle Will," a somber classicist, author of a skillful reminiscence of Mississippi Delta life prior to the

First World War, *Lanterns on the Levee.* No Christian, Will Percy nevertheless adopted Walker and his brothers and gave them a decent upbringing. Having graduated from medical school (1941), Walker Percy specialized in pathology, but in that work contracted tuberculosis, for which there was then no easy cure. Convalescing, he read Kierkegaard, and iron determinism (in which until then it had seemed to him science encased the world) fell away—choice was possible; atheism was not the given. Recovered, Percy lived in Santa Fe, met and married his wife, Mary Bernice Townsend, and in the following year (1947) took instruction and entered the Catholic Church. The Percys lived briefly in New Orleans and thereafter thirty-five miles north across Lake Pontchartrain in Covington, Louisiana. He had long since abandoned the practice of medicine and taken up the writer's task, finding he "had a knack" for it. In 1961 his first accepted novel was published. To the surprise of the publisher it won the National Book Award. This was *The Moviegoer* (Percy, 1961). Thereafter, slowly and deliberately, he continued to write novels for the rest of his life, the last, prophetically named *The Thanatos Syndrome,* in 1987. Percy died in 1990, less celebrated than such Southern novelists as Faulkner, Styron, Welty, and O'Connor.

To understand Percy's themes it is needful to refer to Søren Kierkegaard (1813–55), whose *Either/Or* had sharply distinguished dimensions of life that could not be compressed into one: the *aesthetic,* in which pleasure and feeling reigned, the *ethical,* in which stern duty fulfilled life, and the *religious,* which transcended the other two and could not be reduced to them. What Percy discovered in reading Kierkegaard was that this third stage on life's way was a real possibility that could not be leveled to the stages of immanence. In particular he read an essay, "On the Difference Between a Genius and an Apostle," in which Kierkegaard proposed that a genius (e.g., his philosophical nemesis, Hegel) belongs to the sphere of immanence, purely human; the apostle, though, presents a paradox that cannot be captured by the greatest genius, not even by a Plato or a Shakespeare (Kierkegaard, 1940:71ff). The truth of God might never be comprehended on a merely human level—and might nevertheless be true, a new dimension enabling a new grasp of everything.

The Moviegoer (1961), widely regarded as Percy's most elegant achievement, presents two single cousins-by-marriage, a man and woman in their twenties who are members of one extended 1950s New Orleans family. A failed social worker, she is a drug-user now at her wit's end and suicidal; a stockbroker, he is a Korean War veteran now so profoundly alienated from communal life that he prefers to live in Gentilly (an unglamorous New Orleans suburb). Nightly he survives by attending Hollywood films with whose heroes he identifies and daily by plotting the conquest of consecutive, nubile office secretaries. Here are Percy's Adam and Eve alienated from Eden, he by his metaphysics, she by psychic disorder. The man, Binx Bolling, is narrator and protagonist. We learn at the outset that he is upon a two-part search, vertical (for God) and horizontal (for a meaningful world), "which is what anyone would undertake if he were not sunk in the everydayness of his own life" (1961:13). In Kierkegaardian terms, Binx is an aesthete who copes by remaining at life's surface. Yet there the search is hopeless. His Catholic family understand his state as "loss of faith"—language he rejects (p. 145). A promising trait is his surviving loyalty to his extended family, especially to desperate Cousin Kate, who sees in him her only friend. The plot puts the two aboard a train bound for Chicago; on the slow trip they discover their need for each other and (slowly and awkwardly) discover each other sexually. When they return to New Orleans, his adoptive Aunt Emily, stiff-spined Southern moralist, gives Binx a lecture that might have jarred even a Louisiana playboy into straightening up. Not Binx Bolling. Still unaware that in Kate he has found a way out, he continues his search until in the concluding pages, as in a good comedy, everything comes together for both: he proposes to Kate, they marry, he settles down into medical research (as a less alienated Walker Percy might once have done) and she into therapy (as Percy once did).

In his *Comedy of Redemption* (1988), Ralph Wood, buttressed by Percy interviews, shows from *Moviegoer*'s text that its ending is not pedestrian Hollywood: In a scene at novel's end, Binx and Kate see a New Orleans Negro, middle-class in dress and manner, going to church to receive Ash Wednesday ashes. The Negro symbolizes Binx's perplexing search: Is he merely climbing the social ladder? Or is he, by the grace of God, encountering a present God in a parish church in middle-class Gentilly? Or like Binx "is he here for both reasons: through some dim dazzling trick of grace, coming for the one and receiving the other as God's own importunate bonus?" (1961:235; Wood, 1988:174). Binx Bolling has not escaped the 'aesthetic' stage of skirt-chasing only to go aground at the 'ethical' stage of his Aunt Emily's Catonic stoicism; his search really is fulfilled—yet not by a heavenly vision or a knock-down proof of God; rather Binx is converted to his family's way of faith that comprehends and honors the everydayness he has until then so abhorred. As Wood writes, "Through his love for Kate Cutrer, Binx Bolling discovers that his cynical contempt for the world's unconscious despair will not suffice." Remarkably, the 'sacrament' that Catholic novelist Walker Percy provides for Binx is neither baptism nor eucharist; it is marrying, for "by yielding his will to a radically needy woman" this lost Adam enters Dante's *vita nuovo,* finding, beyond alienation, "true community" (Wood, 1988:173).

* * * * *

In American culture words have come but little closer than paint to expressing a rich artistic response to faith. Though this culture has sometimes called itself 'Christian,' it displays but small claim to faithfulness. The literary artists like the visual ones have in the main been empirical still; that remains true, and I see no extraordinary advance. If gains were made in the succession from Cooper to Melville to Percy that brought other writers along as well, these are as nothing compared with what might be done. Yet (and here is the theme maintained since Chapter One), disclosing a culture's slow grasp of its destiny is not so much a judgment upon the culture as a self-reproach to Christian peoplehood: until we have found our true or faithful standpoint within it, how can the environing culture find itself? A church true to its revealed gospel might even yet provide this culture with the vision it so lacks.

§3. American Music: Grooving with the Gospel

Many Americans never visit an art gallery or read a book. Their interest in painting and belles lettres is at best secondhand—perhaps cinema substitutes for both. The same can hardly be said of Americans and music, for quite apart from deliberate music-making, the sound of music seeps into every cranny of American life. Whether as the mood music for films, or the distracting blast of workers' radios, or the half-heard murmur of a commuter's audio speakers, music is everywhere. Most of it is aesthetically trivial and emotionally banal. It is 'music to ride elevators by,' often mercifully unnoticed. Yet beneath and behind this so-called popular American music, generated as inevitably as a great city's powerhouse generates unwanted urban smog, vibrates another music, distinctly American, that is all that the blur of popular sound is not. This is unique, aesthetically powerful, original *jazz.* It is jazz with its partner the blues that constitutes a distinctly American music, thereby offering American culture (and increasingly, world culture) a fresh art.

Thus it is that any theology of American culture must attend the jazz scene. A theology of jazz is not a scholar's whimsy; it is required work.

This is not to deny other American musics. Europeans brought with them their native songs and dances, and the high European musical tradition has been transplanted into this hemisphere with impressive results. In fact, great urban orchestras and operas have appeared wherever artists of European training gathered—in New York as in Israel, in Chicago as in São Paulo and Tokyo. Nor can the progress of this music on American soil be denied: American performers and composers have joined the topmost contemporary artistic ranks, and more rarely, in the person of a Charles Ives or an Aaron Copland, they, too, have produced uniquely American music (McClendon, 1990:chap. 6). American schoolchildren have been trained in many levels of this European music, from folk songs to band marches to orchestral concertos, and many have found these a source of lasting satisfaction. Yet none of this has fulfilled the primary requirement of a distinctive artistic practice: American 'symphonic' and 'chamber' music remain, as these very terms imply, tributary to the European practices that are their source and paradigm. Ives has not transcended Beethoven. All this deserves further attention (as do other world musics), but here the focus is on the primary American musical practice, and that is jazz.

a. How jazz began.—To follow its spread it is helpful to have some defining sense of jazz as a kind of music. It is not sufficient to identify jazz with syncopation, or with improvisation, or with energetic performance—European music had displayed each of these and sometimes all of them at once without becoming jazz. Wynton Marsalis, New Orleans–born trumpeter and musical entrepreneur, has said on occasion that two things combine to make jazz happen: swing and blues. Like other attempted definitions, this seems inadequate. In what sense are "Muskrat Ramble" and "Tiger Rag" blues? Yet each is paradigmatic early jazz. Marsalis's definition sheds light, though, when "swing" and "blues" are seen as metaphors of this music. *Swing* here refers not to the 1930s Swing era, but to a rhythmic characteristic: (1) not, for example, one, two, three, four, but one *and,* two *and,* three *and,* four *and;* (2) performed with rhythmic liberties such as 'laid-back' notes (played just behind the beat) and 'float' (in which a singer keeps a time that seems free yet stays related to the time kept by the rhythm section); and (3) marked by an energy that musicians and audience sense driving the piece forward. "It don't mean a thing if it ain't got that swing," Duke Ellington liked to say. *Blues* here refers not to the standardized twelve-bar measures and lyric structure of classic blues singers; it is rather the adaptation of the style and expressive quality of these 'secular spirituals' to instrumental playing, employing devices such as the 'blue notes' (bent tones) of a scale that are in no recognizable European key—perhaps a scale with African roots? To oversimplify, the freedom of swing and the passion of the blues, occurring together, make jazz (Sales, 1984:215-19; Feather, 1965:209-44; Tanner, Megill, and Gerow, 1997:3-5).

*i. **New Orleans culture and music.***—"Jazz," said early jazz composer and pianist Jelly Roll Morton, "started in New Orleans." Behind every beginning, though, there are older beginnings. Bond slaves working American plantations produced field hollers, rhythmic work songs that were themselves African-rooted. In pre-Christian days slaves' worship centered on the ring-shout, part dance, part song. As the gospel took effect, the songs became spirituals, speaking the conviction of those who knew not only that God was near but that help was on the way: "Swing low, sweet chariot, comin' for to carry me home." Outside the church a secular version of spirituals, namely the blues, made its appearance. Spirituals and blues were everywhere in the South, but as jazz historian Michael White points out in an important article, other roots of jazz were specific to New Orleans, a city favored in the richness of its musically sophisticated multicultural heritage. Like biblical Galilee, New Orleans was a cultural borderland. South Europeans, descendants of Africans arrived within memory from Africa or imported from the rich African population of Jamaica and resold in New Orleans harbor, largely white-blooded 'Africans' descended from wealthy Creole fathers and gorgeous quadroon mothers, Anglos arriving to make money, build magnificent Garden District mansions, and enjoy the good life—in time all were compressed in the little levee-protected town at the bend of the river, all, with their music, their faith, their passions, their sorrows. The earlier settler heritage was Catholic, but Protestant congregations and vodun (voodoo) practitioners with their own lively rites jostled the Catholic parish churches and cathedral. Music was a major part of the life of 1890s New Orleans not in the thin way in which ubiquitous electronic sound is today a part of America but as the musical fabric of a way of life. There were bands to play for church celebrations and funerals, street parades that required marching bands, dances that needed dance bands; there was Mardi Gras with its bands of paraders. This was the setting in which jazz arose; it became the distinctive music of a city, evolved in answer to its life, not least its religious life, and blended with its culture (M. White, 1991:18-38; cf. M. Williams, 1967:1-25).

The proud Spanish and French families who colonized New Orleans brought with them the instruments and musical memories and skills of the Old World. The more autonomous forms of urban slavery permitted considerable leisure-time liberty even to Africans in bondage, and there was a sizable pre–Civil War free Negro population as well. (When spirituals were mated with white hymns in the Isaac Watts tradition, 'gospel,' a distinctive twentieth-century black church musical form, emerged. 'Gospel' and jazz, then, are siblings, the one usually developing inside the black church, the other outside it.) Memorably, there were in New Orleans Creoles of color, in many cases products of stable sexual liaisons in that non-Puritan city. Some Creole children were afforded a cultural education as broad as that of their purely European half brothers, including European schooling. Long after Federal troops occupied New Orleans, all slaves were eventually freed; Reconstruction and after would see an ongoing African American search for genuine equality and freedom. Yet between the Creoles of color who could claim a higher social status and those ex-slaves who could not, an ethnic barrier persisted. Oddly, the barrier was not broken until an 1894 segregation statute forbade Louisianians to intermarry, race with race, while anyone with as little as one-sixteenth African ancestry was counted "Negro." The consequence was that Creoles of color, who for generations had held themselves a people apart from other African Americans, were pushed behind the color line. These light-skinned Louisianians who "spiritually, socially, and culturally were . . . as isolated from other blacks as if they were a separate race" and 'blacker' blacks who had suffered their own isolation now found themselves conjugally classified together (one of the ironies of segregation) and separated from 'pure' whites. Thereby blacks (often Baptist) who recalled African rhythms and tonalities in church spirituals and worldly blues were introduced to other blacks (often Catholic) whose musical heritage was European. Out of this redeeming mixture—of races, of heritages, of musics—came jazz (White, 1991:19f).

Charles (Buddy) Bolden (1868–1938), son of ex-slaves, was a part-time bandleader who frequently performed in Lincoln Park, then an African American gathering center. Bolden's earliest musical memories were formed by the music of the black Baptist church he attended but also by the African-imprinted rhythms inherited from old Congo Square and by the European-style marching bands that frequently crowded the streets of New Orleans as well as by that city's mania for parties and dancing. His own band apparently incorporated and importantly modified the rhythms, melodies, and harmonies of all these settings as it produced a sound that was none of them alone—neither European nor African—but specifically American, a truly new music. As the New Orleans musicians who came North would later recall, Bolden's band played the first jazz (Marquis, 1993).

b. The spread of jazz.—The New Orleans phenomenon spread like kudzu vine. Other parts of the country had some of the elements that had generated the first jazz (Feather, 1965:3-38). Like Buddy Bolden, others could jazz up military marches and Baptist songs such as "Down by the Riverside," or "Shall We Gather at the River," or "When the Saints Go Marchin' In," for they, too, were heirs to the spirituals and the blues. Ragtime, dance music whose rhythm was given rough edges, was first produced by African Americans but quickly became a rage among white youth eager to dance or to play it. Its 'ragged' features provided an easy transition to jazz. Even as these elements were at work, public jazz performance was moving (in the years between 1910 and 1920) from New Orleans to Los Angeles, Kansas City, St. Louis, Chicago, New York, Paris, and London. As successful musicians traveled, they met new audiences and could match local cultural demands with their own inbuilt artistic drive to excel. In 1917 in New York a white New Orleans band made the earliest jazz recordings; after that, even those far from city bandstands, bars, and brothels could hear America's music sounding (Megill and Demory, 1996:55-88).

Historians of jazz identify several linked stages in its development, starting with the New Orleans style. After the 1920s came swing, played by big, orchestrated bands that smoothed out and codified jazz rhythm and harmonies. These big bands were widely heard on dance stands and on live radio networks reaching national audiences. Jazz musicians found ways to take the banal popular songs of Tin Pan Alley and turn them into powerful music that was nonetheless accessible to the masses. In the form of swing, jazz traveled everywhere in America. It is no accident, I think, that this happened as Americans suffered a devastating depression in the 1930s: jazz had come from an oppressed people and spoke to economically oppressed and defeated people of every race. It expressed defiant good cheer; it spoke from the poverty of its musicians to the poverty of its listeners. Tellingly, it was in the prosperous postwar era that the big swing bands gradually lost out. They were succeeded in the 1950s by enormously popular rock and roll. Meantime 'pure' jazz artistry, led from the 1940s by musicians such as Charlie 'Bird' Parker, developed the angular rhythms, 'dissonant' sounds, and advanced techniques of bebop (or simply bop—perhaps named in imitation of its staccato rhythms). Bebop was not the end of the road of progress, either. In the 1960s, a number of jazz artists, notably Ornette Coleman, developed 'free jazz,' a music that like *avant-garde* European classical music employed various devices to free creative performers from traditional constraints of key, rhythm, harmony, and instrumental timbre. At this point modern jazz pressed toward extreme individualism, recalling a main philosophical theme of modernity (see next chapter). Like its counterpart in advanced European or classical music, free jazz could attract only a small audience; it was not commercially self-sustaining—a problem that dogs innovative artists through the centuries. Another development, beginning in the 1960s, blended jazz with other existing musical styles. When that style was rock, the product became jazz-rock or fusion; when it was classical European music, the product was 'third stream.' After 1967, Miles Davis was a primary player of jazz fusion; earlier, composers George Gershwin and Gunther Schuller had navigated the third stream. Other styles are "crossover jazz" (various hybrids, especially with Latin music), "cool jazz" (subtle and understated West Coast jazz), "funky jazz" (a return to Africanisms, especially those drawn from church music and blues), and more.

Louis Armstrong (1901?–1971). One of the greatest musicians of recent times was born to abject poverty in back-of-town New Orleans, a district occupied by slavery's discouraged progeny, the disadvantaged whose share in emancipation had been little more than entry into a daunting new struggle for survival. Armstrong survived to grow old and rich, but it was his early struggle that gave his life its timbre. Louis hardly knew his father. His formation came from the intense affection of his mother, from the school and black Baptist Sunday school where his mother and grandmother sent him, and from the Colored Waifs Home where he was confined during his early teens after a childish pistol infraction. In the Waifs Home he learned to love discipline and regularity. Given a choice of trainings he chose music, and before long he was lead cornetist and head of the Home's brass marching band. With the singing he had learned at church and on street corners, Armstrong's life skills were in hand (Armstrong, 1986:11, 33-51).

Released, adolescent Louis went to work to support his mother and sister. Eventually he drove a coal cart by day and played cornet in a Storyville (red-light) District bar by night. His big chance came when Joe (later 'King') Oliver tagged him as his cornet successor in Kid Ory's band. After that, there was no turning back from music. In 1922 Armstrong answered a summons to play in King Oliver's Chicago band. (He left New Orleans in an I.C. Railway Jim Crow car.) Louis met Lil Hardin, the Oliver band's pianist, and eventually married her. A fine musician, she held a degree in classical music from Fisk. With her sponsorship and urging, Armstrong set out on an intense drive toward musical supremacy. He went to New York and then in 1925 returned to Chicago, billed as "World's Greatest Trumpet Player." The billing was not exaggerated. As Martin Williams writes, "[T]his man changed the world; he did, at the very least, change Western music—all of it—and the more that music spreads, the closer it comes to being true that he changed all the world's music" (1967:164).

The artistic climax of Louis Armstrong's long career came next, while he was still in his late twenties. With Lil Hardin's help he formed groups (the "Hot Five" and "Hot Seven") that in two years' time recorded about forty-five sides for the OKeh label (78 rpm). "The Hot Five's music retained the essence of New Orleans jazz—the breaks, the stop choruses and collective improvisation in some of the brief ensemble passages—but [paradoxically?] it de-emphasized ensemble playing." These recordings made history; after them jazz could never be the same. Their intensity, artistry, musical excellence set a standard for groups and soloists that Armstrong himself was never to excel. "Time has not erased their splendor" (Albertson, 1978:17f).

Perhaps the Hot Five reached its zenith in West End Blues, named after a popular Lake Pontchartrain resort. A standard blues in structure, it opens with an Armstrong trumpet cadenza, a link to the waif who had once taken up a bugle. Then the full ensemble enters with a swinging, swaying rhythm that evokes dancing couples at the lakeside. The melody, full of melancholy, justifies the blues of its title. Accented by drummer Zutty Singleton's rhythmic use of wooden blocks, trombonist Fred Robinson comes in, but as Robinson plays, the melody moves from sadness to irrepressible joy. Celebration has begun. Now Louis Armstrong floats the vocal over Jimmy Strong's low-register clarinet accompaniment. Armstrong's song (all scat—dah de dee . . .) is melancholy transposed into pure romance. Next Earl (Fatha) Hines solos on piano. His second riff is a staccato strut, moving the action of West End Blues toward its climax. Then the ensemble again—long sustained tones emerging into a new trumpet variation, Armstrong's technical triumph proclaiming triumph of the spirit as his liquid notes declare the goodness of life, the greatness of love—then at finale's end Zutty's single 'clop' on a small cymbal ends the magic. Everyday returns.

Louis Armstrong had a long life still to live. There were new bands to form, new gigs to play, new cities and eventually new countries in which to perform. In the years after World War II he went all over the world, a sort of ambassador of American goodwill. (Though at least once he refused a State Department assignment: When Arkansas Governor Orville Faubus, arch-segregationist, sought to prevent a few black children from going to their newly assigned Central High, Armstrong wrote a scorching letter to the U.S. government and canceled a planned goodwill trip.) There were as well new wives to marry (Lil was only the second of four), and new duties as film star, even a trip to a Memphis jail because his touring bus had allowed a black musician to sit beside a white woman. Perhaps best of all, there were grand homecomings to New Orleans in 1931 and again in 1949 when he appeared as King of the Zulus in the Mardi Gras parade. Some jazz aficionados were disappointed that Armstrong so easily became a mass entertainer, making money but leaving the original New Orleans style of jazz innovation to his successors. Armstrong disappointed himself in that regard. When an imitator told him, "I've been trying to follow you for 20 years," Louis grinned back, "Me and you both" (Albertson, 1978:18).

Armstrong at his best occupied Kierkegaard's aesthetic dimension. His superb gifts were devoted to art. His fleshly vices, which were (given his upbringing) surprisingly few and trivial, barely touched the essence of the man—charming, generous to a fault, loving life—who brought jazz to an all-time high. Perhaps it was the jazz that came after him, though, that revealed the limits of his achievement. Remember that for Kierkegaard the aesthetic is contrasted with the moral, while neither reaches the standpoint of the religious dimension. Yet as we have seen, jazz has a deep religious root as well as a deep worldly root. Armstrong himself had profited from both: he said he "acquired his singing tactics" in Sunday school (Armstrong, 1986:11). After his achievement, the question that remained was whether subsequent jazz could revisit that essential root of its being.

c. The essence of jazz.—Unlike much American art, early jazz successfully brought together reference and transcendence, the earthly and the heavenly, the whole embraced by a narrative frame implied or expressed in this music. It contained the history of the peoples who created and heard it. Louis Armstrong recording in Chicago and New York with the Hot Five and Hot Seven, and Sidney Bechet exporting jazz from the United States to France with his soprano saxophone, were each playing music that was spiritual as well as earthy, music that expressed the barrier-breaking role their origins had conferred upon them. This occupation of the vacant artistic middle space, neither merely imitative of life's empirical givens (though not without them) nor merely reaching for an ultimacy beyond every time and place (though not without that, either)—this narrative spirituality, formed by the (black) Christian church and echoed by African American secularity, had given birth to traditional jazz (M. Williams, 1967).

James Baldwin's short story, "Sonny's Blues," captures the link between this music and the greater narrative to which it belongs. At story's end, Sonny, a damaged son of Harlem's streets, sits in as pianist to play "Am I Blue":

> Then Creole [string bass player—note the name Baldwin gives him] stepped forward to remind them that what they were playing was the blues. He hit something in all of them, he hit something in me, myself, and the music tightened and deepened, apprehension began to beat the air. Creole began to tell us what the blues were all about. They were not about anything very new. He and his boys up there were keeping it new, at the risk of ruin, destruction, madness, and death, in order to find new ways to make us listen. For, while the tale of how we suffer, and how we are delighted, and how we may triumph is never new, it always must be heard. There isn't any other tale to tell, it's the only light we've got in all this darkness. (Baldwin, 1965:121)

The American rise of blues and jazz, though never merely African, was from the outset *African American.* Yet at once this music crossed color lines (and geographical lines). Jazz revealed itself a human phenomenon. America's unique contribution to the world of music could no more stay behind a color line than could the 1963 protest marchers in Martin Luther King's Birmingham (King, 1986:289-302, 518-54; Megill and Tanner, 1995:143f; Megill and Demory, 1996:1-10).

Some features of jazz wherever it appears correspond closely to African American free-church (i.e., baptist) life. *Participation:* In jazz the roles of composer and performer are not sharply distinguished. Some early jazz musicians could not read music—or read at all. The music they learned from others was memorized, and this itself invited variation when memories clashed. *Cooperation:* polyphonic performance required of each player improvisation that preserved the harmonies and rhythms while allowing, indeed requiring, each to embellish it in line with the uniqueness of his or her instrument and imagination. No two renditions of a piece were identical. The resultant polyphony (call and response, in baptist worship terms) was the cooperative achievement of all players. Suppressed in the swing era, this communal and improvisatory structure has returned, as we will see, in some of today's jazz. *Recognition:* Radio disk jockeys typically announce the name of every performer in a jazz band. This contrasts with the custom in classical (i.e., European) music, where players remain anonymous save for a few stars. Equality for all in the church was matched by equality for all in the band. *Inclusion:* Jazz reached across ethnic, racial, and cultural barriers; it was the product of this cross-ethnic inclusion. It equalized peoples as well as individuals. Here again an original Christian idea stands behind the practice ("no such thing as Jew and Greek, slave and freeman, male and female; for you are all one [body] in Christ Jesus"—

Gal. 3:28). Participation, improvisation, cooperation, recognition, inclusion—these are the requirements for Christian worship of the sort commended by Paul in 1 Corinthians 14. They were the features of black baptist church life—which formed many of the early musicians.

*i. **Challenges to jazz.***—Previous sections of this chapter argue that American visual art (especially painting) and American literary art (especially the novel) from their seventeenth-century beginnings to the present display a schism that has divided each practice into separate paths. Some artistry was this-worldly in representation; it tried to tell the empirical truth about the 'given' world. Other artistry sought to transcend empirical reality to tell of a light that never was on land or sea. From the standpoint of Christian theology neither the pictorial-representative nor the sublime-transcendental could achieve its own goal because each had shaved away part of what (by the Christian doctrines of creation and redemption) was indivisibly one. Here the dominant Christian image is the cross of Jesus Christ: it recalls an event that exactly in its horror, and not apart from it, realizes God totally and redemptively present. Now the same question must be raised about the chief American music. Was jazz split, too? Eventually in some measure it did split. When swing in the mid-forties failed to continue as an authentic American music by remaining truly jazz—creative, cooperative, improvisatory, passionate—its divided successors moved in contrary directions. The transcendent and the earthly diverged as they had in other American art.

Rock and roll and bebop were not even perceived as two versions of one music. Rock had its intrusive, earthy rhythms, its powerful electronic amplification, and frequently its exhibitionist solo and group performances dominated by bizarre costume and lighting. Here the representative side of American art, in this case a display of raw human emotion with lyrics that exalted conquest and copulation at the expense of more profound human feeling, expressed a dimension that had been in some degree present at the beginnings of jazz—present both in the bitter passion of the blues and in the barrelhouse piano played in early-century houses of prostitution. Contrastingly, bebop as played by Miles Davis, Dizzy Gillespie, and others, with its angular melodic lines and distant harmonic extensions, made severe demands upon players' musicianship and technique; it sought to transcend all previous achievements (Megill and Demory, 1996:Part 5). Thus bop was head music, played by intellectuals for intellectuals; others could listen if they liked.

Where rock and roll was tempered by appealing personalities, as for example by the winsome Elvis Presley singing "Heartbreak Hotel" or by the touring English rock quartet, the Beatles, singing what became in an album "Sgt. Pepper's Lonely Hearts Club Band," it was less evident that the schism between representation and transcendence had occurred. Such schism is even harder to detect in the late stages of the Beatles' history as their work turned to psychedelic and mystical themes, once again forming an *amalgam* of two diverging elements in Anglo American art (Megill and Demory, 1996:317f). Meantime bop, the less popular and more arty side of the jazz schism, pursued its increasingly intellectual course of development. Though early bop did recall previous small ensembles, it tended increasingly toward solo performance and exalted the individual eccentricities of (sometimes startling) technique. The modern jazz that followed it was still less rooted in the original jazz heritage.

ii. Same old saints?—Some music critics wrongly assume that the history of humankind is a story of 'progress' in which every generation advances on the one before so that in a few centuries we are better, almost infinitely better than our foreparents. This is heresy from a Christian standpoint, for what believer presumes to have improved upon the Christ? While endless progress is no part of Christian theology, on the other hand recovery or looping back is essential to Christianity in all its forms, and expressly so in the case of baptist life and thought. What these three volumes define as the baptist vision ("this is that; then is now") has a counterpart in the development of jazz. At least in this sense jazz is a Christian music. For there is in the history of this music a significant spiraling back to its past. Whether the jazz spiral moves up or downward is probably not ours to judge; such gains and losses are best perceived long after. In any case, return to an earlier style does occur in jazz; this move retains the riches of intervening years yet recovers what may have been lost in passage, going back to the time of origins. Repeated revivals (such as the New Orleans jazz revivals of the 1940s and after) thus required a circling back to recapture the original solidarity of jazz—to rephrase, they required a music that truly *sang*.

Michael Gerard White (1954–), born in New Orleans, genetically embodies both of that city's lines of African American heritage described earlier. His mother Helen Forcia (pronounced For'shay), Catholic, college-educated, a schoolteacher, was related to those Creoles of color who had maintained rich European cultural traditions in South Louisiana. Her kin included as well traditional jazz artist 'Papa John' Joseph (1877–1965). Michael's father, Oscar White, a New Orleans mail carrier, shared the heritage of those working-class blacks who had produced Louis Armstrong, though the White family had attained middle class. In early life a Baptist, Oscar had joined his wife's church later. So Michael was sent to parochial schools and to Xavier University in the city. He played Sousa-type marches in the smart St. Augustine High School band, went to mass as required, and seemed destined merely for predictable academic success via a Ford Foundation fellowship, a Tulane Ph.D. in Spanish, and then, when he finished, a professorial appointment at Xavier—all of which he achieved, but along the way, something else happened. In his last year of college White began really to listen to the jazz that had surrounded him as he grew up in the Crescent City. Through a student friend White met traditional jazz band leader Doc Paulin, who (in his distinctive Creole English) invited Michael to try out for the band. The first appointment came in the spring of 1975—to play for a Baptist church parade in Marrero, Louisiana, across the Mississippi. Parades were a standard structure of celebration for black Baptist churches: Churchgoers dressed in their best—all white clothing for women, all black for men—hired a band or two, and paraded, celebrating the church's homecoming anniversary or some like event. Sometimes a parade would start at one church and end at another. For Catholic clarinetist Michael White the music was new and strange: jazzed-up versions of "In the Sweet By and By," "Sing On," or "When the Saints Go Marchin' In." Nevertheless he marched and played, someone admired his clarinet tone, and a wonderful new road opened before him. After that he played often with Doc Paulin and with dozens of other groups for church parades and funerals, learning from the old-timers who had played with Louis Armstrong, Jelly Roll Morton, Sidney Bechet, and Joe (King) Oliver. Doctoral study in New Orleans provided Michael White with further opportunity to stretch his ears: in his spare time he visited Tulane's superior jazz archive, listened, talked with the gentle curator, Richard B. Allen. Thereafter the gigs came fast; there was a lot to learn; Michael White's musical career (for him as for many, a parallel, second career) was well launched.

New Orleans was changing, though. In prosperous late-twentieth-century America it had become a tourist town. Tawdry tourist traps appeared in the French Quarter, their music a noisy imitation of the authentic New Orleans style. The trouble was with the listeners, perhaps, as much as the musicians: jazz is two-way music, and when the audience was no longer the sharer in local worship and dancing and sociality but became a clutch of assorted visitors who watched as if at a zoo, the mood shifted. Michael White watched these changes occur even as the older musicians retired and died. In 1961 survivors had begun performing at Preservation Hall, a cooperative established to keep the traditional music alive. As his fame grew, "Doctor Michael White" (his working name) found that between concert tours to the East Coast, to Europe, and to the Orient the mantle of leadership for traditional New Orleans jazz was descending upon his shoulders. The task was not to imitate Buddy Bolden or Joe Oliver, though they had taken unforgettable steps on the way. It was to recover a style, a spirit, that had invested the early music, and to create jazz anew in that style. This was what the traditionalists combined to do.

"High Society," recorded in 1991 by a Doctor Michael White group drawn from his original Liberty Jazz Band (Antilles 422-848 545-2), had been composed in 1901 and was commonly played by New Orleans marching bands of that era. (The 1901 march in turn was based upon traditional marches played by village bands in France and Belgium—Chase, 1955:469, 475, 480). Its structure reflects the standard American street march: introduction, first strain, second strain, 'trio,' finale, all linked by transitional riffs. For the session White chose African American musicians with long experience in the New Orleans style. It is interesting to hear what this ensemble has done with "High Society." First, it is longer than earlier versions: at almost four and a half minutes, more than twice the length of an old Sidney Bechet side. A second point is obvious: A string bass and a piano are added to White's band as to Bechet's; the march has been brought indoors. Yet this does not mean tamed! Rather, the players seem liberated to produce an intense, throbbing, swinging version. The lyrical first and second strains are led by Greg Stafford's cornet, while the clarinet adds polyphonic improvisation that promises more to come. Then after a riff comes the 'trio,' climaxing in White's version of the traditional "High Society" clarinet solo. White offers a fast, virtuoso performance in sixteenth notes. Compared with Jimmie Noone's staccato version of this trio and the liquid gold of Sidney Bechet's (these were two clarinet greats who had recorded the piece), White's version is strikingly elegant, and it is swinging elegance. Soaring from high to low registers, maintaining flawless tempo, the solo conveys a passion that does justice to its heritage. This "High Society" is not mere repetition; it is, as White writes in the program notes for the disk, "a continuation and not an imitation of principles and ideas begun in the past." In our terms, it is a secular version of the baptist vision in which 'this is that.' Artistic excellence and cultural passion converge here to make jazz once again a fit answer within the culture to the Good News of the gospel.

In the traditional New Orleans marching funeral, the band played solemn hymns en route to the cemetery (in life we are in the midst of death), but then on the return struck up a lively march, full of the good cheer Jesus said his work had brought with it (John 16:33). Put back on the street again, "High Society" played this way would be a good choice for the march home from the cemetery (even in death, we anticipate resurrected life).

At this writing, as evidenced by articles in numerous periodicals such as *Gambit, The Second Line,* New York's *Hot House,* and the French *Jazz Hot,* 'Doctor Michael White' continues as a leading force in the ongoing traditional revival (Carter, 1991:269-73). His performances of the music of Bolden, Morton, Johnnie Dodds, Freddie Keppard, King Oliver, and Sidney Bechet at New York's Lincoln Center and elsewhere provide even more solid evidence: In White and others like him this music has looped back, recovering, without merely repeating, its own culture-rooted sources. Bookings varying from Manhattan's Village Vanguard to France and distant Asia to campuses across the United States ensure that this new-old music is getting a hearing alongside other jazz. It is too soon to predict the outcome, yet not too soon to characterize White, whom I am privileged to know: if Louis Armstrong occupied Kierkegaard's aesthetic dimension, Michael White occupies his religious dimension. While remaining Catholic (with all that church's treasures available to him), White has picked up the baptist understanding of existence as well; his life and art contain both. This gain came not from the (few) Baptist sermons he heard or (even fewer) Bible classes he attended; it was delivered by baptist gospel music itself, music he heard, understood, reinterpreted. When White plays "God Will Take Care of You" in his unforgettable phrasing ("Be not dismayed, whate'er betide . . ."), he knows what he is playing about. In a sense this music is as old as the gospel in slavery times (jazz musicians sometimes refer to one standard piece as S.O.S.—the "same old saints," still marching in), yet it is music as new as tomorrow for a culture in need of good news.

* * * * *

Art is a kind of action—it does something. The theologian of culture must understand exactly what is being enacted in a given art-form and bring that action under gospel light for better understanding. What, then, does jazz do? To answer, recall the action of the music that preceded it. Work songs supported tiresome labor, ring shouts conjured liberation and release, European dances and marches synchronized passionate bodies in motion, and spirituals, underwritten now by the Great Story as it was re-enacted in troubled slavery times, cried out in faith: "My Lord, what a morning, when the stars begin to fall!" Blues were sometimes complaint songs: they issued Job-like protest against life's sorrows. Early jazz gathered all this up into action that was above all *celebratory.* Its place was the picnic and dance-hall, celebrating the delight of sexuality and the joy of time free from labor; its place was the parades, celebrating public holidays; yet its place was also funerals, celebrating the presence of life in the midst of death. There was always an underside to these celebrations: the time of love is so short and its disappointments are so near; all parades end; funerals remind us of life's brevity. So jazz not only celebrated, it recalled these sorrows and introjected them by way of the bent notes and rhythms of the blues.

In this light, recall every art's constitutive elements: Every work of art has a *dual reference:* it speaks of the world as it is, the world of everyday with its joys and sorrows; it also speaks of the world the art creates, where (in this case) joy overflows and fellowship is unflawed. Again, jazz, as art must be, is overwhelmingly *expressive:* its expressions of the earthly and the heavenly (from King Oliver's "Dippermouth Blues" to Duke Ellington's "A-Train" to John Coltrane's "Love Supreme") may overwhelm listeners who desire a greater psychic distance between such expressions and their own selfhood. Finally, jazz like other art is *conventional:* drawn both from the European dance and march music of Creole New Orleans and from the African American drum rhythms of the sugar plantations, rising both from ragtime and from the rhythms of Christian hope poured out in gospel hymns, jazz transforms its source-conventions to enact the new world (trans-ethnic, trans-cultural, heaven-and-earth-bridging) that it means to celebrate.

§4. Art and Christian Peoplehood

What about explicit Christian art, the art of church buildings and church services and private devotions? Have we discovered here why there is still so little such art in America (and nowadays in the whole wide West)? Can we see why there are not in this 'Christian' land more and greater Christian painters than the Europeans Ghiberti and Grünewald and Rembrandt, why not more and greater Christian poets and novelists after Milton and Bunyan, Donne and Dostoevski, Hopkins and Tolstoy—why not even a Charles Wesley or an Isaac Watts? Why not more and greater church music, Christian music for home and school and festal hours? Admittedly, this has not been the surface question of this chapter. It has asked about art, *not* about Christian art. Yet the chapter is part of a theology that with Jonathan Edwards deems God not only beautiful but the beautifier of creation, deems God the world's original artist—sees redeemable creation as the scene of God's self-giving new creation, drawing for its life upon God's own life—Father, Son, Holy Spirit (*Ethics,* Four and Five; Jonathan

Edwards, 1765; cf. Begbie, 1991:Part iii; Pattison, 1991:chap. 7; Gunton, 1993:chap. 8). In plainer, baptist words, the story of God is by Christian conviction the world's Great Story, and a religion or science—or art!—that misses this fact has not yet come into its own.

Such a claim about art cries out for justification on a wider field than that of American culture. Ancient Indian temples, Chinese Buddhas, pre-Colombian pyramids, African carvings demand a place in the artistic sun, as is long recognized by museums and galleries. So my claim is local and limited, but all the more relevant to the reach of these volumes, which from the outset propose a 'local' theology—the truth of Christ as it appears in our own and our near neighbor's eyes. Yet no vicious relativism follows. For the day must come (I believe, has come and will come again) when the Great Story shapes still other cultures each in its own way, creating worlds that are not our Western world. Enough for us now to ask, *why is it not more fully shaping our own?* As my friend Ralph Wood reminds me, the formal answer is clear: our Enlightenment or 'modern' culture still has presuppositions (see Part II below) that make this culture alien to Christian art, a culture still unhealed via churches whose feeble witness, swerving now toward gnostic transcendence (cf. Bloom, 1992:s.v. "gnostic") and now toward gross experientialism, offers our culture scant nourishment.

The standard of comparison often invoked here is the European Middle Ages, when (it is said) art and life were one, and art was in the main gospel-sponsored art. Nothing said here dare denigrate that achievement, yet that age ended and its art-tasks ended with it. The age ended because it spilled over, burst out at its seams, producing a new politics (from Aquinas to Machiavelli to Jefferson), a new Christianity (reform in its several forms including baptist ones), a new science (so new that its predecessor sciences became unrecognizable as sciences), a new art. The concern of this chapter has been with the local (American and Western) promise of that art, and we have seen its real achievement but its stubborn limits. Visual artists in our era seemed only rarely to paint the Great Story as had their Christian forebears; American literary storytellers from James Fenimore Cooper to Toni Morrison distorted or suppressed or only rarely echoed earth's oldest continuous living faith-story. Yet an exception appears: America's distinctive jazz and blues, poured from the crucible of slavery and molded in the free black church and in multi-ethnic America, showed a distinctive capacity to set the Good News, with its secular analogs, to music.

Given this America, this "new found land" (Donne), artists may have done what they would as well as they could. Jazz proves, though, that the way to Christian cultural greatness is not barred here. Still, as Julian Hartt liked to remind us, final responsibility in this matter lies not with the artist community but with a people that gathers as church. It is this people which is entrusted with the gospel, it is the church-bearing people of God (not excluding Jesus' ragtag baptist people) who must body forth that gospel in their common life. Now as in High Medieval times and earlier times, Christian life with its great holy art-evoking signs—preaching, baptism, the table (cf. *Doctrine,* Nine)—must be shaped to accord with the story these recall, so that the world may believe.

One dimension of the task is the shape of the church's own meeting. This is not only as Yoder would remind us a political meeting, the *ekklesia* gathered to transact the weekly business of the citizenry of heaven; it is not merely, as Harvey Cox once thought, a strategy session or pep rally to shape Christian witness outside the church's walls. It is these things among others, but it is far more. To journey with this community is to come

> to Mount Zion, the city of the living God, the heavenly Jerusalem, to myriads of angels, to the full concourse and assembly of the firstborn who are enrolled in heaven, and to God the judge of all, and to the spirits of good men [women, children] made perfect, and to Jesus. . . . (Heb. 12:22-24)

In such an assembly, by what right do we neglect, by what right disdain artistry that mirrors in the assembly the beauty of heavenly things? By what right diminish our prayers to fleshly whimpers? Turn preaching into prating? Replace our ancestors' stately rites with showmanship and chatter? Diminish the sensibility of little children—God's little children—by surrounding them at church (at church!) with the coarse and the cluttered? Protestant purity (no idols) and catholic comprehensiveness (no isolation) alike have their gifts to contribute to Christian artistry. Both in their uniqueness cry out for the companionship of yet a third, that pentecostal community whose integrity of fellowship bursting with life can weave all our earthly wealth into a new art suited to God's coming day. No insularity of spirit can give birth to tomorrow's art; no indolence suits the cultural witness of the church.

In a chapter on art in his *Christian Critique of American Culture,* Julian Hartt refocuses a Tillichian theme: Art, he grants, uses symbols (in this chapter, read 'conventions') "to show forth reality not otherwise discoverable." The "shadows of art" guide us into "the substance of reality." Hartt is telling us that *any* real art does this, not just 'Christian' art, not just 'realistic' or 'expressionist' art. Hence the very illusions art creates can expose the sick illusions of the given world, the diseases of everyday. In art, "love of truth can lead to . . . transformation and transvaluation of the given world." True artistic creativity is grounded in the real world, and starting there the artist "creates the world anew, afresh" (Hartt, 1967:355-64). This claim assumes the *dual* reference of artistic acts. Of necessity, artists refer to the given world, but their work implies another, a "whole new world" of unrealized possibility.

PART II

PHILOSOPHICAL VISIONS

We are now at the end of an era not just in a calendrical sense—leaving behind a thousand years starting with a "1," and entering a thousand years that will start with "2"—but in a deeper, historical sense. . . . If an historical era is ending, it is the era of Modernity itself. . . . How we ourselves are to feel about the prospects—whether we join those who are despondent at its end and say good-bye to it with regret, or those who view its departure with satisfaction and look forward with pleasure to the coming of 'post-modern' times—depends on what we see as the heart and core of the 'modern,' and what key event in our eyes gave rise to the 'modern' world.

Stephen Toulmin, *Cosmopolis*

I believe that my originality (if that is the right word) is an originality belonging to the soil rather than to the seed. (Perhaps I have no seed of my own.) Sow a seed in my soil and it will grow differently than it would in any other soil.

Ludwig Wittgenstein

And so, if philosophy asks us what reason we have for supposing that we know our neighbors, we have no answer for her except a confession of ignorance. We have no reasons for it, because we have always taken it for granted. . . . In the same way we go on in our religion, taking it for granted that the founding, steadying, invigorating, illumining and enriching of our existence which we find in it, is the action of the God to whom we pray; and who, it appears, extends a similar beneficent action to our fellow-believers.

Austin Farrer, *Faith and Speculation*

Introduction to Part II

Some may suppose there is no role for philosophy in a system that in the spirit of 1 Corinthians 3:11 renounces mere cultural foundations for theological work—"no other foundation than the one already laid: I mean Jesus Christ himself." For consider that philosophy is the self-reflexive work of culture striving to know itself, re-form itself in light of present human knowledge and convictions. It is thus itself a cultural phenomenon. Apostolic Christianity cannot base itself upon that. Nor can the suggestion that a *Christian* philosophy may fill the bill carry the day, for if 'Christian philosophy' means perennial Christian truths that lay rightful claim upon the world alienated from God, there can be no greater assurance of their truth than there is of the gospel upon which openly or perhaps secretly they depend. And if on the other hand 'Christian philosophy' means no more than a temporary, fragile, and contingent readjustment of philosophical content or style intended to take account of the gospel as it appears in a particular time and place, such philosophy may indeed have a useful role, yet this is not and does not even claim to be the foundational work that is here renounced. Philosophy, no less that done by Christians than by others, does its worldly work in light of its worldly knowledge. 'Christian' or not, *philosophy* as a self-reflexive work of culture *provides no external basis for Christian life and faith.* As such a cultural phenomenon, though, philosophy is a matter of perennial theological interest. For philosophy is the world of its time set down on paper; it is the world thinking itself. Thus, even more than science and art (Chapters Three and Four), more than commerce and politics and play (topics passed over here), in its generality even more than religion (Chapter Two), philosophy is the world's tall weather vane; at its best it is culture's thermometer and barometer and wind-gauge. Therefore an attempt to come to terms with culture, discovering the authentic course for faith under way in that culture, staking out the witness of the gospel church to a wanting world—such an attempt must read philosophy's weather instruments in order to keep faith with its own message.

To this point in this introduction, philosophy (or culture or world) has been mentioned as though it were a single thing. This is far from the case, as philosophers know better than most. A dynamic gospel confronts many philosophies at many times and places, registering many changing cultures. A central note of our times is in fact the changing face of philosophy in the West, underlining the changing countenance of the world. This is so of every age. Yet one change or shift—the revision in Western or European American thought from early modern times until now—is the central theme of the three chapters that follow. **Chapter Five provides a preliminary view of this watershed now being crossed, the setting of the sun of philosophical modernity.** No longer is philosophy in the West totally absorbed by modern problems of knowledge and language and omnicompetent science. A new philosophical day presenting a new challenge and new opportunity for the gospel is at hand. Yet from what possible standpoint does anyone now challenge modernity itself? Is that not as vain as the pot denying its own black bottom? Shall birds deny the reality of the air in which they fly? Is modernity not for us unavoidable? **Chapter Six responds by analyzing the modern-postmodern philosophical pilgrimage of a single, pivotal figure, Ludwig Wittgenstein, who achieved a revision of the modernity he inherited.** As it happens, Wittgenstein became a practicing Christian fairly early in his pilgrimage. Certainly the argument here is not that since he did so we Christians must hold his philosophical ways dear, or that his moves authorize parallel ones by the rest of us. That would constitute a cheap victory for the faith, actually no victory, for that argument is fallacious. Rather the claim of Chapter Six is that there is a striking *convergence* between Wittgenstein's changing standpoint from his earlier to his later philosophical work and the simultaneous journey he made from his early doubts to his subsequent mystical transcendentalism (the *Tractatus*) and then on to his ultimate faithful embrace of life in its particulars (the *Investigations*), a *convergence* between the intellectual trail he found and the gospel that found him and to which he held fast. Ludwig Wittgenstein's Christian journey, we will see, was in part flawed; so, it can be argued, was his philosophical one. Yet their convergence is real enough to show us, in a favorite Wittgensteinian phrase, "how to go on." **Chapter Seven considers some modest**

attempts to go on in the limited but important sphere of philosophy of religion, showing, by a contrast of these with older ways of proceeding, how this modern philosophical project has changed in light of Wittgenstein's work. In particular, the chapter considers two nodes of modern philosophy of religion, the question of religious knowledge and the problem of many religions, showing how in both cases these tasks undergo profound changes at the hands of philosophers conversant with the shift in paradigms which in this volume he represents.

The entirety of Part II, then, constitutes a *theological* look at one deep-seated part of culture: it is a brief *theology of philosophy.* Its work is done not by matching philosophical theses with opposed theological ones—a medieval fantasy never fulfilled—but by speaking in a theological voice concerning matters philosophical. Other theological workers will find other things to say about philosophy; here is what one worker says from this standpoint.

CHAPTER FIVE

The Metaphysics of Modernity

British philosopher R. G. Collingwood suggested almost a century ago that the right way to think of 'metaphysics' is not as a mysterious philosophical gaze behind the screen of appearances to penetrate an otherwise inaccessible realm (the really real): Metaphysics is essentially a historical task; it is precisely the discovery of the absolute presuppositions of a preceding era. By absolute presuppositions, Collingwood meant those taken-for-granted beliefs that give form to the entire life of that time and that go unquestioned because they go unnoticed (Collingwood, 1940). (Metaphysical beliefs in this sense are comparable to presuppositional or 'presiding' convictions, those that lie behind even the general or 'doctrinal' beliefs that we typically invoke to identify ourselves ([*CONV.*: 96]). An example of such a presiding or metaphysical belief is the hierarchical view of reality that prevailed throughout the European Middle Ages: by it, all existence is connected in a Great Chain of Being in which each sort of item—earth, plants, animals, human beings, angels, the heavenly bodies, the triune God who is above all—relates to the rest in a comprehensive structure that assigns to each its place and purpose. This picture of reality was not so much argued, then, as assumed, thereby shaping the remainder of human thought in that culture. What we are chiefly interested in here is a more recent set of metaphysical beliefs, those that characterize not the Middle Ages but modernity right up to (and for many, including) the present.

We should note that if Collingwood were altogether correct, this is actually an impossible quest—he held we can discover the metaphysical beliefs only of previous ages, not of our own. Perhaps, though, the presuppositions of modernity present a marginal case: this is so if modernity is indeed a dying age, in process of being displaced by another. In fact this is the character of modernity as the present chapter understands it. So on this ground Collingwood might allow this chapter's project.

A chapter on modernity understood in this way falls into three unequal sections: **(§1) a brief look at the relations of theology to philosophy over the earlier portions of the Christian era, when both disciplines were concerned with presiding convictions, with 'absolute presuppositions' in Collingwood's sense, with metaphysics; (§2) a more detailed look at modernity itself, construing it in rival ways: one, the standard account that locates the beginnings of now-troubled modernity with the work of Descartes and Newton in the 1600s; another, a view that sees a more promising modernity arising earlier, in the Renaissance, with originators such as Shakespeare, Erasmus, and on the religious side, the Radical Reformation; (§3) finally, the question about purported successors to modernity labeled (or at least self-labeled) 'postmodern,' successors that in some cases might better be called 'mostmodern.'** This chapter sets the stage for the remainder of Part II, that is, for the genuine postmodernity that will show up in Chapters Six and Seven.

§1. Before Modern Times

The relations between theology and philosophy are older than Christianity itself. The portion of the Old Testament designated Writings embodies the sort of transcultural 'wisdom' that was a common property of the ancient world. Part moral instruction, part advice on *savoir faire* for young men aspiring to roles in their nation's civil or military service, the book of Proverbs embodies a horizontal philosophy of common good whose corresponding theology is close to the Deism of a later era: "Go circumspectly. . . . God is in heaven and you are on earth, so let your words be few" (Eccles. 5:1-2). The book of Job, a later part of the Writings collection, adapts a cautionary traditional tale of slow but sure divine justice (the prose portions of present chapters 1, 2, and 42). Job inserts within this moralistic story a profound verse drama that offers more complex ideas of JHWH's inscrutable holiness, thus overruling (without flatly denying) the earlier tale's simplicities (*Doctrine,* pp. 173f). These philosophical or universalizing accounts show an awareness within the biblical tradition of concerns that persist in the New Testament Scriptures. Certainly the young Christian movement appeared in a world rich with ideas with which to interact. A foremost example of this ongoing interaction is provided by the concept of divine redemptive purpose embodied in Paul's Letter to the Romans, particularly in the reflection of Romans 8, already discussed (*Doctrine,* Four §2). Briefly, Paul there *resolves* (rather than 'solves') the problem of evil by contrasting present suffering with destined glory: the greater the suffering, the greater must be the glory God foresees and intends that makes the present worth its cost: "[T]he universe itself is to be freed from the shackles of mortality and is to enter upon the glorious liberty of the children of God" (Rom. 8:21). Another example of interaction is the anonymous Letter to the Hebrews, which presents a Middle Platonist interpretation of redemption in Jesus Christ. Following these biblical exemplars as if at a distance came the early Christian apologists, who employed existing Hellenistic philosophical strategies in defending the gospel message against its pagan critics. Perhaps these efforts reached a climax in the reply made by Origen of Alexandria, about A.D. 250, to Celsus's notorious attack upon Christianity. Platonic and Stoic elements shaped most of these attempts at Christian witness to the Hellenistic world.

Yet it was none of these, but the intellectual labor of African rhetorician, Christian convert, and eventual Bishop of Hippo, Aurelius Augustine, that controlled the intersection between the gospel and its world-context from his day to the present. On this account alone Augustine is indispensable for understanding Christianity, and if we add his contributions to doctrinal theology (especially ecclesiology and soteriology) he is the most important Christian theologian between Paul the Apostle and the Protestant Revolt. Indeed, the Reformation itself has fitly been described as a battle between Augustine's (Catholic) doctrine of the church and his (evangelical) doctrines of sin and grace.

a. Augustine of Hippo.—Born into a middle-income household in Roman North Africa, Augustine (354–430) received from his mother a formation that was at least nominally Christian. He was educated at his birthplace, Thagaste, and at Carthage, the provincial capital, and took up a career as a rhetorician, a sort of combination literature professor and orator-for-hire. At age nineteen he experienced an intellectual conversion in reading Cicero's philosophy: its outcome was his resolution to devote his life to the quest for truth. In pursuit of this career he emigrated, first to Rome (by then, A.D. 383, a city of largely symbolic significance in the larger Roman Empire), and then to Milan, where Emperor Theodosius I was often resident, and where Catholic Bishop Ambrose was a key public figure. Already at age thirty Augustine was appointed professor of rhetoric at Milan, a plum indeed. By then he had adopted the philosophical views of Mani, founder of the spreading Manichaean movement. This was a loose form of Christian teaching that by its dualism 'solved' the philosophical problem of evil. From this allegiance Augustine advanced, via Porphyry (an anti-Christian) and Plotinus, into the philosophically sophisticated New Platonism of the time. In Milan, however, Augustine came under the powerful preaching of Ambrose, and in his thirty-third year (August 386) he experienced in a garden a striking conversion to evangelical and Catholic orthodoxy. Thus encouraged, he devoted his life afresh to the quest for truth that he had earlier pledged. Now he began a lifelong stream of books, pamphlets, and letters defining and defending his newfound faith. In 387 he was baptized by Ambrose; in 388 he traveled via Ostia (where with his mother he shared a fresh mystical experience) back to North Africa. There he founded a monastery, eventually was ordained a presbyter, and in 395 was consecrated coadjutor bishop of seaside Hippo, and a year later became sole bishop, an office he would occupy until his death. North Africa, like the entire Roman Empire, was by then aflame with ideological strife both within and without. The 'barbarian' armies threatened Rome; imperial politics was fraught with mistrust and betrayal; the Catholics found themselves only one party (and in North Africa, only a minority party) among competing Christian bodies. Augustine appeared to have unusual power to deal with these competitors, notably with the *Donatists,* who maintained Catholic doctrine and liturgy but yearned for return to the old confessors' fidelity of earlier Christianity (see M. Tilley, 1996), while the rival Catholics now favored a more relaxed standard for church members. Regrettably, Augustine won this battle only at the cost of enlisting imperial troops to stamp out the Donatist populace—sword and torch against their stubborn evangelical heritage. Other chief opponents included the followers of *Pelagius* (c. 355–c. 425), a British Christian come to Rome, who urged a return to the moral purity of earliest Christianity at the expense (so Augustine argued) of the doctrine of unmerited grace (*Doctrine,* pp. 125f, 183). Meantime, externally Augustine confronted the vast political upheaval created by tribal movements (of barbarians all, in patrician Roman eyes) within the now bloated imperial frontiers. These last events paralleled, though they may not have evoked, Augustine's last great literary achievement, twenty-two books named *The City of God,* a work completed only four years before his death.

b. Augustine the philosopher.—The task now is to single out the distinctive philosophical drives in Augustine's strenuous life history in order to illustrate the continued philosophical shaping of the evangel that he professed. Begin with Cicero's influence on the eighteen-year-old youth that led to what is designated his first, or philosophical conversion. Statesman and philosopher Marcus Tullius Cicero (106–43 B.C.) had transmitted Greek philosophical thought to Latin readers, emphasizing no one school such as the Platonic or Stoic but fostering throughout an ideal of human education that would surface again at the sixteenth-century Renaissance. Since the work that Augustine then read, Cicero's *Hortensius,* survives only in fragments, we can come no closer to the substance of this first, intellectual conversion, yet Augustine reports in the *Confessions* that "the book changed my feelings. I altered my prayers, Lord, to be toward you yourself" (III.iv.7), which I take to mean that from his later Christian standpoint, Augustine saw his younger determination to discover philosophical truth as continuous with his quest for the one true God. He felt this truth was worth whatever it cost.

So the late adolescent Augustine was converted to be a truth (or wisdom, *sophia*) seeker, but what did that entail? He was already nominally Christian, and Christians read the Bible, but when now he dipped in, the Bible seemed unworthy compared with Cicero! Some fellow students at Carthage were promoting a teaching that kept the name "Christian" but went on to more advanced religious thought. Mani (c. 216–c. 276), their Eastern founder, had rejected the 'coarse' Old Testament, while he acknowledged Buddha and Zoroaster as apostles of the light as well as Christ. Ascetic, mysterious, professing above all things 'reason,' and always ready to debate, these students attracted Augustine. So, to his Christian mother's horror, he became a Manichee (*Conf.* III.iv.10f). Simply to report this, though, may mislead, for later Christian writers, influenced by the mature Augustine's own revulsion, have pictured Manichaeanism as a viper's nest of vicious dualism. Dualists they were, but that in itself is neither what first attracted Augustine nor later repelled him. We can best understand these 'advanced' thinkers by comparing them to the liberal Christianity of the nineteenth century: for instance, they retained Scripture's triadic language for God but rejected the orthodox doctrine of the Trinity—a move that had curious consequences. It dissolved the gnawing problem of evil that they with other Christians confronted, for by their myth God was pure light, always totally opposed to the world's dark evil. Yet this left the children of light (themselves) helplessly passive; matter was evil, so they were prisoners in their own material bodies and thus perpetual victims of the darkness they professed to abhor. Their appeal to young Augustine, however, lay in their universal claims: they said they had transcended the errors of all ordinary Christians, so it was hardly surprising that their movement had spread as far as distant China (as indeed it had) as well as to Africa. When after nine years Augustine abandoned the Manichees, it was not only because their theology embraced a sophistry—for God remained for them despite everything the source of evil—but because they could not account for the sin he found not merely in his material body but in his spiritual soul: there was darkness there as well. He could pray, "Grant me chastity and continence, but not yet" (*Conf.* VIII.vii.17). So he became instead a Platonist, but that meant remaining a dualist, and indeed the dualism survived, infecting not only him but many centuries of his theological followers (Brown et al., eds., 1998:chaps. 1, 7).

By the time he turned to Platonism, Augustine was a published author and was soon to be Professor of Rhetoric in Milan. The New Platonism that won his allegiance was the creation of Plotinus (205–70), an Egyptian though perhaps of Roman descent, who had come to Rome and won even the emperor's favor, and whose work was available to Augustine through a pupil of Plotinus's, Porphyry of Tyre (died after 301). Porphyry had organized Plotinus's writings as the *Enneads*, six groups of nine treatises each. On his own Porphyry had also written a polemical work, *Against the Christians.* For these New Platonists, knowledge of God is no other than knowledge of oneself, gained by abstracting from all material things. Christ was not for them divine, but only "a man of excellent wisdom which none could equal" (*Conf.* VII.xix.25). So Augustine could learn from these 'philosophers of spirit' (as we might dub them) that "[i]n the beginning was the Word, and the Word was with God, and the Word was God." "But that 'the Word was made flesh, and dwelt among us' (John 1:14) I did not read there" (*Conf.* VII.ix.13f).

Intellectual life in Augustine's Roman world was then dominated by two sharply opposed groups: There were the old pagans, who in the spirit of the recent Emperor Julian (the Apostate) sought to reclaim the civic virtues of old Rome in the name of the time-honored gods—but for Augustine that was idolatry and he shunned it. And there were the Catholics, whose religion by the late fourth century had itself grown old, hardened into dogmas, looking backward to congealed tradition but never forward to therapeutic growth and cultural change. What Augustine found in New Platonism was a way of thought, perhaps religious if not Christian, that offered an alternative to both these. The sermons of Ambrose, chief shepherd of Catholic Milan, seemed to acknowledge this third way. Ambrose read the pagan authors and quoted them in his sermons, finding a place for them in Catholic Christianity. The intellectual dimension of Augustine's garden conversion (August, A.D. 386) was the discovery that he, too, might by God's grace adopt and shape that third Roman way into (Roman) Catholicism.

Classic Christian conversion (*Doctrine,* Three §3) has at the least three elements—moral, mystical, and intellectual. Indeed, Christian conversion is exactly the practice that binds these three into one by its structural features of confession (of sin) and profession (of faith): hence Augustine's own baptism signified all three elements of conversion newly gathered up in his allegiance to Christ. For him the moral element began as his release from a persistent sexual drive that had mastered him (thus the relevance of the Scripture to which the child's voice in the garden sent him, Romans 13:13f: "Let us behave with decency as befits the day: no drunken orgies, no debauchery or vice, no quarrels or jealousies! Let Christ Jesus himself be the armor that you wear; give your unspiritual nature no opportunity to satisfy its desires"). For him the mystical element was plainly miraculous beyond all chance coincidence: a child chants "*Tolle, lege . . . ,*" leading him to open the Book and read, and ultimately to a vision of continence that would allow him to master his sexual drives. But as prominent as either of these, was the intellectual element. This was continuous with his earlier, African conversion, his first commission to be a *philosopher*—only now his reading and discussion led him to claim the Greek heritage for *Christ.* So he would henceforth read the Bible, and follow the path of morality, and take up the full range of Christian practice, shaped throughout by his New Platonism. This philosophical stance may strike some as fortuitous; others will find it rather deplorable, for it was to form the Augustinian doctrines of sin and grace, the doctrine of election and predestination, the dualist theory of human nature, and the doctrine of church as the invisible number of the elect yet at the same time the militant corps under papal command—views and doctrines that for better or worse give form to Western doctrinal Christianity to this day. With this outcome in mind, one might even wish for a Christianity untainted by philosophy so that it could realize its pure nature. But that would be a fruitless wish, for if the present pages have any lesson it is that the gospel's living water is drunk only from earthen vessels—that is, whenever the Christian evangel appears it presents itself in some cultural shape, never in none at all.

c. The City of God.—In the final two decades of his life Augustine was summoned by his Christian followers to take up a project that demanded of him new philosophical skills. It was first formed in sermons and letters, but took its fullest shape in *The City of God (Civ. dei)*, published serially from 413 to 425. Since his youth the Roman Empire had undergone continuing changes that would eventually be interpreted as signs of desperate morbidity: schisms within the imperial headship, barbarian attacks from without, marauding tribes within the empire's extended domain sometimes allied with or against imperial factions—all this reaching at least a symbolic climax when one barbarian army, Alaric's Goths, invaded and sacked the ancient capital, Rome itself (410). It is sometimes reckoned that this progressive imperial decline occasioned the writing of the *City of God*. More to the point, many have claimed that Augustine wrote *City of God* to answer those pagans who accused the Christians of precipitating the demise of Rome. Yet Peter Brown, Augustine's recent, fine biographer, takes a deeper view: Augustine never doubted that Rome would survive; *City of God*'s great question is rather about the character of that survival.

> He had a civilized man's distaste for the Goths: captivity among them was "at least among human beings *even if* (!) among barbarians." He could accept the mortality of all human institutions. But his whole perspective implied a belief in the resilience of the Empire as a whole. (P. Brown, 1969:295)

Augustine meant, not to comfort Roman Christians on the coming loss of the evil empire (it was not that to him), but to offer a final, full-fledged challenge to the opponents of Christianity.

At long last his training in debate found an adequate adversary: not the pious Donatists (Tilley, 1996:vii-viii) or the morally earnest Pelagians or the mission-minded Arians, each of whom embraced more of what Augustine stood for than not, but opponents who were dutiful followers of the old Roman religion such as his acquaintance Senator Volusianus, age about thirty, an urbane refugee from Rome to Carthage.

> These last pagans were anxious to invest their beliefs in a distant, golden past, untroubled by the rise of Christianity. . . . We have here a strange phenomenon: the preservation of a whole way of life in the present, by transfusing it with the inviolable safety of an adored past. (P. Brown, 1969:301)

Volusianus might well have been a model for that pagan of two generations past, Mississippian Will Percy, Walker Percy's adoptive father, whose *Lanterns on the Levee* is just such disciplined nostalgia written to evoke a lost but treasured past.

Against this, Augustine's rhetorical strategy was a very paradigm of Christian refutation: He would devote ten 'books' of *City of God* to *undermining* the pagan dogmas; then twelve more to *overwhelming* reluctant readers by his presentation of Christianity. In the first ten, his long study of the New Platonists came to Christian fruition, for Plotinus was the chosen weapon of these literate pagans in defense of their faith. Augustine knew how to quote Plotinus in refutation of their views: more generally, he was able to invoke the culture he shared with such as Volusianus, making their shared convictions the premises of his counter-pagan arguments. Did pagan New Platonists believe (in this case, following Plato) in *daimôn,* demons? Augustine believed in them as well. But were there 'good demons,' intermediary spirits whose agency might unite pious pagans to an otherwise inaccessible Platonic God? In reply Augustine invokes Plotinus's own teaching:

> We must fly to our beloved fatherland. There is the Father, there our all. What fleet or flight shall convey us thither? Our way is, to become like God. (*Civ. dei* IX.17, citing *Enneads* I.vi.8 and ii.3)

Human estrangement from God, Augustine proceeds, cannot be a matter of measurable space, but is rather a matter of moral beauty, of "immortal purity." Thus demons (who according to the culture had diseased souls encased in immortal bodies) cannot, of necessity cannot, heal human estrangement: That requires a mediator such as the risen Jesus Christ, whose once-mortal body (by contrast with demonic ones) has united him to us, while his true divinity unites him (and with him, us) to God. Whereupon Augustine quotes a relevant New Testament verse, 1 Timothy 2:5, not offering it as an authority the pagans must acknowledge as such, but as giving fit literary expression to the truth their own cultural beliefs imply or require. Where paganism fails, Catholic doctrine succeeds (*Civ. dei* IX.18). So Augustine can recall New Platonism when he needs it even though long ago in Milan he had abandoned it for a higher form of truth. Yet he had not altogether abandoned it, for now at argument's end it plays him false. What he had retained (as indeed did practically all of his Christian contemporaries, as well as Mani and Porphyry and Plotinus) was body-soul dualism. Thus the conclusion of this part of his defense of Christianity is tinged with the old error that had shaped the Manichees' belief: the body is mortal, therefore it is polluted, defiled; only as we escape it can we conform to the likeness of God. Yet even that is not the end of the story, for by Book 14 of the *City of God* a happier theme appears: when the Word became *flesh,* mortality's corruption was overcome for us as well; thenceforth the human body is God's new creation. And in Book 22, it appears that sexual distinctiveness will be included in future, resurrected human flesh as well. Thus in the end Scripture here masters Augustine's flawed cultural context (cf. *Ethics,* Five §3).

That is the larger story of the *City of God* as well. As the work progresses and undermining gives way to overwhelming, the philosophical ground bass is sounded not by Platonism but by a new, narrative philosophy: The long narrative from Adam to the present holds everything together. Augustine becomes in the end not so much a narrative philosopher as a *narrative theologian.* Of course this contribution is not original; it is a theme present in Scripture—powerfully so in Paul, Augustine's soteriological favorite, present also in the rule of faith of early Western Christianity and the ecumenical creeds of the orthodox East. Recovering it as his main thread, Augustine finally completes the philosophical journey that has led him from his first impassioned reading of Cicero to the end of his course. He continues to juxtapose the Great Story of Scripture with the lesser great story that the Romans told themselves about themselves; he acknowledges wherever he can the truth and value of that lesser story, but in the end it must give way to a greater. Once again Peter Brown has said it best:

> Juxtaposition, indeed, is the basic literary device that determines the structure of every book of the *City of God.* Augustine deliberately uses it to contrive a 'stereoscopic' effect. The solutions of the new Christian literature must "stand out more clearly" (*Civ. dei* XV.8, 17 and XIX.1, 9) by always being imposed upon an elaborately constructed background of pagan answers to the same question. It is a method calculated to give a sense of richness and dramatic tension. This accounts for the vast appeal of the *City of God* to learned men in future ages. For, in it, Augustine moves with massive and ostentatious deliberation, from the classical into the Christian world. (1969:306)

Those who recall the mid-twentieth-century appearance of Reinhold Niebuhr's *Nature and Destiny of Man* may recall that its intention, and in some degree its achievement, was to offer just such a challenge to secular doubt. For reasons not to be listed here, Niebuhr's was a temporary achievement at best. Augustine's *City of God* endured, and it did so because more than the other (indeed, what has excelled it?) it immersed itself in the Great Story of God's way with humankind that the passionate Bishop of Hippo had made his very own. In it philosophy of history became, as early-church scholar Massey Shepherd used to say, *theology* of history. Yet the persisting Platonic dualism would recur in the following period in the thought of René Descartes.

Augustine stands both at the end of the ancient and the beginning of the medieval period of Western history. A representative account would next show the relation of philosophy to theology in subsequent medieval thinkers. Yet these successors were predominantly Augustinian (admittedly there are exceptions) until we reach the crisis of the thirteenth century occasioned by the widespread adoption of Aristotelian thought transmitted through Muslim scholars to the 'Christian' West, for it seemed to subvert such central Christian themes as the doctrines of God and creation. Then appeared Dominican scholar Albertus Magnus (Albert the Great, 1193–[or 1206–]1280), who set out to adapt Aristotelian thought to the received Augustinian tradition. In this Albert was followed and surpassed by his pupil Thomas Aquinas (1225–74), whose work in Albert's footsteps initiated the tradition we know as Thomism: Augustinianism modified to cohere with Aristotle rather than Plato. It is Thomas's theological response to the new philosophy, then, that should be taken up next. However I have reported that work in the preceding volume (*Doctrine,* Seven §2*b*), so that here it would be redundant.

§2. Modernity in Search of Itself

a. The standard account of modernity.—Passing so briefly over the High Middle Ages is doubtless a defect in this chapter, but it would have been counted a positive virtue until very recently. Stephen Toulmin (1990:13-17) recounts the picture of Western progress that was current in his own youth in Great Britain between the two World Wars. According to this account, taught even to children in school and taken for granted by virtually all thinkers of the time, modernity, arriving in the 1600s, had *replaced* the outworn Middle Ages. Before that, so this standard account had it, the dual authorities of the church and the secular arm of society had wickedly impeded progress. But at last René Descartes (1596–1650) in philosophy and Isaac Newton (1642–1727) in science had broken the bars of the premodern intellectual prison. Descartes had shown that science and philosophy alike rested not on churchly authority but on a self-authorizing rationality ("I think, therefore I am," etc.). Newton had given material content to the Cartesian argument by joining mathematics to empirical observations in order to explain at a stroke the operation of mechanical nature, from the path of a projectile to the revolutions of the solar system—explaining, as it were, the knowable world entire. Later, Alexander Pope would celebrate the Newtonian achievement in a couplet:

> Nature and Nature's laws lay hid in night;
> God said, *Let Newton be!* and all was light. (Epitaph for Isaac Newton, 1730)

Trusting this picture, Toulmin recalled, the twentieth-century heirs of Descartes (and of Spinoza and Leibniz, other pioneers of modern rationalism) were confident that the end of the Middle Ages had meant the end of superstition along with fanaticism and bigotry—a confidence in 'progress,' by the way, that was about to be tested by the reappearance of exactly those elements in the twentieth-century Nazi phenomenon.

Toulmin sees this standard version of the scientific rationalism of modernity very closely linked with the political rise of the nation-state. France, Germany, and England had come to political self-consciousness in this very period, the 1600s, later followed by the United States, Japan, and Russia (Toulmin, 1990:7). Ironically, many today regard the terrifying power of these nation-states, with their deadly military strength and their economic clout, as a chief threat to the well-being of humanity; many long for some new political system, less chauvinistic, less arrogant, and less dangerous to human well-being, that might bring to an end the era of the nation-state just as this system had previously supplanted the Holy Roman Empire. What form the replacement should take remains less clear.

In contrast to those 1930s cultural optimists, but in step with the close observers of today who realize that political modernity is in serious trouble, there seem now to be certain broad areas of agreement about the surviving culture of modernity: These are (1) what most today know as modern times indeed began (philosophically, scientifically, politically) in the seventeenth century, the 1600s; (2) modernity so understood has lost much of its credibility in the eyes of the best thinkers of today; and therefore (3) a wholesale change of times is in order and already under way. This third agreed point is now commonly hailed in connection with a rising new century, in fact a new millennium, now begun. (Such an arbitrary calendar number could hardly *cause* such profound change, but it may handily symbolize it.)

What is not on all sides equally agreed is what the replacement for modernity is to be. Three options appear: that the world is now entering a *postmodern* era quite unlike what has ever gone before; or that the need of the future is merely an *extension of modernity*, cleansed of undesirable elements so that it can return to the Enlightenment heritage of Immanuel Kant (thus says German philosopher Jürgen Habermas); or that it is time to recover *'premodern' elements* that were submerged beneath modernity's seventeenth-century wave. In effect, Toulmin argues for the third of these: What the other alternatives, continuing modernity or radical postmodernity, neglect, he says, is that the preceding century was no longer merely medieval: in Europe *between* the Middle Ages and Descartes came a lively Renaissance which displayed valuable features that later modernity unwisely discarded. The teachers (and presuppositions) of Toulmin's youth were to that extent wrong; Cartesian modernity never deserved its high billing, but was in human worth a step down from still earlier modern times.

The Renaissance was the period of giants of human thought such as Shakespeare, Erasmus, and Montaigne; it was the age of the voyages of discovery by Columbus and Vasco da Gama; it was the age in which printed books liberated readers from the dead weight of expensive, hand-copied manuscripts; it was the age in which new forms of art (Leonardo, Botticelli), music (the madrigal, instrumental ensembles), architecture (the passing of the gothic), and science (the freedom to replace old paradigms with new) appeared. Replacing the medieval sense of seamless continuity with the past, there came between 1450 and 1599 a new sense of time providing perspective on the nearer past by comparing it with the 'Golden Age' of antiquity. The Renaissance looked back to Rome and Greece (and in some cases to the Bible) as an age in which human life was more authentically human. Whether Toulmin is right or not in his choice of the correct successor to modernity, his claim for the importance of the Renaissance is worth attention here.

b. The Renaissance and the baptists.—Humanist scholars mined the witness of antiquity with the ambition of the space explorers of a later day. They labored not out of mere curiosity, but in hope of recovering lost human good. The Italian poet and scholar Petrarch (1304–74) set the standard for his successors: Aristotelian theory had not fulfilled its promise, Petrarch thought, and must be revised: A new rhetoric must teach men and women to love virtue and hate vice. Such persuasive eloquence must be combined with the study of history, where examples would show the needed moral truth, and with grammar, which would guide effective expression. Poetry had its role: its beauty pointed listeners toward the required moral goals. "Combined in this fashion, the *studia humanitatis* constituted a program of moral reform designed to motivate people to aspire to that dignity uniquely theirs as beings created in the image of God" (Friesen, 1998:23). It was a program that with changes appropriate to their competence could be adopted by the baptists, a radical company just then appearing.

Indeed, by the 1500s alignment with Renaissance thought affected most forms of European Christianity. The Catholic humanists, Lutheran Evangelicals, and Calvinist Reformed Christians all made use of Renaissance scholarship (for example, in the recovery of texts of Scripture and the Church Fathers), and most (though not all) believed that the return to a Golden Age would repair the sickness they perceived in the Christianity of their time. In detail, of course, there were great differences among these Christians, and much hung on them. Certainly Martin Luther (1483–1546) and John Calvin (1509–64) each recognized that new times had come demanding new ways of thought. Luther fashioned a new-style Christianity centered upon the individual's eternal salvation, which was to come *sola fide, sola gratia, sola scriptura* (by faith alone, from grace alone, through Scripture alone). He never wrote a dogmatic *summa,* but expressed himself by commentaries, sermons, and tracts, full of piercing evangelical insights and striking paradoxes. Calvin met the new age rather differently, composing *Institutes* that in successive editions presented a mature theoretic of Reformed faith, relating everything in Augustinian fashion to the majesty of the triune God, the enigma of fallen man, and gracious salvation in Christ. A more relevant case for us is Calvin's Swiss predecessor by a generation, Huldreich Zwingli (1484–1531), a Catholic priest and a disciple of Erasmus the humanist. Zwingli meant by his preaching and writing to return his Zurich congregation to New Testament patterns, employing the new Renaissance scholarship. Loyal Catholics responded to all these other reformers by emphasizing the role of tradition alongside Scripture and the historic connection between the original revelation and current church teaching. While these were all creative responses to new times, they left important questions about church life and the church's relation to culture unanswered. There was room (and from our point of view, need) for another, still more radical, approach.

The case of Zwingli gives a clue here because his parishioners included young Conrad Grebel (c. 1498–1526), son of a patrician Zurich family, student of the humanist Vadian, and reader of other humanists including the influential Erasmus, who had taught at Basel during Grebel's student year there. Grebel was destined to become the first baptist in modern times. After a profligate student life in Basel, Vienna, and Paris, he returned to his family home, got into fresh scrapes, and married against his family's wishes. Meantime, though, he had become

Zwingli's regular hearer, and in the spring of 1522 Conrad Grebel underwent a profound evangelical conversion. Transformed, he became Zwingli's prime follower and ultimately the leader of those who in the name of consistency were to rebel against their pastor. With them Grebel formed a little Bible study fellowship. Eventually (January 21, 1525) group members administered baptism to one another afresh, and thus to Zwingli's dismay became practicing Anabaptists who soon "went everywhere preaching the word." Mennonite historian Harold Bender protests that Grebel did not become an Anabaptist *because* he was a humanist (ME II:239f; Bender, 1950:75), which is correct as far as it goes, but no one denies the chain of events just listed. Later in the twentieth century, other historians showed persuasively that Anabaptists did not stem from Grebel's group alone ('monogenesis'); rather they appeared here and there ('polygenesis'), diverse in conduct and doctrine, but sharing (at the very least) the renewed practice of baptizing only converted believers (ME 5:23-26; cf. *Doctrine,* pp. 341f). This polygenetic account of baptist origins can hardly be the last word, either, for it leaves many urgent questions unanswered, yet it opens a way to the point being made here: there were (*pace* Bender) close parallels between the early baptists and the spirit of the Renaissance that Stephen Toulmin invokes.

Consider as a prime but not singular example baptist connections with the famous humanist, Desiderius Erasmus of Rotterdam (1466?–1536). Since Erasmus's positions on restitution and reform did not coincide with their own understandings, his influence upon Anabaptism was often denied by recent scholars. Yet the baptists shared with Erasmus a spirit of inquiry and a yearning for Christian renewal that set both of them apart from reformers whose main concern was to re-establish Christendom. Significantly, Erasmus minimized the role of the priesthood, promoted pacifism, and made a return to a New Testament style of Christianity the heart of the matter. Take as a primary item Erasmus's attitude to baptism. While never renouncing the received Catholic practice (which permitted baptism of infants), he was deeply dissatisfied with it and in search of a better. Zwingli and his rebellious followers could reasonably have gleaned from one edition of Erasmus's widely circulated *Paraclesis* the impression "that the great biblical scholar wished, in an ideal Christian world, for a baptism based upon an understanding of, and voluntary personal commitment to, the Christian faith" (Friesen, 1998:45).

Bastard son of a Dutch Catholic priest and his mistress, perhaps self-named since he came by none legally (Desiderius and Erasmus are respectively rooted in the Latin and Greek words for erotic love), educated in an excellent school run by the Brethren of the Common Life (emphasizing Christian living ahead of church law and theological doctrine), ordained a priest and taking the vows of an Augustinian monk, released from monastic duties to pursue a career in letters, further educated at Paris, Milan (where he earned a doctorate), and more briefly elsewhere, pioneer editor, translator, and exegete of the Greek New Testament, Hebraist, humanist, popular author, Continental traveler, one of the best-known men of his times, Erasmus brought to expression in his full life some of the central concerns of his day. Toward the end of an ironic little book titled *The Praise of Folly*, in which he lampoons all the stock characters of the era—popes, kings, bishops, noblemen, priests, monks, scholars (he was far from sparing himself from ridicule)—Erasmus contrasts the popular attitude to the eucharist ("the common people think there's no more in that sacrifice than to be present at the altar, and crowd next to it, to have a noise of words and look [upon] the ceremonies") over against what he considered a faithful Christian view: "[T]he death of Christ is represented by it, which all men, vanquishing, abolishing, and, as it were, burying their carnal affections, ought to express in their lives and conversations, that they may grow up to a newness of life, and be one with him, and the same one amongst another" (1509:249f).

Renaissance historian Abraham Friesen gives evidence for the influence of Erasmus upon the baptists of his day, listing both points of doctrinal similarity and evidence of direct influence. One similarity addresses a recurrent question of Christology: How Christlike are Christians' lives to be? (cf. *Doctrine,* Part II, Intro.). The standard baptist answer is well known: the imitation of Christ, *Nachfolge Christi,* is a central baptist theme. Others in Erasmus's day were satisfied with a less self-involving answer, but as an Augustinian monk inclined toward Augustine's sort of Platonism, he understood the Ideal Forms or Archetypes to have been fulfilled in Christ. That sheds light on Erasmus's observation: "If we would be holy, we must go to the sole archetype of godliness, Christ himself. Anyone who refuses to do this is outside the pale" (*Enchiridion,* cited in Friesen, 1998:26). Behind this christological conviction stands also his education by the Brethren of the Common Life, the fellowship that produced the anonymous *Imitation of Christ.*

Not that Erasmus was a covert baptist. On the contrary, he condemns them—in terms that reveal regrettably little direct acquaintance with the radicals' faith and practice (Friesen, 1998:28). Yet on one point there was a direct line of connection. Erasmus's Greek and Latin New Testaments (1516, 1519, 1522), which showed that Jerome's Vulgate was not the last word in texts and translations, with Erasmus's added *Annotations,* notably his vernacular paraphrases of the Gospels and of Acts, came into the hands of the radical leaders and soon became for them standard tools. In these biblical works Erasmus was relatively free of the inherited weight of Augustinian theology and Platonic philosophy; in gospel light the Platonic modes of thought were diminished and evangelical truth prevailed. "It was in the *Paraclesis* [helps for readers of his Latin New Testament and published with it] that Erasmus proffered the proposition that the Bible, especially the New Testament—not the church—alone contained the 'eternal wisdom' from which one could derive a true theology" (Friesen, 1998:44f).

Erasmus's publisher bound together with his freshly translated Latin New Testament the *Annotations* just mentioned, a commentary including paraphrases of New Testament books. These Latin paraphrases were soon translated into vernacular as well. In these *Annotations* Friesen finds the tightest link of all: Erasmus treated the final verses of Matthew 28 (known to us as the Great Commission) as the authority for the evangelical activity of the apostles recorded in Acts, which in turn (according to Erasmus) was the proper model for Christianity in every age. Friesen argues that this Erasmian Renaissance interpretation of the Great Commission was a novel recovery of its original meaning (a claim confirmed by David Bosch in Shenk, ed., 1983:218-48), and that it was adopted from Erasmus by the South German Anabaptists (Mantz, Hubmaier), by Hutterites (Walpot), and independently by Menno (Friesen, 1998:53-65). Hence missionary obedience became the active focus of sixteenth-century baptist energy (Littell, 1952:117-27; C. J. Dyck in Brauer, ed., 1968:218) and is a key example of the baptist vision in practice (*Ethics,* One; see further Chapter Nine below).

The connection between Erasmus and the Anabaptists has been questioned because Erasmus has been remembered as a mere moralist or mystic, yet Friesen shows from Erasmus's own writings that more broadly, he was a New Testament Christian. This illustrates and supports the main point being made here: The baptists of the sixteenth century were children of the Renaissance. Their return to origins was the central motif of their own times; their call for an authentic Christian morality was the very goal of contemporary humanists; their persisting (and if need be, defiant) Christian faith appeared in the midst of an age of renewed faith. Like Christians at other times facing current philosophies, those who encountered early philosophical modernity made more than one response to it. For their part, the radicals found in the cultural themes of their times ways to be faithful to the gospel of Jesus Christ that they had rediscovered. It was a costly rediscovery. It obliged them to face persecution and death, just as their Master had done long before. Yet their acceptance of the suffering, their *Gelassenheit* (yieldedness), was the corollary of their engagement in (rather than any withdrawal from) the life of their age. Later, some descendants of the radicals were driven by persecution into Hutterite or Amish isolation. Not so the earliest baptists; their outgoing love for their neighbors expressed itself in sharing the very means of life—including the means of eternal life. As Mennonite historian C. J. Dyck writes,

> Their missionary zeal was not motivated by a stiff and arid obedience to the divine command but characterized by a genuine love for people and a real desire to see them in the kingdom. Their sharing of material possessions with the needy was a logical corollary of this compassion, a footnote to authenticate their profession of faith and love. (Dyck in Brauer, ed., 1968:228)

c. Christianity and modernity in tension.—If we accept the view that modernity began not once but twice (Toulmin), we need now to take a fresh look at its second wave. For it is this second, less free, more totalizing beginning in the seventeenth century that the standard account hails as the true modernity, yet its onset produced a culture that was most problematic for Christians. This is the age of Descartes and Newton, each of whom set out to organize all human knowledge in an inclusive philosophical and mathematical framework. As a historian of ideas, Stephen Toulmin realizes that his view of the matter is revisionist and is still rejected by many. Yet Christian scholarship has a strong motive to pursue Toulmin's underlying theme: Philosophical modernity from Descartes and Locke to Hume and Kant created a crisis that challenged free Christian existence. This hardly needs to be demonstrated: The history of recent Christianity, to borrow Kenneth Scott Latourette's title, has been "advance through storm." Christians made many an intellectual sacrifice in meeting the crisis, sometimes giving up convictions dearly held, though these defensive gambits often issued in further loss and even despair. The modernity identified by the standard account was so unfriendly to Christian life and thought that a challenge to its sway has been a commonplace of recent Christian theology. Europe, once nominally Christian from Spain to the Urals, has become in our day a mission field, and indeed wherever in the world Enlightenment secularity has spread, to America and Japan for examples, the Enlightenment crisis of faith—religious doubt, the loss of meaning in religious language, a reductive metaphysics of the human self—reappears. So much is this so that in a great turnabout from their longer history (see §1 above), some sincere Christians have supposed the separation between faith and philosophy to be permanent and necessary.

My own view is different. While standard-account modernity certainly created great difficulties for Christian belief, this adversity had its sweet uses as well. Moreover, Cartesian modernity no longer monopolizes the scene, so that the long episode through which the church has passed now recedes into the past, perhaps valued or regretted but no longer the unique threat to Christian existence. To see matters this way, though, requires that with Toulmin we recognize standard-account modernity not as the achievement of timeless philosophical truth but as a contingent response to the circumstances of its own time. The rise of seventeenth-century philosophical rationalism coincided with the time of the Thirty Years' War, and this is but a part of a larger picture of disorder and distress. Although the standard account pictured the seventeenth century as a happy, prosperous, and civilized era in Europe, the known facts do not support the picture. The seventeenth was a century of great political instability marked by internecine wars (not only the Thirty Years' War from 1618 to 1648, but the English Civil Wars of 1642–48 as well as assorted colonial wars fought overseas by rival European powers), by severe economic depression, recurrent plagues, and deep fear of the approaching end of the world. These upheavals seemed to cry out for Christian solidarity to face them, but the reality was a divided faith, Protestant and Catholic. Leaders sought to settle these theological differences by force of arms, while radical Christians were at risk from both sides. Thus the picture of a tranquil era in which reason increasingly prevailed must be replaced by one of a torn and troubled time from which the old Renaissance spirit had vanished—so goes Toulmin's thesis (1990:5-44).

In these circumstances it is easier to see the point of the contributions of Descartes, Newton, and Leibniz. In them philosophy sought to establish a new rationality, a new, universal way of thinking that by its assurance and clarity could banish the dark clouds of human enmity and error. Their work thus addressed the immediate political and social need of their times precipitated by the breakup of trans-national European unity. Powerful nation-states ruptured that unity, backed and encouraged by rival versions of state churches that were Catholic in the South, Protestant in the North, while little middle-European princedoms became prizes contested by both sides.

> Whether for pay or from conviction, there were many who would kill and burn in the name of theological doctrines that no one could give any conclusive reason for accepting. The intellectual debate had collapsed, and there was no alternative to the sword and the torch. (Toulmin, 1990:54)

Small wonder that seventeenth-century philosophers dreamed of a universal *reason*, free of partisan politics and religion, that could restore civility and sanity.

i. The Cartesian solution.—In the quest for certainty none was ahead of René Descartes (1596–1650). Born in a small French village and educated at the Jesuit academy at La Flèche, young René learned little of the preceding era's humanism; his teachers were scholastic Aristotelians. On the other hand Descartes learned a great deal at first hand about the Thirty Years' War, which began about the time he finished his law degree. He served as a military attaché in Holland and then in Bavaria, perhaps fancying that a new military strategy would terminate Europe's woes. Ultimately, in the early 1630s, he turned his attention to devising a new philosophy. The more the political situation collapsed, the more pressing was his need to find a way to escape the doctrinal contradictions that lay behind the religious wars (Toulmin, 1990:62). Perhaps to his own surprise, Descartes in time found a better reception for his teaching in Protestant lands, and he died (at age fifty-four) while serving as tutor to young Queen Christina of Protestant Sweden.

The method of thought that had by that time made Descartes justly famous began with deliberate doubt. If one would only doubt everything that was doubtable, such as the existence of the 'external' world, suspending belief even in the existence of one's own body, what remained would surely be indubitable. So Descartes held, arguing that since what could not be doubted had to be believed, it was also necessarily true. Apparently he repeated his famous thought-experiment many times, but there was a first time to report:

> I was then in Germany [and I] was caught by the onset of winter. There was no conversation to occupy me, and being untroubled by any cares or passions, I remained all day alone in a warm room. There I had plenty of leisure to examine my ideas . . . (1637:10)

The one thing that could not be doubted, he found, was his own existence.

> I soon noticed that while I thus wished to think everything false, it was necessarily true that I who thought so was something. Since this truth, *I think, therefore I am, or exist,* was so firm and assured that all the most extravagant suppositions of the skeptics

> were unable to shake it, I judged that I could safely accept it as the first principle of the philosophy I was seeking. (1637:24)

We could put Descartes's central idea this way: I doubt, but doubting is thinking, and thinking takes a thinker, and that thinker is what I call "me." Or we can employ Descartes's later, Latin version: *Cogito, ergo sum* (I think, therefore I am) is itself a "clear and distinct" idea; hence it is true. So the foundation is firm; from it further construction can follow. How is it, Descartes asked, that my mind contains the idea of God? (You and I might think it was because young René had gone to church, but that is an answer he deliberately ruled out.) After eliminating alternative explanations, "The only hypothesis left was that this idea was put in my mind by a nature that was really more perfect than I was, which had all the perfections that I could imagine, and which was, in a word, God" (1637:26). Not in every case, but in this one perfect case, one can think it only if it is really so. In two easy steps, then, Descartes went from doubting all he could doubt including the external world and the existence of God, to absolute certainty about both of these: I exist; it follows that God and the world exist. The ideas he has of the external world cannot all be illusory, since the God Descartes has proved is by definition no trickster. Admittedly, from Descartes's day onward some have found this reasoning a bit too swift. Was the original doubting adequate? Is the idea of the self, "a thinking being," really clear and distinct? And who tells us that "clear and distinct" ideas are true, anyway? In time, these difficulties became notorious among philosophers, but by then Descartes's place as the founder of standard-account modern thought was secure.

Note some features of his thought that were destined to have a long future. First, Descartes's *dualism:* He believed that his body was dubitable in a way his mind was not. He put it this way:

> For if I judge that [a piece of] wax exists because I see it, certainly it follows much more evidently that I exist myself because I see it. For it might happen that what I see is not really wax; it might also happen that I do not even possess eyes to see anything [since my eyes, like the wax, are material objects]; but it could not happen that, when I see, or what amounts to the same thing, when I think I see, I who think am not something. (1641:90)

The existence of mind is one thing that is quite secure; the existence of matter, though less evident, can be demonstrated, but how mind and matter are connected or interact is a puzzle that Descartes and his successors never satisfactorily solved. Second, note the *role of God:* Here Descartes probably intended to be a loyal son of the Catholic Church and meant his writings to support its theology. Yet his bare-bones idea of God comes down to a series of mathematical infinites, "an infinite substance, eternal, immutable, independent, omniscient, omnipotent . . . by which . . . I myself . . . have been created" (1641:101). Regrettably, this exalted Heavenly Cause of All Else is as different from the triune God of Christian faith as ancient Marduk was from JHWH; Descartes had omitted the very qualities plain Christians find central to God's godhood. Where in this reduction is God the Missionary, God who is Spirit, God who is love? It has even been argued that this barren modern theism is at the root of modern atheism (*Doctrine,* pp. 309-11, citing Michael Buckley). Third, Descartes is confident that his inner sight, glimpsing the ideas he says he "sees" in his mind's eye, is more reliable than sight itself. "Seeing is believing," we tell one another, but Descartes would not have agreed. We only suppose we see things; what we really see are our own ideas, and Descartes believed that our perceptions are secure only because God guarantees a correspondence between our mental vision and the real world—a 'guarantee' later moderns were to reject. Finally, fourth, there is his fascination with *the image of architectural construction.* As Nancey Murphy has pointed out, images of building and construction run right through the *Discourse on Method* and the *Meditations* (Murphy, 1996). In the seventeenth century, up-to-date town plans were arranged with orderly avenues and streets at regular intervals, taking the place of crooked medieval alleys; Descartes's method was meant to bring corresponding order to human thinking (*Discourse on Method,* 1637:10). And as every building has its foundation, upon which all else rests, so must human thought be built on its own 'foundations' (1637:11). These foundations, as we have seen, were the existence of Descartes's own self or at least his mind, backed by the existence of that mind's inferred Cause, the mathematically infinite God.

Note that the seventeenth century marked the first centennial of the Jesuits in Europe and was the birth century of the Puritans in England as well. In both, religious conviction issued in overseas mission, for the Jesuits, to India, China, and the Americas; for the Puritans, to what was to become the United States. Philosophically, both movements rejected the Cartesian thrust, if for opposite reasons: the Jesuits found Descartes too little the Catholic; the Puritans found him too much so. Typically, Jesuits sought to reinstate Aristotle via Aquinas. Meanwhile learned Puritans turned instead to the logic of another French philosopher, Petrus Ramus (1515–72), who wrote voluminously against the Aristotelian syllogism, favoring instead a plain logic closely tied to vernacular speech, the common man, and the 'arguments' to be found in observed nature. This last is instructive, since it may explain why seventeenth-century Congregationalists, Quakers, and Baptists (here

Puritan-shaped) excluded Thomist proofs of God from their confessions and sermons, preferring a Ramist rhetorical style.

ii. Descartes's descendants.—The most influential philosophers after Descartes, however, continued to reject as a source of knowledge any tradition whatsoever (overlooking the fact that doing so constituted their tradition). These heirs fall into two groups: on the Continent of Europe, rationalists such as Leibniz and Kant; in Britain, empiricists such as Locke, Berkeley, and Hume. In summarizing the second-wave position they all shared, it is important not to overlook these philosophers' differences from one another, and important, too, to recall that like Descartes they were children of their own time and place.

Mentioning a member of each group, the empiricists and the rationalists, may help in this recall. Empiricist philosopher *John Locke* (1632–1704) came closest to the Puritan attempt to remake church and state, yielding no ground to Catholic tradition. Son of a Puritan family, trained in scholastic philosophy at Oxford, Locke was thereafter a theorist actively engaged in the political and cultural issues of his day. This led him to two sorts of writing: In the *Essay concerning Human Understanding* (1689), his goal, à la Descartes, was to provide a deep foundation for human thought and conduct alternative to the authorities upon which European culture had so long relied. Locke's new foundation would be a combination of experience (or observation) and reflection. Like Descartes, he assumed that one's knowledge rested exclusively upon one's *ideas.* Wallace Matson notes that philosophers who begin with their own innermost thought ("inside-out" philosophers such as Descartes and Locke) usually find themselves unable to make clear how the ideas apprehend actual things (1987:275f). Nevertheless, Locke asserted, they do apprehend them. Thus at secondhand one could know about the world. Knowledge of God, on the other hand, was merely a matter of (valid and available) proof. Later critics have found Locke's an inconsistent account of how the mind works, but it fulfilled his desire, which, as Matson points out, was "to be at once Cartesian and commonsensical" (1987:321). The drive to common sense was predominant in Locke's political writings, most famously in *Two Treatises of Government* (1690). The *Second Treatise* defended a people's right to overthrow even a hereditary monarch (such as England's Catholic [!] James II) in favor of a constitutional monarchy (as in the Glorious Revolution that installed Protestant William and Mary). His argument was that since the purpose of government was the well-being of the people, when that purpose was not served, revolution was in order. Locke's influence upon the Protestant-leaning Church of England of his day is evident, and of course he was anathema to Catholics. For baptists, though, the matter is more complicated: Those Baptists and others who drifted toward eighteenth-century Unitarianism found encouragement in the *Second Treatise* to adopt a *reasonable* Christianity, by which they meant one tending toward Deism; later, Alexander Campbell, father of the Churches of Christ and Disciples of Christ movements, took similar delight in Locke's Bible-quoting reasonableness. A little earlier, in eighteenth-century America, Isaac Backus and John Leland, like President Thomas Jefferson, also found inspiration in Locke's *Second Treatise;* to the emphasis on representative government and the separation of governmental powers these Baptists added the separation of church and state, and saw it enacted in the United States Constitution's First Amendment.

While the British empiricists depended upon Descartes, even more did their Continental contemporaries do so. These differed from the British on the foundational data out of which true philosophy could be constructed (not bodily *experience* but inmost *thoughts*), but the two groups had much in common and influenced one another. *Immanuel Kant* (1724–1804), for a prime example, was deeply stirred by reading David Hume, his Scottish contemporary (Kant said Hume "interrupted my dogmatic slumber"), even though Kant remained throughout his life in his native city of Königsberg on the Baltic. Both, as sons of the Cartesian turnabout, were determined to liberate Enlightened Europeans from the old bondage represented by the church and its doctrines. They each saw their times in much the same way, yet Hume was early on branded a skeptic and drew so much ecclesiastical wrath that his main writings on religion (the *Dialogues,* the *Natural History of Religion*) could not be published during his lifetime, while Kant, entertaining many like thoughts, came to be regarded as "the philosopher of Protestantism," and eventually a great part of Christian thought was affected by his work. Indeed, the attraction seems to have been mutual: Kant found Christian morality attractive; he even hailed an austere concept of God as "the Ideal of pure reason"; and in what may have seemed good Lutheran fashion he wrote in the Preface to the second edition of his *Critique of Pure Reason,* "I have found it necessary to deny *knowledge* in order to make room for *faith*" (1787:29). A more jaundiced view of what he achieved (for example in his *Religion within the Limits of Mere Reason* of 1794) is that Kant effaced there the ancient landmarks of Christian conviction, replacing them with a bare Enlightenment moralism.

The metaphysical foundation of this heavy reconstruction of both human knowledge and human morality was for Kant as for Descartes the solitary, thinking self. Yet where Descartes, earnestly doubting, vaulted from his indubitable existing self to a provable external world and its Creator, Kant asked what transcendental truths must obtain (what must be the case) if the self was to know the external world. These truths turned out to be the forms of space and time, and a neat dozen 'categories' (such as cause and effect) by which thought understands things. So far, so good: now Kant, like Descartes, had a world. But Descartes was mistaken, according to Kant, to believe that God could be proved from any starting point in pure reason. God could be acknowledged only as a "postulate of the practical [i.e., moral] reason." Though strictly speaking unknowable, God, like human freedom itself, had to be presumed, since morality required both God and freedom.

For theology, Hume was not the bombshell; Kant was. Most believed Hume could be refuted somehow. But the quiet, methodical Königsberg professor, pious to external view, altered all thinking about religion, at least in Protestant lands. Wherever Kant's critical idealism prevailed, modern thinking found that the Christianity it had been practicing was an embarrassment. Religion had supposed it possessed real knowledge of a living God, yet in Kantian philosophy, God was classed with the unknowable things-in-themselves, experiential religion was a contradiction in terms, and Kant offered in their place only an austere morality of duty.

Thus for two centuries not only Locke and Hume and Kant but dozens of other earnest thinkers worked out the heritage of Descartes. Their original goal—a universal mode of thought that could heal Europe's theological and political enmities—was largely forgotten. Anyway, as a political solution the project failed: Europe at the end of the eighteenth century was just as divided into rival camps as it had been at the beginning of the seventeenth. Nonetheless, this second wave of modernity had profound consequences for Christianity. As already noted, some of the modern philosophers were very nearly canonized as intellectual saints by Protestant theologians (e.g., Kant by Schleiermacher and Ritschl), and eventually Catholics, too, were strongly affected by this second wave of modernity (consider the line of influence from Kant to Maréchal to Karl Rahner). Yet whether Christian thought internalized these philosophers or repudiated them (as it so avidly repudiated Hume), their work set an obstacle (a wide ditch, in a phrase from Lessing) in the path of any Christian thinker.

Several years ago (1989) Nancey Murphy and I listed some of the distinctive features that marked this second modernity, distinguishing it from both earlier and later thought. All these features had created difficulties for Christian theology, and some remain barriers to this day. *First,* all the modern thinkers just listed, and others like them, were preoccupied with the problem of *certainty.* The 'probable' conclusions based on authority that had satisfied premoderns would no longer do. Descartes doubted in order to find the *un*doubtable. Whatever that turned out to be, it was expected to provide a known foundation, a certain basis, on which everything else of human value could be reconstructed as necessary. Such a foundation must be universally available, unquestionable, utterly certain. For Descartes, this foundation was the thinking self, the *cogito;* for Locke it was normally observation, what anyone could experience, the facts. For Kant it was the mind's rational understanding, and after that the judgments of the moral and aesthetic self. *Second,* all these thinkers were concerned with making the instrument of knowledge, that is, *language,* a reliable instrument, and they tried to do this by linking words and world tightly together. They hung everything on what we might call the labeling moment in language, its representative role. Kant's first task, in his First Critique, was to establish the zone in which *understanding* was legitimate. This was the zone of space, time, and the categories (which were themselves distilled from the structure of grammar). To leave that zone was to go beyond the limit of the knowable. Locke, likewise, and before him Descartes, taught that for universal knowledge to prevail, the language that represented it must be universally available. *Third,* an implicit metaphysic (now not in these philosophers' sense of the term but in our Collingwoodian, historical sense) underlay all their work, namely the conviction that everything human could be reduced to the human *individual,* and more broadly that such reductions, whether in science or politics or philosophy itself, were the name of modernity's game. Each of these tendencies contrasts with the dominant medieval view of the matter: for the Middle Ages, truth and certainty lay in *authority,* language functioned (on the realist view) by *participation* in that which it represented, and reality was not atomistic but formed a *hierarchy.* On the other hand, Descartes lingering in his warm room on that favored occasion exemplifies to perfection all three modern tendencies: He rejected authority in order to find foundational certainty; his clear and distinct ideas were representable in clear words; finally, he staked all upon the solitary, atomic individual. That self thinks; therefore it is, and all else follows. Of course, before long each of these three features of modern thought would be challenged by other moderns.

iii. A third wave of modernity.—The Enlightenment was not without its critics. Not only were there negative Christian reactions (one of which, as noted, was to reject Enlightened modernity *tout court*); there was that diverse tribe, the Romantics. Kant's student J. G. Herder, with others such as Schlegel and Novalis among philosophers, Schleiermacher among theologians, and Goethe, Coleridge, and Emerson among literary folk, sought to correct the representative or word-thing theory of language and the preoccupation with doubt and certainty of the High Enlightenment. The Romantics embraced expressivist theories of language, and organic or holist theories of human nature. In the Romantics' steps, but more sweeping in his claims, more radical in his criticism of the Enlightenment, and better attuned to the long claims of human history, came G. W. F. Hegel, bringing with him a third wave of modernity that, more than the first or even the second, proposed remodeling both Christianity and society, a goal later adopted in parts of the Two-Thirds World of Marxist revolution and Liberation Theology.

Georg Wilhelm Friedrich Hegel (1770–1831), son of a minor Stuttgart bureaucrat, took up a theological vocation and studied theology and classical languages at Tübingen, but was little satisfied with what he learned there. Engaged as a tutor at Bern and later Frankfurt, he began to write essays that sketched a revisionary Christianity, based on the teaching of Jesus but rejecting later dogma. Moving to Jena thanks to his friend Schelling, he completed the sizable *Phänomenologie des Geistes* of 1807 (*Phenomenology of Spirit*) as an introduction to an even larger projected work of systematic philosophy. Having fled Jena to escape Napoleon's invading army, Hegel next edited a newspaper, was principal of a high school, and eventually became a professor of philosophy, first at Heidelberg, then (1818) at the new University of Berlin. By then he had become Germany's (and perhaps the world's) most famous living philosopher, and students flocked to his lectures. Among other accomplishments, his lectures on religion, together with the work of his great Berlin rival, Schleiermacher, laid down the basis of liberal Christianity for the following two centuries. In 1831 Hegel died during a cholera epidemic in Berlin; by then he was author of a difficult body of writings expounding "absolute idealism." These lines cannot well describe that vast material; at best I can provide some clue to Hegel's controversial achievement.

Hegel scholar Charles Taylor suggests that the early (pre-Jena) Hegel had already adopted three reference points: (1) expressivism in human life and language, (2) the Kantian drive to a free, that is, self-sustaining, morality, and (3) the Christian religion (1975:51). The writings of the young Hegel were meant to reconcile these—a difficult undertaking, to say the least. By the Jena period, he had achieved some resolution, at least to his own satisfaction, and the subsequent major writings continued his effort to produce a philosophy that subsumed all things (God, history, nature, law, culture, art, religion, the history of philosophy, etc., etc.) in systematic coherence. Not surprisingly, one of his works was titled *Encyclopedia.*

All these features set Hegel at variance with the philosophers of the second wave (e.g., Hume and Kant). Despite this, he remained a truly modern philosopher. To see this, begin by comparing his handling of the themes of the preceding modern wave. Since Descartes the search for knowledge had concentrated on absolute certainty based on an indubitable foundation, but for Hegel skepticism became only a preliminary stage in philosophy; he believed, in Wallace Matson's words, that "you cannot fully understand anything until you understand everything," but to his own satisfaction he *did* understand everything. He was thus holistic and integrative where these predecessors had been analytic (Matson, 1987:403). When it came to the philosophy of language, he and they were again at opposite poles: for their word-thing language he substituted the expressiveness he had learned from Herder, in which words with gestures and other signs brought human beings to fulfillment (see Taylor, 1975:82, 19-21). Finally, while second-wave moderns had sought reality in the human individual, following a strategy that reduced each thing to its constituent 'atoms' (irreducible fragments), Hegel looked for wholes without which the parts could not be understood. Thus it was not individual man, but *Geist* (the concrete, historical human reality viewed as a whole) that in Hegel's philosophy was the actual subject.

Geist (literally, spirit or mind) is for Hegel a technical term, difficult to match to any single English word, but referring to the evolving human reality in its historical development. On the one hand, Hegel understood *Geist* as the actual human race in all its diverse parts, viewed throughout time and space. On the other, *Geist* is also the Absolute, that is, God, but this is not the unique personal God of the Bible, but a God who grows with and expresses himself only in what actually takes place in the course of world history. God knows himself, for example, only in the growing self-awareness of the collective human spirit, which culminated (to that point) in post-Enlightenment Europe.

So it is proper to call Hegel a 'modern' philosopher if, but only if, we recognize that his third-wave modernity completed the second wave by (as he would say) contradicting or negating it in order to fulfill it (his technical term is *Aufhebung*—"cancellation and fulfillment"), or as we might prefer to say, by confronting the Enlightenment with its polar opposite: total affirmation replacing their doubt, expressivist form replacing their representative language, the collective reality preempting the individual. On this last topic Hegel, like the later Structuralists, was so far correct—we only see a thing complete, define it, by seeing as well what it is not.

Even the book-length summaries of Hegel's philosophy are intrinsically controversial: he was either helplessly ambiguous or he was deliberately so. Consequently his later disciples soon divided into two main camps: right-wing interpreters who believed he had rescued historic Christianity from its foes, and the left-wing, including Karl Marx, who founded his own early views on a reading of Hegel. Here I intend only to recall the effect of these interpretations of Hegel upon Christian thought, thus continuing this chapter's theme.

iv. Christian reactions to modernity.—So far I have omitted any specific reference to the effect of second-wave modernity upon the baptist movement (save that John Locke's political philosophy resurfaced in the thought of Baptists Backus and Leland in America). But what of Locke's discounting of miracle, or Hume's deep religious skepticism, or Kant's reduction of religion to morality? Could seventeenth-century baptists make no response to these ventures? The answer is that in the main they did not even try. If one consults, for example, the most influential Baptist confessions of that century and the next, such as the First (1644) and Second (1677) London Confessions of the Particular Baptists, or the Philadelphia Confession (1742) of American Baptists (Lumpkin, 1969:149-70; 235-94; 348-52), one finds not a hint that their makers had been reading modern philosophy from Descartes to Kant. Why not? Toulmin suggests that it was a matter of social location. England, first home of the seventeenth-century Baptists, had been torn apart by a civil war, and the eventual restoration of monarchy and the Church of England to their places relegated Baptist and other dissenters to a separate stratum of the national life. Excluded from Oxford and Cambridge, these non-conformists could receive advanced education only in their own academies. "After 1700, then, the framework of [second-wave] modernity did not carry equal conviction, in England and France, with people of *all kinds and classes*" (Toulmin, 1990:123). Instead, these seventeenth- and eighteenth-century confessions were still preoccupied with *sixteenth-century* (i.e., first-wave) modernity, with its appeal to religious liberty and its Renaissance-style return to the sources, notably to Scripture.

It should not be concluded from the silence on this point of early Baptist (and other dissenting) confessions of faith, though, that the influence of more recent modernity was not at work. For the philosophers had signaled what was in the air of modernity itself, and that air was breathed by baptists as by others. Thus (to bring the story along to the present) second-wave modernity's quest for *foundations* eventually found expression among many Christians in the dual foundationalisms of the rival liberal and fundamentalist movements (cf. Murphy, 1996: Part I). Modern reliance upon a referential theory of language (cf. again Locke) was reflected positively in the role of narrative experience displayed in baptist piety (singing "I love to tell the story"), but negatively in a thin and diminishing discourse about God that all but evaporated the Christian mystery, while the religious individualism of modernity captured both these threads and wound them together in a new metaphysical individualism (as in E. Y. Mullins's "soul competency"—see Freeman et al., 1999:chap. 34).

To come now to the trajectory of third-wave modernity as it affected the Christian churches, we must return to Hegel's view of freedom. Recall that for Hegel the acting subject is no longer, as for Kant, the moral self that dares to think for itself, standing as it were outside the phenomenal world to act according to a categorical imperative. Hegel's 'subject' is the collective *Geist,* the corporate human spirit moving through history. Freedom, though still prized, is therefore no longer the moral independence of each individual: freedom becomes the power of the social community to realize its destiny, to fulfill its role as *Geist.* And such communal freedom may very well entail the constraint of individual members of society: jail such dissenters! Despite this evident social conservatism, Hegel's idealism became the philosophy of choice of European freedom movements after his day. Lewis White Beck, commenting on this anomaly, reminds us that "no philosophy of the nineteenth century before Nietzsche's was more Heraclitean, dynamic, or evolutionary than Hegel's" (*Enc. Phil.,* 3:304). And this was just the sense of it that was eventually appropriated by twentieth-century Liberation Theology. Thus Puerto Rican theologian Orlando E. Costas writes:

> It should be pointed out that this obsession with the [second-wave] Enlightenment as an intellectual challenge to faith . . . revolved around the issue of freedom from authority through reason. This obsession is shared by practically all Euro-American theologies. . . . Their primary concern has been the skeptic, atheist, materialist-heathen—the non-religious person. This is why the second phase of the Enlightenment [our third wave] associated with the nineteenth-century movement of freedom from political, cultural, economic, and social oppression has been in the main a peripheral issue in Euro-American theology, including Evangelical theology. Yet this is one issue of fundamental impor-

tance in the theological agenda of the Two-Thirds World. (Costas in Freeman et al., 1999:381f, emphasized)

In Latin America, Liberation Theology was largely Roman Catholic; in Africa it was both Catholic and Protestant; on both continents it was also a baptist movement, as Baptist theologian Orlando Costas's contribution evidences. In all these cases the third wave took effect upon Christians in the Southern Hemisphere; only from there did it spread to various northern liberation movements such as feminist and African American theologies. In its original homes it flourished, thereby becoming part of Hegel's heritage. Consequently, a general word of caution is here in order: Rooted in Hegel (though more nearly in Hegel's left-wing follower Karl Marx), while Liberation Theology enjoyed the strength of this sort of modernity, it inherited some of its weaknesses as well. In my own judgment, on balance this wedding to third-wave modernity dilutes any form of Liberation Theology, just as their bondage to second-wave modernity has diminished the European American theologies of the recent past (see further Chapter Eight).

§3. After Modernity, What?

During the time that theologies of liberation were flourishing in the Two-Thirds World, while meantime analytic philosophy reigned supreme in the universities of Britain and North America, a different series of developments, linguistic, literary, political, anthropological, and philosophical, formed intellectual leadership on the European continent, especially in France. The wellspring of these French developments was Swiss theorist Ferdinand de Saussure (1857–1913), whose theory of language came to be known as structuralism. Under that label he cast a wide influence across academic and intellectual fields for half a century or more. As the twentieth century moved to its close, structuralism spawned a counter-movement, best labeled poststructuralism, that in one form or another attracted leading Continental thinkers. Earlier in the century existentialism had protested the grand European tradition that ran from Descartes to Husserl, but by mid-century it had reached its terminus in the late work of Heidegger and Sartre. There was space for a new departure. My own brief account of structuralism and poststructuralism appears in the second edition of *Convictions* (*CONV.*:chap. 2), so that I will not repeat it here. Many felt that if not through structuralism, at least in poststructuralism philosophy had fully overturned the great European heritage; modernity was therefore over, it was 'deconstructed'; postmodern times had come. Some philosophers in the United States such as philosopher-become-literary-critic Richard Rorty and some literary critics such as Stanley Fish found the Continental postmodernists compelling; in their work the movement crossed the Atlantic, and in this country as in Europe it won adherents in all fields, not only in English literature but in history, economics, and politics as well. By the 1960s there were postmodern power centers in American universities, notably at Yale and Duke. Before long, theologians and other professors of religion in the United States were reading this transplanted Continental postmodernism and invoking its conclusions as their own. It was at about this stage that Nancey Murphy and I wrote the paper mentioned above, offering some rough guidelines for distinguishing any authentic postmodernity from its less qualified rivals. The thesis we worked out there may still be useful here (Murphy and McClendon, 1989).

a. Continental postmodernism.—First, then, a selective look at Continental postmodernism, asking whether it is better to think of it as a continuation of modernity proper (perhaps a fourth wave?) or whether some forms of European poststructuralism actually introduced a new era in thought.

Jean-François Lyotard, one of the leading figures in the post-structuralist and postmodern discussions, was born in Versailles, France, in 1924, and trained with Merleau-Ponty in phenomenology. He began teaching in 1952 in Algeria, and after that at the University of Paris. In the 1960s he was associated with a Marxist group, and at other times he was influenced by earlier thinkers: Freud, Nietzsche, and (especially) Kant. Lyotard was present in Paris during the 1968 upheavals in which students demanded academic and administrative reform that would make the educational system more humane and less bureaucratic; the students were partly successful, and in any case the event made a deep imprint upon Lyotard's own life and thought. Most recently he has taught philosophy at a branch of the (reorganized) University of Paris (viii), located in the suburb of Vincennes. He has also taught widely in the United States, filling visiting lectureships and guest professorships at a number of American universities. He is perhaps not so colorful as Derrida, or so outrageous as the fictional postmodernist, Doctor Mensonge (Bradbury, 1987), but Lyotard's very stability and accessibility make him for us a fair example of Continental postmodernity. (Concerned readers might go on from Lyotard to the even more influential thought of Michel Foucault [1926–84] and Jacques Derrida [1930–].)

Omitting much, I present three theses that the mature Lyotard would likely stand by and that other Continental philosophers might in large measure find congenial:

1. *The alterity thesis (difference):* Human reality is significantly different in its various occurrences over time and place, so that generalizations about the human condition [except possibly this one?] are never in order, since they inevitably obscure the differences their generality is meant to embrace.

2. *The linguistic thesis (pragmatics):* As is fit in a world of 'alterity,' pragmatic human utterance *(parole)* is characteristically complex, issuing not only in a variety of natural languages with their grammars and vocabularies, but in a variety of 'speech acts' and 'language games' by means of which human beings act linguistically. Consequently, the Cartesian quest for foundational certainty is rejected.

3. *The metaphysical thesis (against metanarratives):* No single metanarrative (or philosophical master story) or combination of metanarratives is now possible for advanced European society; with the loss of such presiding metanarratives, metaphysical philosophy and the universities that have sustained it are also discredited and must undergo radical change or perish.

I propose only to say enough about these theses to clarify Lyotard's relation to historic modernity, especially his relation to its second (seventeenth-century) and third (nineteenth-century) waves. Do the theses disclose him as a truly *post*modern thinker, a primal member of a new breed? Or does Lyotard only extrapolate one or more of the previous surges of modernity, perhaps outdoing them as a "mostmodern" philosopher? (Griffin et al., 1989:143). My plan is to answer by reviewing in turn the concerns that Murphy and I found typical of second- and third-wave modernity, starting with the primacy of epistemology. Is certainty available to human thought in Lyotard's postmodernity?

This is the central question of a much-read Lyotard essay (1984). There can be little question that he works here as a conscious *heir* of ongoing modernity from Descartes to Jürgen Habermas, with special concentration upon Kant. The modern tradition, Lyotard believes, founded its truths upon certain grand fundaments, or "metanarratives." Nowadays, though, it is no longer suitable to invoke these (or any other) foundations: in fact, postmodernity can quite simply be defined as "incredulity toward metanarratives." So it would seem that Lyotard is related to epistemic modernity only as a rebel who rejects its chief claim. He says that our knowledge has been captured by a culture that provides it with a new technological logic: now, for example, input-output matrixes control education itself. Society's decision makers "allocate our lives for the growth of [their own] power"; their standard is efficiency rather than truth; following that standard, they will necessarily employ *terror.* To be aware of this historic cultural change *is* to enter "the postmodern condition" (1984:xxiv). Now existence separates into its particles; the unifying whole can no longer be found, does not exist.

Assessing this, recall that the seventeenth-century theme of epistemic certainty arose against a background of profound uncertainty, and brought this disquiet with it into more recent troubled times (cf. Nietzsche). Its epistemic stance was polar from the outset: either skepticism or fundamental certainty. In this regard, Lyotard has only positioned himself on the side of the inherited *un*certainty, and indeed, measured by the skepticism of Hume's *Treatise,* Lyotard is far from extreme. Despite his claim, then, we find here only a continuation of characteristic *modern* features, choosing (as did second-wave moderns), one or the other pole or some compromise between them—in Lyotard's case, choosing modern skepticism rather than modern certainty.

When we come to Lyotard's theories of language and its utterance, though, the picture changes. For him all human utterance falls into two categories: on one hand there are the narrative language games typical of popular knowledge and traditional utterance, and on the other the scientific language games typical of advanced industrial society. By listing both these as forms of "narrative" speech, Lyotard does not mean to withdraw his objection to modernity's "metanarratives." For one thing, the surviving narratives of our species are older than philosophy's and science's "grand stories"; our traditional narratives display skills of "knowing how" (to negotiate the world) as well as skills of "knowing that" (such and such is the case). This is the shared narrative language that constitutes the social bond among human beings (1984:21). The scientific "language games," in contrast, are required for research and teaching. Their stress is upon denotation: they state the relevant scientific facts. Yet science, functioning as it does in this way, does not generate any free-standing or independent truth, for in its turn it depends "on the institutions [such as universities and government departments] within which [it must] deliberate and decide, *and which comprise all or part of the state!*" (1984:30f, emphasized). So behind pure science stand institutional (political) structures, and behind them pure terror always lurks!

As we have seen, Lyotard frequently employs the technical terms invented by J. L. Austin ("speech acts") and Ludwig Wittgenstein ("language games"). Not too much should be made of this fact, though, for Lyotard's facility with Austin's work is both limited and at crucial points mistaken. For instance, he supposes that Austin was still committed, in his mature work, to the performative-constative distinction, whereas in reality Austin withdrew this analysis as unsatisfactory at least as early as 1956, when he gave the B.B.C. talk that became later the paper "Performative Utterances" (Austin, 1961:foreword and pp. 220-40). Lyotard seems equally insecure in handling Wittgenstein's apparatus. Surprisingly, he seems to believe that speech acts and language games are equivalents—two words for a single phenomenon, namely the many uses of language! Despite these reservations, it seems clear that Lyotard's theory of language does depart from the modern track: he is thus by this measure, at least, a postmodern thinker. The best evidence of this lies not in the misused jargon, but in Lyotard's insistence on the *pragmatics* of utterance: words do things. In this regard he seems close, not to Austin and Wittgenstein, but to an earlier Dutch-American philosopher of language, Willem F. Zuurdeeg (cited in *CONV.*, 1st ed., pp. 29-35).

So far, by one of our tests, epistemology, Lyotard is some sort of modern thinker, but by another test, his language theory, he is a postmodern thinker. Which should prevail? A third test may settle the issue: Recall that seventeenth-century modernity introduced a Newtonian cosmos. In its purest form this new view was atomistic and reductionist, bringing with it both a new metaphysics of reality and new conceptions of nature and human nature. For this faltering second-wave view of reality, Hegel and his followers substituted a (still-modern) alternative, which became modernity's third wave: human reality consists, they said, in collectivities—in races, nations, religions, supremely in *Geist.* These bear the weight of history, so that a true philosophy must engage all of them. Well then, if the several waves of modernity have preempted both the individual and the collective, what option remains for postmodern thinkers? One suggestion is that authentic postmodernity presupposes as the subject of inquiry a *communal* reality, formed by intentional (rather than constrained) association. This view proposes as the bearer of human morality *communities,* not isolated selves or nameless masses (Murphy and McClendon, 1989:199). Regrettably, though, by this measure it is difficult to say where Lyotard stands. His emphasis upon the *difference* that distinguishes each of us might only signal his continued allegiance to the old Kantian-modern individualism. On the other hand, his emphasis upon the little narratives that disclose the diverse streams of checkered human life may (or may not?) suggest his turn toward a communitarian postmodernity. Certainly he rejects the dominance of the collectivities Marxism promotes. For the rest, we cannot be sure. Part of the obscurity here comes from Lyotard's employment of certain French words (such as *discours* and *recit*) that his translators with whatever justice render in each case as "narrative," even when the context makes it appear that "presupposition" or even "concept" might have been a more accurate rendering. This ambiguity cannot be resolved here. By his own measure, then, Lyotard exhibits "the postmodern condition" while by ours his may be only a marginal case. Perhaps it is more helpful to assign him, along with others on the recent Continental literary and philosophical front such as Michel Foucault, Paul De Man, Jacques Derrida, Gilles Deleuze, and the like, to a *fourth wave* of modernity, one that shares emphases with the preceding three but like them has distinctive features of its own. As Lyotard himself says (though he promptly qualifies the claim), "[T]he postmodern is undoubtedly a part of the modern" (1984:79).

b. An Anglo American postmodernity?—Consider now the strikingly different philosophical context in Britain and America which arose as part of a many-sided twentieth-century movement, *analytic philosophy.* In this frame British philosophers Gilbert Ryle (1900–1976) and J. L. Austin (1911–60) (the latter my own honored teacher), and even before them Ludwig Wittgenstein (1889–1951), a mid-century Austrian *émigré* who was eventually trapped in Britain by Nazism and war, created a new philosophical style sufficiently distinctive to imply its own 'postmodern' label—they created an Anglo American postmodernity (cf. Murphy, 1997). Richard Rorty, in his landmark *Philosophy and the Mirror of Nature,* claims, in fact, that philosophers from three different twentieth-century traditions, namely *Wittgenstein,* who emerged from British-Austrian philosophical analysis, *John Dewey,* a leader among American pragmatists, and *Martin Heidegger,* whose formation had come from European phenomenology via Husserl, each underwent at mid-career a significant postmodern shift, discarding the received assumptions of late modernity on which each had been weaned to adopt instead, in surprising parallel, new modes of thought (Rorty, 1979:5ff). David Griffin has more recently claimed a similar status for process philosopher A. N. Whitehead (1861–1947), but Griffin's criteria for postmodernity differ from ours (Griffin et al., 1989:141-44). Since I cannot pursue all these (or even Austin and Ryle) here, I leave these tasks to others. The following chapter explores Anglo American postmodernity in the life and thought of Ludwig Wittgenstein. It will come out that at least in his sort of philosophy there is a necessary link between life-narrative and philosophical labor. This is doubly interesting for us because of Wittgenstein's remarkable profession of Christian commitment. It may furnish by example a concrete answer to the question about the relation of Christianity to philosophy in our time.

* * * * *

Why does it matter what is or is not called 'postmodern'? Surely it is only a matter of nomenclature: surely the rose's scent persists, whatever language the gardener speaks? Well, the aim of this chapter has been to expose one part of the cultural setting of today's Christianity, namely, the shape of recent Western philosophy. As we have seen, some of its successive 'modernities' have presented severe challenges to modern Christianity. Such challenges have been countered with more or less success in modern Christian apologetics, and I will indicate some of these traditional responses in Chapter Seven. By then, though, it will be clear that I think Christianity has begun to meet a new sort of cultural challenge for which some strategies of 'modern' response, even current strategies, may soon be beside the point. At that stage it will be helpful to be able to distinguish the characteristics of the old modernities from some new characteristics now appearing in our culture. As long as we do *not* become prisoners of our own labels by supposing that "postmodern" just must refer to some essential quality, so long, that is, as we pay careful attention to our own use as well as others', the term can help us to make the wanted distinction between the old and new strategies required for Christian response. So while labels such as premodern and modern and postmodern are in a sense only arbitrary nomenclature, it does help to use these labels accurately in order to guide appropriate responses. So far, the lesson seems to be that "postmodern" is so variously used as to remain for many a vague term; I need to specify in the following chapter the sort of postmodernity I mean to address.

CHAPTER SIX

Ludwig Wittgenstein: A Christian in Philosophy[1]

A gap, cultural and emotional as well as intellectual and institutional, separated twentieth-century religious thought from science and philosophy. The previous chapter shows part of the reason: A declining modernity had ceased to provide thoughtful Christians with any broad matrix for their thought. Other eras had been so provided, and often this provision had seemed providential: Augustine in the fifth century drew upon and transformed Plato; Aquinas in the thirteenth relied on and transformed Aristotle; Ritschl in the nineteenth presupposed Kant, though without achieving the needed transformation of Kant's system. No comprehensive philosophy shaped more recent Christian thought in a similar way. When an effective Christian theology did appear in the past hundred years, it was likely to be the sort offered by Karl Barth, or in America by the Niebuhr brothers. Though each of these was in some measure indebted to nineteenth-century philosopher Søren Kierkegaard (1813–55), none found in him or anywhere in their own century a philosophical matrix; if anywhere, each sought this guidance in still earlier times. Hence a representative article on philosophical theology published at century's end was obliged to mention only three twentieth-century philosophical icons: Martin Heidegger (1889–1976), the German existentialist, had influenced Rudolf Bultmann.

The Kantian philosophy of Joseph Maréchal (1878–1944), a Belgian Jesuit, had launched the Transcendental Thomism of Karl Rahner and Bernard Lonergan. Alfred N. Whitehead (1861–1947), an English philosopher of mathematics become metaphysician, had charted Process Theology's early course (Brown, "Philosophical Theology," in EMCT). Compared with the famous precedents just mentioned, this list is not impressive. Each of these speculative philosophers stood well apart from the century's dominant philosophical streams. In America, for example, the main currents were analytical and empirical and were closely associated with the growing dominance of science, while a side current continued the pragmatism of William James and John Dewey. Yet these currents received no sustained theological attention. Were English-language theologians overlooking something crucial? Admittedly, the anti-religious tone of these dominant philosophical movements made it awkward for theologians to join their chorus: logical positivism and pragmatism had frequently proclaimed themselves enemies of the faith.

This may be regrettable, but it is too late to change the facts. What has been, has been. It is still worth asking, though, whether theology has ignored elements within twentieth-century philosophy that disclose a better way ahead. For this inquiry there can be no better choice than the work of Ludwig Wittgenstein. In this Austrian-British thinker there appeared a unique convergence of the strongest elements of twentieth-century philosophy. Continental European thought merged in him with the dominant analytical movement in Britain and America, and there were ties to pragmatism as well. Moreover, in Wittgenstein that broad convergence evolved into profoundly new ways of thought, a new conceptual style no longer strictly 'modern.' This combination of features in his work has led some to name Wittgenstein the most significant of all the century's philosophers (cf. Hacker, 1996). Certainly he was among its most provocative! And significantly, Wittgenstein himself was a passionately concerned human being whose philosophical work grew from an intense spiritual journey. I will argue in this chapter that Ludwig Wittgenstein was in fact an authentic Christian (albeit an undogmatic and thus perhaps an irregular one), and that his Christian convictions were symbiotic with the new, postmodern philosophical stance he ultimately took up. Thus one sort of postmodernity, so far from being the enemy of Christian faith, was in his case both the product and the partner of an unconventional yet genuine Christianity. In Wittgenstein modernity was merely mulch soil for reconceiving both words and world—philosophical words and human world—to provide a new understanding of their relation to one another in Christian faith and practice. This view of Wittgenstein will have to be tested, for it is not the standard interpretation of his life and thought. Yet the final consensus on Wittgenstein, whatever it may be, cannot fairly neglect the factors I will explore here. Meantime, this recounting of his journey will help to clear our own path, in the following chapter, to discern a no-longer-modern standpoint in the philosophy of religion.

Readers not familiar with volumes I and II of this trilogy may have their doubts about a biographical approach to Wittgenstein's achievement. Briefly in the preceding volumes and at greater length in an earlier work, *Biography as Theology* (1990), I have argued that at least for Christian theology the interlocking of life and thought, of mind and deed, is not merely illustrative or decorative—such integration is at the very heart of the theological task. A Dag Hammarskjöld, a Jonathan Edwards, a Dorothy Day can be truly heard, theologically understood, only as these passionate, enfleshed Christians' words are connected with their deeds, only as what they think is related to what they are. Readers who want to know more about this relation should consult the volumes just mentioned. Conceded, the method may not work in every case. There may be philosophers, and theologians as well, whose thought is so detached from (or at such variance with!) their lives that the method of biography as theology affords only negative help. Certainly, though, that is not true in this case. If ever there was a philosopher whose puzzling words cried out for interpretation from the life whence they emerged, that philosopher was Ludwig Wittgenstein. Indeed, this has been widely (if not universally) recognized by professional philosophers: brief and longer accounts of his life in relation to his thought have multiplied since his death. Some of these, such as the *Memoir* by Malcolm (2nd ed., 1984), the sketch by von Wright (1982), and the longer biographies by McGuiness (1988–), and Monk (1990) have already become standard sources. What follows depends heavily upon these as well as others cited, though the interpretation of the facts they relate is my own.

This chapter has three sections: **Section 1 (§1)** shows a young Austrian, deeply troubled by the emptiness of his own life and that of his European culture, seeking secure foundations in a logic closely related to mathematics—and finding a quite different standpoint, it seemed by chance, in the Russian Christianity of novelist-philosopher Leo Tolstoy. This find led to **Wittgenstein's conversion**—to become an authentic if quiet Christian. **Section 2 (§2)** begins in the decisive middle period of Wittgenstein's life and thought. Now an established Cambridge philosopher, he sought to reconcile his own disparate logical and convictional footholds just noted. In the painful process, he was forced to find a **new way of thinking** about language and about life itself. The later philosophy of Ludwig Wittgenstein thus came into being. This section displays that philosophy by recalling the three tracks or axes of modernity of the preceding chapter, showing how

Wittgenstein at great cost departed from each. **Section 3 (§3)** considers some **alternative accounts** of Wittgenstein's religion and life in relation to his philosophy, including the widely shared misunderstanding called "Wittgensteinian fideism," and then reflects on the tasks set today's philosopher-Christian by his life.

§1. *Preparatio Evangelica*

Ludwig Josef Johann Wittgenstein—he would drop the aristocratic middle names—was born April 26, 1889, the youngest child of eight in an elegant Viennese family including four brothers and three sisters. The main factors in his home life seem to have been the dominant, forceful role of his father, Karl Wittgenstein, an Austrian industrialist, and the nurture provided their little brother by his older sisters. The family owned three splendid Vienna residences. The father, who had made a vast fortune and taken early retirement from the steel industry he had created, played a significant role in Austrian cultural life. Leopoldine, the musically talented mother, presided over glamorous concert evenings at her home—over the years Johannes Brahms, Gustav Mahler, and Bruno Walter were among her distinguished guests. All the children received first-class musical training, and one brother, Paul, became a brilliant (and unusual) concert pianist. The other sons and daughters excelled in a variety of other ways. Apart from the persistent miasma of anti-Semitism that even then clouded Austria, the Wittgenstein family position could hardly have been more advantageous. They were of Jewish ancestry ("pure-blooded," one of Ludwig's uncles somewhat mistakenly said), though like many other 'assimilated' Viennese Jews they remained indifferent to or alienated from their Judaic heritage. Ludwig, like his siblings, thus received a routine Catholic christening in infancy.

a. The early years.—Coddled by his sisters and overshadowed by his talented family, Ludwig Wittgenstein did not talk until he was four years old. Within that silence, though, a puzzling complexity had begun to form. Though outwardly compliant and appealing, the boy early realized there could be a great gap between what was said and what was so: Was it necessary to tell the truth, or might one lie? One might, he remembered reasoning one day, if there were any advantage in it. On that uncharacteristic note of sophistry, philosophizing had begun. Outwardly, he seemed to lack his brilliant family members' visible gifts, appearing content with mechanical interests. He once made from wood and wire a model sewing machine that actually sewed. Educated by tutors at home until he was fourteen, the youngest Wittgenstein was eventually sent away to school at Linz. This, his father's choice for him, was a *Realschule,* that is, one that would accommodate Ludwig's perceived talent of working with things rather than ideas. This was followed in due course by two years in the *Technische Hochschule* in Berlin, at that time comparable to America's Caltech and MIT. There he received certification as an engineer in May 1908, just after his nineteenth birthday. During this period of scientific training, young Ludwig also began a lifelong practice of writing down his philosophical thoughts in a diary.

To understand his motivation for this writing and thought, it helps to know that while still a schoolboy at Linz he had "lost his religious faith" (Monk, 1990:18). Apparently he had lost confidence in the propositions of received Catholicism that were transmitted to him by tutors and members of his family. His older sister Margarete (Gretl) had once been psychoanalyzed by Freud and was fond of matters philosophical and psychological; she now took the responsibility of explaining religion to Ludwig more fully: Belief in God was a thing to be abandoned once one was mature. Gretl recommended progressing to Schopenhauer's philosophy. (Yet convinced faith, I think, is not so easily abandoned. So perhaps it would be more accurate to say that as late as late adolescence, Ludwig's authentic Christian formation had not truly begun. At most, his interest had been aroused: despite the required school focus upon mathematics, science, and engineering, his best grades at Linz were in the religion courses he took there.)

Philosophy in early twentieth-century Europe, especially in Germanic Europe, meant first of all the heritage of the greatest of the Germans, Immanuel Kant. As it developed, though, Kant's heritage displayed unresolved tensions. From one direction came the writing of Arthur Schopenhauer (1788–1860). For Schopenhauer the world we perceive is the world of appearances subject to our own wills, yet the human will is not an independent player that moves the objects in the world about much as a chess-player moves pieces on a board. "Will" is only another way of talking about our bodies, our selves. We are our bodies, and consequently our selfhood is subject to undisclosed motives and hidden desires. In an important sense, to be sure, Kant was right: the noumenal self, the self behind all appearances, is the will, and it is this human will that is virtuous or vicious, capable of creating good or evil. Yet in another sense, Schopenhauer anticipated Sigmund Freud: the will that rules is not an autonomous power guided by pure reason, but is self-serving and begets evil. To will is to want, and to want is necessarily to be frustrated; only when all willing ceases does good prevail. Thus the outcome of Schopenhauer's philosophy was deeply pessimistic. Human existence stood poised over a chasm of failure into which sooner or later it must plunge. Good cheer appears in his philosophy only in a few mitigating qualifiers: There is an escape from the relentless human will in art as Schopenhauer conceived it, since art invites will-less contemplation. There is yet another escape in felt sympathy for others' suffering; thus religions of compassion such as Christianity and (for Schopenhauer, an even better example) Buddhism mitigate the evil of human willing. When the disciplined will finally abandons its will to live—not by suicide, which does not qualify since it is itself a passionate act, but by complete intellectual self-denial—then at last evil is overcome (Matson, 1987:II:400). In brief summary, this was the melancholy outlook to which lonely engineering student Ludwig Wittgenstein turned as he worked out a way to live and think without God.

Heinrich Hertz (1857–94), a physicist whose *Principles of Mechanics* (1894) was in Wittgenstein's student days a standard required text, had developed another side of Kant's thought, addressed to the role of the sciences. Hertz was a pioneer in modern physics; his name is memorialized in the standard unit of radio frequency (1 hertz = 1 cycle per second). Scientific theory, Hertz held with Kant, does not begin with induction; science begins in some set of constructed presuppositions that must then be tested as a whole by relating them to observation reports. So far, this might have made science straightforward and uncomplicated: briefly, hypothesized systems of axioms are to be confirmed or falsified by empirical tests. Yet Hertz recognized that matters were not so simple. Concepts such as 'force,' for example, were in fact obscure, and existing scientific theories such as Newton's were clouded by these obscurities. The task was to eliminate them, reworking the theories in other terms that eliminated the obscure terms: The 'intuitions' of space and time (posited by Kant as elements of the human understanding) together with mass and energy could become elements of a purely mathematical mechanics, and this in turn could be used to interpret the observable phenomena (see P. Alexander, "Hertz, Heinrich Rudolf," in *Enc. Phil.* III:491-94).

Hertz typifies a main intellectual strategy of modernity—reduce, rationalize, simplify. Ludwig Wittgenstein was imbued with that strategy by the time he completed his work at the *Technische Hochschule*. The Kantian aspect of Hertz's work suggested both this and still another dimension of young Ludwig's future thought. Whereas physicist Ernst Mach had sought to ground physics in sensory psychological data,

Hertz resolutely insisted that the theories of physics must be totally independent of empirical psychology: The intuitions (of space and time) and categories (such as cause) that Kantians believed were fundamental to reason were not derived from nature: they were instead brought to nature by the reasoning mind itself. Hence scientific models are not mere copies of observed phenomena; they are mental constructs, *Darstellungen,* layouts of possible reality to be tested only by subsequent observation. A good scientific theory shows us by its very structure the limits of the experience that can be related to it (Janik and Toulmin, 1973:138-43). In principle the entire world can be rationally perceived in one *Darstellung*—via the universal categories of modernity. These Hertzian strategies would be employed anew in the decisive first book that lay, still unplanned, in Ludwig Wittgenstein's future.

b. An English interlude.—Now, however, the future author was about to add fresh layers of preparation to his equipage. To pursue the challenging new field of aeronautical engineering, he had traveled to County Derby, in central England, where there was a kite-flying research station; then he had enrolled as a research student in aeronautics at the University of Manchester. There he remained from 1908 until 1911, along the way designing an airplane propeller and an airplane engine. Gradually, though, his interest shifted from engineering to mathematics to philosophy. Bertrand Russell, the premier British philosopher of mathematics, was then teaching at Cambridge University. After consulting Gottlob Frege, the mathematical genius at Jena in Germany, Wittgenstein resolved in 1911 to seek Russell out and if possible to become his student.

In 1911, Bertrand Russell (1872–1970) was moving toward the apex of a distinguished philosophical career. He had just completed writing, with A. N. Whitehead, *Principia Mathematica,* a work designed to show that all mathematics could be derived from a few elementary propositions of logic. Russell, a fellow of Trinity, probably the grandest of Cambridge University's old colleges, was launched upon work that would soon make his philosophical reputation known around the world. For present purposes, it is worth noting that by this time Russell was firmly settled upon all three axes of modernity as defined in the preceding chapter. His *theory of knowledge* was foundationalist, though the foundation for Russell, in contrast to the Continental tradition Wittgenstein had absorbed, was empirical: "Sense-data" were immediately presented to human knowledge, and by "sense-data" (a term he and his Cambridge colleague G. E. Moore introduced into philosophy) Russell meant the objects of perception that were 'immediately' or 'directly' known, as opposed to material objects, which one could apprehend only by means of the intervening

sense-data. Further, Russell's *theory of language* was representative: in the earlier stages of his work this meant that whatever could be meaningfully spoken of was real, so that the words of a sentence, whether a true sentence or not, were meaningful only if the words that made up the sentence represented real objects: "The car is in a garage" was a meaningful sentence if and only if "car" represented a car and "garage" represented a garage and "in" represented a real relation. (Russell puzzled over what to say about "the" and "is" and "a": did they, too, represent real objects?) Finally, Russell's *metaphysics,* which at the beginning of his career had been based on Bradley's and Hegel's idealism, was by the time Wittgenstein arrived thoroughly individualist: a little later, Russell and others would begin to call this view "atomism," though the term was used differently here than in modern physics. What existed, what was real, was individual particulars, indivisible fragments, atoms of 'reality,' and the main task of philosophy was therefore analysis, that is, the logical dissolving of the appearances of the world—not only its material elements, but also its social systems, its languages, its ideals, and its supposed last realities. All these appearances could in principle be reduced to the individual particulars or 'atoms' of which they were composed (Wm. P. Alston, "Russell, Bertrand Arthur William [Epistemology and Metaphysics]," in *Enc. Phil.* VII:239-44, 256-58; Matson, 1987:II, 457-66).

On approaching Bertrand Russell, young Wittgenstein was filled with a mixture of self-confidence and self-doubt: On the one hand he yearned to have Russell assure him that he was a brilliant student; on the other, he could not wait a day to point out his new teacher's own mistakes in logic. Russell apparently delighted in both aspects of this intense student's presence; he wrote to his lover, Lady Ottoline Morrell, that "my German" seemed to have become Russell's teacher rather than the other way around (Monk, 1990:36-56).

What exactly was it that Bertrand Russell had undertaken that had attracted Ludwig Wittgenstein? If we recall Wittgenstein's time at the preparatory school at Linz, we remember that by his own account he had there "lost his faith," ceased to believe the conventional propositions of Austrian culture-Christianity. In its place he had found the post-Kantian philosophy of Schopenhauer, whose grand construal of the world as will and idea was deeply pessimistic: only as the will gives up its imagined grip upon the world does evil cease. Meantime, Wittgenstein's engineering training had instilled into him the scientific Kantianism of Heinrich Hertz: It seemed possible to construct a set of logical principles whose clarity and comprehensiveness permitted their application to the data of physics in a way that qualified physics for full mathematical validity. What if the work Russell and Whitehead had now accomplished in *Principia Mathematica* could be applied not only, as *Principia* claimed, to mathematics, not only to physics, but to all the sciences, and indeed to everything—perhaps including ultimate questions of good and evil? Would that not mean that the problem of understanding everything in the world was solved? Not, of course, solved in detail, but in general and in principle? Solved by a set of principles generated from necessary logic alone, and therefore self-evidently true if anything at all were true! And would not such a solution perfectly display its author's greatness, be a work of genius in which his own genius would realize itself? (cf. Monk, 1990:27). Moved by such hopes, Ludwig Wittgenstein registered in 1912 at Trinity College, Cambridge University, first as an undergraduate, later as an "advanced student" under Bertrand Russell, remaining there until 1913.

Cambridge before the Great War of 1914–18 had more than its share of brilliant teachers. Besides Russell, Wittgenstein met and associated with philosophers G. E. Moore and A. N. Whitehead and with J. M. Keynes the economist and with others as well. Many of these belonged to an elite conversation society, the Apostles; Wittgenstein the undergraduate was selected for membership and in fact attended some meetings. However, he shortly resigned—something that was never done! The reason he gave was that he found the chatter of other student members intolerable (McGuiness, 1988:151). Perhaps the deeper reason was that it was hard for him to belong to any community—even that of Cambridge's brightest and best. It was a trait that would later show itself afresh. Human relations for Wittgenstein were always important, but their formation always difficult. An exception was a young mathematics student named David Pinsent. With him he formed an intense friendship that was an elixir of life to the lonely German. A further factor now complicated his life: Wittgenstein's father died in 1912, leaving his youngest son a proportionate share of an immense family fortune. His great business, nevertheless, was to clarify the foundations of logic—if logic justified mathematics, what was it that justified logic itself, or made it relevant to the world? While Wittgenstein struggled to find the answer, the alien English social setting grew more and more oppressive. At last, in the autumn of 1913, he retreated to a remote farm he had discovered northeast of Bergen, Norway. There, as a lodger in a Norwegian household, he could be almost free of ordinary human social interaction and could concentrate on his difficult work. He remained in Norway, struggling with his self-assigned project, visited by only one or two guests from England, until the outbreak of war in August 1914.

c. Finding what really matters.—Europe seemed actually to yearn for the war that was now to shatter forever its way of life. Just before the onset of war there was everywhere a restlessness, a sense that things could not continue as they were. Wittgenstein, too, longed for decisive change. When the war did begin, he hurried home from Norway to Vienna and promptly enlisted in the army of Austro-Hungary as a private soldier. He would sadly lose touch with Russell and Keynes and Pinsent; communication between enemy countries must cease. War with its threat (or promise) of death would claim what had until then been his entire life. He continued the practice of journal keeping, and his wartime notes show him wrestling again with the despair and suicidal urges that had first appeared during school days at Linz. He longed to be sent into danger and asked to be placed in the most exposed outposts, hoping that he would either be killed or in the crisis would find a self worthy of survival.

i. The road to conversion.—The Great War (1914–18) fitfully obliged these hopes. Assigned to an artillery regiment, Ludwig Wittgenstein repeatedly volunteered for a risky forward observation post. His diary records some of his prayers:

> [29 April, 1916:] Was shot at. Thought of God. Thy will be done. God be with me. . . . [5 May, 1916:] Now, during the day, everything is quiet, but in the night it must be *frightful.* Will I endure it?? Tonight will show. God be with me!! (MS 103, cited by Monk, 1990:138)

But what is this? Does the atheist pray? Wittgenstein does, and requests, not safety for himself or victory for his side, but integrity in face of death. To what god, then, are these spontaneous prayers addressed? That question gripped Ludwig Wittgenstein himself as he continued to refine his projected book even during this perilous time. Now the notes that will coalesce in the book introduce a radical new theme, asking ultimate questions: Where does the meaning of the entire world lie? Can that meaning be—God? Is God fatherlike? What does it mean to pray to such a God? (*NB*, 72).

Evidently something preceding these June 1916 notebook entries had profoundly changed them—and him. During the first month of the war Ludwig Wittgenstein had wandered into a bookstore in Polish Galicia. There he had found a German version of Tolstoy's *Gospel in Brief* and, finding nothing better, had purchased it. Apparently, the book changed his life.

The Gospel in Brief is one of the religious writings that grew from the remarkable career of Count Leo Tolstoy (1828–1910), the distinguished Russian novelist (*War and Peace, Anna Karenina*) and thinker. Tolstoy's career as landed estate holder and novelist had been interrupted when in disgust at his own libertinism he was converted to a severe and simple (some would say simplistic) version of Christianity. His later writings, advocating evangelical love, nonviolence, and the renunciation of wealth, gave him a reputation for saintliness, yet in 1901 the Orthodox Church had excommunicated this saint as a heretic. Finding that the four Gospels contained the substance of Christ's teaching, he took a dim view of the rest of Scripture as well as of later church teaching. *The Gospel in Brief* (1881) is a harmonization of Matthew, Mark, Luke, and John, mainly arranged in John's order, since Tolstoy thought it was the most spiritual Gospel.

In succeeding months, as the Austro-Hungarian army suffered severe losses and as Wittgenstein was moved about by military necessity, an ant in an earthquake, he read and reread Tolstoy's book—read it, devoured it, carried it everywhere with him, memorized long passages from it, recommended it to anyone who would listen. As Ray Monk his biographer concisely says, in reading Tolstoy's *Gospel,* Ludwig Wittgenstein was converted.

> What saved him from suicide . . . was not the encouragement he received from Jolles [a Berlin friend] and Frege, but exactly the kind of personal transformation, the religious conversion, he had gone to war to find. He was, as it were, saved by the word. . . . For a time he . . . became not only a believer, but an evangelist, recommending Tolstoy's *Gospel* to anyone in distress. "If you are not acquainted with it," he later told Ficker [an Austrian friend], "then you cannot imagine what an effect it can have." (Monk, 1990:115f)

Genuine Christian conversion, like other matters spiritual, is spiritually discerned (see 1 Cor. 2:14). Regrettably, Ludwig Wittgenstein when he read Tolstoy's *Gospel* had no spiritual advisor, no Christian community, not even a fellow Bible-reader. Perhaps unjustly, he had spurned the company of his coarse fellow soldiers, some of whom may have been Christians as well. Consequently he was quite alone with his thoughts and prayers, his notebooks, and his Tolstoy book. Our construal of his pilgrim journey must accordingly be tentative, for he left only an imperfect record of its progress. Nevertheless, there is concrete evidence that the turn he took was indeed a classic Christian conversion to be compared with those of Augustine and Francis, Bunyan and Wesley, Sarah Pierpont Edwards and Dorothy Day.

There is a parallel between Wittgenstein's turn to Christian discipleship at this time and the turn from the aesthetic and ethical stages on life's way to the religious stage pseudonymously delineated by Søren Kierkegaard. Perhaps, though, as Kierkegaard scholar Heiko Schulz remarked to me, it is here best categorized as S. K.'s "religiousness A." The clearest evidence that religiousness A is Christian comes when it develops into religiousness B, a sub-stage more concerned with a dialectical awareness of sin and redemption. In due course I will show that this development did occur (Wittgenstein, *NB* 81-91; *TLP* 6.43; Kierkegaard, 1846:501f, 555-61).

Evidently, there was at this time some kind of conversion, and in the long run it turned out to be clearly Christian. Consider some of the earliest evidence. Besides the prayers just quoted and others that show him in the very act of submitting his life to God, there are reports from others that signal a change: though he was perfectly willing to risk his life, he displayed no interest in eliminating the enemy as such, or in the political aims of the war. Contrariwise, he carried *The Gospel in Brief* with him everywhere and urged it upon everyone. This was itself a costly practice.

> At one time he was a byword among the soldiers for carrying it—"the one with the Gospels" he would be called. The Christianity that he found in Tolstoy seemed to him the only sure way to happiness, but it was not an easy way. (McGuiness, 1988:220f)

More significant still, as soon as he was free to do so upon release from internment in Italy at war's end, he returned to Vienna, engaged a lawyer, and gave away to two sisters and a brother the vast fortune he had inherited. These deeds echo words of Jesus via Tolstoy:

> . . . the one who owns property cannot be in God's will. (Tolstoy, 1881:105, paraphrasing Mark 10:23)

The divestment completed, Ludwig Wittgenstein had to face his own future. Suicide had slowly ceased to dominate his thought, and yet he no longer sought to become an aeronautical engineer or a great philosopher. Instead, he would perhaps become a monk, or a teacher of children. Settling on the latter, he enrolled for a teacher training course and spent the next six years as a schoolteacher in remote villages in Lower Austria. Here again he must have remembered the saying of Tolstoy's *Gospel:*

> And not one child is lost by the will of the Father. . . . [So] one must shepherd them, and not distract them from the Father and from the life of truth. (Tolstoy, 1881:145, paraphrasing Matt. 18:14)

Against this record of gospel obedience, admittedly, must be set the things the new convert did *not* do: He did not find a new church nor did he reclaim his nominal Austrian Catholicism. He did not enroll for systematic instruction in the faith. He did not (with an exception soon to be noted) partake of the signs of salvation—notably, his place at the Savior's earthly banquet table, the eucharistic meal, remained empty.

The discussion of baptism in *Volume II* has shown how even an imperfect baptism may be significantly reclaimed, 'repaired' by a Christian community in order to bring out its relevance to the new life of a convert (*Doctrine*, 395-97). Had such a community been available to this new believer, and had it reached out to him and he to it—but to list these possibilities is to see how remote they were from the circumstances of his life at that time. The consequence is that the story of this conversion remains from the outset a severely limited one.

In hindsight, these are serious neglects. Yet they echo the example and teaching of Leo Tolstoy, a highly literate and sophisticated writer, well aware of the results of nineteenth-century Gospel criticism and the difficulties educated modern Europeans faced in embracing the content of the Gospels. Tolstoy's strategy was to eliminate or spiritualize those Bible passages (such as nature miracles, teaching about the Devil, and, most grievously, even the bodily resurrection) that he considered irrelevant to his contemporaries. Nevertheless, much remained; enough, Tolstoy felt, to direct his own newfound Christian life. Its flavor may be captured in the German version of Tolstoy's book that Wittgenstein would have used:

> The proclamation of Jesus Christ's salvation is a proclamation of the awareness of Life. ¶ It is an awareness that the Source of life is the complete good. By its power a human being is completely good. To grasp this Source one must understand that the spirit of human life is derived from the Source. The one who was not already there is called into life by the Source. The Source gave mankind wholeness *[das Heil]* and therefore the essence of this Source is Holiness *[das Heil]*. ¶ So if one is not to reject the Source of one's life, one must firmly grasp the only available property of this Source, firmly grasp the blessings *[Wohltaten]* of love. However, human beings can do good to none but human beings. ¶ All individual desire is opposed to the Source of salvation *[Heils]*; therefore one must sacrifice this desire and one's entire life in the flesh, exchange it for a desire for the Source of the blessing, the love of one's neighbor. ¶ Love of the neighbor flows from the

> awareness of Life which is revealed *[offenbart]* through Jesus Christ. . . . (Tolstoy, 1881:196f)

Perhaps to a theological eye this little passage is only a diffuse summary of 1 John, the brief New Testament epistle with which Tolstoy closes his little book. To Ludwig Wittgenstein, however, it was a word of life at a low time in his earthly existence—it was indeed a gospel in brief. In it he found the ultimacy that had so far eluded his deeply personal quest.

ii. The 'final' philosophy.—Alongside Tolstoy, Wittgenstein carried in his soldier's kit two other treasures. One was a set of notebooks or diaries. A surviving fragment of these is our *Notebooks 1914–16* (*NB*), which record at first hand his spiritual rebirth. The other was the text-in-progress, first drafted in Norway, whose final form we know as *Tractatus Logico-Philosophicus* (*TLP*). This was the book that, in Ludwig Wittgenstein's intention, would solve—or dissolve—the main problems of philosophy. What that goal had left out of account, his unanticipated conversion to gospel ways of thought and life, was destined to affect not only the form of the *Tractatus,* but also his subsequent life's work.

Today's American student who picks up the *Tractatus* for the first time is likely to have one of two reactions: The student in the mainstream of recent philosophy may think, "Here is a book full of the commonplaces I have learned already (truth tables, the synthetic-analytic distinction, the impossibility of talk of God, the difficulties of securing referential language)—only, what are these strange pages devoted to 'God,' to an unworldly 'ethics,' to 'the mystical'?" Another sort of student, formed in one or another side channel of recent philosophy, may react to the *Tractatus* in a contrary way. "The references to showing not saying, to ethics as all that matters compared with the world that matters not—these themes are of course valuable, but why so many pages devoted to 'logic' and to 'propositions'?" Either response is credible, given one pre-formation or another. But where did the author stand? Is Ludwig Wittgenstein on the side of current, everyday (Anglo American) philosophy, or is he, too, merely a voyager in a side channel? We must see.

For any reader the *Tractatus* begins portentously enough:

> The world is all that is the case. (*TLP* 1)

McGuiness suggests that this opening is itself a sort of "creation-myth" (1988:299). Certainly it sets the stage grandly: Here begins a metaphysical treatise indeed. So what sense of "world" is intended here? Are we hearing of a hard, exterior world, the same for everyone? Or is this a subjective, idealist world, *my* world? We are not told.

The rest of the *Tractatus* expands that proposition and six more like it (except that there is no expansion of 7):

> What is the case—a fact—is the existence of states of affairs. (2)
> A logical picture *[Bild]* of facts is a thought. (3)
> A thought is a proposition with a sense. (4)
> A proposition is a truth-function of elementary propositions. (5)
> The general form of a truth-function is $[\bar{p}, \bar{\xi}, N(\bar{\xi})]$. (6)
> What we cannot speak about we must consign to silence. (7)

To put these points informally, Wittgenstein is telling us that when it comes to the facts, words and world fit very well, one on one. There are the facts, starting with the elementary propositions (Russell's 'atomic facts'?) upon which all others rest. The complex of these facts constitutes the world. Thus the world can indeed be talked about, and to that purpose everyday talk is well enough suited (5.5563), since its foundation is these elements, the 'objects,' the infinitesimal building blocks of words and world alike. Russell's worries about the role of logic and about whether logical constants 'refer' to something or other can be put to rest; they do not. How we know the facts is not a problem, either; we do. (The *Tractatus,* in this regard unlike British empiricism in general, focuses on what there is rather than on how one 'knows' what there is.) Little is argued; Ludwig Wittgenstein expects that if we understand (and not many will, he thinks) we will accept the whole. In it he has furnished a *Darstellung,* a Hertzian model, for understanding all about everything. Except for some use of technical symbols (as in 6) and for the extreme brevity of the entire treatment, one might almost be reading a simplistic account of the world that the logical positivists would soon be constructing, its play blocks stacked with exquisite care. This sense of this-worldly order pervades until we reach the final pages.

To be sure, from early on the *Tractatus* displays hints of something else, something unspeakable; we were already at its margins when we wondered whether this was a book about words (and word-like thoughts) or a book about hard facts accessible to science, an engineer's world. The doubt, though, is deliberately induced by the author: *Tractatus* is about both of these and properly about their inseparability. While false propositions are just as much a part of the system of language as are true propositions, both are in order, for both together represent the world as it is—one by saying what the world is not, the other, what it is. Here, though, the unspeakable intrudes: this match between propositions and facts is possible because they share a common structure or *form*, yet what that commonality is, *how* words and world are alike, cannot be said; it can only be shown. Nevertheless, this literally unspeakable commonality, this given match between words and facts, is the necessary condition for thinking about any fact at all; without the match, there are no propositions true or false, and thus there is no thought whatsoever. It follows, importantly, that for something to be unsayable does not mean it can be disregarded or set aside.

"Showing" is frequently a technical term in the *Tractatus*. For examples: the application of a sign *shows* its meaning (3.262); propositions *show* how things stand if they are true (while they say that they do so stand) (4.022); propositions "*show* the logical form of reality. They display it" (4.121); number-signs *show* that they signify numbers (for they cannot *say* that they do—4.126); more generally, propositions *show* what they say; tautologies and contradictions *show* that they say nothing (4.461); a grammatical feature *shows* that in the superficial sense of Russell and Moore there is no "soul" (5.541–5.5422); all tautologies *show* that they are tautologies though they do not say they are (6.127); mathematical equations *show* "the logic of the world" (6.22).

In the concluding passages, the notion of showing takes up the task for which its previous uses have prepared us. The final paragraph of the 6's tells us that

> [m]y propositions serve as elucidations in the following way: anyone who understands me eventually recognizes them as nonsensical, when he has used them—as steps—to climb up beyond them. (He must, so to speak, throw away the ladder after he has climbed up it.) (6.54)

One must transcend. So all that has preceded, facts, propositions, truth tables, the excluded subject—all is 'nonsense' of a special sort. It has equipped us to abandon it, readied us as it were to fall on our faces in speechless wonder and awe before something these are not, before the Unspeakable.

Why was this needed? Why all this ladder-climbing? Why not simply devote oneself to live as a Tolstoyan disciple, a radically evangelical Christian, from the outset? Well, when they are understood in a way all too familiar to Bertrand Russell's pupil, the sentences of *The Gospel in Brief* say nothing to jar truly modern thinkers awake, for at best they only present a few facts about the world: Such and such a one—named "Jesus"—appeared, did this and that, and perished (cf. Schweitzer,

1906, ad fin.). To any who, so reading, cannot "climb up beyond," the *Tractatus* offers its wonderful ladder. One can mount it; one can thus be *shown* that which "cannot be put into words."

> There are, indeed, things that cannot be put into words. They *make themselves manifest* [Ogden and Ramsey translate: This *shows* itself]. They are what is the mystical. (6.522)

As Wittgenstein wrote to his friend (and potential publisher) Ludwig von Ficker,

> [M]y work consists of two parts: of the one which is here, and of everything which I have *not* written. And precisely this second part is the important one. (quoted in Monk, 1990:178)

Anyway, the work was done; the war was ended; on his release from an Italian prison camp, Ludwig Wittgenstein could indeed as he imagined leave philosophy behind, its main question answered, give his fortune away, and devote himself to the life of a disciple: perhaps as an ordained priest teaching little children the gospel, or perhaps as a teacher teaching them life according to the gospel. He would actually take the latter path, except that—as he gradually realized with the passage of time—philosophy was not over for him. If the wartime conversion was to endure, there was much still to do and only he could do it.

§2. Exiting Modernity

Wittgenstein's final years in Austria were troubled ones. The *Tractatus Logico-Philosophicus* had been published in German in 1921 and in a bilingual English edition in 1922, but he thought so far no one else understood it—perhaps in a hundred years? His schoolteaching experiment had ended in a crisis over his physical disciplining of a pupil. He had then worked for two years as architect and builder of a house for his sister Gretl. During that time (1927–29) he was sought out by Moritz Schlick, a professor of philosophy at the University of Vienna, who told him of the interest the *Tractatus* had created among members of the Vienna Circle, a group later to be known as logical positivists. These were empiricists who claimed to reject any metaphysics and to rebuild philosophy and science on a logical basis. With them Wittgenstein discussed shared philosophical interests, but he was uneasy in these discussions. He recognized more fully than they the gulf that separated them: after all, what was important in the *Tractatus* was the 'mysticism' that it could *not* express. He startled gatherings of the Circle by turning his back on them at meetings and reading aloud the verses of Indian mystic Rabindranath Tagore. As Circle member Rudolf Carnap recalled, "Earlier, when we were reading [the *Tractatus*] in the Circle, I had erroneously believed that his attitude toward metaphysics was similar to ours" (quoted in Monk, 1990:243).

These contacts, along with a Vienna guest lecture by mathematician L. E. J. Brouwer, led Wittgenstein to realize that there was still philosophical work he must do. At the urging of Frank Ramsey, he returned to Britain, which from 1929 onward was to be the chief scene of his labors. Except for some stretches in Norway, Wales, and Ireland, occasional home visits, and a rare trip elsewhere, he would live and die in Cambridge. He fulfilled the new Cambridge University doctoral requirements, submitting the already-published *Tractatus* as his dissertation, and then in 1930 was elected a fellow of Trinity College and in 1939 Professor of Philosophy at the University. There he was to think out the viewpoint of his so-called later period, culminating in the only other book he ever offered for publication (it was withdrawn, but finally published posthumously), his *Philosophical Investigations* (*PI*). In Britain, too, Wittgenstein would rethink his religious convictions afresh. This is the arena, then, in which the thesis that his Christian standpoint contributed crucially to the development of his mature philosophy (and vice versa) must stand or fall.

Ray Monk said of the 1914 conversion that "for a time" Ludwig Wittgenstein became a believer (1990:115f). Is that all? Assuredly, a conversion can be a mere episode, seed springing up only to perish on a hard path (Matt. 13:5, 20f). Yet there is good evidence that for Wittgenstein conversion lasted, evidence of a sort he himself would have demanded—deeds as well as words. Here is a partial account: Though he shifted from Austrian mountain children to students at one of the world's leading universities he continued until retirement the vocation he had taken up in 1919, his work as a teacher. His inner life (a topic any who learn from Wittgenstein must approach circumspectly) was partly revealed in a lecture on ethics he gave in 1929 that spoke of "feeling *absolutely* safe"—a feeling he had long connected with authentic religion (*LE*, 8; Malcolm, 1994:7f).

A little warning to oversophisticated readers may be in order here. There is no reason to suppose that Wittgenstein in referring to such 'experiences' as these was invoking the old liberal religious apologetic: the feelings he referred to were precisely not offered as examples of a universal essence of religion as in Schleiermacher (CF §§3–4). Nor were these feelings or awarenesses to be taken à la Alvin Plantinga to constitute any sort of epistemic *grounds* for belief in God (cf. Plantinga and Wolterstorff, eds., 1983:78-82). Rather Wittgenstein by mentioning these experiences was seeking to evoke in his youthful but perhaps inert university listeners some grasp of the nearly unavailable *concept* of ethics as it related to the (still less available) concept of *God.*

He frequently introduced into his lectures the theme of belief in a last judgment, and (though he had sometimes let students think these beliefs were not his own) he told M. O'C. Drury as late as 1949 that "[i]f what we do now is to make no difference in the end, then all the seriousness of life is done away with" (Drury in Rhees, ed., 1981:175). In particular, former student Drury records long conversations in which Ludwig Wittgenstein critically expressed his own faith and urged Drury to share and practice it: "There is a sense in which you and I are both Christians," he told Drury in about 1930 while urging that Christianity must be practiced rather than merely professed (Rhees, ed., 1981:129f). (The phrase "there is a sense" acknowledged afresh the unconventional nature of Wittgenstein's own Christianity.) Yet the 'practice' Wittgenstein urged was not for him merely a matter of secular kindness and decency: Norman Malcolm, his most famous American student, tells us that

> [i]n 1931 Wittgenstein lived for a while in his hut in Norway. On his return to Cambridge he told Drury that he had done no philosophical writing, but *had spent the time in prayer.* (Malcolm, 1994:12, emphasis added)

In addition, he had in that time written out a confession of his sins. The old war veteran later told Drury (who by 1944 had become an army medical doctor) that in wartime, "If it ever happens that you get mixed up in hand to hand fighting, you must just stand aside and let yourself be massacred" (Drury in Rhees, ed., 1981:163)—a clear echo of Tolstoy's Jesus thirty years after Wittgenstein's first reading of *The Gospel in Brief* (Tolstoy, 1881:450f, paraphrasing Matt. 5:38-41 and Luke 6:40). This, then, is the quiet Christian whose intellectual progress we are exploring, asking whether and how it coheres with his persisting faith.

a. Displacing modern metaphysics.—Modern philosophy from Descartes to Kant locates the human self in a separate realm; it begins as the disembodied *ego* of Descartes and eventually becomes either the dismantled self of Hume or the transcendental 'I' of Kant and Schopenhauer. This last is also the 'I' of the *Tractatus Logico-*

Philosophicus (e.g., 5.63). The later writings of Ludwig Wittgenstein represent a shift from this Cartesian, bodiless I to a 'we' that is corporate and communal as well. Here we must briefly review this profound change of thought—as it were, watching the metamorphosis of a social self emerging from its transcendental shell.

Recall that the pages of the *Tractatus* are meant to show how words can represent the world—more exactly, how propositions can say (or can even deny) what is the case. Left untouched in most of its pages is the question, Who is it that issues the propositions? This omission is no accident. The logical notation of the *Tractatus* made it unnecessary (and thus by its method impossible) to symbolize or refer to a 'proposer' of propositions, somebody or other who believes some proposition *p*. It follows that "there is no such thing as the soul—the subject, etc.—as it is conceived in the superficial psychology of the present day." Such a "soul" would only be a construct *(Eine zusammengesetzte Seele)*, not a real soul (5.5421). The real Tractarian soul is transcendental, part of the Unspeakable. The self that says "I" and "my" cannot be represented; it is not in the *Tractatus* an object. Nevertheless Wittgenstein writes that it is "my" propositions that represent the world. So the world is "my world": "The limits of my language mean the limits of my world" (5.6). This leads to a certain sort of solipsism (the view that what I myself think is necessarily all there is). In brief, "I am my world" (5.63). Now, however, the "I" (or soul) that is evoked is no longer the self of "superficial psychology" but is a transcendental, Kantian self. To underline the point with a homely illustration, Wittgenstein points out that the form of the visual field cannot include the seeing eye itself. In like manner the metaphysical subject ("the philosophical self") is not part of the world, but "shrinks to a point without extension" (5.64).

The great difficulty here is that this extensionless, metaphysical self is for Wittgenstein, as it had been for Kant as well, the ethical self—the self to which for example the commands of Tolstoy's Sermon on the Mount are addressed. How can this be? How can a transcendental self become a doer of the word and not a hearer only (James 1:22)? What Wittgenstein by the 1930s found needed more thought was that ordinary language consistently brought the words "I" and "my" into relation with a particular human body—one's own.

Facing these puzzles, Wittgenstein in the early 1930s dictated notes to his students in which he concluded:

> These considerations show that the proper name "A" and the expression "A's body" do not have the same use, at least not if we decide to use the above criteria for the identity of A [such criteria

> as possessing memories only A would have]. But now be careful not to think that these considerations show that besides A's body there is something else, another object, which is A. You must refrain from looking for a substance when you see a substantive—but not from thoroughly examining the use of a word. (in Lazerowitz and Ambrose, 1984:130)

For their part, bodies were enumerable. One could count the number of human bodies present at a Cambridge lecture. Could one at the same lecture count the number of souls present? Only if soul and body were logically inseparable. Yet what was inseparable was nevertheless distinguishable: One does not say "my body has a toothache" but always "I have a toothache"—and this despite the fact that aches are themselves bodily troubles! Here the Kantian (and Tractarian) doctrine of the metaphysical soul showed itself inadequate to the way things are (*AMB*:60).

The persistent difficulty (philosophy's *bewitchment* of thought, he sometimes called it—*PI* §109) lay in the doctrine of Cartesian privacy, the belief that the self knows itself, and secondarily knows other matters, from a standpoint of sovereign isolation. If this was correct, then (1) the universe consisted of isolated individuals, (2) language was essentially a private affair, and (3) wanting sure foundations, doubt about everything lurked everywhere. Ludwig Wittgenstein knew now that matters were otherwise, but he could not escape these bewitching claims until he had found a way to show them false or empty. This was what he next attempted—in the lectures just cited, in the student guides labeled *The Blue Book* and *The Brown Book* (*BB.*), and climactically in the first completed segment of the *Philosophical Investigations.* There, in aphoristic paragraphs (1–188), he established enough to refute at least the first of these Cartesian errors—modern individualism was overturned in the autumn of 1936!

From §1 through §136 the *Philosophical Investigations* provides a revised understanding, not of thought itself but of its necessary instrument, language or speech (*Sprache*), and declares (again in the prophetic style of the *Tractatus*) that this revised understanding of language is philosophy's true business. Yet all this serves as prologue for §137, where he addresses the great neglected topic of the *Tractatus Logico-Philosophicus*: who or what is the logical issuer of any sentence? Wittgenstein argues by examples against the reduction of a sentence's meaning to the psychology of a particular subject whose thought just happens to 'fit' that sentence, irrespective of its use in any current language-game (§138). So the crucial move has been made: "Subjects" have been turned into speakers whose roles in language are social. From this will follow later the denial of a private language, and thus the impossibility of solipsism's temptation (§246ff).

The rest (i.e., §§139–88) of this earliest completed segment deals with objections to the standpoint Wittgenstein has here reached. The so-called essential meaning of words is only a superficial, psychological phenomenon (§§140–42); learning a language is not an unfolding of innate linguistic skills (on the relation to Chomsky see Malcolm, 1994:chap. 4) but is finding *how to go on* (§§151–55). This is illustrated by recalling the task (here one remembers Ludwig Wittgenstein the schoolteacher) of learning to read (§§156–71). For linguistic essentialism (portrayed by Paul Feyerabend in Pitcher, ed., 1966:104-7) and mechanistic behaviorism (in which human bodies are mere automata responding to stimuli) are each wrong; they are to be replaced by a third standpoint—one expressed via *roles* and *games* and a self involved with other selves from the outset (§§157–59). Defending this, the *Investigations* develops a grammar of the terms or concepts of *fitting (passen)*, of *being able* (to go on), and of *understanding* that is neither essentialist nor mechanist, but displays a third standpoint (182). The hidden topic here is Wittgenstein's unfolding account of human nature, the natural history of being human (cf. §174).

Such philosophical work had a theological, indeed a religious consequence. No human self was alone in a private world. Solipsism was unthinkable. Logic and language converged to make that clear. It seems ironic that Ludwig Wittgenstein finally hammered this truth out while he himself was mainly alone, having gone to his remote Norway lodging in 1936 at the end of his term as Cambridge don to complete the book that would embody the new understanding. Yet the irony is overturned when we learn that during this stay in Norway he reached out to God and to his fellow *Menschen*—as a Christian must—by making confession of his sins. He prepared written confessions to read out to his friends and family, and he traveled this same year to the mountains of Austria to apologize to those he had harmed there while teaching school (Monk, 1990:367-72). Friends who in some embarrassment heard these confessions recalled a report of mistreating a pupil in Austria and subsequently lying to the principal to save his job. They also recalled the confession of having allowed people to suppose his ancestry was not (mainly) Jewish! Biographer Ray Monk claims the point of all this was auto-therapeutic: "to dismantle his pride" (1990:371). Of course it has that dimension, but Monk misses the *social* nature of Christian confession, its engagement with others—and with God.

In Hebrew and Greek Scripture, confession of sin and confession of faith are not far apart; one does not 'confess' one's fault against God and neighbor without 'confessing' one's share in the grace of God (cf. Psalms 32 and 51, esp. 32:3, 7; James 5:16). From a biblical standpoint one cannot explicitly make either sort of confession without engaging the other—in Wittgensteinian terms, sin and faith are grammatically inseparable in biblical language-games. Anyone can be self-critical, but only in faith can one acknowledge and confess sins (see *Doctrine,* Three).

In 1931 Wittgenstein had written to himself that "a confession has to be a part of your new life" (*CV* 18). No longer pushed toward solipsism, yet lacking a church, he made his confessions to those he had injured and to those nearest or dearest to him—to his sisters, to Fania Pascal, to Francis Skinner, to G. E. Moore! In doing so, he was practicing one of the classic salvific signs (i.e., sacraments) of the Christian community (see *Doctrine,* Eight). A long quotation from the *Confessions* of Augustine had begun his climactic work, the *Philosophical Investigations* (*PI* 1); now the latter-day convert would continue Christian tradition by making his own confessions.

b. A new account of language.—Philosophical interest in language did not begin with Ludwig Wittgenstein; it was as old as Plato's Socrates, who in the *Cratylus* maintains that since the roots of Greek terms have their origin in primal speakers' conceptions of things, one can learn from those ancient roots about the world, about morality, about the gods. In modern times Johann Georg Hamann (1730–88) and Johann Gottfried von Herder (1744–1803) had introduced critiques of language in powerful opposition to Enlightenment thought. And in Wittgenstein's youth, Viennese intellectual figures such as Karl Kraus and Fritz Mauthner had employed linguistic strategies in their battles against the establishment culture (Janik and Toulmin, 1973:chaps. 3, 5). Later, the Vienna Circle offered its own linguistic approach to philosophy.

The thinkers who now challenged Wittgenstein, though, were British. Bertrand Russell's philosophy of language masterfully embodied two main modern themes. On the one hand, Russell, like Frege, took the point of meaningful human language to be *reference.* This alone established a proposition's claim to bear meaning. On the other hand, Russellian propositions were grounded in someone's subjective experiences (feelings or perceptions): Even the most objective claim, "Here is an elephant," sprang from "I am having elephantine sense data here now." Wittgenstein had sought to do justice to the first of these themes in the *Tractatus,* with its related theory of the proposition—a theory (and a book) he had come to believe seriously flawed. Russell's second theme, a characteristically British way of ideas or sense data or interior feeling as the ground of speech, never strongly appealed to Wittgenstein, and he meant to correct it as well.

As we will see, Ludwig Wittgenstein's *linguistic* struggle and his struggle to *live,* to interact with others in fully human ways, to be *decent,* to have *faith,* could not be worked out apart from each other any more than his struggle to confess his sins could be separated from the struggle against solipsism related above. Consider what was going on in his life during the crucial 1930s, the period in which the new account of language took shape: He received his doctorate and began a term as fellow of Trinity College. He formed close, loving friendships—with Marguerite Respinger, the young Swiss family friend with whom he long anticipated marriage; with Maurice O'C. Drury, the Irish Anglican who became Wittgenstein's disciple as early as 1929; with Francis Skinner, a Cambridge mathematics undergraduate who became a devoted companion, taking the place of David Pinsent; with Rush Rhees, who came in 1935 to study philosophy and became an enduring friend; with Norman Malcolm, the Harvard graduate student who first came along in 1938; with Fania Pascal, a radical scholar who helped Wittgenstein plan a never-accomplished move to mother Russia; with Piero Sraffa, the Marxist Italian economist, who encouraged Wittgenstein to form an 'anthropological' way of viewing language (Monk, 1990:255-400). Additionally, he retreated twice to Norway (in 1931 and in 1936–37) to grapple with thoughts he found hard to resolve in the British setting. He endured the 1938 annexation of his mother country by Nazi Germany—he whose family was by Nazi reckoning Jewish. He was elected Professor at Cambridge, and began to serve in 1939. And beneath all this he wrestled throughout the decade with thoughts of God, of sin, of judgment, of a resurrection life to be (*CV* 3-37). The struggle to form his views about human language had to be hammered out in the midst of these urgent and inter-related involvements.

They had also to be hammered out in the context of his longer philosophical task begun in the *Tractatus.* There he had held that the matters he thought most important were simply unsayable. Religion, ethics, aesthetics—the entire realm of value—was the Unspeakable. So was the *Tractatus* just mistaken on this main point? Could such matters be brought to speech? Did they in fact set their own linguistic task, as the Bible, for example, seemed to assume? Two obstacles, well represented by Russell's views, stood in the way: the tenacious modern assumption that language had an essence (such as referring) and the equally tenacious assumption that religious beliefs belonged to a private, inner sphere. For on either of these assumptions, the 'meanings' anyone assigned to utterances in the sphere of value remained will-o'-the-wisp, ungraspable. It followed that the book that would succeed the *Tractatus* had to show that language has no single core but is rather a patchwork of non-congruent though related human activities, while it also had to show that private feelings are never the foundation of language in any sphere. For the first of these tasks, Wittgenstein would provide the descriptive notion of *Sprachspielen, language-games.* For the second, he would offer an extended argument, showing that the supposed interior foundation of language (quintessentially, of any so-called private language), was not available even as a way of speaking of feelings, so that in no case could privacy be the foundation of human speech.

The language-games approach carries over from the *Tractatus* the insistence that words and world are necessarily linked, but now that linkage takes a quite new form. Words no longer make up propositions that picture the world (*TLP* 1); rather words are *part of* the world; they come together in activities, language-games, constitutive of practices that comprise the human world. Thus words are even more tightly related to the rest of reality than were the propositions of the *Tractatus.* These ideas, brought to light first in Wittgenstein's 1930s lectures, then in the unpublished *Blue and Brown Books,* and finally in the *Philosophical Investigations,* were presented through a series of imaginary language-games. In their simplicity these games enabled students to grasp a way of construing word-world relations closer to actual life than the earlier, austere account of 'propositions' and 'facts.' In one game, a primitive builder instructs his assistant by ordering any of four needed stones: blocks, pillars, slabs, or beams (*BB.* 77-79; *PI* §2). In another, children play word-games as they learn their native language (*BB.* 17, 81; *PI* §7). Again, a shopper secures "five red apples" from the greengrocer (*PI* §1). Or a military commander gives battle orders and receives reports (PI §19). In each of these examples there is a relation to the way things are, yet crucially, these relations include the deeds and needs and intentions of the participants. No game can even be understood as a human activity (no proper sense of 'meaning' can arise from its words) apart from the *forms of life,* practices such as building, shopping, playing, or fighting, that make up human endeavors. Together these practices constitute our world (Kerr, 1997: Part Two).

Two sorts of objections likely occur to the modern reader of Wittgenstein's account—the reader imbued with the thought of Bertrand Russell or of the *Tractatus.* One is that while of course such activities provide the setting of human speech, it is always possible to detect within any meaningful setting a central core of reference—to blocks or apples or enemy action in Wittgenstein's examples—and so it is this referential core that (alone) gives their meaning to the words and the games played with them. (The other objection, not significantly analyzed in this chapter, is that 'meanings' themselves are the essential thing, 'meanings' seen as psychological foundations lying behind the spoken or written words.) Together these objections restate the reigning modern theories that Wittgenstein sought to overcome. What he had to show was that such 'reference' and such 'meaning' do not adequately describe the real workings of language. Take reference. It is no part of Wittgenstein's case that we never refer to anything. Of course we do. But referring hardly constitutes an interesting language-game by itself (such a game might merely bore us to death!), far less should we give pride of place to it in understanding our actual language-games, which are characterized not by *one* lordly move, referring, but typically by a rich assortment of moves. In natural languages such as German or English many of these are expressed by regular or customary terms: ordering ("I order you to . . ."), describing ("Can you describe it?"), constructing, reporting, speculating, hypothesizing, presenting, making up, play-acting. . . . (*PI* §23). So why crown "refer" as prince among all its fellow verbs of speech action?

The other temptation was as old as René Descartes. If, as modern Cartesians still supposed, body and soul were two separate items, with soul (or self, or mind) doing all the thinking, feeling, language-generating, and the like, while body merely moved about on soul's instructions, made sounds, took bumps, and so on, then mind-like matters were hopelessly isolated from the available world. The wonder was that there could be effective human communication at all, for there was no guarantee that (for example) what I call my headache is even the same sort of item as what you call your headache. Indeed, on this Cartesian view they are invincibly different: I cannot feel your pain; you cannot feel mine; so who is to say they are both actually *pains*? Communication is thus flawed at its core. Wittgenstein's language-game account overcame the temptation to think in this Cartesian way (for language was social from the outset), yet it was not enough to have offered an alternative account: one must see the private-language temptation as itself internally flawed; then it could tempt no longer.

Wittgenstein's refutation as refined in the *Investigations* was making out the best case he could for the Cartesian temptation (often giving its lines, within quotation marks, to an imaginary opponent) and then case-by-case showing that incoherencies followed. A single example among many must suffice here: Suppose an experimenter marks an S in a diary on each occurrence of a certain sensation. It appears that the recurring sensation is a referent for the investigator's new, private language, in which case S means that and only that sensation. Yet trouble brews here: how can the investigator be certain it is the very same sensation each time? "For he has no criterion of correctness" (*PI* §258). Subsequent remarks through the rest of *Philosophical Investigations* pursue other such attempts until there is nothing left to pursue; the Cartesian project is hopeless; the foundation it meant to offer is not there.

The language-game account of language is hardly what a tidy thinker would have wished for. It is loose and open-ended, designating a wide range of phenomena different from one another in scale as well as kind, and it never defines as "language-games" an exact class of linguistic phenomena, or makes clear what is too slight or too broad to count as one game. J. L. Austin's account of speech acts is more exact and more readily displayed, while it, like Wittgenstein's, diverges from modernity's linguistic track (Austin, 1975; *CONV.:* chap. 3; Murphy and McClendon, 1989). Yet language-games do provide a vocabulary by which certain tempting philosophical traps can be escaped or puzzles dissolved. The great positive gain the Wittgensteinian account offers (this, too, is paralleled by Austin's speech-act account) is to show language not on the *Tractatus* model of propositions picturing clusters of atomic facts, but on a model thoroughly woven into the fabric of human (linguistic and other) activity. Language-games proceed (like other games) according to *rules;* not to observe its rules is to fail to play any game. The rules of a language are so commonly recognized that they have a special name—we call them its *grammar.* Wittgenstein insisted that the word "grammar" in his use was no metaphor (*AMB*:31). The school grammar of correct usage differs from the grammar of the *Investigations* only in this: the former deals with easy-to-correct mistakes such as saying "them" when one needed "they," while philosophy has to grapple with hard-to-correct grammatical mistakes such as implying that the human self can be spoken of apart from its embodiment or presupposing that an investigator is recording the 'same' sensation when there is no way to check the sameness. Such serious grammatical mistakes misapprehend a *form of life.* Once acquired, the vocabulary of language-games serves to describe language as it is used in everyday life—a point Wittgenstein emphasized by saying that (good) philosophy "leaves everything just as it is" (*PI* §124).

The two main themes about the role of language that Wittgenstein struggled to overcome are around again in our own day: Still today there are referential and truth-conditional theories of language (cf. Michael Dummett). Although theories based on sense-data or other psychological features of speakers have not fared so well in straight philosophical circles, they persist among religious philosophers and liberal theologians (cf. David Tracy?). Wittgenstein, at least, knew he must overcome these foundational temptations if language and the thought it shaped were to be freed from the scientism and solipsism of our times, if (to put it positively) language-users were to emerge as full participants in a fully human life.

Christianity, Ludwig Wittgenstein saw, was more to be lived than talked, yet it, too, could be brought to speech. If language was part and parcel of practices that make up the living world, one could make sense of Christianity's teaching as well as of its ethics: "Christianity . . . offers us a (historical) narrative and says: now believe" (*CV* 32). It can hardly be accidental that this memo was jotted down in 1937, a year in which the language-game account of language was virtually complete. Ray Monk tells us that 1937 was a difficult year for Wittgenstein himself. Still in lonely Norway, he endured agonies of depression and self-reproach (Monk, 1990:372-82). His spiritual difficulties might have been eased had he consulted fellow-believers, but he encountered none. Or more accurately, his fellow pilgrims were only the classic Christian writers, not merely the New Testament, but Augustine (already mentioned), Bunyan, Kierkegaard. From them at least he could learn anew that "salvation through faith," for example, was "a real event"—as real as the "consciousness of sin" that beset him in these dark periods (*CV* 28). Kierkegaard's "religiousness B" had finally taken shape in him, too.

Finally, at year's end on the ship returning to Bergen from his Norwegian retreat, Wittgenstein addressed his journal notes to the central Christian doctrine itself (see *Doctrine,* Six)—the resurrection of Jesus Christ from the dead (*CV* 33; Monk, 1990:383f). If Christ was not risen, Wittgenstein reasoned (as another voyager in faith had reasoned long before—see 1 Corinthians 15), there was no good news. "If he did not rise from the dead," the questing Christian wrote, "he is a teacher like any other and can no longer *help;* and once more we are orphaned and alone." In that case we are "roofed in, as it were, and cut off from heaven" (*CV* 33). In that case, God is at best the remote God of the *Tractatus.*

> But if I am to be REALLY saved—what I need is *certainty*—not wisdom, dreams or speculation—and this certainty is faith itself

> *(der Glaube)*. And such faith is faith in what is needed by my *heart*, my *soul*, not my speculative intelligence. For it is my soul with its sufferings, as it were with its flesh and blood, that has to be saved, not my abstract mind. Perhaps we can say: Only *love (die Liebe)* can believe the resurrection. Or: it is *love* that believes the resurrection. We might say: Redeeming love believes even in the resurrection; holds fast even to the resurrection. What combats doubt is, as it were, *redemption*. Holding fast to *this* must be holding fast to that belief. So what that means is: first you must be redeemed and hold on to your redemption (keep hold of your redemption)—then you will see that you are holding fast to this faith. (*CV* 33, translation revised)

At last he was getting the matter right: it was not faith projected in modern fashion upon an inaccessible Tractarian heaven, but heaven's own faithfulness, the resurrection faithfulness of God in Jesus Christ (1 Cor. 15:20-23), that constituted the good news. And with that understanding had come a new understanding of language that made faith speakable.

c. ***Outflanking modern skepticism.***—Most twentieth-century philosophers sensed a high obligation to justify the validity of human knowledge—to fail here seemed to open the door to skepticism. (Religious knowledge appeared specially vulnerable in this regard.) The home station on this modern philosopher's track was foundational certainty. The trick was to take up a position on the track close enough to home to do justice to the claims of reason and experience, yet not so close as to seem indifferent to skepticism's legitimate threat. Wittgenstein was well aware of these required postures—they were the heritage of Descartes and Kant, or in Britain, of Locke, Berkeley, and Hume. All these philosophers had set out in one way or another to place human knowledge on secure foundations. Yet even from the *Tractatus* days Wittgenstein had avoided modern philosophy's preoccupation with epistemology. His great focus had instead been the metaphysics of language and the world it could represent, while the Unspeakable (ethics and aesthetics and ultimately God) had in this earlier work lain necessarily out of reach. (*Wovon man nicht sprechen kann, darüber muss man schweigen—TLP* 7.) It was not until language with its task had been treated anew in the *Investigations* that he could explicitly address his contemporaries' concerns about knowledge and certainty.

The best place to see this development of his thought is in Wittgenstein's treatment of the language of religious belief. The change here is foreshadowed as early as the lecture on ethics he gave at Cambridge in 1929. In it he called attention to some distinctive sorts of human awareness: for example, one might wonder at the very *existence of the world* (not *how* the world is, but *that* it is); or one might sometimes feel *absolutely safe;* or one might experience *guilt* and thus implicitly recognize God's disapproval. Being conscious of any of these ways of experiencing the world amounts to *seeing the world as a miracle.* This particular sort of 'seeing as' cannot be reduced to simply another perceptual datum—to do so would be to treat these distinctive experiences as simply more facts about human nature on a par with the human tendencies to procreate, to define and solve problems, to acquire property or make promises. Such a reduction would deny to this language of miracle its own unique quality (*LE* 9-12). Here, then, is a transitional stage between Wittgenstein's earlier and later thinking. In this Cambridge lecture the role of language-games had not yet appeared in his thought.

In the ten years following, as we have seen in preceding subsections, Wittgenstein fought clear of two powerful philosophical temptations—he replaced the temptation to solipsism with a sense of human community, and he replaced a Tractarian view of language that set words and world exterior to one another by an account of (self-involving) language-games. In each case, as we have seen, there was a corresponding development of Wittgenstein's own Christian life: realizing humanity's communal solidarity entailed for him practicing the confession of sin; seeing language's embeddedness in practices and forms of life freed him to reflect upon Christian doctrines such as the resurrection of Jesus Christ from the dead. Coincident with these developments (1929–39) was the further realization that religious knowing and believing and confessing were all interior to language-games and practices. There could be no settling of the accuracy or verity of religious beliefs as it were from the outside, no validation of religion apart from participation in the forms of life that were constituted in part by these very beliefs. Moreover, religion was a sphere in which differences of belief arose: the existence of alternate (and rival!) standpoints was integral to the account. It was thus no accident that Wittgenstein began his 1938 lectures on religious belief by recounting an episode that evoked disagreement: an Austrian general had once said, "I shall think of you after my death, if that should be possible." Wittgenstein pointed out that some hearers would find the general's remark ludicrous, while others would not (*LC* 53).

This raised the question, How could convictions such as a last judgment or a life beyond death, or language-games that involved speaking about God, be understood by those who did not share these religious forms of life? In the lectures on religious belief Wittgenstein sometimes set himself among the unbelievers (Hilary Putnam suggests that this may have been a pedagogical device—1995:49f). In any case, Wittgenstein's point was that to understand the convictions one must know the grammar of their utterance. It was often the case that religious beliefs did not rest on the ground ordinary or everyday beliefs did:

> There are instances where you have a faith [that] does not rest on the fact[s] on which our ordinary everyday beliefs normally do rest.
>
> [Instances where] what you say won't be taken as the measure for the firmness of a belief? But, for instance, what risks you would take? (*LC* 54)

A good way to describe religious convictions, then, was "having different pictures" (*LC* 55). A preceding chapter has shown how such picturing works (see *Doctrine,* Two, 75-77). To Wittgenstein it made little sense to speak of contradicting or refuting particular cases of picture-thinking, and therefore little sense to think of confirming their pictures in the way one might confirm "there's an apple in the refrigerator." Yet it did not follow from this difference in their grammar that these pictures were *un*reasonable. What had to be checked was the *connections* the pictures required. Religious communities may make blunders, but these are to be detected by the "further surroundings" discoverable within their language-games and practices: "Just as something is a blunder in a particular game and not in another" (*LC* 59).

At this stage readers may be tempted to a mistake that has been congealed in the phrase "Wittgensteinian fideism." This is a term of reproach, first used by Kai Nielsen but widely copied by others, whose point is to claim that Wittgenstein and his followers are "fideists" who believe that if a (religious) language-game is "played," that is all there is to be said about it: no criticism or correction is possible or relevant or in order. This is not what either Ludwig Wittgenstein or even his most ardent followers meant; I will say more in the following section (§3) about why such a reproach is misplaced.

The war years (1939–45), a difficult time for most Britons, stretched over most of Wittgenstein's tenure as Professor of Philosophy at Cambridge University—from 1939 to 1947. They were relatively unproductive years even for his genius. He lectured for several terms, but was eventually granted leave to do medical work, first as a porter at Guy's Hospital in bomb-ravaged London, then as a research assistant to a team studying the physiology of shock in a Manchester laboratory. During these years, nevertheless, he came close to completing a version of the *Philosophical Investigations* fit to publish (the extant Preface is indeed dated January 1945), though at the last minute he withdrew it. Dissatisfaction with his students and his own post-war lectures, along with failing health and the old restlessness returning led him to resign his chair after two more academic years. His needs were few: a friend or two, simple food, a quiet place to read and work, and a few books, besides Street and Smith's *Detective Story Magazine* for leisure hours. All this was available through friends in Ireland, and so he spent most of 1948 there. Much of his work was on the philosophy of psychology, continuing the thought of Part II of the *Investigations.* There came as well the opportunity to relate what he had been doing in philosophy to some traditional Anglo American questions about knowing and certainty.

Ironically, that late treatment produced what some regard as Wittgenstein's most readable book, the posthumously published *On Certainty* (OC). In 1949, already in poor health, he crossed the Atlantic by ship to visit Norman Malcolm in Upstate New York. While he was there Malcolm drew his attention to some papers by Wittgenstein's old friend and colleague G. E. Moore. Moore had said that he could *know* a number of propositions for certain, such as "Here is one hand, and here is another" (spoken while extending his own hands) and "The earth existed for a long time before my birth" (*OC* vi). Wittgenstein did not doubt the truth of Moore's truisms, and indeed was favorably impressed by these papers. They were, he said, Moore's best work. Yet he thought they were still not right: It was a mistake to suppose the integrity of human knowledge was provided by some unexceptionable propositions that kept the rest afloat like pontoons supporting a bridge. 'Knowing' and 'being certain' functioned in human languages in an altogether different way.

Moore's truisms are unexceptionable for us, he thought, not because we have extremely good evidence for them, but because they belong to our picture of the world. This picture is a social possession, a "kind of mythology" (*OC* 94f).

> 96. It might be imagined that some propositions, of the form of empirical propositions, were hardened and functioned as channels for such empirical propositions as were not hardened but fluid; and that this relation altered with time, in that fluid propositions hardened, and hard ones became fluid.

> 97. The mythology may change back into a state of flux, the river-bed of thoughts may shift. But I distinguish between the movement of the waters on the river-bed and the shift of the bed itself; though there is not a sharp division of the one from the other. (*OC* 96f)

The things that we believe and that stand fast for us (Wittgenstein avoided "know" here because of its special role in the language) form a system in which no "sense data" or "logical givens" provide foundations. We can speak of such things only because we possess the whole system. So

> one might almost say that these foundation-walls are carried by the whole house. (*OC* 248)

It is worth noting that this "epistemology socialized," as it came to be called (Glock, 1996:81), could not have been worked out save by an anthropological turn in which Wittgenstein withdrew from modern individualism and save by a linguistic turn in which he discarded modern theories of language. At the end of his life (the last draft entry of *On Certainty* is dated April 27, two days before his death), Ludwig Wittgenstein thus explicitly departed from modernity's foundational theory of knowledge, replacing it with a web of understanding, interdependence, and shared practice that marked his invention of the post-modern world.

When it became clear that the progress of prostate cancer would soon end his life, Wittgenstein was offered an upstairs room in the Cambridge home of his physician. There for two months he continued to work vigorously, until just before his end. Still the naturalized alien, he died apart from his beloved family and apart from the Austrian friends he had maintained over the decades. A few British friends gathered at his bedside, but only after he had lost consciousness. He had left them a message: "Tell them I've had a wonderful life" (Monk, 1990:579; Peter, 1988). After hesitating, the friends agreed that Roman Catholic prayers should be offered at his bedside and at his grave in a Cambridge churchyard. He died April 29, 1951.

If we ask what Christian convictions consoled his dying, the best evidence is the dignity of his last actions. Since his concluding work was *On Certainty*, though, it may be appropriate to refer here to a play that he had for a long time found especially valuable. This was *The King of the Dark Chamber* (1916), by Rabindranath Tagore, the Indian mystic whose poems Ludwig Wittgenstein had puckishly read to members of the Vienna Circle years before. The play was one he had valued so highly that he had attempted with a friend to revise its English translation (Monk, 1990:408-12).

In the play, a country is ruled by a king who is never seen by his subjects, though perhaps sometimes he appears incognito. Some say the king is hideous; others, that there is no king; still others, that the unseen king is the true source of the people's surprising liberty. The king visits his queen, Sudarshana, only in a darkened room or chamber where she cannot see him. Consequently she shares the suspicion that his appearance is revolting. He tells her that she will be unable to bear his sight until (through suffering?) she is prepared for it. Forsaking him, Sudarshana flees. She is sought by others, royal rivals; she suffers greatly; finally she longs again for the king of the darkened room. Sensing his unseen presence with her in exile, she returns down a dusty road. Back with him in the darkened room, the prodigal Sudarshana at last dimly sees the king. She exclaims that he is not beautiful; rather he stands beyond all comparison. He tells her, though, that the game in the darkness is finished, and invites her now to come with him—into the light.

It seems that the author of the *Tractatus* and *Philosophical Investigations* and *On Certainty* was attracted to this parabolic play because it stood for the Unspeakable. In his life there had been much darkness, there had been sins to confess, there had been failures in his struggle to say and to show. These led him to identify with the distraught and sometimes faithless suffering Sudarshana. If his sixty-two years had nevertheless been "a wonderful life," was this not only because he was "a truth-seeker" (see Monk, 1990:3) but also because (as he had once written on a ship en route to Bergen) "redeeming love believes even in the resurrection"? Or, in another's words, was it because of the hope that though "at present we see only puzzling reflections in a mirror, . . . one day we shall see face to face"? Because the King had at last said, "Come with me now, come outside—*into the light!*" (see 1 Cor. 13:12; Tagore, 1916:205).

§3. Assessing Wittgenstein

a. Rival views regarding Wittgenstein and religion.—The preceding documented account of Wittgenstein's Christianity in relation to his philosophy may cause readers to wonder why others have missed so important a connection. Here I consider some interpretations that by their silence or neglect challenge mine. Luckily this will not require surveying the wide field of rival interpretations of Wittgenstein's philosophy; I mean merely to look at some interpreters who, while relating his philosophical work to his life of faith, even acknowledging some of the crucial biographical facts, still pass by them without drawing the conclusions reached here.

William Warren Bartley III. An American philosopher interested in philosophical biographies, Bartley was among the first to focus upon Wittgenstein's Austrian context. He spent time in Austria interviewing surviving friends and family and traveled to the mountains of Lower Austria to talk with some there who remembered the teacher two decades after his death. Bartley reported these investigations in a small volume, *Wittgenstein* (1973), that attracted considerable attention. Although much of the material on which the present chapter depends was not readily accessible when he wrote, Bartley correctly reported the influence of Tolstoy's writings on Wittgenstein during the war of 1914–18, recorded Wittgenstein's 1919 examination of a call to a religious life, and noted his ongoing friendships with devout Austrian and British Christians (1973:18, 83f, 104f, 117). Regarding the momentous discovery of Tolstoy's *Gospel in Brief,* Bartley wrote that "Wittgenstein had been overwhelmed by Tolstoy's version of the Gospels after reading it in Galicia in 1915 [actually 1914], and he had reread the *Gospel* countless times since then, so that, as his friends testify, he could recite large parts by heart." Bartley then proposes a view that foreshadows the present chapter: "That Wittgenstein was engaging in an imitation of Christ is a possibility that cannot lightly be dismissed when one attempts to comprehend his extraordinary life [as a schoolteacher] between 1920 and 1926." Yet he withdraws this proposal at once, since "it is . . . only a possibility and one whose correctness would be impossible to establish or even seriously to test" (1973:83f). Yet Bartley's own account of Wittgenstein's life is framed by an interpretation of two of Wittgenstein's reported dreams! (1973:31-40, 178f). It seems more than a little curious that Bartley could dismiss as evanescent the concrete Christian particularity of a life that he correctly labels "ethical activity and practical philosophy" (1973:84) while reposing such great confidence in his own long-distance psychoanalysis. The latter enterprise may have some value (Wittgenstein himself respected Freud), but the former is the stuff of life itself. In any case, Bartley reported religious data that, for whatever reason, he quickly discounted.

Bartley's book became notorious for another reason: in it, he pictured a Wittgenstein possessed by a (homosexual) demon he could hardly control; in particular, he said that while living in October 1919, in Vienna's Third District, Wittgenstein obsessively frequented the nearby Prater, a park where "rough young men were ready to cater to him sexually," and that this compulsion remained to tempt him throughout his life (1973:47, 51f). Bartley does not condemn Wittgenstein for this alleged promiscuous behavior; indeed, he speculates that in 1919 it may have provided a release that saved him from suicide (1973:46). Yet his claim, if true, diminishes the picture I have presented of a Christian convert struggling not with demonic temptations but with life-shaping vocational choices. The Bartley claim has been uncritically accepted by many who seem untroubled by the total lack of evidence for it, and who consequently scorn or alternatively glorify Wittgenstein as "a homosexual." Setting aside the common (but dubious) assumption that anyone's life can accurately be categorized by others or even self-categorized as "gay" or "straight," it is at least worthwhile to set the facts as straight as possible. Happily, Wittgenstein's tireless biographer Ray Monk has exhaustively investigated the Bartley claim (Monk, 1990:581-86). Monk points out that in a book otherwise well documented, Bartley provided no evidence for his claim, even when later challenged to do so. Even Bartley agrees that (with this alleged exception) Wittgenstein's lifelong sexual behavior was closer to total abstinence. Early on, Wittgenstein was influenced by an Austrian psychological theorist, Otto Weininger, who taught that the price of creativity was chastity. And Monk adds that for his undocumented exception Bartley appears to have relied on evidence that he misread:

> It would be entirely in keeping with what else we know about Wittgenstein that he did indeed find the "rough, young, homosexual youths" that he discovered in the Prater fascinating, that he returned again and again to the spot from where he could see them, and that he recorded his fascination in diary form in his notebooks. But it would also be entirely in keeping with what we know that the youths themselves knew nothing at all about his fascination, and indeed were unaware of his existence. (Monk, 1990:586)

On a different plane, Wittgenstein certainly did form friendships with young women and young men, in whom he took a deep and moral interest. These friendships comforted what might else have been an intolerably lonely bachelor existence. Yet in all this we know of but one 1937 instance, self-scoldingly recorded in his private diary, in which he departed from the Platonic love that was his lifelong ideal (Monk, 1990:376f). In the rigorous confessions that marked Wittgenstein's progress on the Christian journey, promiscuous sex (or any other sort of sex) was not included among the flaws he repeatedly confessed, some of them minor flaws indeed.

James C. Edwards, in his insightful book *Ethics Without Philosophy: Wittgenstein and the Moral Life* (1982), sets out to show that Wittgenstein's central concern throughout his philosophical career was ethics. He starts from the clue to the *Tractatus* provided by a letter to Wittgenstein's friend Ficker:

> My work [the *Tractatus Logico-Philosophicus*] consists of two parts: the one presented here plus all I have *not* written. And it is precisely this second part that is the important one. (quoted in Edwards, 1982:25)

So the *Tractatus* was meant to *show* by its silence that the factual language of science, what Edwards calls "reality-as-representation," is inapplicable beyond the sphere of science; it cannot describe the infinitely more important sphere of ethics, the sphere Wittgenstein there calls "the mystical." Ethics is supernatural: its content cannot be said or stated; it can only be shown. The true goal of ethics for Wittgenstein is to display a "sound human understanding," one that belongs to a "sound human life" (Edwards, 1982:106, 151-59, 216-30). Edwards shows how Wittgenstein pursued this goal in his remarkable 1929 Lecture on Ethics (*LE*) and in the work that followed, culminating in the *Philosophical Investigations.* Ethics as a discipline is concerned not with rules or choices, but with "discovering the permanent sense of human life": it is about what makes life "worth living" (*LE* 5). Thus suicide remains the "elementary sin" (*NB* 91), not because it is the wrong choice or because it breaks a moral rule, but because it

> represents . . . failure to find the sense of life that renders it worth living. And if that sense is not found, then everything is allowed. (Edwards, 1982:83)

Given the centrality of the sound or healthy human life in Edwards's rendering of Wittgenstein, it would seem natural for him to pay considerable attention to the latter's Christian conversion and its consequences. And in fact he does report the "profound impact" of Wittgenstein's reading Tolstoy's *Gospel in Brief* during the war and relates this impact to his service as a schoolteacher in Lower Austria. He even calls this, as Bartley had tentatively done, an *imitatio Christi* (Edwards, 1982:44, 61, 70), an imitation of Christ. Edwards then goes beyond Bartley to identify the moral goal of Wittgenstein's work ("sound human understanding") with "the mystical" of the *Tractatus,* and more broadly with a "religious sensibility" that he admits persisted throughout Wittgenstein's life. This sensibility provided a link between the "Christian" themes of his earlier years and his ongoing attempts to do philosophy without falling into metaphysical nonsense (1982:244-46).

> In [the later Wittgenstein's] adamant refusal to countenance the metaphysical gaze there are present both the Tractarian acknowl-

> edgement of the world's miraculous existence and an ethic of love which continues the Tolstoyan service to the poor. By interpreting the sound human understanding as *a religious vision* we preserve a place for these important features of his thought and character; otherwise their ostensible disappearance is an anomaly. (Edwards, 1982:245, emphasis added)

Edwards's conclusion here is a helpful part of a valuable book. For under the heading of ethics he has placed much that might with equal justice be labeled Wittgenstein's ongoing share in the Christian *religion.* Oddly censored, however, from Edwards's account is any employment of standard Christian terminology: that Ludwig Wittgenstein read the Christian Gospels, that he was converted to follow the way of Jesus, and that (within the limits already noted) he lived a faithful Christian life and died a Christian death. I do not know how to account for the systematic omission of these concepts. Is it Edwards's lack of familiarity with the Christian tradition, or is it rather his unwillingness to acknowledge its terms as Wittgenstein did?

Norman Malcolm, the American philosopher whose *Memoir* (1984) is an important primary source for the life of Wittgenstein his teacher, wrote just before his own 1990 death a second brief work, *Wittgenstein: A Religious Point of View?* (1994), that provides extended evidence of Wittgenstein's ongoing Christian commitment together with a reflection on the relation between his religious outlook and his philosophy. The first chapter summarizes such known facts, not all of them mentioned in the *Memoir,* including the 1914 discovery of Tolstoy's *Gospel,* the prayers recorded in the wartime diaries, the post-war divestment of wealth, the vocational struggle issuing in teaching, the written reflections on the mystical and on the last judgment in the *Tractatus* and elsewhere, the Lecture on Ethics with its references to distinctive intuitions (such as "feeling *absolutely* safe"), the religious conversations and religious advice given to Drury his onetime student, the report of time spent in prayer on a retreat to Norway, the advice on non-violence, the invocation of God's will for his work, the confessions of sin, the repeated emphasis upon Christianity as a matter of practice not theory, the embrace of the resurrection of Christ, the disdain for philosophical proofs of God's existence, the stern self-judgment in Gospel light: "*of course* I want to be perfect" (Malcolm, 1994:7-22). What one does not find is any attempt to string these beads of faithfulness together into a spiritual narrative, or indeed into any other sort of theological overview. Instead, Malcolm turns next to a series of reflections on philosophical themes related to the singular religious point of view he sees exhibited in Wittgenstein's life—reflection, for example, on his friend and teacher's struggle to locate the nature of language (1994: 40-47). Malcolm hopes thereby to explain the saying attributed to Wittgenstein: "I am not a religious man but I cannot help seeing every problem from a religious point of view" (Drury in Rhees, ed., 1981:94). My own reading of that saying is that (while confessing his inadequacy for the role) Wittgenstein cannot help addressing philosophical problems as one who is himself shaped by his Christian convictions. Malcolm takes only an obliquely similar view. He tries to show that there are *analogies* between Wittgenstein's religious attitude and his attitude to philosophical questions such as the nature of explanations: to say that explanations necessarily come to an end is analogous to a Christian appeal to "the will of God" (1994:85-86). Certainly there is something to this: the later Wittgenstein meant to show that human language and thought were set not by timeless logic or metaphysical necessity but by "natural history"—the reality that surrounds us all (*PI* 415; II, xii). That reality stretched from earth to heaven, and gave all our concepts a "pre-linguistic, pre-rational" basis (Malcolm, 1994:92). Malcolm writes:

> Clearly, there is an analogy between Wittgenstein's view that our concepts rest on a basis of human actions and reactions, and his view that what is most fundamental in a religious life is not the affirming of creeds, nor even prayer and worship—but rather, doing *good deeds*—helping others in concrete ways, treating their needs as equal to one's own, opening one's heart to them, not being cold or contemptuous, but loving. (Malcolm, 1994:92)

That 'view,' as Malcolm labels it, might with equal justice be ascribed to a traditional Mennonite farmer or crafts worker or indeed to any number of traditional Christians—including the author of the Epistle of James. It is one among several sorts of typical Christian conviction. Malcolm, though, never went on to identify the 'view' in this way or to display the narrative unity that held this set of convictions together.

The biographies of Ludwig Wittgenstein by *Brian McGuiness* (1988) and *Ray Monk* (1990) have been quarried for information in the first two sections of this chapter, but neither biographer gives the weight to Wittgenstein's Christian standpoint reckoned appropriate here. This is perhaps a premature estimate of McGuiness, who in his first volume has brought Wittgenstein's life only through 1920, the time when he took up teacher training in Vienna. Besides the now familiar facts about the Tolstoy *Gospel,* Wittgenstein's divestment of wealth at war's end, and so on, McGuiness provides many valuable sidelights. For example, he offers an interesting if incomplete impression of Wittgenstein's faith during the Italian imprisonment period of 1918–19 given by fellow prisoner-of-war Franz Parak: Wittgenstein said that he had been reborn (an expression Parak was not sure he understood), but light broke for Parak later, he said, when he read Dostoevski's *Crime and Punishment,* recommended by Wittgenstein, and came to its last paragraph:

> But now a new history commences: a story of the gradual renewing of a man, of his slow progressive regeneration, and change from one world to another—an introduction to the hitherto unknown realities of life. (*Crime and Punishment,* cited by McGuiness, 1988:273)

A parallel example of the detail Monk furnishes is found in his review of the works Wittgenstein was reading during his time as a soldier in the Austro-Hungarian army. This reading included, as well as Tolstoy, *The Anti-Christ* by Friedrich Nietzsche. Monk of course recalls that work's attack upon Christianity, but he then quotes from it a significant passage of another sort:

> It is false to the point of absurdity to see in a 'belief,' perchance the belief in redemption through Christ, the distinguishing characteristic of the Christian: only Christian *practice,* a life such as he who died on the Cross . . . *lived,* is Christian. . . . Even today *such* a life is possible, for *certain* men even necessary: genuine, primitive Christianity will be possible at all times. . . . *Not* a belief but a doing, above all a *not*-doing of many things, a different *being* . . . (Nietzsche, cited in Monk, 1990:122)

Together these valuable biographies by McGuiness and Monk furnish needed lumber for reconstructing this life, but neither provides, perhaps for different reasons (McGuiness because his work is incomplete; Monk because he has chosen not faithfulness but genius as the controlling model for his work), the integration of life, faith, and thought proposed here.

b. "Wittgensteinian fideism"?—While Wittgenstein interpreters who pay some attention to the solid facts of his life have provided only imperfect accounts of his relation to religion, those who totally neglect these biographical facts or pass over them in near silence confront even more serious difficulties. It is worthwhile in closing, since these interpreters are nowadays perhaps most often heard, to note the consequences of their approach. They, too, can be seen to suffer from a neglect of the lively facts cited earlier in this chapter.

Total neglect seals the interpretation of Wittgenstein's religious convictions provided by ***Hans-Johann Glock*** in his (otherwise useful) *Wittgenstein Dictionary* (1996). At the outset the *Dictionary* provides a "sketch of an intellectual biography" that purports to list the main influences upon Wittgenstein's thought. It lists Mauthner, Schopenhauer, Hertz, Loos, Russell, Frege, Ramsey, and many others, but says nothing whatever of Tolstoy and his *Gospel.* Correspondingly, when the *Dictionary*'s entry on religion appears, it only cites some entries from Wittgenstein's *Lectures and Conversations* (*LC*) and his later occasional jottings (e.g., from *CV*), without relating these cryptic notes to the life-story of their author. This is the case, even though Glock writes, citing Wittgenstein, that what gives religious beliefs meaning "is not empirical or metaphysical beliefs but *their role in the practice of the believer*" (1996:32, citing *CV* 85, emphasis added). Glock does not reveal that the believer first in question, Wittgenstein himself, had left a meteor track—his own religious passage—through the dark sky of modernity. Regrettably, Glock's handling of Wittgenstein's religious convictions is all too typical of philosophical treatment of this main twentieth-century philosopher. It is as though in our time a fog of indifference had settled around the phenomena of faith, making such striking faith as that of our subject all but invisible.

> By the same token, religious terms like 'God' do not refer to entities, and to state that God exists is not to make a statement about the existence of a certain entity (*LC* 63; *CV* 50, 82). It expresses a commitment to a certain frame of reference or a form of life, a commitment which is brought about not by argument but by a certain upbringing or certain experiences. (Glock, 1996:321)

On Glock's understanding, Wittgenstein held that religion was not "about" God, indeed, not "about" any entity at all. The role of religion was to "express a commitment," namely the commitment to a certain way of life.

This comment expresses a half-truth that can best be completed by placing it alongside an opposed interpretation, the view that notoriously has proposed the term "Wittgensteinian fideism." This epithet is much endured by Wittgenstein interpreters who attend to Wittgenstein's philosophy of religion—advocate it, debate it, often assume roles as its rightful expositors—yet who omit the biographical facts that shape this chapter. Foremost among those thus abused is the Welsh philosopher of religion ***Dewi Z. Phillips*** (1934–). In a series of articles and books Phillips has offered a penetrating account of Wittgenstein on religion altogether sympathetic in spirit, yet he has not been able to repel the curt dismissal, of Wittgenstein and of his own interpretation, expressed by this charge. Whereas for interpreters such as Glock religious convictions say all too little, being limited (on Glock's view of what can possibly be made of them) to "commitment" without any corresponding content or reference, Phillips's view of religious convictions, like that of Wittgenstein himself, seems to these detractors to claim far too much, since they think Phillips or his predecessors have placed religious language-games beyond all criticism (cf. Nielsen, 1967). It seems that even the careful historian of religious thought Hans Frei understood his fellow Wittgensteinian in this way. Frei classified D. Z. Phillips as typical of those for whom philosophy was irrelevant to the content of religion (Frei, 1992:46-55).

Phillips has been at great pains to display the injustice of these caricatures of his views. Against the claim that religious belief is cut off from the rest of human life (or that religious belief can be understood only by those who are already believers, or that so-called religious language alone determines what is meaningful in religion, or that religious beliefs cannot in any way be criticized, or that religious beliefs cannot be criticized or even affected by personal, social, or cultural events outside themselves—the fivefold form Phillips finds his critics assigning to "Wittgensteinian fideism"), he tries to show that his own writing, presumed to display these features, displays in each case the very opposite (Phillips, 1986:chap. 1). He holds, for example, that religious belief may be overturned by reflection upon the problem of evil. (Just how true to Wittgenstein this particular defense is, remains another matter.) What can hardly be disputed is the melancholy conclusion reached by Phillips himself—that, his protests to the contrary notwithstanding, "Wittgensteinian fideism" remains the irresistible misunderstanding Phillips's work evokes (Phillips, 1993:254).

Why is this so? Why do the majority of philosophical interpreters persist (despite repeated denials, complaints, and protests) in rejecting the religious thought of Wittgenstein and certain of his principal followers as "fideism"? To my mind their mistake is exactly parallel to that made by Glock. What we have is two sides of 'modernity' in the sense of modernity earlier defined. On the one side are those who with Glock are still willing, despite Wittgenstein's long labors, to relegate all religious language-games to pure expressivism, classifying them either with someone's groaning in pain or else with promising oneself to behave better in the future. On the other side (the side of Phillips's major critics though not Phillips himself), Wittgensteinian religious language-games are supposed to constitute an intact whole, but this is a whole that is cut off like extreme sectarianism from the outside world, so that these games are irrelevant to all else. Only by doing violence to all he maintained could this be taken as the actual view of the later Wittgenstein (see §2*b* above). Is not Phillips's difficulty, then, as Brad Kallenberg has suggested to me, (1) claiming that universal justifications of religion are of course impossible, since "justification" does not name any one thing but many things, while (2) nonetheless failing to provide any *particular* justification as required in Wittgenstein's case? *Phillips could have done this by pointing to the Christian life Wittgenstein lived.* (Perhaps his view that philosophy must maintain a rigid neutrality with regard to the truth of religion kept him from this remedy.) Thus he lacks the universal justification that modernity wrongly hankers after, yet fails to provide the one kind of justification that is in this case possible. Lacking both, Phillips is charged with fideism and, though he rejects it, cannot silence his critics.

Doing violence to what Ludwig Wittgenstein stood for religiously is the peculiar temptation of those who neglect the profound life journey of this quiet Christian. Against their misreadings, though, there stands the "wonderful life" itself. Without reckoning with it, Wittgenstein's own religious standpoint will likely meet one of two fates—either be *reduced* à la Glock to opinions of no great philosophical moment, or alternatively, *cast off,* so that his religious convictions may (as by a Phillips) be acknowledged or may (as by a Nielsen) be opposed, yet in neither case be convictions that matter much to philosophy. Only a narrative interpretation of the complex facts of Wittgenstein's life, one that weighs his "wonderful life" and its basic Christian dimension into the task, can provide fair and full treatment of his significance to his times and ours.

* * * * *

Will proper attention to Wittgenstein (thinker, Christian, human being) change for the better the situation of Christian thought in our times? Some continue to hope for a 'Christian philosophy' that can pour foundations *other than Jesus Christ* upon which believers may build. Such essentially modern hopes find no comfort in the achievement of Ludwig Wittgenstein. He was no 'Christian philosopher' and he offers us no 'Christian philosophy,' not even an embryonic one. Had he spoken sympathetically to those with such hopes, he might have offered to teach them how to stop philosophizing! Still other believers despair of philosophy, making themselves practical fideists—their religious practice hermetically sealed from thought's proper tasks. Here Wittgenstein's achievement comes into play: in instance after instance the Christian life he lived and the intellectual work he did are harnessed together. Moreover, in the process he escaped from intellectual modernity without being thrown back upon unacceptable premodern alternatives—without antiquating himself. Thus the twentieth century's gap between its best philosophical insights and its chief religious convictions was closed. To pursue that closure is the task of the chapter next to follow.

CHAPTER SEVEN

After Wittgenstein: The Changing Role of Philosophy of Religion

The twentieth century saw a surprising collapse of philosophy as an ultimate discipline undergirding Western culture. Perhaps the first evidence of this, a signal that the wary might well have heeded, was that early in the century philosophy ceased to be a discipline undergirding the Christian gospel, but became instead its harsh critic and, more often than not, its cultured despiser. In the year 1900 there were still many who believed that a proper philosophical grounding must and could prepare the way for Christianity. Some, the late Hegelians, even taught that true philosophy spoke in its more rational dialect the message that religion with its colorful images was meant to convey, so that philosophy and religion were partners in a common task. Then came the meltdown. Where at the twentieth century's beginning American philosophy departments typically housed actual or nominal Christians or at least philosophers who provided broad support for religion, the entire world of Western thought was about to say good-bye to all that (the sardonic title of Robert Graves's memoir of the First World War). The following philosophical generation called into question all the foundations of the preceding one. For example, close to the summit from 1900 to 1914 were Royce, James, Pierce, and the early Dewey, all supporters of some form of religion. Yet shortly there appeared G. E. Moore, Bertrand Russell, Vienna's logical positivists, and in their turn the generation of A. J. Ayer and W. v. O. Quine, each hostile to religion understood as a truth-bearer, and all at the very eminence of later-century philosophy. In the English-speaking world, the most striking exception to this turn away from Christianity was the career of Austrian-English philosopher Ludwig Wittgenstein (see preceding chapter). With a few others, Wittgenstein looked beyond modernity to another way of construing selves, world, and God, and in his case this turn paralleled a quest for a faithful Christian existence. Yet in this regard as in others he was exceptional.

What was until quite recently less clear, though true, was that philosophy in the course of the century had abandoned any design to serve as a prop for the culture of the Western world, whether that meant standing for religion *or* against it. Among English-speaking philosophers, that foundational role was largely set aside. Philosophy would not guarantee the world's (apparent) metaphysical beliefs.

The task of this chapter, then, is to show the changing role of philosophy of religion in a setting where its earlier tasks have been abandoned as inappropriate or impossible. From the wider range of topics covered by current philosophy of religion, I consider two: **(§1) the problem of religious knowledge (can anyone know about God? *can one know God? if neither, in what if anything can religious knowledge consist?) and (§2) the problem of many religions (why are there so many, and since there are so many, why do they matter?)***. The second problem partly overlaps the first. A third focus of philosophy of religion, the (so-called) problem of evil, does not receive separate treatment, but our sample philosophers' approaches to evil will nonetheless appear. The general structure of the chapter is to show for each of the two chosen problems the way it is treated by a contemporary philosopher who has continued the older or 'modern' paradigm, disregarding the work of Wittgenstein and those like him, followed by the way the same or similar problems are treated by philosophers who represent the new paradigm. Some will want to call the latter examples 'post-modern.'

§1. Religious Knowledge

a. Knowing about God: Alvin Plantinga.—Few if any who have chronicled the changes in recent philosophy from a modern to a putatively postmodern style have offered the work of Alvin Plantinga as an example. Plantinga is more likely to be thought of as a brilliant, albeit eccentric, practitioner of classic analytic philosophy in the style of his mentors and colleagues Cartwright, Alston, Chisholm, Frankena, Gettier, and Quine. To be sure, from his earliest writings Plantinga, a convinced Christian of conservative cast, set his face against the logical positivists, displaying a particular dislike for the verifiability criterion of meaning. Yet this dislike could readily be expressed in traditional analytic terms (e.g., by asking whether the verifiability criterion was by its own standard either verifiable or meaningful). So the consensus about Plantinga reflected in *Alvin Plantinga* (Tomberlin and van Inwagen, eds., 1985), a substantial review of his work at mid-career, seems to be that whatever he may be as a philosopher, Plantinga is not an Anglo American postmodernist. A partial exception may be William P. Alston's contribution, which notes that Plantinga has renounced "classic foundationalism." Yet by itself this renunciation may not be enough to reverse our judgment of his place in philosophy. We must see.

i. The early Plantinga.—In his important early book *God and Other Minds* (1967), Plantinga worked in what is here called a (second-wave) modern style, the heritage of Descartes, Locke, Hume, and Kant. His book's goal was to show that the philosopher's best argument for belief in God (he thinks it is the teleological argument) had the same status, in his words, is "in the same epistemological boat," as the philosopher's best argument for belief that other people exist (the "other minds" argument). Plantinga examines both. The teleological argument for the existence of God, as displayed by Hume and Kant, is analogical: since human contrivance had a designer, must not the beautifully constructed cosmos have had the same? Admittedly, against that argument stands the problem of evil: would a good God have designed a universe containing so much evil? Yet against that, Plantinga continues, stands the free-will defense: the demand for an evil-free universe is nullified once we recognize that human beings cannot be both truly free and guaranteed free of evil. So Plantinga balances the evidence of the theistic against the atheistic argument. Next he examines the argument for other minds, and this, too, is analogical: here the analogy is between the recognizably mind-guided behavior of one's own body and the apparently intelligible behavior of others' bodies; if one's own mind exists, must not others' exist as well? Another displays pain behavior, cries out as if in agony. Is not this (analogical) evidence that the other is indeed in pain? In either case, whether arguing to prove

God or to prove the existence of other minds, the success of the argument depends on *evidence* applied by an *analogy.* The book's argument proceeded, Plantinga later said, "by way of considering the evidence for and against the proposition *there is such a person as God*" (Tomberlin and van Inwagen, eds., 1985:390). In short, Plantinga in 1967 worked as if he were an "evidentialist"; perhaps he was then a "classic foundationalist" as well.

Alvin Plantinga was born in Ann Arbor, Michigan, in 1932, the descendant on both sides of his family of early-twentieth-century immigrants from Friesland, a part of the Netherlands. His forebears were staunch, hardworking Calvinists, and going to church was an important part of Alvin Plantinga's childhood. He was educated at Jamestown College (North Dakota), where his father was a young professor, and then changed colleges when his father moved to teach psychology at Calvin College. Alvin spent a year at Calvin, then a year at Harvard where he had won a scholarship, and then, preferring it, came home to finish at Calvin. There he came under the influence of Harry Jellema, Calvin's influential philosophy teacher, and made friends with fellow student Nicholas Wolterstorff. For everyone Plantinga knew, the life of the mind was a serious matter, but in the summers he went west and learned to love hiking, mountaineering, and rock-climbing. After a master's degree in philosophy at Michigan, he went to Yale for a doctorate. There he learned more about the history of philosophy, but found little encouragement to do philosophy himself. That came when he was invited to his first job, teaching at Wayne State in Detroit. Colleagues there, such as Robert Sleigh and Edmund Gettier, spent every day arguing through the current problems of philosophy. At Wayne State the rigor and love of formalization of Plantinga's philosophical style were formed. In 1963 he was invited to replace his retiring teacher Jellema at Calvin. He richly enjoyed the Christian scholarship there, was widely invited to guest teaching assignments elsewhere, formed with his friends the influential Society of Christian Philosophers, and gained through his writings an international reputation as a convinced Christian philosopher. In 1982 he moved to the University of Notre Dame, where as of this writing he still teaches.

ii. The later Plantinga.—In 1983 Plantinga accepted a chair in philosophy at the University of Notre Dame. His inaugural address, later published as "Advice to Christian Philosophers" (1984), signaled a change in his work. No longer, he said, was the philosopher Christian to assume with secular philosophers that belief in God must be proved by the preponderance of evidence. Evidentialism was about to be succeeded by 'Reformed epistemology,' a quite different stance.

The advice in the address was that 'Christian philosophers' such as Plantinga himself must now sense new circumstances in the world of thought. Accordingly, they must display more autonomy. That is, they must address in their work not only questions that preoccupied current secular philosophers (the question of radical indeterminacy of translation, for example, or the status of artificial intelligence), but particularly those philosophical questions that naturally arose in the life of the Christian church at the time: such questions as what confers his or her (undoubted) "epistemic rights" upon a Christian believer in God (that, and not *whether* God exists), or the relation between faith and reason (that, and not the attempt to construct a worldview or 'faith' built upon scientific knowledge alone). In short,

> the Christian philosophical community ought *not* to think of itself as engaged in this common effort to determine the probability or philosophical plausibility of belief in God. The Christian philosopher quite properly *starts from* the existence of God, and presupposes it in philosophical work, whether or not she can show it to be probable or plausible with respect to premises accepted by all philosophers, or most philosophers, or most philosophers at the great contemporary centers of philosophy. (Plantinga, 1984:260f)

So Plantinga had recognized and appropriated a change in the philosophical weather. My question is how this climatic shift relates to the change in Anglo American philosophy described in the preceding chapters. Has Plantinga's "Advice," presumably addressed as much to himself as to any, been provoked by the shift, in particular the epistemological shift, represented by Wittgenstein?

Perhaps not. Already in *God and Other Minds,* Plantinga had vigorously renounced Wittgenstein's argument against the possibility of a private language, which as we have seen was a central move in Wittgenstein's resistance to the doctrine of the solitary self or solipsism (Chapter Six above; Plantinga, 1967:199ff). As regards his indifference to Wittgenstein, I find no evidence of change. Yet that is only part of the story. Already in 1981, two years before the Notre Dame inaugural, Plantinga had published an article that summed up his changing epistemological strategy regarding the knowledge of God. "Is Belief in God Properly Basic?" (1981) distinguished his doctrine of *properly basic beliefs* from the beliefs of "classic foundationalism" ancient and modern. In classic foundationalism, all beliefs, to be rational, must either themselves be foundational (meaning either self-evident or evident to the senses in the ancient and medieval version, or meaning "either self-evident or incorrigible for [a person] S" in the modern version), or if not that, must be based upon such foundational beliefs. At latest by 1981, Plantinga in contrast held that *many* of person S's beliefs are properly basic and are not based on *any* other beliefs. Plantinga's examples, "2 + 1 = 3," "I am seated at my desk," "there is a mild pain in my right knee," show the sort of thing he has in mind (1981:41); these are basic though not foundational.

Now consider the move for which this prepares us: For a Christian, *belief in God is properly basic.* This does not mean for Plantinga that it is an unreasonable (indefensible, or groundless) belief; the Christian if well trained may indeed know *why* he or she believes in God. Basic beliefs are just those on which many other beliefs may properly be based, while they themselves touch bottom; no other beliefs are more available or reliable than they are. So from 1981 or earlier Plantinga is no longer an evidentialist in the philosophy of religion; then if not sooner he rejects classic foundationalism ancient and modern; he has come to a new place.

How should we describe the new place? Well, it is not vulgar relativism. Plantinga does not doubt that theists (he includes here Christians, Jews, and Muslims) disagree with atheists, and further, he does not doubt that the theists are right and their opponents are wrong. Nor is his view covert foundationalism: for foundationalists all religious—or irreligious—beliefs to be rational must be founded upon unexceptionable premises that are universally shared. Nor is Plantinga's new view fideism: reasons still count, only they are not evidentialist reasons, put forward as a preponderance that must win the argument. Just how all this works out is best seen by consulting Plantinga's later writings, starting with his long essay, "Reason and Belief in God" (1981; reprinted in Plantinga and Wolterstorff, eds., 1983:16-93).

iii. Advice to Plantinga.—From the present standpoint, then, the Plantinga of 1984 ("Advice") still occupied a halfway house. Consider the following gentle criticism of Plantinga's program offered by his Reformed philosophy colleague Merold Westphal—criticism that I support (Westphal, 1999): (1) Once Christian philosophers discover that they have their own agenda and methods (thus the "Advice"), they must prepare to go beyond this to "a more *dialogical* interpretation of reason" (1999:176). Discovering one's own assumptions may be a useful first step, but it must not be the last. (2) It is time for Christian philosophers to give up the assumption that "propositions are the coin of the realm in which we carry out our philosophical business" (1999:176). Propositions are what it is said a sentence in English ("It is raining") and a matching sentence in German ("*Es regnet*") have in common—these two sentences express only one proposition. This, Westphal warns, is philosophically risky, for it is highly questionable to think that meanings are independent of the natural languages in which they are expressed. Thus when Christian convictions or any other convictions are filtered into propositions abstracted from the speaker's natural language, something crucial to their sense may be irretrievably lost. And Westphal might have added that a further irresponsible reduction occurs when the propositions themselves are reduced to place-holding symbols, for these are still further disconnected from natural human utterance in all its particularity. Plantinga, one might note, took a step in the right direction when he noted in his 1981 article that the actual properly basic beliefs of Christian believers are not likely to be "God exists" (that philosopher's football), but such livelier beliefs as "God is speaking to me," "God has created all this," "God disapproves of what I have done," "God forgives me," and "God is to be thanked and praised" (1981:46). (3) Another Westphal suggestion is that religious language is richer than assertions alone. "When God speaks to us we are more likely to be dealing with promises, warnings, commands and the like than with mere assertions of fact" (1999:178). Cohering with this is his reminder that proper Christian utterance is not so importantly talk *about* God as it is address *to* God: "in prayer, in praise, in confession, in gratitude, and so forth" (1999:178). This leads to a further admonition: Authentic Christian talk is never mere talk but is in every case embedded in the *practices* that constitute Christian existence. Prayer is not mere thoughts, even uttered thoughts, but exists as the *practice of prayer;* gratitude is not mere thank-yous timely spoken but consists in a way of life that is formed by a grateful awareness of what God has done for us. And thus to recognize practices is to be reminded that real Christianity is involved in practical as well as theoretical reason. Westphal goes on to remark that Plantinga's inaugural address has gone a long way toward closing the gap between philosophy and theology, "between metaphysics and spirituality and between metaphysics and politics" (1999:178-80).

To these measurements of Plantinga's progress I add one more. Though happily he has not become a vulgar relativist (a position, as others have made clear, that entails severe internal difficulties—Bernard Williams, 1972:chap. 1), his new acknowledgment of the distinctive singularity of Christian beliefs lays Plantinga open to the challenge of relativism in a new way: If as he says "the Christian philosopher has her own topics and projects to think about," others (secularists, Hindus, Muslims, Marxists, for examples) will find that they, too, have topics and projects distinctively their own. Thus the dialogues that Westphal favors may be diverted by a preliminary worry: can there even be such dialogues in a plural world in which the topics and projects of various groups are so plainly disparate? The further task of the Christian epistemologist, who among his other beliefs is convinced that God, the Father of Jesus Christ, is maker of heaven and earth and thus of each of these diverse sorts of believers and thinkers, is to provide an account of the plurality that will not be reduced to vulgar (i.e., hard) relativism or any other outlook that gives up on all but one's own group of believers. Once Plantinga's first step is taken, philosophers who take it can no longer shrug aside the challenge of relativism. What can still be attempted is to *defuse* it.

Exactly this project had been undertaken in the 1970s in my work with James M. Smith, gathered up in our *Convictions: Defusing Religious Relativism* (*CONV.*, 1st ed. 1976), which expounded the philosophical points Plantinga was to put forth in his inaugural as well as those added by Westphal in 1999.

b. Knowing God as God: Diogenes Allen.—While Plantinga began his work in the philosophy of religion from a distinctly modern standpoint but in time evolved a different approach, Diogenes Allen came to the tasks of philosophy of religion in a non-modern manner from the start. It is no accident that Allen was influenced by Ludwig Wittgenstein at the outset of his philosophical studies.

Diogenes Allen was born to parents of Greek ancestry who had been expelled from Asia Minor (Turkey) by Kemal Atatürk ten years earlier, along with a million and a half of their fellow Greeks. Some of these immigrants were reunited in Lexington, Kentucky, and there, in 1932, Diogenes Allen was born—his first name evidently Greek but his last after that assigned his parents by United States immigration officials. During his childhood the family shunted back and forth between the Orthodox and Episcopal Churches. Allen loved these liturgies but ended up in the Presbyterian Church, largely because he liked its respect for the intellect. He completed a bachelor's degree at the University of Kentucky, won a Rhodes scholarship, earned another degree at Oxford, and met and married an Englishwoman. He progressed to Yale Divinity School, where he trained as a minister and served a rural parish in New Hampshire for three years, eventually taking the Ph.D. in philosophy at Yale and returning to Oxford in the late sixties to write the dissertation that became *The Reasonableness of Faith* (1968). After three years' teaching at York University in Toronto, Allen moved to Princeton Theological Seminary as professor of philosophy; there with his wife and their four children he worships in an Episcopal parish church. This journey led him to focus on the philosophical import of the Christian's spiritual life. A prolific scholar, Allen has already published some fourteen books and fifty articles.

i. The believer's reasons.—Allen means to show how someone who wants to know whether his or her nominal Christianity is actually trustworthy and true, may come, in a phrase borrowed from the New Testament, to "the full wealth of conviction" (Col. 2:2). A central theme is learning to understand the proper role of evidence in such a quest. Modern philosophers have argued that the weight of evidence either justifies or fails to justify "theism," a standpoint that "Christians, Jews, and Muslims are said to share: belief in one God, who is all-powerful, all-knowing, and good." A deep difficulty, though, is that even if one accepts such theism, this constitutes in itself no *reason* to believe in any one of these three religions. So perhaps faith is called in to fill "the gap between a warranted case for theism and an unwarranted case for Christianity (or Judaism or Islam)"? (Allen, 1989:15). On this modern view faith and reason unite in a marriage of convenience; they need have nothing more in common. In contrast to this, Allen depicts faith as a

> response to the good promised to us by God, preeminently in Christ. In that response, we interact with God and begin to receive that good. We do not move from the evidence we can muster for theism to an actual religion by a leap of faith, understood as a substitute for evidence. On the contrary, it is with an "initial faith" [thus Austin Farrer] or with a full faith (each of which usually develops through interaction with a believing community) that we look critically at nature, history, human nature, and Scripture. There is thus no "gap" to be closed by "faith" after we have engaged in critical study. (1989:15f)

Scholars will recall that Allen's theme here—the believer's reasons based on spiritual need and its spiritual fulfillment rather than on mere extrinsic evidence and argument—was also adopted by British philosophical theologian Austin M. Farrer (1904–68), constituting a noteworthy shift in his intellectual journey. (Earlier, Farrer had approached the knowledge of God via a post-Kantian Thomism—see *CONV.*, pp. 115-18, for Farrer's earlier view.) In *Faith and Speculation,* the volume that signals his turn, Farrer credits the turn to Diogenes Allen (1967:10). Already in process of change, Farrer read Allen's completed dissertation while he was at Oxford and found it persuasive. Behind both stands the influence of Ludwig Wittgenstein, whose posthumous influence was felt at Allen's Yale and Farrer's Oxford during the 1960s.

The new view shared by Diogenes Allen, Austin Farrer, and others made it clear that their knowledge of God could not be separated from the content of Christian doctrine. The philosophy of religious knowledge was not a separate prelude to Christian belief or disbelief, but would consist in the critical philosophical examination of Christian convictions themselves. This raised for Allen and his allies the problems of relativism: why this faith and not some other? If there were all these others, why any one of them? This cluster of problems (addressed in part in §2 below as the 'problem of many religions') could be met, Allen thought, either by analyzing the concept of relativism (see Chapter One §4 above) or by finding a standpoint that accepted the problem but sought to show how Christian faith could resolve it. Allen chose the latter strategy, which involved exploring the reasons for the beliefs that were intrinsic to Christian experience. Though these reasons could be condensed, in a phrase of Farrer's, into a need and its satisfaction, the actual course of faith's journey toward "the full wealth of conviction" was most likely to involve development over several stages. Farrer wrote compactly that "the gospel offers God to me as good, not simply as fact. In embracing the good I am convinced of the fact" (Farrer, 1967:10). Yet that offer and that conviction are for most believers the summation of a pilgrim journey rather than the report of a single, explosive awakening. Philosophy's role, then, becomes the critical examination of each stage of the journey.

This approach rejects two alternative views of 'experience' that persist even in recent Christian thought. One of these invokes *supernatural experiences* in which (it is claimed) God is self-revealed. Extended from Scripture into church history, this emphasis authenticates Christian faith by miracles in the lives of biblical and later saints. An alternative view, made famous by Schleiermacher, treats religious experience as an underlying quality of all human life, present whether noticed or not, so that religious 'experience' is simply an *interpretation of universal human experience.* This view persists to the present in the work of Chicago theologian David Tracy as well as others. Allen, though, has a different sense of religious experience. Certainly, extraordinary events may occur in the Christian pilgrim's life. Yet these events are valuable neither as proofs of religious truth nor as soundings of a substratum of religious feeling. They may, however, illuminate the whole of one's ordinary life, shedding interpretive light upon a believer's everyday.

This requires some clarification of what was said above about the believer's reasons for belief. As noted, a believer can say that he or she had a need, that the gospel of Jesus Christ met that need, and that the resultant satisfaction is reason enough. Yet not just any sort of satisfaction will do. There are basic human needs—for food and shelter, sociality and adventure, survival and love, for examples. The gospel may satisfy some of these, and surely the gospel encourages us to attend to such needs in both friend and stranger (Matt. 25:35f). Yet that is not

Allen's point here. For typically the gospel awakens the very needs that it satisfies. Thus the gospel in its cognitive dimension does not merely satisfy random curiosity. Rather it awakens a yearning to know our origin and our last end, to know life's true goal—and then it answers *that* intellectual yearning. Again, it is not mere need of sociality that the gospel fulfills, something that might be met by random fun and games. Rather the gospel evokes awareness of the deep alienation that separates us from God and one another, alienation we learn to label as shame and guilt and sin—and it meets *these* needs in the forgiveness and reconciliation it provides. (One is reminded here of Yale Professor Julian Hartt's "ontological essentials"—see Chapter One §3*b*.) Nor is it merely a need for some costly adventure and self-risk that the gospel satisfies (something skydiving might do for some). Rather the gospel sets before believers' eyes the cross, and summons us in Jesus' name to *that* adventure: "take up your cross and follow me." Allen does not deny the gospel's relevance to earthly physical needs, but its satisfactions address these needs only in company with the distinctive fulfillments it requires and provides (Allen, 1968:Parts I–II).

ii. Allen's interpretation of Simone Weil.—Still, there is a worry here. Is the "satisfaction" the gospel yields so remote from the needs of everyday that it is for many people irrelevant? An answer I find adequate appears in Allen's recent accounts of the life and thought of Simone Weil, the tough-minded mid-twentieth-century Frenchwoman whose philosophical writings emerged from her intense and outwardly very difficult life journey.

Simone Weil (1909–43) was trained in the French tradition of literature and philosophy, and was a competent mathematician as well. She employed all these skills in expressing her religious thought. But the latter development came slowly, since she was devoted to rigorous honesty concerning religious questions (Weil, 1973). Afflicted most of her life by severe, blinding headaches and other ills, nonetheless whenever possible Weil took a job as a factory worker lest she be separated from the working class. At one stage she fought against the fascists in the Spanish civil war of the 1930s, and later she served in the 1940s French resistance against Hitler's armies. Weil died at the early age of thirty-four, leaving behind a treasure of highly independent philosophical and religious thought.

A brilliant student, Weil early on had set aside "the problem of God" as beyond solution; she was unwilling, she said, to embark on a quest that could not be resolved with strict honesty (Weil, 1973:62). Although her conception of life's moral requirements was Christian (embracing, for example, the spirit of poverty and the demand for justice for the poor), she was unwilling to add Christian dogmas to these practical convictions lest the dogmas compromise her intense need for honesty. Nevertheless, on three occasions in her lifetime she experienced deep mystical moments for which her existing convictions had not prepared her. During the last of these, at a holy week liturgy in Solesmes, she said that "the thought of the passion [i.e., suffering] of Christ entered into my being once and for all" (1973:80). From this experience she concluded that "Christianity is a religion primarily for those who are wretched, and one finds in it a force that is elevating. This elevation comes in the midst of suffering" (Allen, 1994:293).

These mystical events, Allen thinks, show how a particular experience may illuminate the whole of a life. To appreciate his interpretation one should if possible first read Weil's own account of these developments in her *Waiting for God* (1973). What he draws from Weil's Solesmes experience, namely "the intersection of wretchedness and love," is the light it sheds upon the correct philosophical understanding of Christianity. It is not a mystical experience standing alone, he writes, "but the light it sheds on Christian dogmas and through Christian dogmas [on the rest of life] that brings conviction" (1994:294). Thus the intersection of wretchedness and love, so evident in the story of Christ's passion, becomes (via Weil's mystical vision) *a Christian interpretation of suffering* itself. To interpret suffering, though, is to interpret life; it is to interpret a dimension of everyday and by interpreting it to transform it, for all of us suffer in one way or another.

> Necessity and compulsion (the forces which act upon nature) are not lovable, but we can love the world because of its beauty. The intersection of necessity and beauty follows the pattern of gravity and grace, or of wretchedness and love on the cross. We may thus come to see nature as obeying God perfectly, and learn to obey God, in a way appropriate to human beings, with the same perfection as does the natural world. (Allen, 1994:297)

Following Weil, Allen found a way of looking at everyday human needs, drives, and capacities that led to a rediscovery of their significance. He found her vision transforming his own. He is reminded by this of a Wittgenstein journal entry we have had occasion to consider before:

> So this [love that believes the Resurrection] can come about only if you no longer rest your weight on the earth but suspend yourself from heaven. Then *everything* will be different and it will be

> 'no wonder' if you can do things that you cannot do now. (Allen, 1994:299, quoting Wittgenstein, *CV* 33*e*)

"Then *everything* will be different." We in turn might be reminded of an exclamation made by the apostle Paul as he explored a similar line of thought: "For anyone united to Christ, there is a new creation: the old order has gone; a new order has already begun" (2 Cor. 5:17).

§2. Many Religions

a. 'Many religions' from David Hume to John Hick.—Why are there religions, and why are there so many religions? In the Enlightenment these came to seem proper philosophical questions, often pursued without regard for the Christian conviction that true religion was a gift from God (James 1:17f).

i. David Hume on religion.—David Hume set out to show that such faith could not be founded on philosophical arguments. Neither a miraculous revelation (Hume's "On Miracles" in the *Enquiries: Concerning Human Understanding,* 1777*a*) nor a reasoned theism (see his *Dialogues Concerning Natural Religion,* 1779) provided such a foundation. One sort of religious claim remained: religion like morality might have its root in human nature itself, so that faith, though otherwise unprovable, was validated by the *consensus gentium,* the common consent of humanity. Yet in *The Natural History of Religion* (1777*b*), Hume undermined that claim as well: the origins of religion, while indeed human, sprang merely from the mistaken hopes and fears of primitive peoples.

On Hume's view the essence of religion was always a set of *beliefs,* though it involved rites and other practices as well. (Perhaps this focus on belief was a distant mirror of the Calvinism of his native Scotland, which had elevated faith as right belief over the rejected Catholic heritage of sacrament and ceremony.) Had Hume confronted the twentieth-century thesis of the myth-ritual school—that rites came first, and only afterward the myths that gave narrative expression to them—he would have rejected it. Religious beliefs, in every case mistaken ones, were the real source of religious practices.

His problem was how to account for such beliefs and attitudes, since many of them arose prior to recorded history. Hume held that they did not spring from any special religious drive paralleling primary human drives—self-love, or sex, or resentment of injury.

Religious beliefs were secondary, being only human attempts to survive in a world full of lurking dangers. As a primitive device for expressing helpless fear and dealing with real and imagined dangers, however, religion had long since served its purpose; scientific explanations of the phenomena of nature were now available. Hence religion could be abandoned by Enlightened thinkers without any cost save perhaps the opprobrium they would endure in the eyes of the pious. (Such public disapproval in fact prevented Hume's publication of the *Natural History,* which appeared only posthumously.) All religions were variations on a single theme: they expressed or assuaged ignorant human hopes and fears.

> We are placed in this world, as in a great theatre, where the true springs and causes of every event are entirely concealed from us; nor have we either sufficient wisdom to foresee, or power to prevent those ills, with which we are continually threatened. We hang in perpetual suspence between life and death, health and sickness, plenty and want; which are distributed amongst the human species by secret and unknown causes, whose operation is oft unexpected, and always unaccountable. These *unknown causes,* then, become the constant object of our hope and fear; and while the passions are kept in perpetual alarm by an anxious expectation of the events, the imagination is equally employed in forming ideas of those powers, on which we have so entire a dependance. (Hume, 1777*b*:28f)

Hume's pioneering work marked the road taken by other philosophers as well. Together with the French encyclopedists (Diderot, Voltaire) and the German *Aufklärung* (Lessing), it set the pattern for the philosophical approach to religion for two centuries to follow, and for much subsequent social-scientific study of religion as well. All these agreed that since all religion was variation on a single theme, there must be a single account of its cause. Hume believed that this causal source would be disclosed by examining the data of the religions. By later standards, his sources for study of the religious phenomena were limited—he had access to the ancient Greek and Latin writers, and there were the more recent Eurocentric accounts written by travelers to distant lands. In his philosophical writings Hume never refers to his own firsthand acquaintance with religion as practiced in the Church of Scotland, and he says little enough of Roman Catholic belief and worship, which he mentions only to disparage. Nevertheless, here was a precedent for two enduring patterns of philosophical thought about religion: *the search for a rationale or basis for religion*, coupled with study of its *empirical phenomena*.

ii. Kant, Schleiermacher, and Hegel on religion.—A prime example of this pattern was the work on religion by Immanuel Kant (1724–1804). Kant was challenged by Hume in this as in other ways. Descendant of a Scottish family that had immigrated to Königsberg in East Prussia, Kant in his mature thought regarded the moral substance of Protestant piety a thing of value, though religious metaphysics itself could not survive in his critical philosophy. Like Hume, Kant regarded religion as a single phenomenon. Yet religion was not a kind of belief but a kind of action—so it must be treated with the practical reason. Kant wrote in the preface of his *Critique of Pure Reason* that he had "found it necessary to deny *knowledge*, in order to make room for *faith*" (1787:29). That is, he had refuted the rational proofs of God's existence; God was only the Ideal of *pure* reason, but belief in God as a demand or postulate of the *practical* (i.e., moral) reason remained necessary (Matson, 1987:II, 399). Thus the religion of morality was true religion, and Kant thought that Christianity, though sometimes, alas, debased by its Jewish origin, approximated that truth, provided it was understood as morality expressed in symbolic language. His book, *Religion within the Limits of Reason Alone* (1794), spelled out this approach. Religions could be divided into those that like Christianity reflected the moral ideal and those that merely attempted to win favor from on high (1794:47). Kant's attention to the details of Christian practice partly complemented Hume's second emphasis, the empirical examination of religions.

Friedrich Schleiermacher (1768–1834), in some contrast to both Hume and Kant, set religion close to the center of philosophical understanding. The relation of humanity to the All or Whole was not at its root a matter of understanding or thought (as with Hume); nor was it a matter of morality (as with Kant), though both reasoning and moral action are entailed by religion. The primal relation was a religious sense or awareness of the Whole, and religion was the "sense and taste for the infinite," or more fully, it was "the immediate consciousness *[unmittelbar Gefühl]* of the universal existence of all finite things, in and through the Infinite, and of all temporal things in and through the Eternal" (1799:39, 36). This account of religion set Schleiermacher the task of explaining the variety of religions (Hume's second task), which he took up in the fifth of his *Speeches* addressed to religion's "cultured despisers." Since in history there are varieties of human beings, each variety produces a different sort of "positive religion," and all the positive religions, taken together, constitute the one religion philosophers sought (1799:217f). Thus Schleiermacher, while maintaining like others a single theme in all religion, which for him was religious awareness or *Gefühl,* by this emphasis on religious variety encouraged empirical study of what came to be called "world religions" or "the religions of mankind."

Georg Wilhelm Friedrich Hegel (1770–1831), Schleiermacher's contemporary and great rival, identified philosophy with the history of human culture and thought. An evolutionist half a century before Darwin, Hegel taught that the history of the cosmos was the history of the emergence of Absolute Spirit. In religious terms, God had evolved, achieving self-awareness only in the self-consciousness of the highest forms of religion. God on this view was not another entity separate from the world and its Creator as in traditional Christian teaching; rather God and world were inconceivable apart from each other. In his *Phenomenology of Spirit* (1807) and in more detail in his *Lectures on the Philosophy of Religion* (1832–40), Hegel painted on a grand scale the development of human culture with its evolving religious dimension: there were the religions of *nature,* exemplified by awareness of Spirit as it indwelt plants and animals; there were the religions of *art,* in which artistic skill created sculpture and other representations that displayed Spirit; and finally there was "absolute manifest religion," which realizes that God is *pure Spirit*—the special achievement of (Lutheran) Christianity. Yet religion's truth was even better expressed in philosophy, notably in Hegelian philosophy. Religion can only represent or mirror what philosophy has the power rightly to conceive (Welch, 1972–85, I, 91-99).

iii. John Hick's interpretation of religion.—We might conclude this survey with philosopher-psychologist William James (1842–1910), save that in his classic Gifford Lectures, *The Varieties of Religious Experience,* James exempted himself from considering institutional religion: the lectures focused on the religious life of individuals (1902:12). Or we might as in Chapter One (§1) turn to the new social sciences including the so-called sciences of religion *(Religionswissenschaften),* but these lead us too far from our philosophical focus. Or we might as in Chapter Five (§3) attend to recent French philosophers such as Foucault, Derrida, and their American counterparts. These take modern thought to what seem utter extremes. Yet these 'mostmoderns' have paid relatively little attention to religion. Thus our concluding example of philosophy in pre-Wittgensteinian style will come from the more recent Gifford Lectures of John H. Hick (1922–), published as *An Interpretation of Religion* (1989). These gather up much recent philosophical and social-scientific work while presenting Hick's own distinct field theory of religion—his comprehensive overview of the entire field of study (1989:xiii). He claims his is a uniquely *religious* approach, though not confessional—a distinction he rather surprisingly denies to Kant, Schleiermacher, Hegel, James, and the like. It would be more accurate, I think, to say that Hick's distinctive note is his own idea of "religious pluralism." To see what this is, some preliminary points must be observed.

Hick finds that all the great religions are salvific; that is, all have as their aim the ultimate well-being achieved by the "moral transformation" of their adherents. The "great world religions" such as Buddhism, Zoroastrianism, and Christianity have thus shifted concern from the tribal or national religions' social stability to "salvation/liberation" (1989:10). They express this common concern in a variety of ways, some with a God or gods, some without, so it is better to say that all aim at the transcendent or, as Hick names it, "the Real." The great religions give the Real a variety of names, "God," "Christ," "Nirvana" or nothingness, and still others, none of which adequately expresses their real referent, though all together (it seems a familiar modern theme) signify that which none alone can: "the great post-axial faiths constitute different ways of experiencing, conceiving, and living in relation to an ultimate divine Reality which transcends all our varied visions of it" (1989:236). The Real has many faces—including facelessness! Purely "naturalistic" understandings of religion are false, and the religions would do well to get together, learn from one another, and share their common aspirations. According to Hick, this view is not "inclusivism," which grants one religion an advantage over all the rest, and of course it is not "exclusivism," but is, in his own sense, "pluralism."

So brief a report can do little justice to the complexity and genuine riches of Hick's book. Though it remains firmly fixed within the modern paradigm, it is, I believe, the best such work from that standpoint. Jesus said of John the Baptist that none ever born was greater than he, yet the least in the kingdom of heaven was greater (Matt. 11:11-14; Luke 7:28), thereby signaling, I believe, the change of the ages that he came to fulfill; so John Hick's treatment of religion incorporates—and sometimes excels—the best of modernity, yet the times cry out for a messenger who in this new age will do religion philosophical justice as Hick has done it for his. I believe that the pages that follow next show the road such a pioneer will have to take.

b. 'Many religions' in post-Wittgensteinian perspective.—The new standpoint presented here assumes the *practical theory* of religion

(*Doctrine,* Ten §1*a*): Religions are not as Hume had assumed simply correct or incorrect accounts of the gods, be they one or many; neither are religions as Schleiermacher had supposed only versions of a universal sense of utter dependence. There is indeed 'cognitive content' in many religions, and certainly feeling as well. But religions are best approached as active clusters of *practices* (such practices as worship, neighbor love, community formation, teaching, and still more) that embody the profound life-shaping *convictions* of their communities. Practices are not merely actions, deeds done in one way or another; they are complex communal actions shaped toward particular goals and deliberately employing rule-governed means of pursuing those goals. Thus Jewish reading of Torah is a practice of the synagogue, having its own goal and its own rules, while a church baptizing candidates engages in another practice with other goals and rules. Motorists reading advertisements posted on highway billboards, on the other hand, are *not* so engaged, since what they do lacks communally established goals and rules and requires no distinctive skills—anyone who can read can do it (see further *Ethics,* Six §1*a*.ii). Reading is a skill, but not in itself a practice.

In the strict sense of "conviction" employed throughout this trilogy, convictions are just those beliefs or states of mind that for their holders are persistent and life-shaping. To recognize that religious practices embody such "persistent, life-shaping" convictions is to see why they matter: practices that are internally tied to convictions matter (by definition) to their practitioners (on the relation of practices to convictions, see further *CONV.,* pass.). One hardly needs Christian theology (or any other sort of theology) to account for the importance of religion if by definition religion is identified with certain of its practitioners' *convictions.* So this understanding of religion provides at the outset the sort of theological neutrality many students of religion have vainly sought: here religions are recognized as cultural phenomena, but as phenomena with a particular, deep relation to what matters most to people within that culture. Ninian Smart, a scholar in religion whose work reflects this post-Wittgensteinian outlook, in a similar way speaks of the study of religion as "worldview analysis," rightly grouping under "worldview" both 'religious' and 'secular' convictions (Smart, 1983).

In what follows I mean to show this changed philosophical standpoint regarding religion, thus exploring the philosophical changes that underlay the view of religion and culture already illustrated in Chapter Two above.

i. Wittgenstein on many religions.—We have seen (Chapter Six) that religion was a matter of existential concern for Ludwig Wittgenstein, so that his philosophical lens repeatedly focused upon it both in the *Tractatus* (1922) and later. The *Tractatus,* composed in the wake of Wittgenstein's 1914 conversion, treated "ethics" and "the mystical" as topics of concern that lay beyond human speech: *das Mystische* evoked only speechless silence. "What we cannot speak about we must consign to silence" (*TLP* 7). Later he believed that religion (and indeed magic!) might provide a useful gate of entry into the revisionary metaphysics that he sought to explore: "I think now," he wrote in 1931, "that the right thing would be to begin my book with remarks about metaphysics as a kind of magic."

> But in doing this I must neither speak in defense of magic nor ridicule it.
>
> What it is that is deep about magic would be kept. (*RFGB:*vi; cf. Monk, 1990:chap. 14)

With this in mind, Wittgenstein began reading the volumes of pioneer British anthropologist Sir James Frazer's *Golden Bough.* His notes show that he respected the contents of this encyclopedic work. Yet in at least three ways Frazer's assumptions aroused Wittgenstein's opposition, even his scorn. (1) Frazer persistently treated magic and religion as kinds of primitive (mis)information, mistaken views of the world that required correction by enlightened Western understanding. (2) More broadly, Frazer accepted an evolutionary theory of the development of human culture: it had progressed from a magical stage to a religious and then to a scientific stage, each stage rendering its predecessor obsolete. (3) In keeping with both these assumptions, his accounts missed the depth, the mystery, the enduring *numinous* quality of the data of magic and religion that Frazer had ineptly examined. For Wittgenstein's thinking, magic and religion indeed had something valuable to say, but what they said could be understood only in connection with what they required of their adherents and what they gave them—only from their own standpoints. Sir James Frazer (1854–1941) had attempted in *The Golden Bough* to summarize the substance of magic and religion in all its forms. Its underlying methodological argument, repeated in successive editions between 1890 and 1922, had by Wittgenstein's day become a standard part of modern culture: Science can produce laws that determine the workings of "the primitive mind." Similar customs in different societies around the world display these laws and reveal the similar motives of diverse peoples, stretching from pre-classical cultures to the "modern primitives" of peasant Europe in recent times.

For example, "primitive minds" blended nature's changing seasons and the growth and withering and regeneration of plants with the magic employed to stalk game and the sexual congress that produced offspring. This entire blend of natural rhythms, vegetable, animal, and human, seemed to them magical; they reflected its magic in primitive myths of gods who died and then lived again. Semitic peoples, Greeks, Egyptians, and many others represented to themselves the "supposed death and resurrection of this oriental deity," who existed, Frazer said, under a variety of names—Osiris, Tammuz, Adonis, and Attis (1922:325).

It was clear in all this that the real though unspoken target of Frazer's work was none other than "the supposed death and resurrection" of that supposed God-man, Jesus Christ. As Robert Ackerman writes,

> Finally, however, Frazer was interested in even bigger game than primitive epistemology. For although in his survey of the dying-and-reviving gods of the eastern Mediterranean Frazer never mentions the name of Jesus, only the slowest of his readers could have failed to make the comparison between the pagan rites that result from an imperfect (because irrational) understanding of the universe and contemporary Christianity. . . . Frazer papers in the library of Trinity College, Cambridge, contain many unsolicited letters from readers, educated and otherwise, that thank Frazer for having finally dispelled the veil of illusion from before their eyes as to the "real" nature of Christianity. (Ackerman, in *Enc. Phil.* V:416)

Wittgenstein, never altogether the Briton, was visibly irritated by this smug British scholarship.

> What narrowness of spiritual life we find in Frazer! And as a result: how impossible for him to understand a different way of life from the English one of his time! ¶ Frazer cannot imagine a priest who is not basically an English parson of our times with all his stupidity and feebleness. (*RFGB*:5e)

More to the point, Wittgenstein found Frazer locked into a philosophical error: he could not distinguish a people's causal reasoning from their accompanying religious practice, or rather Frazer assumed that 'savage' minds helplessly confused these two. (Later, Wittgenstein could refer to these as different language-games.) For his part, Wittgenstein did not find Frazer's 'savages' so pitiable:

> The same savage who, apparently in order to kill his enemy, sticks his knife through a picture of him, really does build his hut of wood and cuts his arrow with skill and not in effigy. (*RFGB*:4*e*)

The so-called primitives he had patronized were on Frazer's own evidence not gullible children but participants in a life-world of their own that employed both cause-and-effect reasoning *and also* magical or religious responses.

Still, it may be asked, *what is the point* of religion or its close relative, magic? Here as elsewhere in his post-*Tractatus* work, Wittgenstein resists any general or theoretical answer—one must look and see, religion by religion, case by case. Take as an example the paradigm case with which Frazer introduces *The Golden Bough,* the story of the "king of the wood," that strange ancient tradition of a succession of priest-kings who inhabited a grove on the shore of a lake at Nemi, not far from Rome. It was told that each of these priest-kings gained his place only by killing his predecessor and held it only until he himself was murdered by his successor (Frazer, 1922:chap. 1). This curious tale serves Frazer as a vehicle to introduce a wide range of magical and religious phenomena from every part of the world: tree-worship, taboo, the "corn-spirit," eating the deity, scapegoats, fire festivals, and more. Yet Wittgenstein points out that in reporting these traditions Frazer consistently overlooked their numinous element. Wittgenstein's German words for the story of the priest-king of Nemi are *furchtbar, grossartig, schaurig*—terms that, like English "shudder," "monstrous," and "fearsome," convey a tone that the civilized Frazer had simply missed. If we turn from this primal case to Wittgenstein's own religious sensibility, we may recall that from *Tractatus* days onward, religion was for Wittgenstein a topic to be approached only with awe and wonder. He found *The Golden Bough* and work in its style a belittling of holy things.

Ultimately, Wittgenstein abandoned the plan to introduce his projected book with reference to magic. Yet he never lost interest in the consequences of his work for the philosophy of religion. He offered no synoptic overview of the many religions. The task was rather to dispel the systematic confusion that arose in connection with the study of religion as it did in other studies. What remained would "leave everything as it was"—employing for the understanding of religion a logic that was internally related to its actual practices. Thus two motives ran through his life and work. On the one hand, there was his own deeply self-involved participation in Christian faith and practice (see Chapter Six). Here his great concern was to be consistent—not failing to live out the faith he had adopted as his own. Consider a 1946 notebook entry—written thirty-two years after his Tolstoyan conversion or turnabout:

> I believe that one of the things Christianity says is that sound doctrines are all useless. That you have to change your *life.* (Or the *direction* of your life.) ¶ It says that wisdom is all cold; and that you can no more use it for setting your life to rights than you can forge iron when it is *cold.* ¶ The point is that a sound doctrine need not *take hold* of you; you can follow it as you would a doctor's prescription.—But here you need something to move you and turn you in a new direction.—(I.e. this is how I understand it.) Once you have been turned round, you must *stay* turned round. ¶ Wisdom is passionless. But faith by contrast is what Kierkegaard calls a *passion.* (*CV* 53*e*)

The other motive paralleled the first: it was the demand for respect for other sorts of religion than his own—including even the startling practices reported by Frazer in the tale of the priest-king of Nemi. Here again there must be no severing of what religions seek from the *practices* they entail: if Christian doctrine *(guten Lehren)* missed the point when detached from the work of setting one's life to rights *(das Leben in Ordnung bringen)*, did not the *Golden Bough* account of the priest-king of Nemi commit just such an error—separating so-called primitive mistakes from their location in a very different sort of engaged practice?

For Wittgenstein, then, the 'problem' of many religions—which is best, or are they all the same?—could not arise. He had *nowhere to stand* to ask such questions, and those who thought they did were attempting to stand nowhere at all. Such philosophers attempted to describe the view from nowhere! In the absence of such a standpoint, the many religions (including one's own religion or one's rejection of religion) are incommensurable.

ii. Wittgenstein's follower Peter Winch.—Seven years after Wittgenstein's death, Peter Winch, a British social philosopher, published *The Idea of a Social Science* (1958), once again attacking the assumption that anthropology (or sociology, or any social science whatsoever) could provide a foothold for the objective study of alien cultures—or even of one's own culture. While religion as such was not front and center in Winch's book, it was an important concern there. His central idea can easily be made clear to those familiar with the Wittgensteinian theses already presented. Cultural practices proceed according to rules internal to those practices. Failure to grasp the rule in a given case makes following that rule impossible, makes it impossible to know when one is doing the same thing as before, which in turn makes impossible the goal of most social science, namely understanding the practice in question. Such Wittgensteinian pronouncements are not arbitrary, Winch thought, but are entailed by the very concepts of 'practices,' 'rules,' 'following,' and 'understanding.' Far from being arbitrary, they are necessary accounts of the character of human cultural interaction wherever it occurs. Winch finds an example in the biblical parable of the Pharisee and the publican (Luke 18:9-14):

> Was the Pharisee who said "God, I thank thee that I am not as other men are" doing the same kind of thing as the Publican who prayed "God be merciful unto me a sinner"? To answer this one would have to start by considering what is involved in the idea of prayer; and that is a *religious* question. In other words, the appropriate criteria for deciding whether the actions of these two men were of the same kind or not belong to religion itself. Thus the sociologist of religion will be confronted with an answer . . . not taken from sociology, but from religion itself. (Winch, 1958:87)

Such considerations had presented few difficulties for those living in an earlier period of scientific thinking, when scientists, whether they studied stars, starfish, or the Star of Bethlehem, were likely to be either themselves Christian or at least to be imbued with Christian habits of thought. But when modes of thought no longer Christian came to occupy center stage in the West and when anthropologists, Christian or not, began to attend to religions and cultures other than those of the West, they exposed a profound difficulty: were they even *capable* of understanding these strangers whom they studied?

> A psychoanalyst who wished to give an account of the aetiology of neuroses amongst, say, the Trobriand Islanders, could not just apply without further reflection the concepts developed by Freud for situations arising in our own society. He would have first to investigate such things as the idea of fatherhood amongst the islanders and take into account the relevant aspects in which their idea differed from that current in his own society. And it is almost inevitable that such an investigation would lead to some modifi-

> cation in the psychological theory appropriate for explaining neurotic behaviour in this new situation. (Winch, 1958:90)

All the more is this true, whoever the investigator may be, if it is Trobriand Islander *religious practices* that are in question.

See why this is so: the argument is classic Wittgenstein. For anyone to know what a religious (person or) group is doing, the knower must at a minimum know when the action being examined is the same thing as before and when it is not, must know how to identify particular acts or practices. As Winch puts it, "Statements of uniformities presuppose judgments of identity" (1958:83). To know what is meant by anyone's words, one must have learned how those words are used, and this cannot be achieved simply by ostention, that is, by pointing to what is meant, for there will remain the question, exactly *what* is being pointed to—a certain mountain range, or one of the mountains in it, or a climber on that mountain, or the color of the climber's anorak? 'Meaning' is not constituted by ostensive reference, but is a function of a shared language that makes the ostension possible. So meaning is necessarily communal (Wittgenstein's private language argument again). Once this guiding principle is overlooked or rejected, once meaning and knowing and following a rule become isolated decisions made by separate individuals, human rationality is poisoned at its source: following a rule has been divorced from the reactions of others to following it, and without those reactions it will be impossible to assign any reliable sense to the expression "the same"—same mountain, same rule, same religious practice (see Winch, 1958:chaps. 1, 8). To this argument G. E. M. Anscombe adds a powerful further twist: some activities differ from others in that they cannot be understood by non-participating observers. Anscombe believes arithmetic is such an activity: a non-arithmetical observer might see someone else making marks on paper, might even be able to 'read' each of the written symbols, but, without having acquired at least some of the skills of arithmetic, could not know what was going on (from an unpublished paper, cited by Winch, 1958:109).

In short, Wittgenstein's work had a profound consequence for the philosophy of religion traditionally conceived. "On my view," Winch writes, "the philosophy of science will be concerned with the kind of understanding sought and conveyed by the scientist; the philosophy of religion will be concerned with the way in which religion attempts to present an intelligible picture of the world; and so on." If those conclusions are correct, the old questions (§2*a* above) will not simply have new answers. The case is more radical: These questions *cannot* be answered because they cannot meaningfully be asked. The problem of 'many religions' will no longer exist.

Yet readers may feel considerable discomfort here. Surely this is an unsatisfactory outcome? Even Winch goes on, in the passage just quoted, to say that religion and its philosophy, science and its philosophy, and the like, with their respective aims, "will be mutually compared and contrasted" (1958:19f). Yes, but how? If, as Winch's interpretation of Wittgenstein has shown, religions are incommensurable, and if there is no standpoint such as science or philosophy from which anyone is entitled to judge the religions or choose the 'higher' or 'highest' among them, must adherents of existing religious standpoints choose between a stubborn, irrational retention of their faiths or an equally irrational renunciation?

Here again the specter of relativism looms large. If there is no standpoint that evidently rules over all the rest, and if consequently the religious (and social and political and artistic) practices of humankind are none of them able to justify themselves by an appeal to such a privileged standpoint, it appears that in Othello's words "chaos is come again"; the human situation seems desperate because meaningless. No wonder there was passionate resistance to Wittgensteinian developments in philosophy as well as to the later, overtly irrational claims of certain kinds of French deconstruction (i.e., Jacques Derrida) that seemed to outsiders to be saying what they thought Wittgenstein already had. (But was it what Wittgenstein had said?)

These fears are understandable, but they are misguided. As a first point, it is worth recalling that even during the period in the West when medieval and then modern rationality seemed to rule, it did this at a great price. The price was paid, not only by the maintainers of a single rationality supreme over all, but by those whose positions were overrun because they did not comply with the establishment's intellectual claims. These victims of imperial rationality included the many peoples of the world who were not part of the 'rational' West. It did not make the situation more comfortable to discover that Western rationality was accompanied by Western jingoism, was backed by Western gunboat diplomacy, and in too many cases was followed by Western missionary imperialism (but on this last see *Doctrine,* pp. 424f, and more comprehensively, Shenk, 1999). The price was also paid by minority groups in the West itself, where Europeans and North Americans who were not part of religious or ethnic majorities came to dread the monolithic 'rationality' that either excluded or persecuted them—one thinks of the sixteenth-century Anabaptists, but also of carlier and later communities of conviction down to the present time. Rationality was interpreted by those who had power as the justification of their power and its use against those without power. No wonder a Nietzsche appeared in nineteenth-century Europe to deny that there was any rationality save power itself (cf. *Doctrine,* Seven §3*a*.i). Not least, the price of imperial rationality as a standpoint was paid by its own sponsors, scholars such as James Frazer. Their encyclopedic goal was to know the whole world and all that was in it, but their assumptions kept them from doing so because large parts of the human world were on their view irrational, *could not be understood* as they really were.

Yet we ought not to become Nietzscheans if there is a better way than his to acknowledge human frailty and the plurality of kinds of human community, and (most important) a better way to show that the end of 'rational' imperialism is by no means the end of all reasonableness in human affairs. To be sure, there is no understanding of 'primitive' societies or of religious or political views not one's own from a standpoint outside that of the 'primitive' society or other convictional group itself. Understanding has to be internal. Nevertheless, judgment (and justification) remains possible. For its part, anthropology had been following Winch's prescription for some time prior to his philosophical argument in its favor. Anthropologists had learned to visit a 'primitive' group, share as nearly as possible its life, and interpret its practices and its outlook from that vantage point rather than from the external standpoint of a James Frazer. Perhaps for the sake of anthropology no more need be said. These investigators do their sympathetic work and record their findings. Even there, though, problems appear. What if a tribe member is attracted to the life of the Western world as mediated by the anthropologist? What if she wishes to become an anthropologist herself? A problem of professional conduct now arises: Should the anthropologist welcome such a 'convert' to his own culture, or must he reject such overtures on the part of those he has come to study? Whichever he chooses, here will be one more instance of the imperialism that was supposedly left behind. Neutral, uninfluential interaction here turns out to be only a myth, a very modern myth indeed.

iii. Defusing relativism.—A quarter-century ago James M. Smith and I sought to show what comes after Peter Winch. We showed that cultural interaction can lead to new or revised convictions that are justified (or justifiable) even though there is no universal science, no imperial rationality, to tell the participants what they *must* think *(CONV.)*. These premises will seem familiar to those who have followed the present project to this point. Human beings are both united and divided by the convictions they share—united, for convictions form strong bonds that unite those who share them; divided, for not all have the same convictions, and the divisions go to the very heart of communal self-understanding. Arabs and Israelis who cannot easily surmount deep barriers of heritage and conviction, Catholics and Protestants who fought to control Europe with opposed Constantinian strategies, colonial European Americans who confronted ancient cultures on two continents—all these found that their convictions bonded them to their own group while separating them from others, religious convictions being a prime instance. The very words we speak, the languages we use, are signals both of human community and of human dividedness. Shall we say Danzig or Gdansk? Florence or Firenze? Leningrad or St. Petersburg? The differing names of these cities imply different worldviews. They are evidence of the diverse webs of meaning and practice that bind peoples together and split them apart. Uttered words are not mere labels changeable at will, but constitute speech acts that engage their users in networks of practice (*CONV.*, chap. 3). Yet words, speech, not only divide; they can also provide a therapy for healing the deadly divisions, grievous to Christian believers (and to many others) who yearn for "peace on earth"—to quote the angels' song.

Two related problems must be distinguished here. How is communication, mutual understanding ever *possible* across these lines of convictional division? Why is it ever *desirable*? In Christian application, is real evangelism or mission ever possible? If it is, is it ever legitimate? The answer to the second question depends in each case on the first, but we will see that the two are interdependent.

Take the first question—can there be authentic convictional intercommunication? An answer is found in three persistent features of human social life: (1) Consider first the just-mentioned feature of human existence as language-bearing. We are inevitably language users, and communities of conviction are linguistic communities as well. On its face this may seem inaccurate: do not Buddhists (as a community of conviction) speak many languages, Thai, Chinese, English, and more? The point, though, is that Buddhists engage in *similar language-games,* whether they speak these—or Japanese or French. Yet all languages are translatable, and consequently so are the language-games that employ them. If someone replies that languages are not perfectly translatable (witness English speakers' chronic use of non-English expressions to make their meanings clear), we should concede this but insist that perfection is not the goal here. Languages and language-games are sufficiently translatable to permit their *adoption* by outsiders. To take a ready example, some Westerners have adopted Oriental practices of meditation, incorporating these into their daily lives. And Asians can and frequently have adopted Western medical practice alongside their own traditional medicine. Yet both practices, meditation and medicine, embody convictions. What may have seemed theoretically impractical is thus achieved in actual practice.

Some self-styled postmodernists claim that convictional communities are indeed closed systems, so that no conviction set can be translated into the terms of another set of convictions. It seems likely that what these folk rightly reject is the notion that a belief system can harmlessly be superposed, *wholesale*, upon another, or that both systems point to a deeper, more 'genuine' reality, and hence can be interchanged. Yet one does not violate the integrity of a set of convictions when one comprehends and makes use of one of its language games in one's own set. To lend and borrow is the very stuff of human neighborliness.

And so it is with two other enablers of convictional interchange: (2) Widely invoked *loci of values* seem to reach across convictional lines again and again: "That isn't *fair*" belongs with "it's not *yours*" and "she's your *sister*" as demands for decent human behavior that transcend cultures. Indeed, the appeal to 'decency' belongs to this very class, as do even more rarefied loci of appeal such as 'justice' or 'honor' or 'love.' Yet to mention those concepts is to be reminded why we must not make too much of them: the *content* of each of these loci is itself disputable. An inquiring lawyer seemed ready to accept Jesus' capsuling of God's law: "love your neighbour as yourself" (Luke 10:25-37, citing Lev. 19:18). But he needed to know how Jesus interpreted this. Who *is* my neighbor? The concept 'neighbor,' like 'sister,' entails obligations—and opportunities for human nearness—that reach across convictional lines. Yet just what those obligations and opportunities are differs sharply from culture to culture, differs even from family to family. After all, how *are* sisters to be treated? Anthropologists are too fond of reminding us of existing tribal cultures which lack concepts that are for us everyday—such concepts as 'forgiveness' (at one extreme) or 'revenge' (at another). Such observations do not permit us to rest easy with the idea of universal, univocal human values or rights. (Even if the latter were to appear, who could guarantee that they were the right rights?) What we are left with, though, is not worthless: no one, no tribe, no people operates totally without such loci of value, and in many a case of convictional difference an appeal to a particular locus, with all its conflicts, may be just the ticket. Seeking justification of our convictions, we do appeal to such standards as 'truth,' 'consistency,' and the like, even though we know that not only our truth-claims but our very understandings of 'truth,' the concept itself, may differ. For 'truth,' too, is a matter of conviction (*CONV.*, 154-62).

(3) Finally, if the convictions of opposed groups are melded, this always happens within some narrative setting. Call that setting the *social matrix* of their convictions. Within a community, for example, a reformer appears. Reform is a matrix that sometimes yields change.

Or on a broader narrative canvas, one community of conviction encounters another—meets it to trade or to make war or to evangelize. Will there be understanding—or blind misreading of the other? This third factor has a strong narrative dimension. It typically invokes the true story that is being presently lived out. It may also employ the previous two (the translatability of language and the widespread sharing of loci of value) to work its magic of convictional transformation. In the course of their respective histories, for example, many Christians reconsidered their origins and achieved a Reformation; many pagan Arabs were converted to Islam; many Buddhist Koreans were converted to Christianity. In each case, a social matrix lubricated the change.

Against all this it can be objected that transconvictional encounters of this sort may not work. The people may reject the reformer ("A prophet is not without honor, save . . ."); the evangelist may return to the fold without even one lost sheep in his arms. Yet my point is not to show that transconvictional communication and reasonable persuasion are inevitable; it is only to show that they are possible. If we admit that they are, we see how the second question (is such persuasion, etc., legitimate?) bears on the first: Lacking as we do 'universal' standards of rationality, is not interconvictional exchange including persuasion and conversion nevertheless often desirable? Desirable, that is, instance by instance and community by community, rather than overall and forever. Here, by the way, a principle of fallibility (*CONV.*, 112) has its place among the convictions of any community. This is not the skeptical assumption that our community of conviction *must* be wrong, but only the wise admission that somewhere we *may* be. If the North African pagan Arabs just mentioned had stood by their earlier paganism, how could the word of the Prophet have swayed them? If Koreans confronted with Christian missions had adamantly refused the Christian witness, how could the gospel have taken Korean form?

Consider the hard case of a community enduring military defeat and mistreatment, and in the face of its suffering reshaping its own convictions. At least two paths are open: the oppressed may perceive the victors as foes to the death, and their own convictions may harden around that perception. Sometimes, though, something different happens. Jews captured and deported into Babylonian oppression learn to "seek the peace" of their captors' city (Jer. 29:7), and by this new-learned openness they become Babylon's scientists, its administrators, its architects and poets. In such cases it is often the conquerors rather than the conquered who undergo the more profound convictional change

(*CONV.*, chap. 6 §3). These illustrations remind us that the justification of a set of convictions, like its understanding, can occur only within the community or for the individual that holds those convictions. "Justified" means justified in their holders' eyes or it means nothing. Here a relativist might read "in their holders' eyes" to mean that no one can by any means transcend his or her own perspective. Smith and I thought differently:

> [O]ne does not deny the logical necessity that *I* shall confirm my beliefs [or that *we* shall confirm ours], but one holds that people may be conscious of their convictionally plural existence in such a way that that consciousness contains the possibility of transcending the singular perspective of its owners. [Here] "in their eyes alone" means "in the eyes of those who see that theirs are not the only eyes." (*CONV.*, 173; cf. pp. 4-13)

In sum, relativism fails, is defused, not because the fact that it seizes upon (a plural world in which convictions differ from group to group) is mistaken, but because relativism cannot tell what to do with that fact. Like imperialism, but coming from the other end of the spectrum, it ends up with only one imaginable way of seeing things exactly because it suppresses the facts that give rise to it. It tries to occupy a standpoint ('the view from nowhere') from which it can survey all possible standpoints and find them all 'relative,' while at the same time it claims that there is no such standpoint. To see this relativist misuse of the facts and correct it *is to defuse relativism.*

It is helpful to see here that my own aim is neither to defeat relativism out and out (which might be simply to reinstate imperialism) any more than it is simply to defeat imperialism (which might have the opposite result). What both relativists and imperialists commonly fail to see is that theirs are not the only two options. Thinking this way, each viewpoint supposes that our rejection of its errors requires us to champion its polar rival. Denying that our viewpoint exists, each commits the same error, though from contrary directions (*CONV.*, chap. 1).

In due course the consequences of this post-Wittgensteinian way of thinking have been taken up by other laborers in the philosophy of religion. Joseph DiNoia showed in a 1981–82 article, and subsequently in a book, that the diversity of religions could not adequately be treated by assuming either that one side was right and all the others wrong or that none of them could have anything fruitful to say to one another apart from demands for conversion (our "imperialism"). For the *aims* of various religions differ, as do the means by which they pursue those aims (DiNoia, 1981–82; 1992). Yet this requires rethinking the preoccupation of philosophical discussions of the phenomenon of many religions with the quest for "salvation," a term that has a coherent meaning in biblical perspective but seems to mean something vastly different when considered outside that context (*Doctrine,* Three, 422-26; Heim, 1985; Hick, 1989:chap. 3). It follows, DiNoia sees, that Christian doctrines about other religions should be neither "exclusivist" nor "inclusivist" nor (in John Hick's sense) "pluralist," for each of these terms presupposes a single aim for the many religions, whether that aim is their own or is another imposed upon them. Christian doctrine should include a theory of dialogue that provides room both for interreligious dialogue and for (non-imperial) mission aimed at conversion (*CONV.,* chaps. 6f; *Doctrine,* Three, Ten; DiNoia, 1992:chap. 4). George A. Lindbeck, when he came to adopt views similar to these, argued against "propositional" and "experiential-expressivist" and in favor of a "cultural-linguistic" understanding of religions (1984:chap. 3). His "cultural-linguistic" approach is close to what is here called the practical theory of religions—meaning that religions are to be identified by their shared practices. In line with my work with Smith and like DiNoia, Lindbeck asserted that "one can . . . think of [other religions than one's own] not as objectifying poorly what [our own] objectifies well . . . but as cultural-linguistic systems within which potentialities can be actualized and realities explored that are not within the direct purview of [one's own] witness, but that are nevertheless God-willed and God-approved anticipations of aspects of the coming kingdom" (1984:54f). This is a theological application of the theme of productive encounter we had argued in *Convictions.* Although Lindbeck and DiNoia are still controlled by the notion that every *religion* somehow provides 'salvation' (leaving only the miserable secularists in the lurch?), their work on the whole moves in our direction.

It appears that the idea of "the many religions" as rival claimants, to be refereed by an impartial philosophy, was a double mistake: (1) it mistakenly assumed that there was no difficulty in confronting the 'claims' of one religion with those of another (cf. *CONV.,* 166-68; and earlier, W. Christian, 1972); and (2) it mistakenly assumed that religions themselves are free-standing belief systems, free, that is, of the cultures they inhabit, so that religions can be either all false (thus Hume) or all in a fashion true (thus Hick), or so that some one of them is supremely true while others approximate it in varying degree. But in the whole course of modernity, none of these claims was made good by any philosopher to the satisfaction of those holding rival philosophical views of religion, or theologically made good to the satisfaction of those embracing other religions than that of the theologian. In brief, no Archimedean place to stand ever appeared from which these matters could be judged in this way. Perhaps it is time for the widely used but distinctively modern sense of the term "religion" to change once more, just as it has previously changed in past centuries (see W. C. Smith, 1963:203-45 and chap. 2; *CONV.*, 14). The term's current use, to identify phenomena somehow all alike (though no one can say just how) has hit many snags. Consequently those social scientists who insist on treating religion as a diverse *cultural* phenomenon may be exactly right! In that case, too, the reluctance of Karl Barth (and Dietrich Bonhoeffer) to make of 'religion' a main theological concern was entirely justified.

iv. Barth and Bonhoeffer on religion (again).—The preceding volume's report of Barth and Bonhoeffer on religion was incomplete. There these theologians were grouped with the old Christian view that all human religion was of the devil—they only added that Christianity *as a religion,* as a human attempt to climb godward, was condemned with all the rest (*Doctrine,* p. 421). Yet that was not the whole story. While Barth's account of religion through his long career was consistent, it was consistently complex. In *The Epistle to the Romans* (2nd ed., 1922), he transposed what Paul says about the law into terms earlier twentieth-century readers could take to heart: the Christian religion now occupies the role of Jewish law. No one is saved by law or by religion; at best these can only bring the consciousness of sin (Rom. 4:19f). Yet, as Paul says, this is a double-edged identification, for "the law in itself is holy and the commandment is holy and just and good" (7:12). Thus Barth's view of religion (and Paul's view of the law) is dialectical (1922). Bonhoeffer followed suit (1972:280-82 et pass.). Barth reinforced this view in the *Church Dogmatics,* using Hegelian terminology. The title of §17 (in CD I/2) should be translated "The Revelation of God as the Remaking *(Aufhebung)* of Religion." The German word Barth uses means at once to cancel and to transform. Regrettably, this title in the English version of *Church Dogmatics* ("The Revelation of God as the Abolition *[Aufhebung]* of Religion"—CD I/2, p. 280) overlooks the dialectical complexity of Barth's analysis: According to Barth, God says both no *and yes* to religion. In this connection Garrett Green comments that Barth's critical treatment of religion as a phenomenon of human self-help is much closer to the work of secular critics such as Émile Durkheim (1915) and Sigmund Freud (1927) than to the vaguely apologetic treatment of religion in the liberal theologies of the nineteenth century (Green, 1995). Barth and perhaps also Bonhoeffer, who is less clear, were close to the 'practical' understanding of religion advocated in *Doctrine:* "a set of powerful *practices* that embody the life-forming convictions of its practitioners" (p. 421). Perhaps some have been misled by the examples of Judaism and Christianity, which *sometimes,* admittedly, appear to fit into the host culture (Babylon or Rome) and are even lost to sight within it, but which are truer to the biblical heritage of prophet and apostle (from Abraham to Paul) when they remain countercultural phenomena, refusing divine kingship (1 Samuel), rejecting rampant Zionism (Jeremiah, Ezra) and militarism (Daniel), and supremely, refusing Messianic kingship (as did the Jesus of the Gospels). If there were ever justification for studying a religion as a separate entity *apart* from its host culture, then Judaism and Christianity would appear as prime candidates. Yet even these are misunderstood except in relation to the cultures they inhabit and the counterculture they create.

* * * * *

The reader of the preceding pages might suppose that learning about the philosophy of the modern period would be a waste of time for today's Christian student. This would be a serious mistake. The earnest prolegomena of the systematic theologies of the past, with the criticisms they evoked and the 'philosophies of religion' they generated, did much to clarify thought in their time, so that we would not be where we are today had this work not been done. That things are done differently now, that (for example) the present volume is not the equivalent of these modern prolegomena, should not diminish our gratitude and respect for them. Yet this is not merely a matter of pious regard for the past. The work of philosophy vis-à-vis Christian convictions in every period has left a deposit of knowledge that cannot wisely be ignored or forgotten. From all these, believers have learned and should have learned more about the intellectual content of their own convictions. To write about these debts would require another volume.

Here I simply mention three such contributions from Christianity's engagement with philosophy in the past. (1) There is philosophical reflection on the nature and being of God. The arguments meant to show whether "God exists" is or is not a true proposition have doubtless had little effect upon belief and disbelief that are more deeply ingrained than these arguments. But these 'proofs' and 'disproofs' have taught us much about the nature of the One whom believers serve and worship. Anselm's argument, sometimes called the ontological argument, is sure to deepen the appreciation of those who examine it. What does it mean to speak of that "than which no greater can be conceived"? In what sense "greater"? Can there really be such a limit (or is it a limit?) upon thought? Is the Holy One limitless? In what sense "limitless"? One who begins with such queries may, like Anselm their author, find that the fit mode for their expression has to be prayer! (2) Philosophical and scientific discussions of human nature: What does it mean to be *human?* From early on there was an urge to adopt Greek dualism as the proper expression of Christian self-understanding: we are souls; we merely have bodies. Yet this apparent dualism came into profound tension with certain parts of the biblical heritage, and certain aspects of the doctrine of redemption. How this tension could be resolved was a philosophical question that persists today (Brown et al., 1998). (3) The question of religious language—talk about God and about the world's relation to God: Are such utterances best understood as mythical? Are they assertions of fact on a par with reports of everyday experience, or assertions of value on a par with our moral convictions, or . . . ? The matter has seemed more complicated than any of the earliest theorists assumed, so that William Alston concluded at the end of a 1967 article in the authoritative *Encyclopedia of Philosophy* VII:173), that "talk about God is much more complex than is recognized by any of the existing theories." Yet that was about the time that the influence of Wittgenstein and Austin was on the rise in America. These philosophers complicated things still more. Wherever the theologian turns, then, there are compelling reasons to be attentive to the philosophical task. Not least has been the theme of this Part, namely philosophy's role as cultural weather vane.

This brings up the changing relations between theology and philosophy, which for a number of reasons are closer to each other now than in the not-so-distant past. As philosophy acknowledges that it is not immune to the convictions of its practitioners, cannot provide self-evident universal foundations, and (to repeat a phrase) is not the view from nowhere, it is freer to recognize that its work not only examines human convictions but embodies some of them. Every philosophy has its time-and-place setting. Meantime, all this and more is true of theology as well. No more than do philosophers do theologians attain the God's-eye view. Consequently, theology and philosophy often ask identical questions, employ the same methods, and reach conclusions that if not identical at least invite interdisciplinary dialogue as moves made on the same board. Should theology, then, give up its claim to distinct status and operate as just another philosophy? Or should philosophy recognize that if not overt theology, it is at least a kind of theoretics (*CONV.*, chap. 7)? Yet if this is so, it is all the more required of workers in each discipline to recognize their disciplinary limits. At this writing the warning seems to apply especially to 'Christian philosophers,' who have recently seemed to suppose that their skills equip them to replace theology wherever they please. The mistake here is a serious one: those who disregard the biblical, historical, and social-scientific skills required of today's theologian are not likely to do theology better but to do philosophy worse. And of course a similar warning is in order for theologians, a point that will become clear in the next chapter, where we will see that one of the ways of organizing understanding of the world's current Christian theologies is by grading their dependence upon, or independence of, philosophy.

PART III

A THEOLOGICAL VENTURE

Each party continues to maintain that the special functions which the term 'work of art' or 'democracy' or 'Christian doctrine' fulfills on its *behalf or on* its *interpretation, is the correct or proper or primary, or the only important, function which the term in question can be said to fulfill. Moreover, each party continues to defend its case with what it claims to be convincing arguments, evidence and other forms of justification.*

W. B. Gallie

Catholicity is not "looking for a home" in the sense of a vagabond who "once lodged will no longer roam"; it is a lived reality that will have its place or "location" wherever all comers participate, in the power of the Triune God, in proclaiming to all nations (beginning where they are) all that Jesus taught. Only if the avowed agenda is that broad and that open can we claim the promises of the Lord who pledged that he would accompany us to the end of the age.

John Howard Yoder

The seed is in the ground.
Now may we rest in hope
While darkness does its work.

Wendell Berry

Introduction to Part III

As a metaphor for its task, this book's three volumes reject the image of a building resting upon a universal foundation. The building Christians are to care about, the Apostle tells us, has no other foundation than Jesus Christ himself (1 Cor. 3:11), and that is not the sort of foundation that philosophers used to demand. Yet this book is not without its images. I compare its task to a little-explored coastline, requiring the respect and caution a good seaman exercises when approaching a strange shore—in this case, the coasts of a world that wants redeeming. A different image envisioned a traveler coming home from a remarkable journey. This returning Marco Polo finds his home city now strange, its language bewildering, its customs unaccountable. Yet his business here is to make known the new that comes in Christ—in this image, to report on the new land he has found. A third, parabolic image came from John Howard Yoder, who recalled the familiar tale of an Alexandrian vessel bound for Italy (Acts 27:6). Among the ship's involuntary passengers was a prisoner-in-transit, Paul the Missionary. Yet when a crisis at sea ended in shipwreck, this prisoner was indispensable, for it turned out, in Yoder's words, that he had read the weather better than the captain of the ship and had more authority than the centurion. Thanks largely to this 'Messianic Jew,' all hands survived and came safe ashore. Admitting that the parable made its point more strongly than he would like, Yoder nonetheless drew a lesson: the "good news for society . . . provides relevant wisdom and enabling vision, precisely because its substance is not [society's] own. . . . The New World that is on its way, and is anticipated in the confessing, baptizing, reconciling, thanks-giving, serving community, is also . . . the future of the yet unhearing world." A final image was Jesus' parable of the sower and the seed (Mark 4:2*b*-9 and par.): If, in Matthew's words, *"the field is the world"* (13:37f), witnesses to the gospel must be aware that cultures differ: not every soil provides well for gospel seed. Discernment and discrimination are required of the theology of culture. Thus in parable and metaphor this volume sketched its goal. The present task is to pursue that goal to the end by sharpening our focus on theology.

Is *theology* also a cultural phenomenon? To say that it is may reawaken the anxiety about relativism supposedly laid to rest in earlier chapters. Yet if theology is not (among other things) also part and parcel of the culture in which it is created, much of its interest evaporates. Augustine's *Civitas Dei* is a register of the ancient Christian world about to become the Middle Ages. Anselm's *Cur Deus Homo?* reflects along the way tribal ideas of justice and the medieval Catholic practice of penance. Schleiermacher's *Reden* is a chapter in the struggle of German romanticism to surpass the lukewarm faith characteristic of the Enlightenment. And so on. We read these texts correctly not by ignoring their cultural dimension but by including it in our understanding of them. Should reading today's theologies be any different? Indeed not. One of the objects of a theology of culture is to see *theology* as a cultural indicator alongside philosophy and art and science and the rest. In line with this entire volume, then, the present Part aims to investigate existing theologies as data for the theology of culture.

So we have here a reflexive task. To list the Christian theologies of the day one must know what Christianity is. What counts as (truly) Christian? What are the bounds or limits of (authentic) Christian theology? Yet these are themselves theological questions; to answer them is to take up a position in Christian theology, to be a participant and not merely an observer. This reminds us of the tasks of *Volumes I* and *II:* they had to say how the church must *live* to be the church *(Ethics)* and *(Doctrine)* what the church must *teach* to be the church—*now.* So these two volumes implied definitions, admittedly disputable ones, of "church"; one might say they constituted an extended ecclesiology. *Witness,* the present volume, contemplates the church as it confronts the world. Thus it understands the church as a witnessing community and the world as culture standing in need of such witness. These two understandings are interdependent; the world can only realize its faltering freedom to be the world when the church's faithful witness enables that discovery. Thus this Part's thesis is that *for it to identify and address culture at a given time and place, Christian theology must rediscover Christianity then and there, must discover itself afresh.*

Chapter Eight will concentrate on locating the available theological options that point to Christian identity; Chapter Nine will sketch a theology of witness that takes its share in that identity-quest; it is my summary contribution to a theology of culture.

CHAPTER EIGHT

The Search for Christian Identity

Chapter One claimed that giving a true account of the culture in which Christians dwell is a *theological* task. We may and should learn from social science; may and should take notice of such cultural indicators as the religions, science, and art produced in that culture; may and should treat its philosophy as a cultural telltale showing which way the wind blows now. Yet when all that is done, our task is not ended; to be intellectually faithful to the gospel of Jesus Christ we require theology. Accordingly, this chapter investigates theology itself (or more accurately, theologies themselves). This is not a task altogether separate from the broader investigation of Christianity. Note, though, that the broad investigation must include theology proper. To say convincingly what Christianity is, what counts as truly Christian, it is necessary to consider at least Christian history and the antecedent history of the people Israel. This entails studying Scripture, for on its human side Scripture is the self-testimony or witness produced by the Hebrew and Jewish and Christian story (see *Doctrine,* Eleven §2). Supremely, such a study must consider that story's heart, which is Jesus the risen Messiah. In its elemental form the truth of Christianity is this: Christianity is Christ. Yet to come up with such a result—to find here the heart of the gospel, or the essence of Christianity as some used to say, demands theologizing, doing theology, not just reporting on it.

So the structure of this chapter is as follows: **Section 1 (§1) is a survey of current theologies, intended as one sort of clue to Christian**

identity today. It will come out (hardly a surprise to readers of the preceding chapters) that in making the survey theological neutrality is not even an option; it is *grammatically* ruled out. Any catalog of theologies will reveal the theological standpoint from which the catalog is undertaken; it does this in the very act of displaying the standpoints of others. If we undertake the task anew, we, too, should be prepared to acknowledge our standpoint—saying just what we take true Christianity to be and what part our theological commitment plays in our perception of others' theologies. **Section 2 (§2) reviews two related and unresolved problems of today's Christianity: on one hand, the search for Christianity's origin; on the other, the search for the indispensable element or elements of Christianity—two tasks that turn out to be one.** The outcome of the search and the discovery of the indispensable element, we will find, are alike contestable; they share a chicken-and-egg dilemma: How can we find Christianity's origin until we know what that is whose origin we seek? But how can we know what it is apart from knowing its real source? This chapter seeks a single, distinct answer to this double-edged question.

§1. Cataloging Today's Christian Theologies

This section will tell of some recent and current efforts to display the entire collection of current Christian theologies. That puts me in the unenviable position of providing a summary of summaries, something like a catalog of cookbooks: it risks loss of touch with appetite and flavor and human nourishment—the very things good cookbooks, and in their way good theologies, offer. Good Christian theologies speak to us of the love of God, the grace of the Lord Jesus Christ, the fellowship of the Spirit. They speak of life that is natural and earthy, of communities that struggle for authentic humanity, of a resurrection (of Jesus Christ from the dead!) that remakes both nature and culture. Far from being stale or dry, good theologies throb with living convictions that grapple with ultimate truth. If theological works are dull or drab, they are *theologically* deficient, not merely short on style. A catalog of them should show what's what by catching the live scent of living theologies, whiffing their animate perfume and sharing it with readers willing to do the work. So if this present chapter succeeds, it will present today's theology-catalogs, these recent inventories of current theologies, in such a way that readers can grasp the current theological enterprise as a whole—no small accomplishment—and in doing so, find another, crucial clue to culture.

How do recent Christian theologies qualify themselves as authentically Christian? While a long-established tactic called for tracking orthodoxy through the centuries (so that the question was, what is orthodox?), here primary space and thought will be given to some twentieth-century developments. Earlier, it seemed evident to most writers that their own tradition was the unique answer to this question of authenticity (or truth), but twentieth-century developments in *ecumenism* and, still earlier, developments in Christian *mission* have quietly but surely reshaped the task. It has become important to provide an inventory of many sorts of Christian theology. The identification of the (or a) true theology demands such sorting. A genre of books devoted to this task has appeared, while older sorts of theological self-location slip into oblivion. For example, the *encyclopedia* of the eighteenth and nineteenth centuries is hardly attempted today. (This was not today's familiar alphabetical encyclopedia of entries, but a work that organized the full scope of theological studies, showing how its parts, biblical studies, practical studies, historical studies, systematic studies, and so on, were distinguished and related to one another and to other academic and religious concerns.) Before the encyclopedia came the *summa,* Aquinas's being the most famous, and still earlier there was the *rule of faith,* a gathering up of Christian essentials to provide a norm for teaching and a shield against heresies. Today, though, we meet the theological 'map' or *inventory,* and this change tells us something about present Christian self-understanding: no single 'encyclopedia' or summa or *regula fidei* has visibly captured the whole truth, for that is sought now by cataloging the possibilities and finding part of the truth in their complex mutual relations. This seems a change for the better, since it slights fewer participants, yet (like its predecessors) the inventory method leaves some questions unanswered.

Here is a hint: the 'inventory' approach is closely related to the modern fascination with the problem of many religions (see Chapter Seven §2). Modernity assumes that since they are many they must all have something in common, and 'religious studies' take up the task of discovering the common element or elements in all religion. This tactical assumption, which seems to be shared by many theologians and most religionists, has been labeled "experiential-expressivism" by historian George Lindbeck (1984:31f). But what if that modern assumption is false? Then one sort of religious study is mistaken and should be abandoned. And when it is abandoned, the inventory approach to Christian self-understanding may need to be reappraised as well.

a. Tracking orthodoxy through the centuries.—First consider what still seems to many the regular way to locate true theology (and true churches): Start from the apostolic beginnings and trace orthodoxy's path to the present. This method was taken for granted by two of the most influential theologians of the nineteenth century, Protestant Friedrich Schleiermacher (1768–1834) and Roman Catholic John Henry Newman (1801–90).

*i. **Friedrich Schleiermacher.***—Schleiermacher's way can be condensed into a sentence or so: first, recognize the division between the Eastern and the Western churches (though this is not very interesting since he considers the Eastern church of his day "torpid," not theologically active). Then recognize the schism between the two branches of the church in the West, the Catholic and the Protestant. Though he means to draw support when he can from the earlier East (notably from the ancient Greek creeds and John of Damascus) and from early Roman Catholicism (notably Augustine), Schleiermacher decisively casts his own lot with Protestantism. Next he takes theological account of the two constitutive Protestant branches, the Evangelical (i.e., Lutheran) and the Reformed (i.e., Calvinist). But why settle for these and not for one of what Schleiermacher rejects as "the natural heresies," namely the Docetic and Ebionitic, the Manichaean and Pelagian (CF §22), or for some other Christian 'deviation'? What 'scientific' basis had he for excluding these others and concentrating upon the divided historic churches of the East and the West and finally on just one of these? The answer is that these churches fit his definition of authentic Christianity as others did not. Famously, by that definition

> Christianity is a monotheistic faith, belonging to the teleological [moral rather than aesthetic] type of religion, and is essentially distinguished from other such faiths [Judaism or Islam] by the fact that in it everything is related to the redemption accomplished by Jesus of Nazareth. (CF §11)

In other words, for Schleiermacher Christianity is a religion of redemption (rather than, let us say, a religion of culture-maintenance or a religion of individual self-help), and this religion's founder is distinguished from other founders (Mani, Moses, Muhammad, et al.) because uniquely "the originator of the Christian communion is the Redeemer; . . . its members become conscious of redemption through him" (CF §11, p. 56). So how is one to know that this definition of Christianity is correct? In what sense is it a scientific *(wissenschaftlich)* proposition? Schleiermacher's answer is that Christianity is based upon the continuing effect of the founder "upon the self-consciousness of those into whose circle he enters" (CF §10, p. 50). One senses that his definition is also an intuition springing from Friedrich Schleiermacher's own religious experience, for that the "effect" has occurred, as his definition requires that it is otherwise verified only by a few historical references (CF §11; cf. Sykes, 1984:243).

It is on the basis of the Redeemer's shared self-consciousness, then, that orthodoxy in every generation must rest. The project of *The Christian Faith* is to explicate that orthodoxy for the Protestant community of Schleiermacher's day. Religious awareness *(Gefühl)* is defined at the outset as "the consciousness of being absolutely dependent *(schlechthin abhängig)*, or, which is the same thing, of being in relation with God" (CF §4). This is at the theological center, and the propositions of doctrinal theology are the several expressions of such basic religious awareness. More exactly, the propositions of theology must exhibit a twofold connection: first and foremost, they are "the direct description of the religious affections themselves" (§31); second, and by no means a matter of indifference, they must also "approve themselves . . . by appeal to Evangelical [i.e., Protestant] confessional documents," which in turn appeal to the New Testament (§27). This second connection, which was Schleiermacher's best claim to orthodoxy, was to be validated as just described: Protestant confessions were taken to be the privileged bearers of authentic Christian experience and formed a link with original Christianity. In principle there should be no conflict between the first and second connections, between the awareness and the historic link with Jesus.

ii. John Henry Newman.—More explicit than Schleiermacher's was the claim to orthodoxy made by John Henry Newman, in his youth an evangelical convert, in middle years a leader of the Oxford (or Tractarian) Movement, which attempted in a series of essay-like 'tracts' to re-catholicize the Church of England *without* a return to Roman Catholicism, and (after 1845) a member, then a priest, and in the final eleven years of his life a cardinal of the Church of Rome. If Schleiermacher's summons to orthodoxy constituted an appeal to the heart, Newman's made an appeal to the head, yet both these assessments require qualification, for Schleiermacher is the most rational of experientialists and Newman the most passionate of rationalists, while both (and this is the present point) ground their appeals in historical claims. For both theologians, every attempt at Christian theology must be validated by Christian history: at bottom, each claims to occupy the true stem of the live, growing Christian tree.

Newman was by nature a controversialist: while he was producing

Anglican tracts he disparaged the pretensions of the papacy; when he became a Roman Catholic convert he reversed himself, writing polemically against Anglican polity. This trait does not count against his integrity; Paul, too, was a controversialist when need arose; so was the Jesus of the Fourth Gospel. And a change, even a reversal of loyalties, if motivated by a persistent search for full fidelity to Christ, can only be admired by a Christian. As Newman wrote in his *Essay on Development*, "In a higher world it is otherwise; but here below to live is to change, and to be perfect is to have changed often" (1845:39). My aim now is not to criticize Newman but to display the method by which he sought out orthodoxy, a method that required him (far more than Schleiermacher found it necessary) to canvass the pages of history. Newman's practice is best exhibited in the *Essay on Development* (1845), composed in the interval between his departure from high-church Anglicanism and his reception as a Roman Catholic. The *Essay* was written to justify that change and more generally to justify the claim of Roman Catholicism to original orthodoxy.

For Newman, as for Hegel a generation earlier, every important human phenomenon was formed by its presiding *idea*. Thus there was an idea of the divine right of kings, or an idea of democracy, or an idea of Platonic philosophy, and each of these was many-sided and complex. In like manner there was an idea of Christianity. In no case could this leading idea be reduced to a phrase or single proposition, though such verbalizations were often useful in giving a rough indication of the idea. (Newman believed, for example, that the central aspect of Christianity was indicated by incarnation; from it three thrusts of Christian teaching, the sacramental, the hierarchical, and the ascetic, arose.) This approach gave him a way to express the difficulty he felt any sort of present-day Christianity, whether Catholic or Protestant, must resolve: how was it that these current expressions were each so different from earliest Christianity? The answer was that an idea might develop, and might necessarily develop. Earliest Christianity, the Christianity of the apostles and the church fathers, was a true but not a complete expression of the Christian idea. Subsequent development would disclose more fully what the early expression had contained just as the acorn contains the full-grown oak tree. Consequently, it was necessary for Newman to find a rule of discrimination, since (unlike oaks and acorns) original Christianity had historically been the source, not only of its 'true' successor, but of every variant and heresy that had since appeared, as well.

How, then (this looks like Schleiermacher's problem again), was real Christianity to be distinguished from the others? This question set Newman's task in the *Essay on Development*. While Tractarianism had claimed correspondences between itself and the first five or six centuries of recorded Christianity, these claims made no allowance for development—and were consequently unable to account for Tractarianism's own departures from early Christian teaching. Catholic development, on the other hand, not only displayed the apostolic origin; it exhibited "the notes of a true development." These 'notes,' conveniently seven in number, were *preservation of type, continuity of principles, power of assimilation, early anticipation, logical sequence, preservative additions,* and *chronic continuance or vigor* (1845:57-93), each of which, Newman went on to argue, came into view when one compared the early church with subsequent (continually developing) Roman Catholicism. He recognized that each 'note' called for a historical judgment; about each, one could be mistaken. So in the end, to discover that if taken together the 'notes' identified the Church of Rome but disqualified all Protestant churches required of an inquirer (what Newman would later call) the illative sense, that is, the capacity to draw true inferences from data that did not in themselves constitute apodictic proof.

It was not, though, others' lack of illative capacities but two difficulties internal to Newman's program that in time suggested to others the need for alternative schemes for linking present theologies to original Christianity. One difficulty was Newman's presumption that there was some *one* ecclesial institution, one 'true church,' which had merely to outshine its rivals in order to authenticate its claim to truth. And this in turn rested upon a second questionable presumption—that the 'idea' of Christianity was at its heart doctrinal, that it was a *teaching* or set of teachings which, when duly preserved, brought Christ to present light. "Theology is the fundamental and regulating principle of the whole Church system" (1877:I, xlvii). The beauty of Newman's scheme was that it made it more clear what an adequate account must provide, even if for the reasons just mentioned it failed to provide that account itself.

Newman's argument turns on *development,* a concept he introduced into modern theological discussion, opportunely employing it even before the appearance of "development" and "evolution" as key terms in Darwinian biology. Newman's *Essay* was completed in 1845. The following year Philip Schaff, the masterful Swiss-American Protestant church historian and theological encyclopedist, published *What Is Church History? A Vindication of the Idea of Historical Development* (1846), which recognized the importance of Newman's thesis but protested that his idea of development in defense of Roman Catholicism had not reflected the spirit of the gospel. Subsequently, still other controversial replies to Newman appeared, yet most of these, like Schaff's, conceded the indispensability of Newman's concept: *development had become a firm fact of church history.* Curiously, Catholic theologians were slow to appropriate this gift from Newman. As late as the close of Vatican II, Karl Rahner reported that there was no unanimity among Catholic theologians in answer to the question, in what sense if any a doctrine [such as Roman primacy, or the assumption of the Virgin, or the doctrine of purgatory] that had been absent from Christian profession in apostolic days was, as Newman said, implicit in the whole deposit of Catholic faith (Rahner and Vorgrimler, 1965:125f).

iii. Theology as culture.—It is no discredit to the labors of either Schleiermacher or Newman to point out that these attempts to discover and defend a central orthodoxy as a theological homing beacon in each case reflected and were expressions of the culture of their place and time. Friedrich Schleiermacher labored in the aftermath of the European Enlightenment epitomized by Immanuel Kant and shared the Romantic reaction to it. Had it not been for his richly emotional conversion, he himself might have been one of the "cultured despisers" of Christianity whom he addresses in the *Speeches.* Thus, though his theology was a theological response addressed to his time and place, it was also a product of that same time and place. Its power lay in the way Schleiermacher understood his era and spoke to it. In the best sense of the term, then, his *was* a theology of culture. Its claim to orthodoxy and to antiquity must not conceal its local and temporal standing.

Even more than Schleiermacher, John Henry Newman was a denizen of his cultural place, the University of Oxford, where from being a student in Trinity College to a fellow of Oriel College to a preacher at St. Mary's, the University church, he labored not so much for himself but as a servant of the entire University community. His 1845 move to Rome's communion, though, by custom and by law entailed the withdrawal of his Oriel fellowship and of his membership in the university. Despite this leaving, he continued to reason and sometimes to write as if the university audience remained his own. His lectures titled *The Idea of a University* (1873) were formed and in many passages were implicitly addressed to his old academic home, though formally they grew from the (never-fulfilled) attempt to establish a Catholic university in Dublin. When later his old Oxford college, Trinity, made him once again an honorary member, in celebration Newman gratefully dedicated the second edition of the *Essay on Development* to Trinity College's Anglican president. The persuasive power of Newman's theological writing, like Schleiermacher's, lay not in its detachment from its culture but in its critical attachment to it. By sounding the particular, each of them struck a universal note.

b. Confessional maps: Braaten and Jenson.—Consider now *A Map of Twentieth-Century Theology* (1995), a volume of readings edited by two of America's ablest Lutheran theologians, Carl E. Braaten and Robert W. Jenson. These readings are apt selections from the work of thirty-six theologians, from Karl Barth to Carl F. H. Henry. Here we meet a fresh way of relating and evaluating theologies. The *Map*'s initial evaluative act (and the place our grave doubts should arise) is simply the selection of these and only these thirty-six from a larger number of theologians at work during the century just ended. Certainly some of the omissions are neither trivial nor obvious. No reading by such distinguished Scottish theologians as the brothers John and Donald Baillie is provided; Karl Rahner is included but not Bernard Lonergan, his fellow transcendental Thomist; no Two-Thirds World theologian and (from America) no black or feminist theologian appears; indeed no twentieth-century female theologian such as the pioneering Georgia Harkness is included; no Eastern Orthodox thinker, and (a matter of particular disappointment) no twentieth-century Methodist or Pentecostal or Disciples or Quaker or Mennonite theologian shows up, though less prominent Germans such as that "great exponent of Lutheran theology," Werner Elert, do (1995:248f). Admittedly, some of these choices merely reflect a cut-off date rather early in the century, though that itself is a bit surprising for a work copyrighted in 1995. What seems difficult to reconcile with the Braaten and Jenson collection is their promise that the chosen readings will provide "the generative ideas of *the leading schools of thought*" from the century's beginning to the present (1995:ix, emphasis added). Leading whom? Leading where?

Surely the best answer is that these selections provide the "generative ideas" of the school of thought to which Braaten and Jenson themselves belong. Nor is there anything wrong with such a choice, provided that students of theology are not made to think that the world of Braaten and Jenson is the whole world of Christian theology, with everything else so many crumbs to be brushed from the table. *A Map of Twentieth-Century Theology* is divided into two parts: Part I, "Dialectical Theology and Its Descendants," delineates the course of true theology. Its entries are all German and largely Lutheran, from Albert Schweitzer and early Karl Barth down to recent post-Barthian Eberhard Jüngel, while Part II, "Alternative Paradigms," offers a random group of twenty other religious thinkers.

These remarks do not indicate that the Braaten and Jenson selections are of value only for those who share their theological position. This is far from the case. For one thing, their own position as already noted is certainly one to be reckoned with. Jointly and singly Braaten and

Jenson have published outstanding work in recent years, and their influence reaches beyond mainline Protestant circles. The authors they have selected, even if they fail to cover the "map" of the theological world, are in many cases of great influence, especially if we include those in Part II. What is missing, I think, is the frank acknowledgment that the world of Braaten and Jenson is a social world, a subculture, so that this collection can be understood as a proper cultural indicator. Next, though, one must ask how adequately this line of thought can constitute an outward-looking theology of culture that addresses the wider Anglo American religious world? At least Braaten and Jenson deserve credit for representing the academic culture they share, a culture more Chicagoan than Ivy League or Pacific Rim or Southern. As noted, Part I presumably indicates the favored portion of this theological map. Thus it was not the Karl Barth of the *Church Dogmatics* who set the agenda for Braaten and Jenson; it was the severe tensions of the century's very beginning reflected in Barth's *Römerbrief* that provide their orientation. If so, even as late as 1995 these authors' idea of theology in our time remained persistently Western and 'modern,' reflecting a social world preoccupied with secularism, with scientism, and with epistemology. How, they seem to worry, can there be a *wissenschaftliche* discipline called "theology"? Indeed, how can there be religious knowledge at all? But this is a typical nineteenth-century question (cf. Welch, 1972–85:II, 266-308). It is as if for Braaten and Jenson, despite the mighty labors of the later Barth and others, theological time had stopped in the nineteenth century, with Ernst Troeltsch, perhaps, speaking the last word.

Next, how satisfactory is the *Map*, viewed as an inward-looking *theology of culture* for today's Christian community? Here even less that is favorable can be said. Consider one example: If the developing free-church ecclesiology of the latest volumes of Barth's *Church Dogmatics* is a guide (as I am convinced it is), then there appeared at mid-century an ecclesial standpoint, a theology of culture, willing to allow the world to be world, to be no longer simply the Holy European Church (including its overseas, American branch) attending to its customary civil tasks. To raise these 'Constantinian' issues, though, is to invoke John Howard Yoder's reading of Karl Barth, an approach that Braaten and Jenson pass by in silence. For their Lutheran map makes no room for such a reading of Barth, and clearly it does *not* provide space (to name but two) for Stanley Hauerwas or John Howard Yoder.

To prevent misunderstanding (and consequent ill will, that *odium theologicum*) that the preceding paragraphs risk evoking, I add that I intend no condemnation, either express or implied, of German-centered theological surveys or of confessionally formed ones. Hugh Ross Mackintosh's *Types of Modern Theology: Schleiermacher to Barth* (1937) was a classic and unbiased account of existing theological types that (save for Kierkegaard) confines itself entirely to German-language theological work of the nineteenth and early twentieth centuries. This little book, which a generation or so ago introduced many students to issues of current theology, simply reflected the judgment of its author that in his day, "the air is mostly filled with German names" (Mackintosh, 1937:3). As a historian of theology as well as a constructive theologian, Mackintosh was surely free to enter his judgments on the Germanic developments reported in his book. Again, a reasonable restriction to his own Roman Catholic communion is found in Mark Schoof's *Survey of Catholic Theology, 1800–1970* (1970), a work that, though closer to historical narrative than to the format adopted by Mackintosh and by Braaten and Jenson, is again a respectable theological survey with a limited compass. Schoof, a Dutch Dominican scholar, shows the developments within European academic and ecclesiastical theology that paved the way for Vatican II, with special reference to the achievements of the Modernists, the Catholic Tübingen school, Newman's contribution, and the little-celebrated but profound preparatory work done at Le Saulchoir and at Fourviere, with the important theologians associated with each of these schools as well as others (on this see Fergus Kerr in Ford, ed., 1997:105-17).

c. Total inclusion? Hans Frei and David Ford.—In Chapter One we met the concept of *correlation,* popularized by Paul Tillich, as a measure of theological adequacy. Some version of Tillich's idea—that theology meets its environing culture point-by-point in an extended dialogue between cultural questions and Christian answers—has become common in theological use, and, together with the (somewhat self-commendatory) equivalent claim of producing "public theology," is now treated by many as the standard. It remained to Yale theologian Hans Frei (1922–88), however, to arrange 'correlative' theologies in a series depending on how much it was philosophy (one end of the scale) that was dominant, or how much (at the other end) the tables were turned and theology proper dominated—or even ignored—philosophy. Many found this way of scaling and comparing theologies both accessible and helpful. Frei's posthumous book, *Types of Christian Theology* (1992), explains the method and provides numerous examples. David F. Ford, who had been Frei's Yale student, employed it as the first of several classification schemes in his voluminous survey of twentieth-century theologies, *The Modern Theologians* (2nd ed., 1997:2ff). After briefly reviewing Frei's scheme I will assess Ford's complex ordering of the world's Christian theologies.

i. Hans Frei.—Begin with Frei's *type #1:* Here theology's express goal is intelligibility. By emptying its language of anything specific to itself, theology becomes simply a part of the mental culture and had as well be described as philosophy. Anything other than this, any attempt to give a special Christian sense to the word "God," for example, is according to type #1 a sectarian move. As Frei describes it, "Christianity is given meaning by its inclusion in and contribution to a larger cultural heritage"; it is merely "one expression of a universal and inalienable human capacity or necessity"—perhaps the capacity and need to be religious? (Frei, 1992:30). Thus theology is treated by type #1 theologians as a philosophical discipline, and after all the term "theology" did find a home inside philosophy from the ancient Greeks to Immanuel Kant. Frei's contemporary example, however, is Harvard Mennonite theologian Gordon Kaufman, for whom "God" is no other than a human construct in face of life's mysterious unknown. Frei's *type #2* is similar, but makes a step toward reckoning with the specificity of the Christian religion. Here the example is David Tracy, whom Frei quotes defining contemporary Christian theology as "philosophical reflection upon the meanings present in common human experience *and* the meanings present in the Christian tradition" (Tracy, 1975:34, my emphasis). Correlation is the explicit goal for type #2: "[T]he Christian 'fact' . . . has a real specificity of its own and in its integrity has to be *correlated* to common human experience, the other source of theological reflection" (Frei, 1992:31). "It is interesting," Frei comments, "that the Church as the necessary context for the use of Christian concepts and language plays no part at all in Tracy's layout of his method" (1992:33). Come now to *type #3,* in which there should be a perfect mating of philosophy and theology, each contributing equally to the product. Frei's deeply admired example is Friedrich Schleiermacher: for him Christian theology is an *academic* discipline that to get under way must borrow propositions from the study of culture, from the philosophy of religion, and from apologetics, each of these being part of the academic curriculum that according to Schleiermacher is independent of Christian teaching, while on the other hand Christian theology is "Christian self-description within the religious community called the Church" (Frei, 1992:35f). The theologian's task is to meld these two, or (to use the current vocabulary) to *correlate* academy and church.

In *type #4,* however, a divide has been crossed: here Frei's (equally admired) example is Karl Barth. It is often rather glibly said that Barth renounces philosophy, and to be sure he does not in the manner of a Kaufman or a Tracy ground theology in some philosophical anthropology. Yet, Frei points out, Barth is fully persuaded that in theology "we cannot do without some such formal categories and categorical distinctions as those between meaning and truth, sense and reference, description and explanation"—elements of the technical philosophical vocabulary. Again, in his book on Anselm, Barth uses a conceptual scheme borrowed from medieval realism; the same scheme is implicit in his subsequent doctrine of justification by faith. What Barth refuses, Frei insists, is to make this *ad hoc* dependence of theology upon philosophy systematic (Frei, 1992:41). Finally, *type* #5 should on its face be a plain enough category: here the theologian has simply to eschew philosophy altogether. Yet Frei complicates matters by choosing as his exemplar his fellow Wittgensteinian, D. Z. Phillips, a choice that seems mistaken, since Phillips, as I pointed out earlier, is glad to engage in philosophical clarification of theological 'confusions' and does so regularly (e.g., in Phillips, 1965; see above Chapter Six §3). In any case Frei's type #5 seems clear enough, for examples of it could surely be found among those who invoke Scripture as their only and sufficient theological source. As he points out, though, the scheme of types is circular; in coming to type #5 one has nearly returned to type #1, where there is again no distinction between theology and philosophy. A limit to all of these schemes is the assumption that philosophy adequately represents the worldly counterpart of correlation theology.

Frei's five types are formally similar to the typology of his senior colleague at Yale, H. Richard Niebuhr, whose lectures published as *Christ and Culture* (1951) took up the task of correlation by locating two extremes, "Christ against culture" and "the Christ of culture" and inserting between them intermediate types, his implicit favorite among these being "Christ transforming culture." The outstanding difference between Niebuhr and Frei, I think, is that for Niebuhr in that book "culture" is monolithic, simply *there* like the Rock of Gibraltar; the only possible variable among types is the *response* Christians make to that rock (on H. R. Niebuhr's typology see Chapter One §3). For Frei, on the other hand, "philosophy" is a place-holder, an x, to be filled in by theologians in a variety of ways.

ii. David Ford.—Frei's student and currently Cambridge professor David F. Ford (1948–) has produced in his edited volume *The Modern Theologians* (2nd ed., 1997) what seems the most inclusive or comprehensive of all recent efforts at theological inventory. Surely, one supposes, the best theology of culture must appear somewhere among the hundred or so theologians and theologies described in its pages by the many contributors—among others, Robert Jenson on Barth, Fergus Kerr on Congar and de Lubac, Christoph Schöbel on Pannenberg,

William Werpehowski on American ethicists such as Hauerwas, Ann Loades *and* Rebecca Chopp on feminist theologies, Rowan Williams on Eastern Orthodoxy, Rebecca Chopp (again) on Liberation Theology, and on and on: prominent writers, outstanding topics. Nor is Ford wanting in organization; he employs a variety of organizational schemes ranging from Frei's types to a geographical canvass of the Christian theologies of the wide world with due attention to the Eastern and Southern Hemispheres and finally to a topical treatment of natural and social sciences, music, the visual arts, the theology of religions, and Judaism—can one doubt that what one of these patterns misses, another will pick up?

With so much so well done, it is hard to picture the shock, and probably the discouragement, with which a Baptist, or Mennonite, or Adventist, or Pentecostal student, or any other heir of the Radical Reformation, must turn through Ford's pages looking for the current representatives of his or her own heritage. Among the many flavors, the many approaches to a theology of culture, can Ford and his reputable team nowhere find this flavor? The baptist student (and in many a case, the baptist teacher) may conclude that his or her theological forebears, even quite recent ones such as John Howard Yoder, are unworthy guides to Christian thought. Why else would so knowledgeable an authority as Ford exclude them all? Such a student is likely to sense that she or he can undertake theological ventures only by working in some borrowed tradition. Saul's armor, it seems, is obligatory dress here.

d. The issue of power.—These catalogs or inventories of theologies are not the only sort of approach to theology today. Besides the individual works they themselves pick out and describe, there is, for example, Stephen Sykes's *Identity of Christianity* (1984), which will be of use in §2 below, and perhaps there are still other approaches. But the inventories are prominent, and they typify the way theology is currently taught: either as a sequence leading up to an implied or evident winner (thus Braaten and Jenson) or as an indiscriminate catalog (à la Ford) with the implicit invitation to take one's choice since there are no winners. What theology seems to lack is any procedure by which decisive choice could be made and results settled. (Perhaps it is this lack of decision procedures that discredits theology in an age of scientific reasoning—cf. Murphy, 1990.) In the absence of such procedures, theology seems too often a matter of power only—power to publish, power to attain influential chairs and offices, power exercised within strong (advocates might say 'healthy'?), well-monied church boards and bodies. There are relevant lessons to be drawn from the very existence of the inventories, and theological conclusions to be drawn even from those catalogs that crown no champions. A first observation: Christian theology occupies a smaller academic niche than previously. In the nineteenth century, apart from the mushroom rise of natural science, Christian theologians continued to set intellectual and cultural standards for other scholars. Schleiermacher and Ritschl, Newman and Loisy, together with a few less-known Americans such as Horace Bushnell, were intellectual pacesetters. In encyclopedic learning, in literary criticism, in study of cultural evolution, in the history of religions, in all the *Geisteswissenschaften,* these giants of the 1800s dominated faculties via their brilliant (terminal) flowering of modern religious thought. Then came the Great War, Germany's defeat and the exhaustion of its European allies and rivals, the light all extinguished, lives shattered, continuities broken. The European American culture that followed was no longer Constantinian at its core, no longer organized around the old cultural centers. A vast duplication of the Great War in a higher key, World War II, paralleled by a genocidal attack on Europe's Jews, primary bearers of its fragile civilization, had the collateral consequence of sapping the spiritual vision of its generations. By the 1950s and 1960s Christian thinkers began to see themselves more as scattered partisans, out of touch with one another and somewhat cowed by the spirit of the age.

A second observation: Despite this decline in prestige and confidence, there continues to be a kind of elitism in current theologies that hardly becomes scholars (i.e., disciples?) of the crucified Lamb. There is a gap between the academic social group to which professional theologians belong by virtue of their training and position, on the one hand, and on the other the religious community that in many cases has sponsored and nurtured these very scholars. No doubt some of this separation between scholars and other believers is inevitable. Extended professional training in any field creates its own solidarity of shared experiences and knowledge. Yet in this case the gap seems to have been widened into a chasm by modernity's effect on both sides. If the theologian sees himself or herself as the advocate of truth and honesty in a religious world of confusion and error, the church or its agencies frequently counter by treating all thoughtful scholars as advocates of infidelity and betrayers of the received faith. Two current instances show how it goes. The Catholic Theological Society of America, an organization to which most leading American Catholic theologians belong, has as I write come under official fire as "a wasteland" because of some criticism within it of Catholic doctrine; for a longer time the theology departments of leading Catholic universities have been forced to suppress creative theological faculty members on the same ground. (I speak from personal experience here.) This is a familiar script for theologians in seminaries and colleges under Southern Baptist auspices as well. The latter have experienced purges that in one case eliminated up to 90 percent of an existing faculty on the same charge, namely its purported failure to sustain the recently announced doctrinal standards of the sponsoring denomination. (Ironically, once again I speak from experience.) What both groups have experienced is tension—erupting into open warfare—between what J. H. Newman saw as two necessary aspects of the institutional church: its "prophetical" and "episcopal" functions (Newman, 1970:254f). According to Newman, both aspects had *teaching* responsibilities. The "episcopal" duty was doctrinal leadership, the practice of primary theology, imparting the "things most surely believed," able to make the flock "wise unto salvation." By the "prophetical," on the other hand, Newman meant that academic enlargement of teaching, standing in the Old Testament prophetic tradition, which enabled Christians to read the signs of the times and by their light to think the faith anew. This is here called the practice of secondary theology (cf. Sykes, 1984:109ff; *Doctrine,* 24). Must primary theology (in the churches) engage in a power struggle with secondary theology (in the academies) as though each were a hired gladiator, indifferent to his opponent's welfare?

Both of these functions, however we care to name them, are christianly necessary. For baptists they might be called the *pastoral function* (grounding faith in knowledge of the old, old story) and the *educative function* (exploring by faith the possibilities of Christian existence in a particular cultural setting—such as America at the onset of a new millennium). Both are needed; Christian life could not flourish if it lacked either one. Yet as Newman saw already during his Tractarian period, the two do not always nicely dovetail. Then the outcome is conflict of the sort both Catholics and Baptists have lately experienced. Yet this is but another instance of the theological conflict (as I will soon argue, the *essential* conflict) that the church must wage with itself if it is to be truly a witnessing church. How much must this be a *power* struggle, sending losers into exile?

If such conflicts between 'prophetical' and 'episcopal' elements not only do occur, but need to occur in every lively Christian community, what sort of conflict management is in order? What can prevent painful outcomes in which professors are dismissed without just cause, schools of theology are crippled for a generation or more, and bishops (or boards of trustees) are held up to public ridicule for their purges and dicta (all in their eyes undertaken to fulfill Christian obligation)? My response follows in Section 2 (§2), but a preliminary reminder is the need on both sides for a *principle of fallibility* (*CONV.*, 111f). Conventions (and bishops) can be wrong. So, God forgive us, can professors. And it is not far-fetched to believe that in many a recent conflict both sides have exposed their fallibility to public view.

§2. Rethinking Christian Identity

At mid twentieth century, philosophy in the English-speaking West turned intensive light upon language and the concepts it embodied. Linguistic analysis sometimes became conceptual analysis, seeking to clarify concepts in daily use (e.g., the concept of mind, the concept of prayer) and, by clarifying meanings, to bring order out of the muddle of philosophical (and everyday) thought. Though it was a project as old as Plato, this renewed effort did yield some new clarity, but before long a difficulty arose: while some concepts had lost a clarity that could be recovered, others were born vague. There were words in English, for example, that were never meant to be clear—such a word as "nice" in its everyday use, where "that's nice" meant "mildly approved by the speaker, who can't (or won't) say why." And still another difficulty appeared: there seemed to be a class of concepts that clearly meant one thing to some but equally clearly meant another to others! Within this class British philosopher W. B. Gallie distinguished *essentially contested concepts,* whose meaning would in the nature of the case never be clarified by conceptual analysts, since the meaning was necessarily in dispute. Gallie offered as examples 'science,' 'fine arts,' 'religion,' 'justice,' and 'democracy.' Here 'Christianity' also found a place (Gallie, 1964:chap. 8).

Stephen Sykes nicely summarized Gallie's tests for essentially contested concepts: What distinguishes them from pointless verbal wrangles are seven conditions: (1) that the concept is appraisive in signifying or accrediting some valued achievement; (2) that the achievement is of an internally complex character; (3) that the explanation of its worth therefore includes reference to respective parts or features of the whole; (4) that each party to the contest recognize that its own use is contested by others, and agree to participate both aggressively and defensively; (6) that there be an acknowledged exemplar from whom the concept is derived and whose authority is agreed; and (7) that there be a plausible case to be made for supposing that the fact of contest enables the original exemplar's achievement to be sustained and developed in optimum fashion. Gallie, followed by Sykes, shows that Christianity nicely qualifies on all seven points, so that (to mention the final one) "there is an approach to the optimum realization of Christianity through the different, competing interpretations of it" (Sykes, 1984:252f).

This section will illustrate the aptness of Gallie's discovery. The first implication of this placement of 'Christianity' among the essentially contested concepts is that *their proper use always requires dialogue.* No one can talk in a judicious way about 'justice,' for example, without recognizing that there are a variety of understandings (theories, definitions) of justice. To speak of justice simply, without such acknowledgment, is to commit the intellectual sin of carelessness: justice under socialism is not justice under capitalism; the justice of Teutons was not the justice of Romans, and neither one, Bible readers could see, was the justice of God. Of course a given discourse need not engage every remote voice. The Code of Hammurabi may or may not be relevant to discourse concerning Rawls's *Theory of Justice.* So part of the wisdom required to grasp and use the concept 'Christianity' will be recognition of the voices that are relevant for its present discussion. In this section I will examine three aspects of the current discussion about authentic Christianity (formally stated, about the right use of the concept 'Christianity'). The three are **the link to the past, the claim to catholicity,** and **the role of the future** in ascertaining Christian identity. Each will turn out to illustrate Gallie's thesis.

a. The link to the past.—Establishing the authenticity of a Christian theology or of the Christianity it examines by links to the Christian past has already been invoked above: John Henry Newman's theory of development is a prime example. Against his former Anglican comrades Newman pleaded the marks of a true development he said their church lacked, yet they shared with him the conviction that to be genuine, a Christian body's continuity with the past must be organic and *institutional*—as when previous bishops had unfailingly consecrated successors through the centuries. These were not the only claims to continuity. At the Protestant Reformation, magisterial reform set out to *restore* a diverted or lost Christian existence. What previous generations had neglected or let lapse would now by the grace of God reappear in the church evangelical. Radical reform made a different claim. Its continuity with Jesus and his disciples would be identified by *repetition* of the original in the current generation. The radicals' continuity was not institutional or reformative but typological and mystical: *this is that,* they confessed, the evidence being both inward and external—inward sharing of the apostolic convictions together with visible display of such marks of original Christianity as believers baptism and a voice for each in the church (*Volume I,* One §2).

In a motto, Christianity is Christ. The burden of proof of participants in this realm is thus twofold: who are we? and who is Jesus? The radical path to apostolic continuity just listed, mystical identity, has been the working assumption of the present trilogy. I have attempted to lay down a pattern of ethics and doctrine and witness that partly describes, partly lays its demand upon the present church in the belief that this pattern and this demand answer to the original pattern and demand reflected in the New Testament. Newman's theme of development is never denied, but it is never made central to the inquiry. The measure of a historical development is just that it answer or not the original practice and teaching. The goal was to envision a church that, where its faith and works are not, through the baptist principle of "this is that," those of the apostles, will measure its failures by these standards—and will seek to remedy them.

i. Which is the true past?—Christian origins begin with what the Bible considers the middle of human history—with the resurrection of Jesus Christ from the dead. So this trilogy inquires about his identity in the middle chapter of its middle volume, a chapter titled "Jesus the Risen Christ" (*Doctrine,* Six). He was a man among others, fully and truly human, born, living, dying as one among the billions of *Homo sapiens*—the blind and the bewildered, the suffering and the strong—to each he was a fellow. He was among us as one of us, was for us by being with us. Yet the account is unfinished. For he arose, and in that resurrection was made known as God's own Savior, Son, Messiah. How this could be, how true divinity could come to us as true humanity, received a variety of explanations, each of which sought to satisfy three permanent doctrinal demands. Christian doctrine must teach *the lordship of Christ* (answering the question, What right has any one among us to this place of absolute sovereignty?); it must teach *the unity of God* (showing how the earliest Christians, who were Jews, could subscribe his absolute lordship without denying their theological heritage, God's oneness); it must teach *the reality of believers' share in his risen life* (answering the question, How Christ-like must believers' lives be?). The New Testament writings, taken together, met these demands; subsequent Christian teaching as it confronted varied missionary cultures had to do the job afresh. This issued in changing christological models, notably a *logos* model that attempted to correct preceding Gnostic and Ebionitic distortions, a *two natures* model designed to square Christian confession with Hellenistic metaphysics, a *historical* model shaped to confront modernity's demand for historically certain knowledge in every sphere, and (latest, and so less well tested) *revelation* and *two-narrative* models, each designed to challenge modernity itself (*Doctrine,* Six §§2–3). All these, we can now usefully add, arose in particular cultural settings, and each aimed to make Christian sense of the biblical witness confronting new cultural occasions.

The present point is that each christological model functioned as the password of the day for any viable church. If this is who Jesus was and is, the current model in effect asked, in what sense is your theology Christian? Much more is at stake here than the proud claim to continue original Christianity (as by a Newman) or to restore a lost gospel (as by a Luther or a Calvin) or to re-enact the original (as by assorted baptists): A truly human, truly divine Christ can be truly confessed only with a true idea of human nature and a true idea of God. The culture to which Christian mission is addressed must, says the gospel, discover in itself that true humanity; the gospel mission must bear witness to that God who is like Jesus. At bottom the identity of God is humanity's final question: Christology can do its job in any age only by testifying to the identity of God (cf. *Doctrine*, Seven).

Nonetheless, some will suppose that the question about Jesus' identity is no longer theological: A scientific history can tell us all that can be truly known. This (characteristically modern) deliverance has its point to make. The quest of the historical Jesus, pursued with undeniable religious zeal, cannot be overlooked. (Indeed, this was the chief point of the *historical* model of Christology just listed.) Yet what is the earnest Christian to make of this passionate scholarly task that seems so often at odds with the biblical picture of Christ? What are we to make of convinced scholars who (at one stage or another) questioned Jesus' ever having lived, or denied his miracles, or doubted his sanity, and often rejected his resurrection? A preliminary point that should now be evident is that these 'quests' of the last two hundred years have themselves been shaped by the prevailing modernity of the times with its own assumptions about causes, about human certainties, about what can really happen. Aside from recognizing its existence, it is not part of the present work to review this extensive Jesus-quest literature any further. A useful compendium is Colin Brown's encyclopedic "Historical Jesus, Quest of" (DJG 326a–341b). It cites literature from all points of view including the "conservative" responses to ongoing Jesus research. It describes the method of the well-publicized Jesus Seminar, whose results question most Gospel records, making it necessary in the Seminar's view to reprint the Gospels in a format that displays their sweeping doubts. Brown notes that while methods differ, most late-twentieth-century projects suppose that Jesus was "a historical figure whose life and actions were rooted in first-century Judaism with its particular religious, social, economic, and political conditions" (DJG 337b). The single recent work that perhaps best achieves the goal of historical research without undue ideological bias is Ben F. Meyer's *Aims of Jesus* (1979). Meyer does locate Jesus in his Judaic, Palestinian setting, and yet he carries his inquiry back to the full Hebrew canon of Scripture as Jesus' forerunner, while he says in conclusion that the task remains incomplete until "in the tradition generated by Jesus [i.e., the Christian movement] we discover what made him operate in the way he did" (1979:253). In other words, even if with Meyer we bracket the continuing presence of the risen Lord Jesus with his people, the question about the aims of the earthly Jesus *cannot be adequately addressed* until we examine the movement he set on its course. Hence the results of Jesus-of-history inquiry (at least in the capable hands of Ben F. Meyer) converge with the present theological task. Effectively, Meyer and we are partners, not rivals.

ii. Models of historical identification.—What is Christianity? The degree to which historians' projects are controlled by their methods, exemplified by the varied Jesus-of-history quests, should make us conscious that models shape outcomes. I call attention now to two models for relating present Christianity to its beginnings. The first and more familiar of the two compares the growth of the Christian movement (as many would say, the growth of 'the church') to a living, growing tree, which sends down roots into the soil while erecting one or more trunks or stems, each dividing into branches. By analogy, the roots draw upon the Old Testament (or upon Hebrew-Jewish culture and religion); apostolic Christianity is the stem from those roots; the branches are the many divisions of subsequent Christianity. The model's advantages are evident: it displays the organic kinship of every living branch even while it provides a way of depicting a 'true church,' one that merely extends the apostolic central trunk, so that other branches can be shown as departures. As imagery, to be sure, the model has shortcomings: Is it so evident in an actual tree, say the California live oak that spreads over my patio, which branch 'continues' the main stem and which ones do not? Not to my eye. Again, how can the tree model depict known *failures* to extend the original tree? Will every twig not have an equal claim to authenticity, drawing its sap from that one root? And again, what if the actual 'apostolic' stem is not single but (as some historians now believe to have been the case) is multiple, like the multiple stems of the California redbud growing beside my front door. The immediate post-apostolic stage of Christian existence was already a divided reality in which the 'Catholic' element was not even the oldest (Bauer, 1934), and similar diversity is found in the New Testament age as well (Dunn, 1990). Yet if "early, undivided Christianity" is actually a modern myth, this first model fails to depict the real history.

Consider, then, an alternative model. Along any watershed, rivulets form that flow in a single direction, toward the plain or sea below. Some of these unite to create streams, and these in turn may empty into a larger body of water, a lake or sea. On this rivulet-and-river model of Christian history, varied Christian formations began, but their outcomes are not identical. Some streams dry up; some go underground for good. Others flow on in majestic solitude or flow together to constitute a deeper, wider stream of ecclesial life which may combine with yet others before the course is run. On this model, Christian unity is a *future* goal, not a reality lost in the past. This model has its own advantages. It provides a way to depict the rise and decline of heresies (e.g., Gnostic Christianity) that made a contribution to some lives, but disappeared—perhaps to rise afresh? Although for this model there need be no single true stream of Christianity, every stream will be judged by its outcome, its yield. There may be good reason, then, to float our hopes on some particular stream, though we had better hope as well for a still-coming unity of waters of Christian faith (cf. Freeman et al., 1999:2f).

The rivers model coheres happily with the sort of Christian continuity affirmed by Reformation theology, and especially with radical reform. The tree model, on the other hand, best depicts the continuity claimed by Catholic theorists. So who is right? The difficulty is that such a discussion falls too easily into claims of superiority: our style of continuity, our link with original Christianity, surpasses their link. Certainly that is not the intention here. Displaying alternative models of continuity is useful only when it reminds Christians that theirs is not the only one. For a better standpoint than any of these, one might turn to Matthew 25:31-46, where at judgment time the King asks listeners why they did not feed him when he was hungry, clothe him when he was naked, visit him when he was in prison. All disclaim having omitted (or done!) these deeds. Whereupon the King explains, "[A]nything you failed to do [or in the opposite case, did] for one of these, however insignificant, you failed to do [or did do] for me." Deeds of love and kindness, unconsciously serving the King! (Matt. 25:45). It is worth noting that the King never asks what model of continuity with primitive Christianity the "sheep" employed that the "goats" had not, nor how they traced their genealogies back to the apostles and to himself.

b. Catholicity.—The word "catholic," like the word "church," with which it is often linked, has meanings that are frequently overlooked. "Catholic" (Greek, *katholikē*) never appears in the New Testament's text, first showing up in second-century documents. In perhaps its earliest use, the *Martyrdom of Polycarp* (probably written soon after 155) the term means "whole or complete" (*Mart. Poly.* 16:2). To be catholic in primitive Christian Smyrna was to embody a way of life—its beliefs, its worship, its morals. To be irregular in any of these regards was to be uncatholic. In this way of speaking, a church was catholic exactly when it had this well-rounded or complete quality, and the same could be said of a 'catholic' bishop: he would be well-rounded, complete, a fully Christian bishop (cf. E. S. Abbott et al., 1947. Signers of this Anglican document include Austin Farrer and Gregory Dix).

i. Strategies of catholicity.—Of course the earliest use of a word need not be its only use: before long, ancient Christians used the word "catholic" in a second way: it came to mean authentic Christian existence *fully extended* in space and time. Now "the catholic church" was the entire authentic new people of God, and a catholic bishop or other member would be one whose congregation was a part of that whole. Cyprian, who died in 258, could say *extra ecclesiam nulla salus*—apart from having a share in that peoplehood no one is saved. Remember, though, that the second use grew from the first, not vice versa. And rather quickly (indeed, already by Cyprian's time, so that we are not sure in which of the latter two senses to construe his words), there was a third use: a certain subset or party of those calling themselves followers of Jesus now claimed that they and only they were the (true) Catholic Church.

In ancient Christianity, once it had appeared, each of these three senses could function meaningfully without obscuring the others. (In the same way, our word "band" means a thin strip of material that binds something or other together, as with a headband or rubber band, but it also means a group of people joined in a purpose, as in a marching band, and yet again, in physics it means a range of frequencies, as in a shortwave band.) Though ancient Christians were not confused, the three or more senses of "catholic" may be confusing today. The confusion is partly ended if we use a capital C for the third sense and a small c for the second. Yet that leaves the first sense (complete or authentic) with no special mark, so that it often gets lost. Another tactic, then, is to give each ancient sense of "catholic" its own subscript: the early meaning, whole or *authentic,* will then be written "catholic_a"; all-inclusive or *universal* catholicity will become "catholic_u"; and the claim of one particular *party* to be in itself all-inclusive will be written "catholic_p" (or "Catholic_p").

John Yoder and I once pointed out that this specialized terminology is convenient in describing alternative approaches to Christian unity (McClendon and Yoder, 1990:562-65). There is the approach of catholic_p catholicity, in which some Christian network, perhaps venerable but perhaps newfangled, declares that its unity is the *true* Christian unity. This league, this confederation, this 'Church' as it may call itself, presents itself as the true league, true confederation, True Church, true people of God. It may be Eastern Orthodoxy; it may be the signers of the Formula of Concord, it may be the Holy Apostolic and Catholic Roman Church, it may be the Landmark Baptists, who had the concept if not the term. (Perhaps Evangelicalism as an organic movement is also such a Catholic$_p$ strategy for unity; perhaps the World Council of Churches, despite profession to the contrary, really presumes such a strategy as well.) In any case, Catholic$_p$ unity is only one understanding.

Another strategy is not so much a strategy as the expression of a hope or faith: This is for catholic$_u$ unity; it is, I believe, the unity prayed for in John 17; it is surely the unity sung in the hymn "The Church's One Foundation":

> Yet she on earth hath union
> With God the Three in One,
> And mystic sweet communion
> With those whose rest is won.

It is also, I believe, the unity that is rightly aimed at in the modern ecumenical movement. The trouble with catholic$_u$ unity is not that it is undesirable, but that it does not tell us how it is to be realized.

This returns us to the earliest recorded Christian use of the term "catholic," a catholicity which is not first of all the wholeness of belonging to a league, or accepting a hierarchy, or sending delegates or messengers to a convention, but is rather *the character that is complete or authentic or prototypically Christian.* It includes within itself those apostolic qualities that make Christianity Christ-like. This is the character that made the church in Smyrna a "catholic" church, or that made Polycarp an "apostolic and prophetic" teacher and bishop—for the senses of "apostolic" and "prophetic" and "catholic" in the second-century *Martyrdom of Polycarp* overlap; together these words indicate what made those suffering saints in Polycarp's Smyrna model Christians (see Rev. 2:8-11). Here, then, we have another approach to Christian unity: Let us all, congregation by congregation, local church by local church, Christian group by Christian group, seek to embody the completeness that is found in Christ Jesus and in his true saints ancient and modern. When we do that we shall of necessity come closer to one another. J. H. Newman approached Christian unity via what I am calling Catholic$_p$ catholicity. This was his chosen path to catholic$_u$ unity. Admittedly, it was a controversial path—which does not mean it was unworthy. Yoder and I made an alternative, and likewise controversial, claim: that catholic$_u$ Christian unity, the unity of "the universal church" or "the whole people of God" is best approached from the direction of catholic_a (for authentic) Christian existence. That is what the first-century Christians sought when they set out to follow Jesus; that is what the monastic movement sought; that is what the Czech Brethren sought in the fifteenth century, and the Anabaptists in the sixteenth, and large-B Baptists in the seventeenth, and the Campbellites in the nineteenth. It is, by the way, the sort of unity the working pastor and members of any congregation must struggle week-by-week to achieve, unity first of all with one another.

In any case, some sort of catholicity is a widely agreed test of Christian identity: we are truly Christian only if we are truly 'catholic.' Catholics in the East (the Orthodox communion and its offspring in the West) and Catholics in the West (Roman Catholics, principally) recognize this truth by incorporating the term "Catholic" into their names. The magisterial Reformation bodies confess it whenever they recite the ancient Christian creeds such as the Apostles' Creed, which avows, "I believe . . . in the holy catholic church." Finally, baptists, widely scattered over the continents, enormous in number yet unstructured by such hierarchy as Catholics have or such creeds as Protestants profess, are nonetheless committed in fact (if not always in name) to what is here called catholic_a wholeness; it is a baptist path toward (catholic_u) Christian unity.

Since avowed baptist catholicity is less well known (indeed, will seem to some a mere oxymoron), it is worth noting that this avowal was a strong emphasis of the earliest English Baptists. Thomas Grantham (1634–92) was among the early leaders of the General Baptists, the cluster of little churches first drawn together by John Smyth (1570?–1612) for English refugees in seventeenth-century Netherlands. Grantham became a pastor and eventually a messenger or *episkopos* in this fellowship. As Curtis Freeman writes, "In his magisterial work, *Christianismus Primitivus,* Grantham contended that the faith and practice of 'the baptized churches' (i.e., Baptist) and primitive Christianity are the same. Yet his account of ancient religion is catholic and sacramental" (Freeman et al., 1999:88). Among these early Baptists there was indeed a catholic spirit, which they voiced in their "this is that" baptist fashion, thereby identifying themselves with all true Christian churches in every age. The Orthodox Creed of the General Baptists (so named because they affirmed a general or universal atoning work of Christ, who died, they said, for all people, not merely the elect), confessed that their congregation was part of "one holy catholick church, consisting of, or made up of the whole number of the elect, that have been, are, or shall be gathered, in one body under Christ" (Lumpkin, 1969:318; see discussion in Thompson, 1999). General Baptists eventually lost out in England and America to Particular Baptists ("particular" in their belief that atonement was limited to the elect), a band that though strongly influenced by Mennonite (and thus, Anabaptist) convictions (Stassen, 1998a,

1998b), was shaped in part by members' prior adherence to Calvinist congregationalism. Yet on the present theme the Particular Baptists used language in their chief confessions of faith almost identical to that of General Baptists, speaking of Christ's kingdom on earth as "the Church, which he hath purchased and redeemed to himselfe . . . which Church, as it is visible to us, is a company of visible Saints" (thus in the First London Confession, 1644) and more explicitly in the Second London Confession (1677 and 1688), which acknowledges "[t]he Catholick or universal Church . . . the whole number of the Elect" (Lumpkin, 1969:165, 285).

Such a conviction (sometimes avoiding use of the dread word "catholic," but with evident attempt to retain its sense) is found in Baptist confessions up to the present. However, one senses in more recent confessions, such as the Southern Baptist's "Baptist Faith and Message," a progressive loss of meaning when compared with these earlier Baptist confessions (see Lumpkin, 1969; Loewen, 1985). It appears that Baptists at present are more likely to comprehend their identity in mildly Calvinist Evangelicalism or alternatively in an individualist version of Christian liberty or "soul competency" (cf. Ammerman, 1990:chap. 4). I suggested above that Evangelicalism makes a catholic_p approach to unity. E. Y. Mullins, though, proposed a catholic_a approach: "If the evangelical bodies which have added to their systems those elements which contravene the axioms [of religion that are sometimes realized in the Baptist movement] will discard them, Christian union will come of itself" (Mullins, 1908:232).

It might seem, then, that the McClendon and Yoder analysis should carry the day. If the link to beginnings is vital to Christian identity, all should return to the earliest sense of *katholikē* by way of the baptist vision. Yet this is a bit too swift. For the analysis consisted in dividing the kinds of catholicity into at least three compartments, subscripted *a* and *u* and *p* (John Yoder would gladly have subdivided still more), and then choosing among them. Yet if that procedure could settle the matter, Christian catholicity is not after all an essentially contested concept as we had supposed. For none who lay claim to catholicity will be long content with such a division. Roman Catholic claimants will not grant that they neglect *authentic* catholicity; baptist claimants have not set aside the appeal to a baptistic *party* as a truly universal party, representing in its time and place "the whole number of the elect, that have been, are, or shall be gathered in one body under Christ," as their Orthodox Creed put it long ago. Certainly, Reformation Protestants have not been inclined to give up either of these claims. Yet all this is just as it should be, Gallie tells us, *if 'catholic' is an essentially contested concept.* A dispute that can be settled by portioning out a slice of the concept to each contestant is just what an essentially contested concept is not. The wholeness or unity that comes in Christ Jesus is not to be thus divided. And that is also the conclusion that was reached by the McClendon and Yoder discussion itself. There we said that obviously no side

> has shown itself so clearly to be the true path that the other side has closed business of its own accord. Our pragmatic suggestion, as lovers of peace and despisers of violence, is that we continue to reason together but that, meanwhile, we each allow the other way to flourish alongside our own way, waiting to see which will in the long run lead to the mutually recognized goal. We ask of those who believe the other way is better only that they refrain from crowding our way out of the one earth upon which we both must live. If the other way agrees to this kind of openness, it has already come closer to our own. (McClendon and Yoder, 1990:579f)

ii. The silence of the baptists.—This chapter inquires, theologically, What is genuinely Christian? It seeks the theological standpoint (among available options) that best witnesses to Christian identity. Both primary and secondary theology deal with *contested* convictions. This is true of the quest for Christian origins, represented here by Christology (*Doctrine,* Six). It is also true, we have now seen, of the quest for catholicity—Christian identity understood as authenticity, or wholeness, or universality. Both Christology (or 'Christ') and catholicity (or 'church') are essentially contested concepts. If Gallie is right, the ongoing contest over these central Christian concepts is not only inevitable but desirable. Indeed, we should expect that when all users of these concepts recognize their contested character, the general level of understanding will rise! Believers who share the dialogue will benefit from it, and so will other Christians who share the convictions Christians profess. As Gallie writes, "[T]his would mean *prima facie* a justification of the continued competition for support and acknowledgement between the various contesting parties" (Gallie, 1964:188).

Here, though, is a crucial hitch. What if, due to whatever cause, one main party is *silenced*? Then, it would seem, that party's cause is injured, but *so is every cause.* The general level of dialogue is lowered in quality, and future understanding of the contested concepts is diminished. Yet we saw in the inventories of current theologies (§1 above) that strangely, baptist participation in the dialogue had been up to the present foreclosed. One may ask whose fault this is, or less judgmentally, may ask its cause. Here are five possible causes of the theological silence of the baptists; perhaps there are others. (1) It is obvious to most readers of this volume that baptists have been *wrongheaded* (and not merely wrong) about some central moral and religious issues in our time. One is segregation and racial prejudice in the United States and in South Africa. This impression needs some correction, to be sure: it was *white* Baptists in both places who were (mainly) wrong on this score, while other, African-ancestry Baptists, such as Martin L. King, were (mainly) right. Yet the wrongheaded thus excluded both themselves and their innocent fellow-baptists from the theological dialogue on other matters. (2) baptists share *no great university*. The great ones they began were eventually secularized; other baptist universities have not attained such greatness. Yet since the late Middle Ages, the universities have served as powerful theological choke valves, admitting or emitting only theology that served their current interests (another case of power shaping theological outcomes). See further Chapter Ten below. (3) The baptist movement from early on has with some reason often deplored existing theologies, and yet it has scorned or repressed its own considerable theological capacities—a kind of collective *failure in self-esteem*. The brightest baptist students, for example, attend good universities, where they imbibe the attitude that theology must be done in others' formats if at all; one's native dress is assuredly unworthy. (4) These disabling factors have long roots. *The so-called Anabaptists* and their successors were regarded as not merely wrong but dangerous. This discredit carries over to today's rare baptist theologian; sometimes the discrediting is done by other baptists! (5) There is in all this a strong element of class consciousness and *cultural segregation*, and baptists have usually belonged to the 'lower' ranks. The consequence of these and other factors has been to discount baptist theologies as nonexistent or worthless. Yet is not the same true of other disregarded voices—of women, of non-Western ethnic or racial communities? We need to admit the strange voices to the common room, need to hear the Pentecostal voice speak of the Christian life, need to hear Mennonites and Quakers speak of peace and good works, need to reckon that even (outrageous) Methodists and (still more outrageous) Campbellites and Baptists may have something theological worth listening to. Until these voices are heard, there is actually no such thing as theological catholicity (cf. Freeman et al., 1999:7-9).

c. Identity via hope.—If the search for Christian identity is not confined to the past, with its recall of Jesus and his fellowship, if it also embraces the present with its quest for catholicity, may it not also be open to the *future*? Bear in mind that a main recovery of Jesus-of-history research was Jesus' prophetic role; he proclaimed a kingdom coming (Meyer, 1979:129-53). If Christianity is Christ (at least a guiding motto here), then Christians to be his must have eschatology in their doctrinal bloodstream. In *Volume II,* eschatology was set first among Christian doctrines in hope that its forward thrust would give shape to all that followed (*Doctrine,* Two). The risen Christ is the same not only yesterday and today, but forever, *eis tous aiōnas,* literally, in the coming aeons (Heb. 13:8). This reminder stabilizes Christian faith and conduct—"so do not be swept off your course by all sorts of outlandish teachings," Hebrews goes on (13:9). This eschatological promise of his persisting identity also assures readers that no present difficulty is permanent, for it is Jesus to whom the future belongs.

All the New Testament writings are eschatologically oriented—not merely the Apocalypse, but staid 2 Timothy, whose Pauline writer is "Confident of [Christ's] power to keep safe what he has put into my charge *until the great day*" (1:12); not merely John's Gospel with its "stay until I come" (21:23), but also Matthew's: "Like a lightning-flash, that lights the sky from east to west, will be the coming of the Son of Man" (24:27), and the rest as well. Behind all this literature, shaping it as genes shape organic growth, stands one incomparable Jewish prophet, Jesus of Nazareth. By his own testimony, he journeys before his people as Lord of the age to come; he himself was the coming Son of Man (Meyer, 1979:200, 209). "Children, this is the final hour," sings the First Epistle of John, written in an early time of troubles. The New Jerusalem Bible sets that entire letter as verse:

> My dear friends, we are already God's children,
> but what we shall be in the future has not yet been revealed.
> We are well aware that when he appears
> we shall be like him,
> because we shall see him as he really is. (1 John 3:2 NJB)

Here "final hour" does not mean that human history shall now end, but that the time has about it the quality of decision. John implies that his readers fail to see themselves aright because they do not see *the coming one* "as he really is." By this measure, clear-eyed Christian identification clearly belongs to God's future.

Yet this orientation has not been dominant in Christian theology. Certainly from time to time futurity has surfaced: Montanists in the late second and early third centuries, claiming under the Johannine term "Paraclete" the Spirit's present gifts and firm discipline, taught a kind of realized eschatology that identified the progressive adaptation of the dominant churches with the powers of the current age (Harnack,

1896:II, 94-108). Joachim of Fiore (1130–1202) laid out a triadic scheme of history in which the ages of God the Father (the Old Testament period) and God the Son (from the New Testament until Joachim's clergy-ridden day) would soon be replaced by a final age, that of the Spirit, in which believers would live purely spiritual lives modeled on the monastic ideal of Benedict of Nursia. The papacy would then wither away; Spirit-filled lives would shape the world anew. Consider also the case of Hans Hut (c. 1490–1527), who in the light of his baptist conversion came to see his sixteenth-century era as a threshold beyond which social justice and equality would be realized in the inbreaking rule of God. Judgment was therefore at hand; its imminence shed light on the meaning of current events of Hut's day such as the Peasants' War and the Turkish occupation of southeastern Europe. For Hut the Anabaptist, "then" (i.e., the coming age) was effectively "now"; consequently disciples must live in brotherly and sisterly love, together practicing God's commandments (*Doctrine,* pp. 94-97). Once more at the beginning of the twentieth century, certain earnest Christians came to recognize themselves as "pentecostal." They, too, were sharers of the baptist vision in its second formulation: "then is now." The pressure of last things controlled their present; the age of the Spirit's latter rain was at hand (Anderson, 1979:chap. 5).

A cheap theological move is to sum all this Christian history up as mistaken: the Christian prophets anticipated an end that failed to come. It seems to me more sound, though, to judge that like the prophets of Hebrew Scripture these latter-day fore-seers were in general correct: in most cases the end they promised or warned of did come; they were right about the fact and wrong only about details of its character or extent. The eras in which they lived displayed signs available for any willing to read; the signs were fulfilled; their respective ages ended. The world of the prophets ended; the New Testament age ended; Joachim's medieval time (which he credited as part of the age of Jesus Christ) ended and was followed by another. If we suppose our times are an exception, think that our Spirit-prophets are wrong, it may be not these but ourselves who misperceive reality. "What we shall be has not yet been disclosed." What are the relevant signs of *our* times? With what right do we who are alive today pass over the promises concerning what lasts and what comes last? (cf. *Doctrine,* Two §3*c*).

One sort of sign is the indication of modernity's ending explored in Part II above. Not a full investigation, it used philosophy as a cultural bellwether, asking what the world might be if the persistent yet impermanent metaphysics of modernity were outgrown. Some suppose that such an outcome must consist in a return to premodernity. The evidence I presented (e.g., the life and work of Ludwig Wittgenstein) signals instead a sort of postmodern world (supposing as before that "postmodern" is not shrunk to the standpoint of mostmodernity). What might such an authentic postmodernity mean for the disciples of Jesus, the worshipers of his Father, enlivened by his Holy Spirit? This is to be a presiding question in the next chapter.

* * * * *

This chapter has sought to understand today's theology as an indicator that displays both sides of the church-and-world encounter that is central in this volume. Theology today tells us (however indirectly) about the world in which it arises. Theology also tells us (however imperfectly) about the Christianity that is this present age's witness to the gospel of Jesus Christ. The world's identity and Christian identity stand face-to-face; they measure and define each other. What we can see of the world is blurred; our vision of it is incomplete and in some measure incorrect because our own sense of identity, our knowledge of who we are in relation to Jesus Christ, is so painfully imperfect. This incompleteness, we saw here, is systemic. "Christianity," like "Christian" and "catholic" and "evangelical" (and, we should in honesty add, like "baptist"), is an essentially contested concept. Clarity about the concept springs from the contest that each such concept requires of the concerned. Christianity is Christ, Christianity is Christian history, Christianity is the present community of faith and hope, yet each of these is subject to the same contest, the same struggle to be true. What can be done next is to supply another, baptist voice, making up in some part for the recent silence, future-oriented as best it can be, speaking as others have spoken to the authentic or true or actual gospel of Christ Jesus. In that effort I shall of necessity speak of the world to which our witness is addressed, as well.

CHAPTER NINE

A Theology of Witness

Why should 'witness' orient this (or any other) theology of culture? The answer begins with some well-known Christian history. When in the sixteenth century earnest Christians undertook from many directions a Reformation, the earliest focus was an appeal to Scripture, to the *word.* Thanks to the new printing press (culture once again shaping religion) the Scriptures were for the first time available to every reader. Reformers argued that since the Bible was the word of God, all traditions, customs, and religious beliefs must be measured against it, *sola scriptura.* Martin Luther, to be sure, made a necessary distinction between the living Word of God and the written word of Scripture; it was the former that saved, yet the two were intimately related: "Truly, no comfort but that of God's Word is possible to the soul. But where will we find God's Word except in the Scriptures?" (Luther, ed. Kerr, 1943:10). Calvin's doctrine of the authority of the word was more explicitly text-focused: in a section of the *Institutes* subtitled by its editors "the Word of God as Holy Scripture," Calvin writes that "by his Word, God rendered faith unambiguous forever, a faith that should be superior to all opinion" (*Inst.* I.vi.2).

The Old Church's reaction to all this was formulated at the Council of Trent (1545–63). That council's first business was to reclaim for the Roman Catholic Church "the written books, and the unwritten traditions" that it had preserved and that it alone lawfully interpreted (Trent, Fourth Session, 1546). With that ground reclaimed to the assembled bishops' satisfaction, Trent next confronted admitted abuses and widespread misunderstandings of Catholic doctrine and practice, strongly focusing (it seems in retrospect) upon *worship*. Justification by faith, the Council declared, was but a part of Christian teaching regarding salvation. Perseverance was required as well, and this called for "a cessation from sins . . . but also the sacramental confession of said sins . . . and sacerdotal absolution; and likewise satisfaction by feasts, alms, prayers, and the other pious exercises" (Sixth Session, Chap. XIV, 1547). This decree was followed in subsequent years by sessions devoted to the sacraments (especially baptism and confirmation), to the training of priests and the duty of bishops, to the eucharist, penance, extreme unction, the mass, holy orders, matrimony, purgatory, and the cult of saints—all elements of a common fund of corporate prayer they said had been discarded or distorted in the Protestant revolt but was now reclaimed as essential Catholic Christian practice (Hughes, 1959:chaps. 6–7, pass.).

So there were two approaches to reform, focused (in motto, anyway) upon word and worship—the Protestant Book, the Catholic Mass. There was as well a third way of reform, called "Anabaptist" by its enemies but by other names, such as "baptism-minded" *(Doopsgesinde)* by its friends. Where did this radical reform focus? Here the primary testimony comes not from the published writings of scholarly Reformers or from a protracted council of bishops, but from the preserved criminal court records of much of Europe and from surviving tracts, some old hand-written chronicles, and a few early songbooks. Perhaps the oldest of these hymnals is *Het Offer des Heeren*—The Lord's Sacrifice (1562). This Dutch collection began with an account of the martyrs followed by a collection of songs memorializing them. If we remember that the life journey of Jesus, culminating in his self-sacrifice, is commonly called the work of Christ (*Doctrine,* Five), it makes sense to call these martyrs' sacrificial journeys their *work*. Alongside Protestant *word* and Catholic *worship* this third Reformation focus, *work,* means here not bland 'good works' (which the baptists certainly practiced but did not make central), but the holy self-sacrifice of saints through the ages, their *Offer* of life itself.

This focus on suffering and sacrifice may puzzle, even repel, modern Christians. The puzzlement may disappear on finding in the Gospels Jesus' summons to his followers to a discipleship that entailed a cross—self-sacrifice, suffering, death, shame. This had been a summons, not to psychological *askēsis,* but to action in the world. Jesus' own humiliating execution presented a difficulty for the earliest Christian evangelists. For was the Christ they preached not an executed outlaw? Paul in a letter to the church at Rome had to encourage members not to be ashamed of the gospel (cf. Rom. 1:16). The alternative to such shame, though, lay in imitating the Master by taking the way of the cross, oneself. Indeed, Jesus in the synoptic Gospels demanded this: "Anyone who wants to be a follower of mine must renounce self; he must take up his cross and follow me. Whoever wants to save his life will lose it" (Mark 8:34-35a); the same demand is expressed in the Fourth Gospel in the image of the planted seed: "[U]nless a grain of wheat falls into the ground and dies, it remains that and nothing more" (John 12:24). Paul presents Jesus' journey to the cross as a pattern to be followed by the church at Philippi (Phil. 2:5-11) and then states that he himself has followed that costly path: "I count everything sheer loss, far outweighed by the gain of knowing Christ Jesus my Lord, for whose sake I did in fact forfeit everything" (Phil. 3:8). The Epistle to Hebrews sets forth a traditional martyrology, from Abel slain by his brother, to prophets stoned, sawn in two, and put to the sword, and finally to Jesus, "the pioneer and perfecter of faith," who "for the sake of the joy that lay ahead of him . . . endured the cross, ignoring its disgrace" (Heb. 11:1–12:2). It seems the radicals had recovered an invariable New Testament theme (Yoder, 1972:95-97; Stauffer in Pipkin, ed., 1994:chap. 12). Unwelcome as it may be to a modern Christian, costly suffering, even to death, is not a marginal but a central part of the heritage.

This baptist martyrdom was neither sought nor self-chosen; it came at the hands of state authorities. Speaking rather loosely, the heirs of Anabaptism sometimes blame Catholics and Protestants for what they endured, but this may mislead: The civil arm enforced the banishments, jailings, drownings, and burnings-at-the-stake; many church officials encouraged these actions but normally they did not execute them. Put more broadly, it was society, or, as we say today, it was the surrounding *culture* that imposed these cruel penalties. *See, though, what follows: the costly work of the martyr as such* ***engaged*** *both believer and culture, both 'Christ' and 'world.'* In contrast, such engagement did not necessarily follow from alternate Reformation foci. While Reformers' focus on the word should have had missionary content, in practice it seldom did. Likewise, concentration on worship need not embrace non-worshipers, though of course from a gospel viewpoint it surely should (see 1 Cor. 14:23-25). Yet in martyr Christianity, the opponents of the faith are as fully involved as are their victims. Thus the radical work of martyrs cannot be primarily inward-looking—disproving the often-heard charge that baptist practice was 'sectarian' and self-preoccupied. Their focus required disciples to engage the spiritually needy other, to confront the antagonistic other. Martyrhood is of necessity a work of *witness*. Taking up the cross was central to the baptist witness, and the fact that it was *enforced* by the civil authorities makes it no less *chosen* by the witnesses themselves, and all the more *engaging* of the surrounding culture.

The word "martyr" comes from a stem that means simply "witness"; the resultant meaning, "one who suffers," is derivative. In ancient legal documents preserved on papyrus, the 'martyrs' were the witnesses whose signatures attested the transaction, be it a last will or a conveyance deed.

If early baptists focused upon 'martyrdom,' this can only mean that they were set to be witnesses for Jesus and never mind the cost. It did not mean that they were masochists who enjoyed suffering; indeed, their witness is preserved for us in many cases by the court records in which baptists defended themselves against their accusers and tried to avert the penalties; they sought not death but acquittal, and sometimes (though rarely) they actually won it. A song in the old Swiss hymnal, the *Ausbund,* memorializes the martyrdom of a certain Jost Kindt, who was burned at the stake in Kontrijk, Belgium, in 1553 after contesting his fate in five separate trials (ME III, 120).

> For this teaching, true and dear
> I'll march freely into fire,
> Confessing this truth gladly.
> Though on truth they pour out scorn,
> And for it set me blazing. (*Ausbund,* Lied #14, v. 19)

The hymn celebrates truth not merely in word but in act (see 1 John 3:18). For Jost, it was truth worth dying for, should that be required.

Were the baptists, more than others, then, the evangelists and missionaries of that century, providing an effective third way of focusing Christian convictions? A skeptic might raise an eyebrow. To be sure, sacrificial martyrdom is a kind of witness, and assuredly, "Precious in the sight of the LORD is the death of his saints" (Ps. 116:15 KJV), but honestly, how many magistrates, Anabaptist-catchers, torturers, and executioners were converted by this heroic testimony? Doubtless few, indeed. Yet martyrdom-to-the-death was only a part of the radicals' witness. Unnoticed by American scholars until Franklin Littell published his Yale dissertation (written for Roland Bainton), these brothers and sisters, almost alone among the Christians of their century, took up the old Christian work of witness to all comers, at home and far away, as an essential part of discipleship. For them, "not only was the missionary mandate obeyed most seriously, but it was given sweeping application. *It applied to all Christians at all times*" (Littell, 1952:112). It meant a *living* witness—going, telling, persuading, baptizing, teaching—not only a dying one. The witness of martyrdom was perhaps the first, but certainly not the only, expression of baptist witness.

In the Reformation century, Catholics continued their standing practice of overseas mission (De Vaulx, 1962), but considered Europe a field already evangelized and thus without that need. The magisterial Protestants sponsored neither sort of outreach. If we ask why the radical reformers differed from both, four reasons seem relevant: (1) To become a baptist was to accept the disciple's role, including witness, particularly in light of the approaching end of the age. "The pilgrim, familiar seeker of the Middle Ages, was transformed in the fiery experience of the 'evangelical Täufer' [i.e., the baptists] into an effective evangelist and martyr" (Littell, 1952:110). (2) A key Gospel text for these Christians was the Great Commission, which in one version said, "Go therefore to all nations and make them my disciples; baptize them in the name of the Father and the Son and the Holy Spirit, and teach them to observe all that I have commanded you. I will be with you always, to the end of time" (Matt. 28:19f). While scholars had long since 'explained' that these words applied only in the apostolic generation, or only to missionaries arriving in new lands, these plain sixteenth-century believers understood that it was addressed to them (Shenk, ed., 1984:pass.). Here was a key application of the baptist vision: "this is that." The rule for the apostles was their rule as well. (3) Their practice of baptism (*Spättaufe,* conversion baptism, but *not* merely 'adult' baptism) was tied to evangelism by a regular salvific pattern in which human action coordinates with divine action. In a formula Balthasar Hubmaier (1480?–1528) often recited, this pattern was "(i) Christ, (ii) word, (iii) faith, (iv) confession, (v) water baptism, (vi) church" (Hubmaier in Freeman et al., eds., 1999:38). For Paul Glock (15??–1585), the Hutterian poet and preacher who was imprisoned for nineteen years in (Lutheran) Württemberg because he refused to renounce such convictions, baptism was "integral to salvation, and since faith follows teaching, an individual's baptism does not precede either having been taught or the personal confessing of faith; baptism instead follows" upon these (Leonard Gross in Shenk, ed., 1984:112). Itself an act of witness, baptism was also a pledge to continue sharing the good news with others. (4) The likelihood of suffering burning (or strangling or drowning) that they obviously risked meant witnesses were sure to be taken seriously. Just as the early Franciscan friars' practice of poverty won them a hearing (for accepting that yoke implied the brothers' sincerity) so the spreading awareness that 'Anabaptism' was a costly way gained it a hearing at a time when monasticism had lost its authentic charm for many. Admirers of the Protestant and Catholic models from the Reformation century may insist that these, too, were witnesses. I have no objection to this plea. Whosoever will may come. Yet the weight of evidence here points to the baptists.

Such a view of mission and witness entailed a *people* with a goal or *end,* and this in turn grew from a (true) *story.* This is the line of direction I mean to follow now. The story continues. Broadly put, the witness is to a story being lived out by those who know it best, a story that can be entered here and now by its hearers. The relation of gospel and world, of church and culture, is best unfolded in such terms. Thus in the Sections that follow: **(§1) 'Following' is a key that links story, history, and theology tightly together; (§2) the gospel appears in a world of clashing stories, yet by a narrative rationality these clashes may be resolved; (§3) the end or goal of the storied history Christians live out is inseparable from sharing its way of life with one another (hence the need for a devoted unity of God's people) and with outsiders (hence disciples are of necessity witnesses).** These headings can be summed up more simply as **(§1) a storied witness, (§2) a contest of stories,** and **(§3) story's end.**

§1. A Storied Witness

No one today should invest too heavily in the movement called "narrative theology," for it was only a protest that arose in the later twentieth century as the fires of modernity burned low and thoughtful folk noticed omissions it had made and corrections that were required. One of these corrections was the restoration of narrative to its ordinary and proper place in human reasoning. Modernity, especially in the exaggerated form labeled modernism, had deliberately suppressed the narrative content of human understanding. Examples of this can be found in the twentieth-century suppression of narrative painting, the disappearance of narrative verse, and (in step with all the rest) theological abandonment of the narrative content of Christian belief. All that 'narrative theology' really had to do was to call attention to this missing dimension in modernity. It certainly did not need to offer stories as replacement for the rest of proper theological work, or (worse still) to suggest that Christian faith and practice itself consisted chiefly (or only) in *telling* stories! Never mind the worship and service of the one God, might it have said? Never mind Jesus Christ and his rule; never mind the church with its mighty signs, its deeds of sacrificial service, its sins and its righteousness? Was it possible that all this could now be replaced by storytelling? It was not possible. Consequently what this Section has to do is to indicate the partial but real role of narrative in authentic Christian theology, in order to show how that role supports a recovery of the church's mission in culture. Like the narrative theology movement itself, this is partly a corrective chapter. If the correction is well and properly accomplished, we will only have begun the work of witness that awaits us.

a. History and narrative.—Christian theology has a big stake in the historicity of what it professes. It will not do to say of the exodus from Egypt, or of the proclamation of the prophets, or of the life and ministry of Jesus of Nazareth, or (center of it all) of his resurrection from the dead, that these are only edifying tales; think on them and be edified. For a fictional past yields at best a fictional God, not a God who is GOD. It follows that among all the human disciplines it may be history that is nearest and dearest to the Christian mind. Thus one of the ironies of the twentieth century was that history as a professional undertaking, a labor that required academic rigor and integrity, found itself challenged regarding the role of narrative in its own task. To outsiders, the matter must have seemed preposterous. What were historians for, if not to tell the true story of the past? But inside the profession the question was seriously raised, and advocates insisted that if history were to be or become scientific, it must come up to a higher level of inquiry: like other sciences, it must have theories, and verifications, and therefore be able to make predictions (or 'retrodictions'). Explanation was its business; tale-telling could be left to underlings. This challenge was met by British philosopher W. B. Gallie, who led a counter-offensive: story was in fact essential to history. The essence of historical understanding (and thus, one might say, the truly 'scientific' or better, truly 'philosophic' element in history) was in fact the mental activity of *following*. History's first concern was with the past, which was what it was. Yet the past was not here now, was not the present, so historians must 'follow' it, not merely in the sense of coming along later, but in the sense of tracing out the past, recovering it by faithful imagining. Explanations there might be (and predictions, too, perhaps), but they were not the main thing; they were only supplemental clarifications offered in hopes of helping others get the story straight. Thus Gallie's argument in *Philosophy and the Historical Understanding* (1964) dealt in successive chapters with story, history, historical understanding, and only then with explanations in history (1964:chaps. 2–5).

Most present readers will find that point so obvious that it hardly required a book: of course history tells a story. The crucial question (and the crucial point for theology as well) is this: How does a historical story differ from other stories? Here Gallie walked in the steps of his predecessor R. G. Collingwood, whose *Idea of History* (1946) had appeared a couple of decades earlier (and had thus preceded the rumpus about storyless history). According to Collingwood, historical narrative had three distinguishing features: (1) its narrative referred to a particular time and place; (2) that time and place were not part of another world (a dream world, a fantasy world) but were connected to the one world to which the rest of history referred; and (3) "the historian's picture [of the past] stands in a peculiar relation to something called evidence" (Collingwood, 1946:246). Only if all three of these are in place can a narrative properly be called historical.

Gallie illustrates the role of following by an illustration drawn from cricket (Gallie, 1964:34ff) that we can just as well, for American readers, convert into baseball. Every player and fan knows what it is to follow a particular game on a particular afternoon. Whether it is the players on the field or at bat, or the spectators in the stands or watching on television at home, all share a common mental activity of following the game, that is, knowing what is happening from play to play, from inning to inning, and knowing (in some degree) how each play and each inning affects the outcome of the game. This is not, Gallie insists, just a matter of knowing the rules; one could know all the rules of baseball (or cricket) and yet be totally unable to follow the game on the playing field, just as one might know the ingredients of rabbit stew but be quite unable to take the first step in preparing it. And on the other hand, it is clear that some players play, and some spectators watch, without being able to formulate the rules—yet unless they are indeed following a game, their 'playing,' even their 'watching,' is idle. As 'players' those who do not follow the game are only triflers, perhaps picking up a bat or mitt but having no idea what to do when (Suits, 1978:44-48); as 'spectators,' they are as remote from the game as if they watched it as a kind of outdoor ballet (Gallie, 1964:37). Now consider, says Gallie, that in fact there are various degrees of skill in following: there will be the idlest of followers, who barely knows how the game is going (but does, barely), up through more knowledgeable spectators and players, on up to the "local expert," one who can follow the game better than any, knowing its ins and outs, strategy and tactics, who understands why fielders change positions when a certain batter comes up, knows why the coach has chosen this relief pitcher rather than that, and who can even predict (but only subject to future contingencies) the outcome of the game. Consider now two further features of following a game: (1) The local expert is often in position to *explain* the progress of the game to less savvy watchers; he can aid their following, but he does so, not by introducing considerations other than those that are part of following (not by introducing, for example, the laws of evolution or the principles of Renaissance art); no, he explains by pointing out features of the followed game itself. "He may explain, e.g., what the captain [or coach] is up to when he sets an unusual field or makes a surprising declaration. But he will do this only on the assumption that his younger friends have *failed* to follow what is happening" (Gallie, 1964:34). (2) It is possible to have an interest in the game that does not require following. This might be the role of a gambler who (taking a tip he knows he can depend on) has bet a substantial amount on the game. The gambler need have no interest in baseball as such, need not follow the game on which he bets or any other game, yet his behavior may be in a certain sense rational: he has made his bet and waits to discover the outcome (1964:35).

Now see how, according to Gallie, following a story is like following a game. There must be intrinsic interest in the way the story goes, play by play, we might say. "What following a game presupposes is, rather than a knowledge of the rules, some sense of the point and purpose of the game, of what makes it 'go,' of what makes it move towards its climax, of what counts most, [namely] winning or losing (or drawing or tie-ing or abandoning) a game; playing a good or worthwhile (as opposed to a flat or farcical or bad-tempered) game; and then a whole range of [other] contingencies" (1964:37). Finally, he emphasizes the importance of the look toward the outcome as of paramount interest, whether in following a game or a story. Of course in baseball or cricket the outcome is usually winning or losing; in stories these concepts may not apply; nevertheless, as Gallie says, following "is a teleologically guided form of attention, with the peculiarity that the end towards which it is guided is essentially open; it could always be either victory or defeat" (1964:38).

Gallie, it seems to me, plays down too much the role of rules in both following and outcome. For as Bernard Suits rightly says, there is *no such thing* as winning apart from winning by the rules (1978:25). It may occur to Gallie that stories are not usually so rule-constricted. Yet if we think of the stories that Christians must follow, stories whose substance is engagement in human practices, then (since practices have constitutive rules without which they would not even exist) rule-keeping of a certain sort is as crucial to story-following and to story outcomes as it is to game-following (Ethics, Six §1a).

b. Theology and stories.—Let us bring these issues to bear upon theology. Here once more our guide is Julian N. Hartt. Writing a decade after Gallie (and so three decades after Collingwood) and with full awareness of the discussions of history and story just noted here, Hartt anticipated the course of the narrative theology that came after him, even forewarning against its abuses. First of all, he recognized the centrality of history to Christian faith. Quietly refuting his Yale colleague H. R. Niebuhr, Hartt said that "*revelation* traditionally bespoke a range of *divinely determined historical events* rather than a human elevation of quintessential wisdom to the order of eternal truths" (1977:223). For us, God is inescapably a God of history, and we ourselves are by nature historical beings (one recalls Gallie's claim that 'following' is a characteristic part of human thinking). Neither of these ideas is a novelty for Christian thought. Now, however, Hartt introduces a new consideration: If understanding history entails understanding a narrative, is there not a remarkable similarity between the understanding we can gain from the world's storytellers (novelists, short-story writers, narrative poets) and the understanding we can gain from historians? Consider, says Hartt, the art of Southern writers William Faulkner or Flannery O'Connor. They do not write history. Though their stories have (or at least seem to have) time and place, they lack the connection to the rest of history and the "peculiar relation to something called evidence" that history requires, lack the intention to produce history that impels historians' work. Nevertheless their power, what separates Faulkner and O'Connor as artists from (say) Margaret Mitchell or Stephen King, lies in *truthfulness, verisimilitude,* the power of their work to show in its (as it happens, Southern) characters the human condition. This power of truthfulness that enables us to raise questions about our own share in the human adventure enables me (for example) to ask whether my own family (or I myself) stand with the Snopeses of this world, or with the Compsons, or the Sartorises, or where?

Still, Hartt has given us here what seems but a truism. ("Of course," we say, "that is of course what great fiction writers do.") Yet now he provides an important enlargement. When the writers of the Bible provide historical narrative—or as Julian Hartt (1977:242ff) and Hans Frei (1974) put it, when Scripture presents us with *reality-intending stories*—these have power to speak to readers as somber discursive prose never does. Shakespeare has Hamlet exclaim, "[T]he play's the thing / Wherein I'll catch the conscience of the king" (act II, scene ii). Because we human beings are historical beings, and because history is essentially a narrative sort of rationality, then *primary* theology, the theology that must guide the Sunday school teacher and the Christian counselor, must inform the liturgy and the sermon—this theology has to speak to us in story if it is to speak as deep calleth unto deep. That is the truth that 'narrative theology' meant to recover.

Next, Hartt introduces a valuable consideration for modern readers regarding biblical stories: these may be more accessible as stories (and thus perhaps only as stories?) than they are as purported history. When such a reader comes upon a tale about demons that interact with human beings, or when he or she reads that "the Holy Spirit led Jesus out into the wilderness," the modern reader may be so distracted by peripheral worries (are there demons?) as to miss the point unless reminded: it's a story, see. For as Hartt says, such a cause of events as the Holy Spirit "is filtered out by prevailing canons of rationality." The X-ray eyes of philosophers can quite likely pierce such filters; they know that "prevailing canons of rationality" are not the eternally given metaphysical truth. Yet for ordinary readers it may be helpful to take up such stories without first demanding to know whether they are (metaphysically?) 'true.' If what they are to read has *only* the life-shaping quality that the stories of an O'Connor do or the different life-shaping quality those of a Faulkner do, may not reading the biblical stories successfully bring their readers to ask whether the 'world' of these stories contains more truth than the world available through modernity's filters? This wondering may lead such readers to an unanticipated alternative: *God the Spirit,* Hartt reminds us, can "cover every detail and the whole run of human history" (Hartt, 1977:233). That is, history may be related through its length and breadth to what God is doing in the great story that issues in Pentecost.

Someone may nonetheless have concluded in light of these suggestions about narrative that Christian witness could be reduced to the effective telling of certain stories, and never mind whether the stories were really true. Yet that is not Hartt's (or my) intention, so it is time to correct course here. Return to the baseball analogy, considering now the big difference between the best of spectators' ability to follow the game and the sort of following required of the least of actual players. Sooner or later, every player comes up to bat; no spectator does. As a batter, even though he be, say, a .285 hitter, it is still necessary for each player to *follow*—not merely to know baseball in general, but to follow the play in *this* game—know the pitcher and fielders who are out there now, see where they are, know what players on one's own team are on which base, know the inning and withal (this one has become a metaphor!) know the score. Without such following, the batter will be an indifferent, perhaps even a "flat or farcical or bad-tempered" player. So far, admittedly, our batter's need to follow approximates that of the 'local expert' in the stands. Yet there is one big difference: the batter must bat. More generally, a player's following engages his or her *action* (action shaped by the rules, part of the game) on the field. Spectators sometimes act, of course, but this action is not part of the game: they may applaud or deride or even run out onto the field (and be ejected). No spectator's action counts as part of the game, while the weakest batter's turn at bat, taken with others' actions, *constitutes* the game. Only followers are in position to judge the truth about the game, and part of that truth is whether one is a player or only a spectator. Telling the story locates the teller's role in it.

Our interest here is in Christian witness. Attentive hearers of the Christian stories, biblical and other, may be only spectators. They hear or read; they may be moved, even as O'Connor's or Faulkner's readers are moved. In these terms, hearers of Christian stories *have been witnessed to,* and their following the witness may affect their lives in some degree. Yet what of the hearer who is not a hearer only, but who joins the action of the story, becomes "a doer of the word" (James 1:22-25)? For these, following has become not mere attentive perception, but life itself; now following is called *discipleship*. Moreover, the Christian story being what it is, such active followers will follow *by the Christian rules for following*. For what I have described here is in theological terms conversion, the turn or turnabout *(metanoia)* that by Christian rules (i.e., in line with Christian faith and morals) constitutes taking the way of Jesus as one's own, since that is where the story leads.

c. Some theological correctives.—We have noticed three or four things in our search for a storied witness to Christian faith. Yet each requires qualification or correction, and that is the next business. First, there is the centrality of (true) story in Christianity. Can there be any doubt about this? Surely not; the gospel comes in narrative form; we who receive it are historical beings whose reality is not timeless, placeless essence (whatever that might be); we have each a before and an after, our own time-and-place-bound relation to the rest of history that makes of every human being a storied creature. The gospel that saves is not an escape from time and place but a teleological encounter with what is most real and most true in all time and space. In entering the gospel story we come to Jesus; we come to God; by the power of the Spirit we come to ourselves as well, prodigals who at last recall their home country (Luke 15:17). Now, though, comes the qualification: followers come to the Master each in his or her own way, and those ways differ sharply. One may hear the gospel story at church; another may hear it outside. One may read Scripture and be persuaded; another's persuasion may come from the example of a saintly friend—or stranger. In brief, we need not overcome our illiteracy, if that is our state, in order to come to Jesus: it may be the other way around. (Christianity, at least on the fine scale of present discussion, may be for some a religion *without* a book, as was the case, for example, in cultures such as early medieval Europe's, where visual art had a big role in conveying the gospel's truth.)

thoughts of Haiti . . .

Second, the preceding discussion points out the advantage to some moderns of encountering the gospel as if it were (profound and moving) fiction. If Scripture's stories were only stories, they might nonetheless engage our lives, and those whose worldview makes gospel truth seem impossible might nonetheless be attracted to the insight, the verisimilitude, the truthfulness of the gospel viewed as story. Twentieth-century theologian Rudolf Bultmann made much of this insight; for him the Christian way was an existential attitude; the Gospel stories (for prime example) need not be (historically) true in order to evoke a truthful response (Bultmann, 1960:9-21, 183-201, etc.).

An example among thousands is the conversion story of Frederick Buechner as told in his *Sacred Journey* (1982). Brought up in a secular home, facing in childhood his father's suicide, Buechner discovered at Princeton that he had a talent for writing. One story, though, eluded him: what of his own life? Change came when he began to write his first novel and struggling to shape its plot found to his surprise that life itself—even his own life—had a plot: "[T]he events of our lives, random and witless as they generally seem, have a shape and direction of their own, are seeking to show us something, lead us somewhere" (p. 95). In time, seemingly random events imprinted themselves on his mind, until "what I found finally was Christ" (p. 110).

The Bultmannian insight, though, requires sharp correction. For when it comes to actual *entering*, the story has to be a real, a true one. In contrast, readers of Arthur Conan Doyle's fiction may imaginatively enter the world of Sherlock Holmes. They may become 'Baker Street Irregulars.' With other enthusiasts they may meet to retell the Doyle tales, may wear deerstalker caps and smoke meerschaum pipes, call one another "Holmes" or "Dr. Watson," and in general play at being participants in the Holmesian world. Yet according to apostolic Christianity, no such fictions can constitute the disciples' life. Paul warns his Corinthian correspondents about this in no uncertain terms:

> If there is no resurrection, then Christ was not raised; and if Christ was not raised, then our gospel is null and void, and so too is your faith; and we turn out to have given false evidence about God, because we bore witness that he raised Christ to life. (1 Cor. 15:13-15*a*)

Faithful witness must distinguish between a path of *approach* to the gospel (in which the seeker need only ask, what would my life be if these things were true?) and a path of *following* it. 'Virtual reality' is not enough; we live by having a share in this truth.

Again, the account of becoming a follower (a disciple) just provided is defective if it denies the primary, all-sufficient role of God, the role of grace, the role of the Holy Spirit of promise, in the matter. Viewed from outside, it might seem that discovering God's story and entering it so that it becomes one's own is simply a matter of human performance: 'everything is up to you.' Yet that is only how matters seem in prospect. As Hartt reminds us, God's godhood can be extrapolated "to cover every detail and the whole run of human history," not least one's own turnabout from darkness to light. Yet a mistake like the one rejected here does in fact tempt some Bible readers. In one story, an inquirer asks Jesus what deeds are prerequisite to eternal life. Some evangelical devotees may be disappointed that Jesus does not immediately reply, "Never mind about deeds; by grace are you saved through faith." Yet a more perceptive reader will see that Jesus' pastoral evangelism in no way cheats this lawyer-inquirer. Rather, the response is deep indeed; Jesus' encounter with the inquirer becomes a narrative of grace in action. The inquirer is led past his inept presenting question, "What must I do to inherit eternal life?" and again, beyond his effort toward the right ordering of God's commandments ("What is *your* reading of the law?"), until he has come to the question of the right ordering of his own life. Employing a story within the story ("A man was on his way from Jerusalem down to Jericho"), Jesus asks, "Who counts as a real neighbor?" (Luke 10:25-37 and par.). To open that question, though, may lead on to thoughts about God's own neighborliness, about God's gift that precedes all our human giving. In retrospect, one may come to see that 'everything was up to God.' God is the good Samaritan; God is love. We are not told how matters ended up for the inquirer in Luke 10; rather we are asked, "What is God going to do with *you*?"

§2. A Contest of Stories

a. The gospel confronts American culture.—There are many sorts of storied existence, and most of us play a role in more than one communal narrative. Children easily recall the story that forms them as Americans. Michael Goldberg reviews this 'consensus history':

> [I]t begins with tales about Pilgrims who set out in search of freedom. Later, the story reaches its climax with chronicles of revolutionaries who struggled for their independence. Afterwards, it continues with an epic about a civil war waged to liberate all

> those within the nation's borders. The American story next moves forward with legends about rugged individualists who pioneered those hard-won liberties in uncharted new frontiers. And throughout the story as a whole, we repeatedly hear of American men and women willing to fight and, if necessary, die to defend their cherished freedoms. (Goldberg, 1995:8)

Goldberg contrasts this American master story with the Exodus story of liberation. Special to each master story is the *hope of the future* that it generates. The American story supports the *American dream* of opportunity: Freed from whatever oppressed them in the past (King George, or slave-owning Southerners, or foreign totalitarianism), Americans can live out their dream of 'making it,' even of getting rich—at least until another threat requires another fight (1995:9). Similarly, the Exodus story supports its own dream (in theological jargon, its own 'eschatology'). Exodus is not a sheer beginning, but is linked to an earlier chapter in the story, one we find in Genesis. God had said the human creature was to "be fruitful and increase" (Gen. 1:28); in Egypt, accordingly, the Hebrews flourished. Indeed, that was part of the trouble: as they multiplied, "the Egyptians came to loathe them" (Exod. 1:12). God's universal directive (be fruitful and increase) was being overruled by an Egyptian story that split the populace into two groups. Egypt sponsored a world of "us" versus "them." So in the Exodus events more was at stake than the survival of Abraham's seed. "At stake also is the survival of a storied plan bearing hope for the whole world" (1995:11). This becomes clear as the narrative continues. Persecution set in, but the Hebrews did not form into guerrilla bands to destroy the Egyptians. They kept on at forced labor until God allowed them simply—to leave. That was the Exodus, deliverance for Israel, but pure disaster (natural disaster, moderns might say) for Egyptians who tried to prevent it. And here another distinctive feature appears: "Israel's deliverance from Egypt is literally unimaginable without a Deliverer. Indeed, it is precisely Israel's deliverance that makes its deliverer known *as God*" (Goldberg, 1995:13). A poorer storyteller than the author of Exodus might have concluded here, saying, "So they went back home to Canaan and lived happily forever after. The end." Yet that was not the way it went. God's leadership required a meeting at Mount Sinai, and a covenant there, and then the long desert apprenticeship, the learning of a covenanted way of life fit for the new land. At the center of that covenant-forming relation between God and Israel came words even more important than the Ten Commandments: At Sinai JHWH said:

> You yourselves have seen what I did to Egypt, and how I have carried you on eagles' wings and brought you here to me. If only you will now listen to me and keep my covenant, then out of all peoples you will become my special possession; for the whole earth is mine. You will be to me a kingdom of priests, my holy nation. (Exod. 19:4-6*a*)

The Sinai covenant did not authorize a kingdom *with* priests (what nation did not have such?) but a kingdom *of* priests, one in which by God's commission *all* were holy. Had they merely had priests, mediators between themselves and God, Israel as such would have had no commission. As it was, *they* were priests—priests to the whole of humanity to whom God in Genesis had originally said "be fruitful and increase." Now Israel is to "minister to the deity by . . . bringing the whole world into his service" (Goldberg, 1995:15).

To a remarkable degree the children of Israel have done just that. On six continents Jews have been agents of morality, of civility, of literacy (witness the role of *Torah*), of clean living (witness the food laws) and pure worship (witness the synagogue). Despite some failures and with interruptions, Jewish people have continued to live out the story of Exodus. Interestingly, they have done so more fruitfully when they failed as an ordinary nation, as in the repeated destructions of their little state, than when they seemed to succeed, as in the kingdom of David and Solomon. Peaceful diaspora Judaism, the late John Yoder liked to point out, was authentic Judaism, most nearly living out the Exodus story which began with a peaceful departure (Yoder, 1997:chap. 3). Yet getting away, surviving, was not the end of the story, either. Why, as Goldberg so poignantly asks, *should* Jews survive? (1995:chap. 7).

> Those Jews' primary concern was not 'survival': It was truthfulness. God had guaranteed that the Jewish people would survive. That was not the issue. The issue instead was how to live truthfully with God, that is, true to the terms of the covenant made between God and their ancestors at Sinai. (Goldberg, 1995:162)

When Pharisees came along, one of their innovations was to insist on washing their hands before every meal. They did this not because of germs, but because the priests in the temple had ritually washed their hands *before offering sacrifice*. The idea was that all Israel shared the priesthood, so that all, by washing up before eating, would symbolize as God had said "a kingdom of priests." More broadly, the priestly service Jewish people are to perform for God and for the world is "to serve God by bringing others into his service also" (Goldberg, 1995:168). And this is different, one must grant, from a master story that says get free so you can realize the American dream—even if you have to kill to do it.

A Christian who feels strong sympathy with this missionary understanding of Jewishness may want to extend it still more, yet the Christian master story must first say Yes to the Jewish one ("It is from the Jews that salvation comes"—John 4:22). Since it is Israel's business to be "a light to the nations" (Isa. 42:6; cf. 60:20), Jesus is truly the son of David and the Son of God only if he carries forward that very business. Consequently, the Christian master story reaches full flower not at Bethlehem or Capernaum, not even at an execution site outside Jerusalem or at a tomb whose stone door has been rolled away, but only at the next great Jewish feast day that followed these events after fifty days. (Appropriately, Pentecost in Jewish practice commemorated Sinai.) At Pentecost the risen Lord's promise to his disciples (Acts 1:8) was fulfilled: "They were all filled with the Holy Spirit" (Acts 2:4). Present when this happened (says Acts 2:5) were "devout Jews from every nation under heaven" (to what other people could the Spirit so readily have borne witness?) who heard from the first disciples the summons of the continuing master story:

> "Repent," said Peter, "and be baptized, every one of you, in the name of Jesus the Messiah; then your sins will be forgiven and you will receive the gift of the Holy Spirit. The promise is to you and to your children and to all who are far away, to everyone whom the Lord our God may call." (Acts 2:38f)

We must not overlook the subsequent sad and painful parting of ways that in the following century separated both Jewish and non-Jewish Christians from the enduring people of Israel who should have remained their staunchest allies. Yet according to the New Testament it was not that way at the outset. If we believe in "this is that" Bible reading, neither should it be that way now. Jesus was a Jew; so was his mother; so were the Twelve. In New Testament light, the gospel is God's Jewish gift to a lost world (see further *Doctrine*, Eight §2).

I do not belittle the American master story; it has meant life and hope to millions of families including my own. At least at one point, though, it contrasts sharply with the biblical master story just reviewed: In the story Americans tell themselves, every great problem from independence to slavery to totalitarian threats is finally resolved by the *ultima ratio* of war. No wonder the film Western has been so popular: at noon on Main Street the white-hatted hero finally meets the villain and blows him away so everyone can live happily forever after. Does that mythic tale embody our "last, best hope"? Not even the best of the bearers of the American legend (Lincoln?) have escaped its inbuilt savagery. In surprising contrast, the biblical master story pivots upon a slave people who ran away "in urgent haste" (Deut. 16:3), upon a Savior who enters the capital city riding on a donkey and who is called the Prince of Peace; today it demands a living witness to that peace.

b. Sorting out our storied identities.—Now, however, the matter is complicated, indeed. Those Americans who are Jews or Christians must ask in wonderment, Which story, the cultural or the biblical one, really engages me? Is the answer both? Yet at some points, such as that about war and peace just noted, the American story conflicts with the Christian one. Can one consistently follow both? Consider a case philosopher James Dunn-Smith suggested to me. Suppose the expert on cricket attends a baseball game, though he previously knew nothing about baseball. There will be similarities: there are a 'bowler' (pitcher) and batters, fielders who catch and throw batted balls, outs and overs (turns at bat), a current score, and of course winning or losing. The cricket expert makes some allowances for American eccentricity and observes the play closely. Can he *follow* the baseball game? Perhaps, to some degree. Yet inevitably there will come times when the differences in the two games make following one game by the other game's rules impossible. See the parallel for the American reader of the biblical stories. Such a reader will not be without resources for following the story. Just as stories by Faulkner or O'Connor (or Melville or Twain) speak to the human condition, so do the Gospels. In them as in the larger narrative in which they are episodes, many a reader may come to know self and world better than before. Yet now comes a hard question: can such a 'literary' reader of the Gospel truly *follow* it? Particularly if one is committed to a master story as attractive as the American story is, can one learn to follow another, different story?

There is both a similarity and a difference between 'following' as the essence of historical understanding (Gallie) and 'following' as the heart of reading the Gospels aright. Consider the saying of Jesus: "Anyone who wants to be a follower of mine must renounce self; he must take up his cross and follow me" (Mark 8:34). Gallie takes us a certain distance along the road: one cannot follow baseball—or a historical narrative—without the interest and skills that make baseball possible in the one case or make history as a form of human understanding possible in the other. Yet farther down that road there is another station: Finally, one cannot follow the story of the Gospels on its own terms without the interest and skills and commitment of a *disciple.*

We seem to have reached firm ground: if there is a clash of stories, check out the facts, and see whose story best fits the facts. The God who answers (not with fire, but) with facts—doubtless *that* God is GOD (cf. 1 Kings 18:24). Here is the strategy of much conservative Christian apologetics. Yet readers of the preceding chapters (especially those in Part II) will sense in this fact-finding strategy a new complication: Those who live by different sets of convictions (embrace different master stories) are unlikely to agree on just what the relevant facts are. As contemporary scientists put it, facts always arrive theory-laden; there are no theory-free facts, no convictionless facts, no facts save those constitutive of one story or another. Realizing this has driven some into hard relativism. It need not, but to overcome or defuse such relativism (while sticking with 'the facts') may require a struggle, and certainly hard work. Such work is all the more important because (another complication) the rival or clashing stories we are considering are not neatly parceled out to two sets of owners. Most American Christians have internalized both the American *and* the Christian stories. (Those who live in other lands may find their own parallels here.) We conceal their clash from ourselves as long as we can. Sorting them out is more complicated, often more painful, than we might wish.

c. An appeal to 'principles.'—Consider now the proposition that there is a straightforward way to resolve any such dilemma, namely an appeal to principles deeper than any particular narrative. An example comes from Julian Hartt, who once identified some "ontological essentials" that we accept simply because we are human. For Hartt, these inescapables are most simply "death and taxes"—one standing for the claim nature makes upon us and the other for the claim culture makes. He also proposed a longer list: *death, love, creativity, anxiety, and guilt,* elements of human existence that engage everyone, but which Hartt says the world disguises with its lies and illusions (Hartt, 1967:70; see Chapter One above). Others offer similar proposals: Bronislaw Malinowski offers a list of seven "basic needs" of individuals: metabolism (nutrition), reproduction, bodily comforts, safety, movement, growth, and health (1944:91). In *Ethics* (Three §3*b*) I reported French philosopher Simone Weil's list of "needs of the soul." A similar concept appears in James Smith's and my *Convictions: Defusing Religious Relativism,* where the so-called essentials are designated as *loci* (the plural of *locus*), that is, *places* to which humans regularly turn to justify their beliefs and convictions (*CONV.*, 106f, 154-62). Looking at the lists mentioned here and others like them, one notices how varied they are. Is it not pretty clear that, far from being ontological (or metaphysical) 'essentials' for all people everywhere, the contents of these lists are actually culturally determined indicators of what seemed essential to some people at some time and place? (Smith and I were careful to provide no such list.) This cultural dependency is apparent, for example, in Hartt's mid-twentieth-century list: writing in an age of anxiety (nuclear weapons, war and the threat of war, selves thrashing about in Freudian disquiet), Hartt's essentials look backward in anxiety more than forward in hope. So if I offer here yet another list, we can expect it to reflect current cultural assumptions; I find that current hopefulness about the future in a new millennium comes only with nagging doubt of anyone's ability to know what the future will be.

i. Three current 'principles.'—Here, then, are three trial 'loci' by which current master stories may be measured—not a complete list nor an inescapable one, but a list that may express some current *hungers* of humanity. The three are *love, forgiveness, peace*—things we want if we want anything; things we think our master story should enhance. Will these do as principles superior to any narrative?

Love is a notorious trickster: the Greek god *Eros* (Roman Cupid) was famous for cupidity as well as for his erotic gifts. Love is a realm in which Christianity has not found it easy to make itself clear—not even to Christians. Augustine tried to distinguish *amor* from *caritas;* in the twentieth century Anders Nygren argued (in part, against Augustine) that true Christian love was always *agápē,* never *erōs;* literary critic C. S. Lewis said matters were more complicated: there were "four loves"; and so on. But the common Hellenistic Greek word for love, *agápē,* like English *love* and German *Liebe,* can stand for any or all of these variations. Thus when I discussed love in a chapter of *Ethics,* I could make the necessary distinctions clear only via alternative *narratives* of love. There was for one the romantic narrative, in which love always yields passion, disappointment, separation, and (in the end) death. It was well represented in the High Medieval romance of Tristan and Isolde, but it persists in recent sentimental films such as *The Bridges of Madison County* or *Titanic.* For another, there was the Freudian narrative, which reduced all love to sex and all sex to the oral pleasure of the sucking babe. Of course there are differences—Freud's project is to discover them—but the differences cannot be sorted out without recognizing the continuities between these various sorts of attachment. While evidently romantic love has to express itself in story form, *Ethics* argued that the same was true of Freudian love: it originated with the painful narratives unfolded on the clinical couch, and it issued, by way of theories Freud formed over a lifetime of work, in narrative reconstructions of these lives. I contrasted both these with the Christian narrative of love, of which Augustine's was an early (but flawed) version, while "the romance of orthodoxy," with which the *Ethics* chapter ends, once again requires narrative unfolding to become clear (*Volume I,* Five). In short, to recognize the human hunger for love leaves it unsettled as to which narrative of love supports it (and us) best. Though we live amid a strife of narratives, if we have none, 'love' is at best a place holder and at worst a symptom of the lies and illusions with which we conceal ourselves from ourselves and from God (cf. Gen. 3:8ff).

A similar account can be given of *forgiveness.* At least dimly we recognize that forgiveness is inseparable from love itself. Love draws human beings together in a yoking that is attempted in passionate unions yet never fully realized. We 'sacramentally' express our hunger for oneness, yet our love remains imperfect and therefore dissatisfied (*Doctrine,* Ten §3.*b*.ii). We want remedy for all our failures in human relations, not merely the transient failures of human intercourse but the lasting failure to be as one—in biblical language, failure to love the other as ourselves. Here forgiveness comes in, offering to cancel not only our betrayals of one another but even our sins against God, the source of all human good. Forgiveness is love's medicine, its everlasting therapy. Yet as with love, forgiveness is only the name of muddled human hungers until it finds its place in a narrative that can define and direct it. As with love, a chapter of *Ethics* (Eight) spelled out that need and showed a line of gospel direction for its fulfillment. The intensity of need for forgiveness, though, is by no means limited to the religious. As these lines are composed, an amnesty court meets in the new, post-apartheid, post-police-state South Africa, seeking a way forward for a country divided by its memories of a racist, repressive past. What is to be done with a retired prime minister who authorized these cruelties, or with his minions, or with the surviving families of their dead victims? Men cry "justice," but what sort of justice can make for peace here—to say nothing of love? Amnesty (literally, forgetting) is a legal device, a justice device: admit all your crimes before this court and you will never be prosecuted for them. It seems the best that can be done. Yet beyond amnesty stands forgiveness; it is as personal as immunity from prosecution is impersonal; it is legally unenforceable, as far beyond the courts as gospel is beyond law.

Finally, the same account can be given of *peace* as a principle deeper than all our master stories. The very term "peace" takes on different substance in other languages: *shalom, salaam, eirēnē, pax, Friede*—all are translated "peace" but each bares its origin whenever it is spoken. For the variant terms are supported by variant stories. John Yoder, in a pamphlet titled *Nevertheless* (1971), listed twenty-five sorts of religious 'pacifism,' no two identical, each supported by a paradigmatic narrative that shows how on its terms peace is realized. It is too far from our present course to inspect all these sorts of religious pacifism, each with distinctive strengths and weaknesses. All of them, as Yoder says, "nevertheless" have their strong points. Consider only his "pacifism of the messianic community." Unlike others, this standpoint requires acknowledging "that Jesus is Christ and that Jesus Christ is Lord." Its central idea is that God's way of peacemaking has come to us, not in a written or even in a prophetic message, but "in the full humanity of a unique and yet complete human being," namely Jesus (1971:124). This way also demands "that peculiar way of living for God in the world, of being used as instruments of the living of God in the world, which the Bible calls *agápē* or *cross*" (1971:125). It brings us back, then, to the centrality of love and forgiveness mentioned above. It differs from some approaches, though, in its inescapable sociality; it is the pacifism of the messianic *community*.

ii. The real role of 'principles.'—At least in the cases of love and forgiveness and peace examined here, the engaged or lived-out story is the thing wanted. The shortcut to principles never turns out to be short. Yet this does not mean that the appeal to these three loci or to others such as justice or rights or human dignity are without value. For though these loci do not escape the need for a master story, and though they provide no way for our story's 'logic' to triumph over all others, they succeed in another way: they serve as bridges linking the concerns of the world to the concerns of Jesus' people. Hebrew-speakers in the Middle East who seek *shalom* and Arabic-speakers who yearn for *salaam* do not have identical concepts of peace—their respective stories are different enough to prevent that. Yet *shalom-salaam* in its very breadth forms a bridge by which they can come to respect each other's yearnings and find a common way to fulfill them. Perhaps that is what Julian Hartt meant when he called these appeals "ontological essentials" and what Simone Weil meant when she listed "needs of the soul." To see the importance of this conjunction of recognized human need with the gospel's witness, consider now a recent work of literature.

d. Culture at work on gospel ground: "Juneteenth."—Jesus came to bring not peace but a sword (Matt. 10:34), came, that is, to challenge the world with the self-giving way of the cross. To miss that challenge is to miss the gospel itself. Yet his challenge, the 'end' of the story he brought to crisis at Calvary, was not merely that his followers should struggle—and fail. From time to time, the sowers of gospel seed are likely to hear the world say Yes. That is apostolic optimism; that is an evangelist's faith. It is right, then, for the gospel's witnesses not only to perceive challenges but to recognize flags of welcome whenever they flutter atop culture's old towers. Such a flag is flown by the late Ralph Waldo Ellison, distinguished American novelist.

Ralph Waldo Ellison (1914–94) was born in Oklahoma City, the son of Lewis and Ida Millsap Ellison. He attended the local (segregated) high school, was attracted to jazz, and enrolled as a music major in Tuskegee Institute in Alabama. Before finishing that program, he went to New York to earn money, met Langston Hughes, the Harlem Renaissance poet, and Richard Wright, the novelist, and never returned to college. After he published *Invisible Man,* which won the National Book Award, he was granted the *Prix de Rome;* it supported his life in Italy for several years. Returning to New York, he was launched on a literary career in which he wrote stories, essays, and criticism, interpreted music and painting, and established himself as a preeminent man of letters. He taught at Chicago, Yale, Rutgers, and New York University, and at his death left a great sheaf of incomplete manuscripts.

Ellison's first novel, *Invisible Man* (1952), was a cry of protest from black pre–Civil Rights America. The book took the literary form of a *Bildungsroman,* a story of a youth's development into maturity, only the youth was Negro (Ellison never relinquished the term) and his 'education' consisted in the young man's encounter with the powers-that-be of a racist society, South and North. He learned he could not accept his identity from them; he must be what he was, even though that meant that a race-crazed society would no longer be able to see *him.* Being himself, he would therefore be to it invisible. Ellison published this novel to critical acclaim; he then spent intervals for the rest of his life, over forty years, writing a second novel that ran to thousands of pages but was never published. His literary executor, John F. Callahan, was urged by Mrs. Ellison to extract from that vast store of pages enough to represent what might have been Ellison's book, with its own beginning, middle, and end. Callahan's selection, only 348 pages, is *Juneteenth* (1999). It tells the story of a baby of uncertain race (but of unmixed white appearance) who is adopted by a former jazz trombonist become Christian evangelist, the Reverend Alonzo Hickman. He rears the child in the black community, naming him Bliss (alluding to his unknown origin, since ignorance is bliss) and helping him achieve a Christian formation. He makes Bliss a child evangelist and his assistant. Eventually, though, the boy is fascinated by the advantage of his own white appearance and runs away, becoming first a moviemaker and later a politician. He rises to become a United States Senator, Adam Sunraider, who conceals and denies his black ethnic upbringing. Sunraider becomes, in fact, a racist demagogue, so that eventually his life is threatened by angry black militants. But Reverend Hickman has quietly kept track of his adopted son and now comes to Washington, D.C., to warn him of his danger. The warning fails; the Senator is shot. Perhaps mortally wounded, Sunraider-Bliss summons Reverend Hickman to his hospital bedside. The novel unfolds from this point, as in conversation, silent thoughts, and private dreams the two protagonists, the jazz player become evangelist and the child evangelist become racist, recall the past they share.

On this small canvas Ellison's book attempts an American epic. Each protagonist is a symbolic type: Bliss is America, reckoning that its substance lies in its whiteness and denying the powerful African American component in its own past; Hickman is the black church and (more broadly) he is the Negro people, suffering rejection by European America yet bearing that rejection in a patience and wisdom that may outlast it. Bliss is the prodigal who has refused to return; he has lost his ability to understand his foster father, but father Hickman understands his prodigal son.

> Oh, all I've been talking about is human, Bliss. All human weakness and human pride and will—didn't Peter deny Christ? But you had a choice, Bliss. You had a chance to join up to be a witness for either side and you let yourself be fouled up. You tried to go with those who raise the failure of love above their heads like a flag and say, 'See here, I am now a man.' You wanted to be with those who turn coward before their strongest human need and then say, 'Look here, I'm brave.' (Ellison, 1999:164f)

The prodigal's journey is by no means the only Christian theme here. The failure of spirit without flesh (p. 112), the eucharistic continuity that binds human beings to one another and to Jesus and to God (pp. 133, 136, 162-66), the conflict of science and faith (p. 274), the human longing for revenge transcended by the gospel requirement of sacrifice (pp. 284-99), conversion as the emergence rather than the cancellation of humanity (pp. 297-319), God who discloses himself as redeeming love (pp. 300-304), the American struggle to realize a peoplehood made of all peoples (p. 353)—all these and more appear in Reverend Hickman's persuasions and self-examinations as he seeks, the good pastor, to reclaim his wounded son. These Christian themes appear in a frame of authentic African American church life, beautifully related, set out in perfect preacherly English, perceived through the faithful eyes of the old evangelist.

It is remarkable that Ellison casts his symbolic portrait of America needing reconciliation, a homecoming, in language drawn directly from the Negro church. This becomes more remarkable still when we realize that the novelist, though so skilled in the authentic use of Christian language and inner reflection, is the same who issued the shrill cry of secular protest in *Invisible Man.* And it is most remarkable if we consider that Ellison himself, though raised in the Christian home of a black schoolteacher in Oklahoma, left his church after childhood and never returned. His is the voice of secular America; it is from the side of culture, not the side of the Christian witness, that this prophetic cry of hope for America comes.

John Callahan was asked to draw from Ellison's storehouse a beginning, a middle, and an end. As it came out on the page, the Washington assassination attempt establishes the beginning, bringing together at the hospital as in a drama the Senator and the clergyman, unconscious white America and suffering, gospel-shaped black America. The middle is constituted by their Job-like debate of memories as Hickman and Bliss together and in private thought reconstruct the past they share—America's unacknowledged past, in our terms America's true master story. And what does Callahan produce for an ending? A long, troubled dream. Sunraider-Bliss slips back into sleep, and in his dreams, good and evil struggle for mastery: which will control the story's end? The Senator "found himself wading through a sandy landscape bathed in an eerie twilight." Dream scenes follow until the dream's center, a sequence in which the Senator, full of pompous insincerity, is approached by a child dressed as in a painting by Goya (p. 339). At first the man attempts to manage the child, deflecting its nastiness with the skills of adult avoidance. Yet the child (the prodigal child? the child who is Bliss becoming Sunraider?) persists in nasty, insulting behavior until the sequence ends in dream-like destruction. Again the scene changes; Bliss dreams of a church service from long ago. A storm has broken over the meetinghouse, with hail and lightning; there is darkness as the power fails. But Hickman redirects the service: he lines out a hymn. Soon everyone is singing "Christ Arose." "He 'rose . . . Heroes! / He 'rose . . . Heroes! / He 'rose . . . Up from the dead!" There are two ways to read the song: it sings of Christ's resurrection, or it sings of earthly heroes. In the dream, these are conflated, indistinguishable; there is no way to select one meaning over the other. But need we do so? Is not the ambiguously printed hymn the very model of a God-mixed world, in which earth's true heroes are soldiers of the cross, chanters of its resurrection hymn? Bliss's dream shifts into nightmare mode, but when the nightmare is at its darkest (as I read the text) Bliss awakes "*and seemed to hear* the sound of Hickman's consoling voice, calling from somewhere above" (p. 348). Here the novel ends. Does Bliss recover; does the prodigal come home? The ending's ambiguity represents our own: Is it America's time of reconciliation, or not?

Ellison's *Juneteenth* (the nineteenth of June in Southern black culture is an annual commemoration of emancipation) has not met with unmixed acclaim. While novelist Robert Stone (in *New York Review,* August 12, 1999) gives it high marks, quoting with approval editor Callahan's claim that the work evokes "a broader and much more diverse world for those who take their provisional identities from groups," literary critic James Wood writes that it is "a lavish disappointment; a false sunset" (*New Republic,* June 28, 1999). Wood doesn't like all those "sermons" (the very element Stone finds superior). One need not set it on a par with *Huckleberry Finn* (which had its own difficulties with its early critics) in order to realize that *Juneteenth* has achieved that rare union of transcendence and immanence, that integration of the divine story with the human one, that answers from within the culture the voice of the gospel itself, thus fulfilling once more art's promise (see Chapter Four §2).

Literary critic Ralph Wood tells me that when Ellison spoke at Wake Forest University in the 1970s, his chosen topic was the civilizing role of the Negro parsonage: home of books, of culture, of dignity and decency. No parsonage appears in the selected text of *Juneteenth,* but in a note to himself that its editor prints, Ellison wrote:

> Proposition: A great religious leader is a "master of ecstasy." He evokes emotions that move beyond the rational onto the mystical. A jazz musician does something of the same. By his manipulation of sound and rhythm he releases movements and emotions which allow for the transcendence of everyday reality. As an ex-jazzman minister Hickman combines the two roles, and this is the source of his leadership.

And then again, dialogue that does not appear in the edited text:

> [T]he law's facts have made us *outlaws.* Yes, that's the truth, but only part of it; for Bliss, boy, we're outlaws in Christ and Christ is the higher truth. (Ellison, 1999:354)

§3. Story's End

The 1980s film *Witness,* directed by Peter Weir, is set on the margin between two versions of American culture. As a young Amish widow and her small son wait in an urban Philadelphia railway station, the boy by chance observes a drug-related murder. The detective assigned the case soon realizes that as a key witness the boy is in danger and that the drug ring he has encountered has ties within the corrupt police department. So he drives mother and son to their home country, where he himself hides, assuming Amish clothing and identity to evade the police and protect the boy. Another sort of witness now appears, as the city visitor's Old Order Amish hosts disclose the attitudes that shape their peaceable way. Thus the film is about story versus story, urban violence (cops and criminals) in a struggle with Christian non-violence. At story's end, it is hard to say who won. Though the film seems to make heroes of the pacifist Amish and villains of those with city ways, the story line turns on the triumphs of the violent. In the California theater where I saw *Witness,* the audience cheered exactly when the tough detective deserted his non-violent Amish pose to smash a teasing bully's chops. At the climax the detective, now armed with a shotgun, gratuitously slays the chief drug-dealer. A story that seemed in position to lift up a small, archaic Christian culture ends (as perhaps American viewers would demand) by reverting to the cultural master story of justice achieved by deadly violence. Nevertheless, in a denouement the chief crooked cop, also armed with a shotgun, is faced down by unarmed Amish folk, witnesses to another way. He recognizes the imprudence of using the gun in the sight of all those witnesses and surrenders it. So both messages are present—in some measure the truth of *Witness*'s story lies in the eye of the viewer. Implicitly, it asks how Christian witness on a broader scale is to flourish in the world of today.

a. A confession.—The story I tell next is not easy for me. I grew up in Shreveport, Louisiana. (Some suppose Shreveport is on the Gulf, but the "port" in its name refers to its situation on the Red River in Louisiana's northwest.) The population in my boyhood was about one-third black, but segregation ensured that I actually knew no African Americans save the domestic workers in my parents' home. This Southern location not only prevented my knowing the real-life equivalents of the Reverend Alonzo Hickman, namely the leaders of the 'Negro' Baptist and Methodist churches of Shreveport; it also led me to believe that this segregated state of affairs was ordinary and proper.

(Had I known it, the rigid segregation arrangements were no older than my parents' lifetimes, having been imposed only in the last decade of the nineteenth century—see Chapter Four §3*a*.i.) Of course, we knew things had not always been as they were: Blacks had formerly been slaves, but that arrangement having been ended by a still-remembered Civil War (so went the unspoken argument), the segregated status quo was both orderly and just: 'They' (i.e., African Americans) had 'their' place; 'we' had 'ours,' and a very pleasant place 'ours' was. No message from church or Bible ruffled this European American contentment, at least, none that I heard. My father was a steward in Shreveport's First Methodist Church, South, and my mother was a teacher and active Woman's Missionary Union member in (Southern Baptist related) First Baptist Church. ("South" and "Southern," though accurate enough, went unspoken; we merely said "Baptist" or "Methodist" when identifying our religious connection.)

In many ways my mother's church, which became mine as well, was a splendid one. Outsiders judged its choir the best in town. We worshiped in a grand old building capped by a tower in which hung great European bell chimes. The central meeting space ("sanctuary," today's Protestants would call it) was a many-lobed, high-domed 'auditorium' in Byzantine style; its crannied balconies delighted a small boy, and its curving rows of seats fronted a matched curving table that at communion was covered with a white tablecloth and gleaming silver service. Behind the table stood a dark wood pulpit, then came the choir loft, and finally, above all but in full view, the baptistry where I had followed Jesus "down into the water" and been baptized in God's triune name. And the people! Every Lord's Day (i.e., Sunday) the spaces, even my favored crannies, were occupied by many, male and female, rich and poor, smartly dressed girls (a point of interest, indeed) and (less interesting) old men with high collars secured with collar buttons front and rear. All sorts and conditions of folk—save only that all were white like me.

Did I sense that something was wrong here? That the segregation ordained and customary on city buses and theaters, the exclusion of blacks from restaurants, schools, libraries, doctors' offices, parish courthouses, had exceeded the proper reach of the principalities and powers when it came as far as church? Memory says I felt no discomfort, no guilt, no shame, on that account. And yet there is this memory: One of our African American servants, a cook I believe named Rebecca, enjoyed conversations on Christian themes with my mother, Mary. Once a visiting speaker came to First Baptist Church to conduct meetings through a week. Mary told Rebecca how inspiring he had been;

Rebecca expressed interest. "Why don't you go hear him, yourself, then?" Attendance, to be sure, was not 'integrated'—to use a word we did not know. Yet, my mother said (and I think in good faith believed) that Rebecca would be welcome to sit in a certain balcony. Colored folk, she had heard, were permitted there, as in the balconies of theaters in town. Urged by Mary, Rebecca agreed to go and to sit in (as it happened) one of my crannies. Next day, though, she came to work distressed. She had gone at the appointed time, had sought the suggested licit seat, but some boys (white, of course) had told her she was in the wrong place and must leave. She had withdrawn. Mary was angry at the nameless boys and disappointed in the outcome. I was neither disappointed nor angry—at least not as I remember it—*but I was profoundly ashamed.* Yet how could I have been ashamed of what I had neither caused nor consented to, this turning away of God's African-descended child from a Christian house of prayer, away from a church that claimed to be of her own Baptist faith? It was not the boys, it was not even my mother's rather constrained hospitality (sending when she might have escorted Rebecca?). No, though I could not have named it, I was ashamed of the *system,* the whole wrong entrenched system of division in Christ's church. Somehow, uninstructed child though I was, I knew that what happened was wrong. As I sit now in my comfortable California home and write, the shame persists. Nothing can indemnify Rebecca; with her generation she has gone on to glory. And the system itself has partly changed—my boyhood church eventually came to boast members of color. Yet I think the separation, the division, rather like my own shame, persists: Sunday morning at eleven remains the most segregated hour in American life, at least as far as Baptists and Methodists are concerned. God has not "made the two one" and "broken down the barrier of enmity which separated them" (Eph. 2:14).

b. Peoplehood and mission.—Why is this so? Why, despite a few exceptions here and there, do European American Christians and African American Christians, be they alike Baptists or alike Methodists, nonetheless continue to exist as separated peoples, perpetuating the pattern of my childhood shame? Why persist, though European American attitudes of superiority and African American fears of unacceptability have diminished? To answer requires the concept of *Christian peoplehood* (*Volume II,* Chapter Two §3*a*).

The biblical doctrine of peoplehood, reappearing also in §2 above, recalls that God drew out of all peoples one that would be God's "special possession; for the whole earth is mine." This is the people whose appointed destiny was missionary priesthood to the nations (Exod. 19:5f). It was a conception that apostolic Christianity, however cool it might have been to some parts of its Hebrew heritage, did not desert. Paul in Romans 9 through 11 wrestled with the mystery of an Israel that had shown itself in his day too largely indifferent to the gospel of Messiah Jesus. Later Christians have sometimes assumed that while once God had been God of Abraham and Moses and the Jews, now God had made a new choice, replacing Israel with 'the church.' Yet this 'supervenience' theory distorts Paul's words and intent. "Has God rejected his people? Of course not!" (Rom. 11:1—the Greek negative, *mē genoito,* is even stronger). Whereupon Paul unfolds a complex account of "partial hardening" that will providentially issue in full redemption for all God's people. Yet there could be no blinking the reality of separation, not in congregations where both Jews and non-Jews worshiped Christ together. So the (Pauline, if not Paul's) Letter to Ephesians crowns the recognition of separated peoples with a proleptic celebration of their reunion: "For he is himself our peace. Gentiles and Jews, he has made the two one, and in his own body of flesh and blood has broken down the barrier of enmity which separated them; for he annulled the law with its rules and regulations, so as to create out of the two [Jews and non-Jews] a single new humanity in himself, thereby making peace" (Eph. 2:14f). In Galatians (6:15f) Paul himself speaks of "the Israel of God," by which I take him to mean the inclusive whole that embraces both God's original Israel and the engrafted peoplehood of Gentile disciples (*Doctrine,* Eight §3a). So the biblical precedent is for a single people of God made up of diverse peoples, and that makes sense of much Christian missionary history: Roman Christians and Greek Christians, 'barbarian' Christians and 'civilized' Christians, Oriental Christians and Occidental Christians, Latin and Anglo and African Christians and more. In *Doctrine* appears the familiar image of tree and branches: a single stem on which many shoots appear (p. 365). A better image may be diverse streams flowing on a single watershed, taking their rise at different points but meandering in the same direction, sometimes converging to create greater rivers of water, sometimes diverging to expose islands of difference, but all with a grand surge toward the destined sea (Freeman et al., eds., 1999:2f). Both images, tree and streams, are useful; neither is without its limits. For understanding the black-and-white diversity of American Christianity I prefer the streams image, for it represents (as the tree does not) the union of the separate elements at story's end.

Michael Cartwright's study of Christian peoplehood led me to say in *Doctrine* that such historic peoplehoods as Baptist, Methodist, and the like "are justified only if they serve as provisional means toward that one great peoplehood that embraces all, the Israel of God" (p. 365). Elsewhere, Cartwright points out that the churchly sickness addressed here, our failure in peoplehood symbolized by the story of Mary and Rebecca and me in 1930s Shreveport, has a combination of causes: hermeneutical, cultural, ecclesial.

Hermeneutics: Blacks and whites in this country learned to read the same Bible differently: For African Americans Scripture unfolded as a two-voiced story which spoke *historically* of slaves liberated from Egypt and disciples liberated by Jesus, but also spoke *presently* of slaves liberated by God's sweet chariot swinging low, of disciples who now were free though their earthly masters knew it not. At about the same time, for European Americans the Bible was losing its double voice; it began to speak of a history that was only history, of a redemption frozen in the past (Chapter Two §3). For some whites, that freeze was deepened by dispensational premillennialism, which declared the present to be only a great parenthesis not covered by the Bible's story: already separate, the church would soon be utterly separated from the world in a 'rapture' (a term the theory could not find in the text of Scripture but sprinkled throughout its footnotes) that would finally show who the saints were. Though Cartwright passes over it here, a similar freeze occurred by courtesy of liberal historical-critical exegesis, whose attempts at recovering 'biblical history' often issued in a hodge-podge of exegetical confusion that led frustrated European American Christians to relegate the Bible to the 'experts.' These frozen reading strategies made it unlikely that blacks who heard Scripture's double voice (its "this is that" and "then is now") and whites who did not could read Scripture together (Cartwright in Okholm, ed., 1997:88-97).

Culture: Alongside the different reading strategies of black and white Christians, entwined with them, there grew another cause of separation: existence within two cultures. Their different histories yielded two American cultures (among not a few others, but now I speak of these two)—one with an African and the other with a European root, one with a history of 'owning' human beings and the other with a history of being 'owned.' The separation is far from absolute, even under the most severe conditions of segregation. W. E. B. DuBois spoke of Negroes' double vision, their ability to see through their own eyes and (by a shift) to see through the eyes of the white other (DuBois, 1903:364). More recently some have pointed out the abiding presence of blackness within white culture (prevailing black ways in American English, black music forming America's listening ears, not infrequently black genetic strains in 'white' America). Yet remaining differences find their way into Christian peoplehood in America. Here I mention only one striking difference: African American history has characteristically employed as its bulwark non-violence (Dr. King's movement was an example not an exception); European American history has typically employed violence. Of course there are exceptions, and much can be made of the exceptions: Denmark Vesey's insurrection, Nat Turner's bloody rebellion (Freeman et al., eds., 1999:chap. 29). Yet these are just that, exceptions. Also on the other side there are exceptions of which this book has made much: the historic example of the Reformation baptists; the peaceable ways of later baptist groups (not to exclude many white Methodists) in America, including their willingness to go to jail in resistance to the military draft; the participation of European Americans in the freedom marches and nonviolent demonstrations of the 1960s. Yet to recall these is to recall that culturally speaking they were exceptions. From the long wait through slavery to the humble endurance under segregation North and South to the freedom rides and non-violent direct action led by Martin Luther King in the fifties and sixties, black culture in the main fought its battles as did Hebrew slaves facing Egypt's might or Christian martyrs facing Rome's. Here exegesis and culture converge: how is it that the first African American Christians managed to discover the way of the cross when their European American fellow Christians were of so little help in the matter?

Ecclesia: The third factor that separates European American from African American churches is church life itself: not differences in doctrine or polity, which are close to identical, but differences in discipline. Though from the very first conversions of Africans in America until toward the end of the eighteenth century, black Baptists and Methodists shared a common congregational life with whites (though seldom as full equals), there followed in the next two centuries a growing separation that has persisted. During that time the European American churches gradually discontinued practices of discipline that were once common property of both races. Cartwright explicitly treats Methodist churches, whose disciplinary practices were spelled out in widely honored documents such as the Wesleys' *General Rules for the Societies,* later followed in American Methodism by the *Social Creed and Social Principles.* Although these continued to be printed and distributed in the European American denominations, the practices they required, such as the mutual admonition of members to lives of holiness, steadily evaporated. There was slippage in African American communities as well, but a wide difference opened between these two ecclesial histories, black and white, compounding the differences in culture and the reading of Scripture (Cartwright in Okholm, ed., 1997:71-114; Cartwright, 1999). As practices diverged, the master story that should have governed both peoples came to be lived out less faithfully—by whites, often not at all. For discipleship meant following the story, and without these practices, following became increasingly harder.

Addressing this concern, Stanley Hauerwas summons Christian peoplehood not merely to discipline but to *devotion* (a term I myself much prefer for its less militant, more religious ring). He finds in his Methodist heritage the desirable centrality of the "journey" motif, explicit if imperfect in the writings of John Wesley. Better still is one of Wesley's forerunners, high-church Anglican mystic William Law (1686–1761), whose *Serious Call to a Devout and Holy Life* (1728) Hauerwas finds still available as a guide to disciplined devotion. He quotes Law:

> [B]ecause in this polite age of ours we have so lived away the spirit of devotion, that many seem afraid even to be suspected of it, imagining great devotion to be great bigotry; that it is founded in ignorance and poornesss of spirit, and that little, weak, and dejected minds are generally the greatest proficients in it: It shall here be full shown that great devotion is the noblest temper of the greatest and noblest souls, and they who think it receives any advantage from ignorance and poorness of spirit are themselves not a little, but entirely ignorant of the nature of devotion, the nature of God, and the nature of themselves. (Law, 1728:299)

In the substantive essay where this quotation appears, Hauerwas shows how Law's pattern of devotion is currently applicable to Christian wholeness or 'perfection.' Against those who fear the Pelagian tendency of such attention—not only to deeds of love and forgiveness and peacemaking (to name again three current loci) but to the habits of soul that make such deeds conceivable in a world mastered by a very different story—Hauerwas argues that these acts and attitudes are the very substance of Christian existence rather than mere means to a 'salvation' extrinsic to them all (Hauerwas, 1998:chap. 7).

Our theme is witness, and there are those who fear that summoning the peoples of God to reconciliation, in the present case particularly to racial reconciliation, will distract from the main task of Christian witness, the call to go into all the world and make disciples of every nation (Matt. 28:19). This objection fails to see that what may seem only a struggle for order within the household(s) of God is actually a struggle between the church and the world, or "to invoke the strange mythological language of the New Testament" is a "wrestling with the principalities and powers (Eph. 6:12) of our time"—that and not merely a matter of domestic housekeeping (Cartwright in Okholm, ed., 1997:103). This quest for reconciliation is in truth a profound contest of stories to see which will be our master story. We can be very sure that *this* witness will not go unobserved in the world outside the church.

Think of the Western missionary in Africa or Asia who must explain why, despite Ephesians 2:14f and Galatians 3:27f and despite the cross of Jesus and despite Pentecost, the members of the Israel of God are to one another strangers still. The theme of this section is essential to complete the preceding two: (§1) we are a storied people; (§2) ours is a contested story while the world lasts; and now (§3) the aim, the end of this story is *an actual oneness* with God in Christ that, reflecting even in its dimness God's own unity, must appear so "that the world may believe" (John 17:21).

Given its threefold difficulty (Cartwright), the emergence of "one new humanity" in this case is not to be assumed as a cost-free outcome of Christians' good intentions. Rather than 'integration' (a concept of legitimate use at law but perhaps of little use in the quest for the new humanity) a valuable first step is crossing over, that is, the deliberate choice of some from each people to connect with a congregation of the other people. This crossing over need not be for a lifetime, and it will not be without its distinct joys, but only those who have attempted it are in position to tell the rest of us its expense.

c. "Then comes the end . . ."—One of the most painful moments in a Christian theologian's life may be attending those funerals in which the doctrine of last things ('eschatology') is shrunk to a frail picture of the departed one leaning over heaven's ramparts, blissful to be sure but mainly absorbed in observing the sorrows and joys of those present in the service. What matters seems only the here and now, *our* sorrows and joys; eschatology's best chance seems only to transform the dead into watchers of the lucky survivors. This chuckle-headed theology has no grasp of the story that constitutes disciples now (a story in which the dear departed may very well have had a lively share), far less can it grasp what the Apostle calls "the sufferings we now endure," which, he goes on, "bear no comparison with the glory, as yet unrevealed, which is in store for us" (Rom. 8:18). My point is that the Christian sense of an ending is available only to those who have learned to 'follow' (thus Gallie), only to those who regarding death or any other human concern can penetrate the worldly 'lies and illusions' that conceal its reality. Are we destined at death to become mere observers, players dismissed to watch from the grandstand?

i. The practices of Christian witness.—The 'last things' that Christians need to know about are those that, because they are God's own, will come last because they do last. In the final volume that he saw from the press, John Yoder, as he had previously done in his pamphlet-sized *Fullness of Christ* (1987), once more offered a short list of practices that serve a double function: these were on the one hand of the essence of Christian existence; they were on the other hand practices that could make sense to the world outside the Christian community. In other words, they were practices of *witness.* I list his five, showing their link to what has previously been said here.

(1) The *rule of Christ* (based on Matthew 18, especially verses 15ff), well-known not only to the so-called Anabaptists but also to Luther and Calvin and their allies, means that Christian community is formed through reconciling dialogue. Yet "it is also the model for the ways a wider society should make decisions and resolve conflict." In the wider culture the familiar terms are "conflict resolution" and "mediation." (2) Almost lost to sight in ecclesiastical struggles over what happens to bread and wine when certain words are said over them is that for New Testament disciples "the *primary* meaning of the eucharistic gathering in the Gospels and Acts is economic." The second practice, then, is *primeval socialism,* a commonwealth of possessions and their use. "At the Lord's Table, those who have bread bring it, and all are fed." (3) Closely linked to both these, and supported especially by Ephesians' discussion of how Christ forms one people out of peoples previously separated, is what Yoder names *the New Humanity.* "Interethnic reconciliation is a part of redemption. It is not a social idealism supported by an appeal to creation or reason. It is the result of the cross." The firm ground for racial reconciliation is not an appeal to what God did in creation (an appeal easily distorted by an Ian Paisley in Belfast or by Afrikaners in South Africa). Nor is the ground Enlightenment-based claims for human dignity ("self-evident truths"). It is the costly work of God discerned on the cross. "It took the cross to break down a wall. In the movements of Gandhi and King it took freely chosen, innocent suffering to renew in our century the possibility of reconciliation between peoples." (4) Congregational ecclesiology is a staple of baptist life, but it is a hollow formality without the emphasis that in Ephesians is named "the fullness of Christ" (cf. Eph. 1:23) and in Paul's Romans (12:6-8) and 1 Corinthians (12:4-11) is celebrated as the distinctive portion of grace which gives *each member a role in the community.* This fourth practice is the death of clericalism; it is the life of a community of witness. Yoder comments that today, ironically, "this vision is more widely operative in the rest of society than in the traditional churches." Town-meeting democracy and freedom of assembly, speech, and press are its fruits. (5) Matching the opening 'rule of Christ' is Yoder's fifth practice, which some call *the rule of Paul.* By it, in the meetings of the fellowship, "all present should be free to take the floor." Nothing in nature or creation makes this rule evident;

it is the outcome of God's reconciling work, "which ascribes status to the underdog and the outsider" (Yoder, 1997:44-46).

My present point is not to argue that these five practices constitute the essence of Christianity (indeed, standing alone they do not, but they are grammatically linked in Christian discourse to such doctrines as the godhood of Christ). I mean rather to say that as Christian practices they will be reclaimed whenever disciples constitute themselves a witnessing people. For it takes but little reflection to see that these five are also internally linked to those loci of appeal that disclose the world's authentic hungers: *love and righteousness and peace.* And that is Yoder's point as well. His list of loci of common concern is a little different—he puts servanthood where I have listed peace—but the claim is that together they indicate "a model for how any society [can] form its common life more humanely. The church is called to live, and is beginning to live (to the extent to which we get the point), in the way to which the whole world is called" (Yoder, 1997:46).

ii. Then how will it all end?—This section began with a confession of sin and ends with a confession of ignorance. When it comes to the future, we speak concerning what we do not know. "My knowledge now is partial" says Paul, "then it will be whole, like God's knowledge of me" (1 Cor. 13:12). I claimed in *Doctrine* (Two §2) that God, nevertheless, has graciously given us end-pictures to provide warning, comfort, and hope—only we must be careful not to freeze these into constructions that chart the future as if it were already past. I conclude here with just one such picture among the many.

What follows was in different words part of my contribution to the Yoder Festschrift (Hauerwas et al., eds., 1999), and before that it appeared, again differently, in *The Believers Church: A Voluntary Church* (Brackney, ed., 1998:192-95).

A familiar passage in Ephesians opens with a celebration of the great confessional unities: one body, one Spirit, one hope, one Lord, one faith, one baptism (4:4-6) and concludes with an appeal to "fully grow up into Christ. He is the head" (4:15). The end-picture I have in mind appears near the middle of this paragraph, in verse 13. In the New Jerusalem Bible this reads:

> until we all reach unity in faith and knowledge of the Son of God and form the perfect Man, fully mature with the fullness of Christ himself.

Here the striking phrase is "perfect Man," words unacceptable to the (gender-suppressing) translators of the New Revised Standard Version, who when they reach the Greek word *andra* simply skip it, no doubt because *anēr* is not their favored term *anthropos,* not "man" in the sense "human being": to their evident discomfort, Ephesians uses instead the distinctively male Greek word. Yet I think the New Jerusalem Bible, though it shamelessly says "Man," misleads as well, for it implies that this "perfect Man" is merely a collective term for God's holy people, the many being treated as one. In truth we face in verse 13 a genuine puzzle for translators. Who is this *andra teleion,* this "perfect man," whom Ephesians says faithful readers are to "meet" *(katantēsōmen)*? Markus Barth, in the *Anchor Bible* commentary on Ephesians, takes us step-by-step to a fresh reading that solves the puzzle (1974:II, 484-96). The main verb, *katantēsōmen,* ordinarily means that we may arrive at a given point, or sometimes that we may meet somebody. In every use of this Greek verb, Barth writes, "movement is presupposed" (p. 485). But who or what *moves to encounter a perfect (male) human being*? In answer, Barth draws two images from the ancient world. The first of these envisions "a festival procession that is under way in solemn fashion for a solemn purpose. Those partaking in the cortege go out to meet a very important [traveler, who will bring] them bliss, joy, security, and peace" (p. 485). Such a cortege might, for example, go outside the city gates to receive their king as he drew near their city. Psalm 68, just quoted by the author of Ephesians five verses above (verse 8), describes just such a royal approach. There is, though, another possibility: the movement of *mechri katantēsōmen* (our going until we should meet) might be that of a bridal party going outside the city walls to welcome an arriving bridegroom. Both sorts of solemn march were customs familiar to the first readers of Ephesians. Barth tells us we need not choose between them, since in Psalm 45, again in the Song of Solomon, and in the rites of many ancient cultures as well, the two sorts of procession, marital and political, were frequently combined: a city provides a bride for its approaching king.

Markus Barth's exegesis of verse 13 is not widely accepted; for example, the learned Andrew T. Lincoln, in the Word Biblical Commentary on Ephesians, explicitly discounts this reading, saying that the meaning Barth finds "is not in view" (Lincoln, 1990:255), and Lincoln is in line with standard English versions. I do not think, though, that Barth's labors here have been adequately taken into account by these versions, or that "not in view" is an argument.

Of course, the movement of the procession toward the Expected One was matched by his own approach to them. Next, Barth reminds us that the "coming of the Lord" is fundamental to the life, faith, confession, worship of the church. The saints pray, '*maranatha,* [our] Lord, come!' (1 Cor. 16:22; Rev. 22:20). The hoped-for coming of Jesus Christ is usually called his "*parousia*" (1 Thess. 4:15-17; Matt. 24:27; etc.) (p. 486f).

Here, then, is a picture that may instruct God's people in the coming millennium, indeed, instruct them in any century from first Advent to last Advent. Together we are to move toward the full knowledge of the *huios tou theou,* the Son of God—so says Ephesians 4:13 as Barth (and I) read it. Only when that last, full meeting comes will our goal be reached. But all is not then ended, for as Markus Barth points out,

> just as a king or bridegroom, by his advent and through his meeting with those expecting him, fulfills the hope and changes the status of many, so according to Eph 4:13 does the Son of God, the Perfect Man, the Messiah. He makes his people participants in his perfection and riches. All that is his becomes theirs. The transformation of the many, effected by the meeting with [this unique] Man, is in this case distinct from a gradual improvement. It resembles a sudden change comparable to the effect of forgiveness and sanctification. (p. 487)

Paul in Romans calls this still-awaited "sudden effect" glorification. When that comes, the assets of the Coming One will be bestowed upon the citizens or upon the bride, so that (in the language of Ephesians) the Messiah himself is perfected by incorporating his people into himself, making one body, one Christ. Thus the New Jerusalem Bible and the New Revised Standard Version are not all wrong, even though their translations fall short, for finally what they proclaim will also come true—they have simply skipped ahead of Ephesians to reach the final stage! (M. Barth, 1974:II, 495).

What will that great and sudden change in the people of God be? But Ephesians has given us the answer. For 4:13 serves as the center, the fulcrum, by which we may understand the paragraph that is its context.

> *9* What else does the term "he ascended" [in Ps. 68:10] imply except that he also descended down to the earth? *10* He who descended is the one who ascended far above all the heavens in order to fill all things.
> *11* He is the one who appointed
> these to be apostles and these to be prophets
> some to be evangelists and others to be teaching shepherds

> *12* to equip the saints for the work of service
> for building the Messiah's body
> *13* until we all come to meet
> the unifying faith and knowledge of the Son of God,
> the Perfect Man,
> the perfection of the Messiah, his bride, our humanity made whole.
> *14* No longer are we to be babes, tossed by waves and whirled
> about by every doctrinal gust, [and caught] in the trickery of men
> who are experts in deceitful scheming. *15* Rather by speaking the
> truth in love we shall grow in every way toward him who is the
> head, the Messiah. *16* He is at work fitting and joining the whole
> body together. He provides sustenance to it through every contact
> according to the needs of each single part. He enables the body to
> make its own growth so that it builds itself up in love. (Eph. 4:9-16, M. Barth trans., 1974:II, 425f, altered)

Progressive changes, crowned by a final change! The changes that Ephesians (4:1-16) mandates are already under way in the lives of members of the cortege who are moving outside the city walls to meet their coming Prince. They are central to its witness. Some of these changes have been explored in this chapter. None is independent of the presence and help of the Coming One: he whom we are to meet, the True Witness (K. Barth), is himself quietly, as if incognito, already present in our midst.

RETROSPECT

The term [studium universale; *later,* universitas] *does not become common until the beginning of the thirteenth century. [It] seems to have implied three characteristics: (1) That the school attracted or at least invited students from all parts, not merely those of a particular country or district; (2) that it was a place of higher education; that is to say, that one at least of the higher faculties—theology, law, medicine—was taught there; (3) that such subjects were taught by a considerable number—at least by a plurality—of masters.*

Hastings Rashdall, *The Universities of Europe in the Middle Ages*

Truth has two attributes—beauty and power; and while useful knowledge is in the possession of truth as powerful, liberal knowledge is the apprehension of it as beautiful.

John Henry Newman, *The Idea of a University*

The future of the earth hangs on whether we can develop ways of knowing that can deal directly, respectfully, and precisely with the life and beauty of nature, rather than talking about these vaguely and then in practice, if not always in theory, reducing them to the inanimate, the quantitative, and the mechanistic. Similarly the renewal of religion depends on whether we can speak in knowledge, and again with precision, of the immaterial, non-sensory realm that is the source of nature and the heart and substance of religion alike. The touchstone will be whether knowledge of the one will have consequences for the other.

Douglas Sloan, *Faith and Knowledge*

CHAPTER TEN

Theology and the University

Each preceding volume's closing chapter offered a fresh perspective on its achievement. Thus the last chapter of *Ethics* reviewed it by assessing the volume's narrative construal of ethics, while the last chapter of *Doctrine* raised the question of authority in doctrine, examining the kind of authority presupposed throughout. In concluding this final volume it seems appropriate to review all three volumes, and to organize the review as a theology of the university—concretely, the university as it has appeared in the Western world from about the twelfth century to the present. Implicit earlier, the idea of the university now becomes explicit, requiring me to say some new things. It is particularly appropriate that this theme should appear at the end of *Witness,* since the university is one place where the two cultures, that of the gospel and that of the world, may meet.

Still, this will seem to some an exercise in irony. Is not the history of the university that of its gradual but now almost complete *separation* from theology? Has not the university in America as well as Europe become positively the *secular* university? For a common assumption is that the Enlightenment progressively led higher education to divest itself of theology just as it had once divested itself of astrology: one does not expect to discover a chair of alchemy at Harvard, or to find courses in astrology in the University of Chicago catalog, or to find a department of theology at the University of California. There are even yet divinity schools at some of the older, church-begun universities, but they are nowadays so disconnected from of the university in which they are housed as to challenge their right to survive within the main body, while the appearance of 'religious studies' departments at some of these institutions (though not at Berkeley) only proves the rule: such departments permit the examination of religion among other human phenomena without introducing theological standpoints no longer acceptable. As for church-controlled universities, George Bernard Shaw wittily remarked long ago that "[a] Catholic university is a contradiction in terms," and one can substitute "Christian" for "Catholic" without blunting the point of his thrust. Long ago, it is said, universities were indeed "Catholic" or "Christian"; for them to remain so now is to surrender their claim to university status. There is no 'Christian geometry,' no 'Christian astrophysics'; neither, then, can there be a 'Christian university.'

So far, the widely embraced assumptions. Pious college and university administrators may resist them, but they are in the position of that ancient British king who ordered the tide to halt. The secular university, all theology excluded, has to all intents become the university, simply. This chapter, then, faces by its very title a difficult, many would say an impossible task. Yet face it I must, for if the viewpoints just expressed not only read the past correctly but forecast the future, it is not only the university, that meeting place of ideas and lives, treasurer of the public's heritage and harbinger of its hopes—not only the university that is divested of the theology that was once its center; the very idea of a theology of *culture* is evidently an anachronism, born too late to be of service to either church or world. If the university, to be itself, must be secular, then Christian witness is banished to various side-street warrens and upstairs hideaways where (at the best) it will await a better day, while (at the worst) it is already brain-dead, ready for life support to be withdrawn. When the Truly Human One (the Son of Man, *huios tou anthrōpou*) returns, Jesus asks his disciples, will he find faith on earth? (Luke 18:8). That core question underlies this chapter.

My strategy is as follows. I will argue that **the living heart of a university, any university, is theological;** secularity is not as its advocates suppose faith-neutral; it is in every single case conviction-based. As it happens, the intellectual tools employed in the preceding volumes and explicated in this one (e.g., Chapter Seven §2) make such an argument not only plausible but irresistible. If, then, the secularizing of the university did not as its managers intended expunge the university's theological dimension, but only (and oddly) ignored it, it is time to reconsider what in the long run universities are about. Can theology, which willy-nilly is present in even the most secular setting—the denial of God, for example, must be theological if the affirmation of God is—can theology construe itself afresh so as to be once again serviceable in the academic halls from which it was banished? Do the present volumes speak to such a fresh construal? I claim they do. The three sections of this chapter, then, may be summarized as follows: **(§1) A brief reminder of the nature of the university, based upon its history: how we got universities, what happened to them, what their true idea is. Originally, the university was the church's (really the gospel's) gift to culture; having made that gift, what remains for the servants of the gospel to do about it now? (§2) Explicitly, if the university must now be construed afresh, what is required of theology? (This entails a brief review of the three volumes.) (§3) Finally, how will a remade university be true to its long heritage? Concretely, what of art, what of science, and (right along with the rest) what of theology?**

§1. Justifying the University

A Christian theologian is all too likely to cast a baleful eye upon the modern university. He or she may of course retain hope for a special breed, the so-called Christian university, which is regarded as an exception. This chapter, though, takes a contrary tack. It argues that hope lies not in 'Christian universities' (who can even say what they are?) but in recovery of the *real* university, an institution worthy of the venerable name without a qualifying adjective. On that path, we shall have to abandon the concept of the 'secular university' as well; that, too, is only an oxymoron. To see that this is so, however, requires more careful, perhaps more radical thought than the topic has so far received.

a. University origins.—As the Roman Empire crumbled, the Hellenistic-Roman civilization, the adventurous first home of missionary Christianity when it reached beyond its Jewish base, crumbled as well. Barbarian kingdoms swept across old Roman Europe, devastating it and setting in its place new laws and customs sustained by tribal peoples. Christianity responded in two ways, an advance and a withdrawal, each indispensable. In the advance, missionaries went among the tribes in order to win their allegiance to Christ and his church; meanwhile, other Christians withdrew into monasteries in the Benedictine style, creating defensive fortresses of faith and learning. Between them, the mission and the monastery established a counterculture that offered resources for a new Europe. In the helpful scheme of Andrew F. Walls, this was the barbarian stage of Christian missions (Walls, 1990:18f). Evangelists, many from Ireland, traveled across the European continent, winning the allegiance of whole tribes and peoples, converting them to a gospel way perhaps only half understood. Missionary bishops who needed assistance in ministry established schools, drawing on the more stable monasteries for instructors. These 'cathedral' schools worked with available materials, mainly remnants from the Greco-Roman age, to form a syllabus of studies that would become the 'seven liberal arts,' perceived as the preparation from which students could move on to advanced work in theology, law, or medicine.

From ancient Varro the schoolmasters inherited the idea of seven liberal arts, divided by Alcuin into a trivium of grammar, logic, and rhetoric, and a quadrivium of music, arithmetic, geometry, and astronomy. Grammar meant in present terms the study of Latin, a language that students not familiar with it would learn to speak as well as to read and write. Logic or dialectic drew upon as much of philosophy as was available at the time, and rhetoric reached beyond both these to shape effectual communication. The infant sciences of the quadrivium (little from the classical past, even of Aristotle's science, remained) were those most useful to churchmen—music supported the liturgy, for example, while arithmetic with astronomy enabled the calculation of the date of Easter (Rashdall, 1895:34f).

In time these cathedral schools were invigorated by certain powerful thinkers whose organizing intellects changed the crude mission scholarship into a practice of inquiry that would gain its own momentum. At Paris Abelard (1079–1142) turned the placid text-bound instruction in the arts and later, in theology, into a ferment of debate and reflection. His pupils would become professors of the still-to-be-born University of Paris. Meanwhile, at Bologna, Gratian (fl. 1140) was bringing rational order to the study of church law ('canon' law) and like Abelard had attracted pupils from all over Europe. Gratian's fame was preceded in civil law by his fellow-Bolognese Irnerius (c. 1055–c. 1130). Thus two schools, of civil and of canon law, evolved at Bologna. These joined with other disciplines to make of Bologna Europe's first true university. Paris, focused on theology, followed almost at once, and after that came Oxford (Rashdall, 1895:pass.).

Strictly speaking, a *universitas* was not of necessity occupied with learning but was any collection of persons, any company, treated as a unity: thus the earliest academic 'universities' of Bologna were student organizations, formed as societies for mutual protection and for the employment of professors to lecture to them. When these student 'universities' came together with others in liberal arts and theology they formed a *studium generale*, that is, a university in the later sense. According to Rashdall, a medieval *studium generale* invariably displayed at least three features: students were received from all parts, at least one higher faculty (theology or law or medicine) supplemented the school of liberal arts, and more than a single master taught these subjects (1895:6f). Whether the initial organization was formed by the students, as at Bologna, or by the masters, as at Paris, the two types converged, since instruction of course required both. Bologna, Paris, and Oxford were the earliest true universities in this sense, and on their model the rest of old Europe's universities were formed.

In broad terms, what happened in twelfth- and thirteenth-century Europe was that *the church gave a precious gift to the culture: the university itself was that gift.* By the early thirteenth century, it had its own officers, elected by its members rather than appointed by the bishop. Thus it progressively separated itself from local ecclesial control. In today's terms the university grew on its own to constitute a *powerful practice* (*Volume I,* Six §1), endowed with its own energies, goals, means, and rules (and of course, with its own potential for productive development or for corruption). Despite this independence, we should not think of the medieval university as in any sense anti-Christian. Its members without exception were bound to their roles and duties as master or student by oaths that invoked the Christian God as their witness. Rules set by students or by masters required all members to conduct themselves according to church law and bound them to the sacramental worship of the Christian church. Typically, as at Oxford, the residential halls and colleges built and maintained chapels devoted to this purpose. From all this there grew a third force, in our term a third practice, alongside those of the state and the church. (*Sacerdotium, imperium, studium,* Rashdall tells us, were regarded by medievals as "the three mysterious powers or 'virtues,' by whose harmonious cooperation the life and health of Christendom are sustained"—1936:2.) At culture's base, the arts curriculum of the university provided two indispensable capacities—a means of communication (thus the *trivium*) and a science relating human life to the natural environment (the *quadrivium*). The higher schools fulfilled three further needs: *medicine* for health, *law* for social solidarity, *theology* for life in the Spirit. In changed form the university so constituted would outlast its age and take on new forms, new tasks, without abandoning these.

b. The university in a secular world.—This gifting process was repeated in the New World of the Americas. Here, too, the university pattern was a gift from the church (more accurately, from the churches); here, too, it attained maturity apart from and sometimes in opposition to its ecclesiastical mother; here, too, its benefit to the culture could be distinguished from the missionary energy that had motivated it.

i. Beginnings.—The earliest North American efforts in higher education were made by colonists who had themselves been educated at Cambridge and who intended to provide similar benefit for coming generations of New Englanders. While college education of clergy was a primary goal, other students were accepted as well. From these beginnings grew Harvard (1636), Yale (1701), Princeton (1746), Brown (1764), and others.

Three bonds linked these colonial institutions to the gospel, and as we note developments it will be helpful to keep the three distinct: First, there was *sponsorship:* Puritans in New England, Baptists in Rhode Island, Friends in Pennsylvania, Presbyterians in New Jersey, and Anglicans in Virginia founded colleges and maintained tight links with them. After the federal union, the newer evangelical denominations, notably the Methodists, followed suit. In the coming century churches and churchmen made hundreds of new starts in higher education; some survived and flourished. Second, there was the *character* of teachers and the intent to convey that character to students. The president of the university was typically a clergyman; professors as well often were. Chapel services with attendance required structured weekdays, and the Sabbath was a day of worship and rest, a pattern aimed at making good the raw material of incoming students. Third, there was explicit *theology.* Courses in Bible culminated in a respected moral philosophy course taught by the reverend president for all the seniors. It was understood to be the summit of the curriculum; it aimed to show how Christian convictions united the whole realm of knowledge. Initially these three, sponsorship, character formation, and theology, were tightly linked.

Supporting higher education, a wide array of primary and secondary schools grew up, most of them church supported. The famed New England Primer ("In Adam's fall / Sinnéd we all") and later the McGuffy textbook series typify the Christian orientation of the schools well into the nineteenth century.

As in Europe, America's universities were the church's gift to the culture, and as there, the afterbirth of church sponsorship was cleared away in due course, leaving the new American colleges and universities on their own—a powerful practice distinct from church and state. Yet in two related ways the American pattern was novel. It began not in the Middle Ages but in the Enlightenment. Thus the new universities were subject from their beginning to strong anti-religious forces. European universities felt these pressures also, but they had accumulated centuries of tradition that served as ballast, a stabilizing factor less evident in North America. Second, though most of the colonies officially established one denomination of Christians (e.g., Congregationalists in New England, Anglicans in Virginia), a convergence of factors led to disestablishment in the new federal government and gradually to laws granting religious liberty in the individual states. Thomas Jefferson, third President, led Virginia to end its ecclesiastical establishment, and he persuaded his fellow Virginians to create a University of Virginia not related to any church. Jefferson, we have noted, was not irreligious; like most of the Founding Fathers he was a Deist (Chapter Two §2). He made sure, though, that the University of Virginia curriculum did not include theology, urging instead that the denominations locate seminaries nearby so as to benefit from university learning. The Northwest Ordinance (1787), and later the Morrill Act (1862) helped even the newer, western states to provide universities on this detheologized model.

ii. Secularization and reaction.—Current theologically sophisticated discussions of the subject have lamented the progressive estrangement from religion of the American university. To assess these laments, however, it is helpful to place them against the work of the previous generation, and so first I turn to the work of *William A. Clebsch* (1923–84), historian of religion and university administrator at Stanford in the 1960s and 1970s. None of these recent laments notes Clebsch's work, yet both as historian and as builder of a religious studies department he exemplifies the outcome some now protest.

For his part, Clebsch was impatient with any dismay at the decline of religion in universities. He rather saw a larger process in American history in which aspirations for an improved life arose again and again *within* the church but then *migrated* into the wider culture for their fulfillment. Though the churches were often the creators of institutions such as schools, hospitals, colleges, and universities, these eventually took on lives of their own, deliberately separated themselves from the sponsoring churches, and in the end even bared sharp teeth at their churchly parents. Clebsch traced this process in various facets of American life: provision for the general welfare, accommodation of groups to cultural pluralism, participation by all in an open society, and still others (Clebsch, 1968:14f). As these social improvements moved beyond their origins, the churches sometimes ceased to recognize their own cultural creations, even opposed them, so that the realized aspirations became "religious campaigns waged, won, embraced, and condemned" (1968:13).

> To the mature adults of American education—the university and the state school systems—religious leaders reacted jealously and zealously, attempting to reclaim parental prerogatives such as demands for compulsory devotions in public schools, school-time or released-time sectarian instruction, on-campus facilities for denominational activities (including worship), and even, in the form of more than one theologico-pedagogic theory, detailed plans to save the university from the pluralism which was its very lifeblood. (Clebsch, 1968:16)

Recounting the 1850s ministry of Congregational missionary George Henry Atkinson, founder of Oregon City's Female Academy and Tualatin Academy and Pacific University, Clebsch quotes Atkinson's stated policy: "Our whole spirit now is free thought; free inquiry, in all directions; the discovery and development of all possible knowledge, under the guardian of faith in the Bible, as God's changeless Word, & under the influence of prayer, the Sabbath, & the preaching of the gospel" (1968:122). Clebsch reckoned that though the minister's "Bible, prayer, sabbatarianism, and gospel preaching" were unassailably sincere, they were of little value in promoting free thought. Surely, though, that depended on the way the Bible was understood, on the content of the prayers, on the substance of the sustaining gospel itself?

It is doubly instructive to discover Clebsch's viewpoint on these topics as he unfolds it in *From Sacred to Profane America* (1968), for even as he wrote it he was creating the religious studies department at Stanford, a little more than a century after Atkinson's Oregon efforts. Leland Stanford Junior University, founded (1885–91) by a rich California couple in memory of their son, had from its beginning a "vaguely Christian nontheological, nonsectarian, theistic, romantic, moral idealism" (Marsden, 1994:254) and a splendid Byzantine chapel whose Protestant chaplain was expected to offer religion courses. Clebsch had come to the faculty in 1964, though, and soon began to create what became the new department. This happened at about the time other American universities were doing the same. For Clebsch, the business of the department was to look primarily, not at the self-descriptions offered by the religions, but at "the function of religion and religious ideas in the common life" (1968:ix)—university studies of religion must discover, in a Jamesian phrase, religion's cash value. For Clebsch, the true or functional role of higher education even in early America had been to meet "social needs," not the least of which was the creation on this continent of a "common set of values around which stable community life could be built." Even at the outset, then, it had not mattered *what* religion the schools taught, but only that they taught *something*. The only limit was that their sectarianism not offend the population or restrict inquiry (Clebsch, 1968:115)—a strange rule, one might think, to propose to followers of the unsettling Jesus of Nazareth. The cash value of such an understanding of religious studies at 1960s Stanford, though, was that methodological atheism overruled free inquiry in a department most of whose members, like Clebsch, were practicing Christians. At the outset these included theologians of considerable power, including Michael Novak, a Catholic, and Robert McAfee Brown, a Presbyterian. But as 'free inquiry' proceeded, they departed and were not replaced by their like. Later, Clebsch came to emphasize the comparative method, in which any religious standpoint examined must be set alongside another for contrast. Strangely, though, departmental secularity never had to be paired with *its* contrary. By these rules, the church's gift to the culture, namely, the university itself, could not be understood as an *intellectual* gift at all. The place of theology in the university could only diminish until, at happy last, it vanished.

Now consider the recent reactions mentioned above. Douglas Sloan, a professor of history and education at Teacher's College, Columbia University, published *Faith and Knowledge* (1994), while the same year saw the appearance of George M. Marsden's *Soul of the American University* (1994). Four years later, James Tunstead Burtchaell, former University of Notre Dame provost, brought out his substantial *Dying of the Light* (1998). Their concerns were similar, yet the three chose different tactics: Burtchaell investigated the history of the relation of seventeen separate church-founded universities and colleges to their sponsoring religious bodies, from Congregationalists to Catholics. He included younger as well as older schools in his study. Marsden, a University of Notre Dame historian, concentrated on the older Protestant schools, frequently finding his examples at Harvard, Yale, or Princeton, though sometimes mentioning Chicago, Stanford, and the state universities. Marsden's interest was in the changing tone of these institutions as reflected in required chapels, curricula, and faculty members' religious allegiance. More broadly, he was concerned with the spirit (as he says, "the soul") of American universities. Sloan's focus was different: he investigated the so-called theological renaissance in mid-twentieth-century American Protestantism, with Tillich and the brothers Niebuhr its main exemplars. What was the content, Sloan inquired, of this "renaissance"? What happened to it? why did it fail, theologically fail, to save the day? Thus these volumes explore the links to the gospel forged by the early American institutions of higher learning and find that one-by-one they have snapped. Against Clebsch's celebration of secularity, these are lamentations of religious failure and death, largely agreeing with Clebsch as to the facts, but reading a contrary message. Church sponsorship ties have eroded across the board, though some more rapidly than others (Burtchaell); the character of teacher and student and that of the Protestant institutions they inhabit is less and less Christian (Marsden); for exact theological reasons the university-nourished American theologies failed to halt the decline (Sloan). It might reasonably be concluded from both these generations of studies, Clebsch's and his successors', that there is currently no such thing as "theology *and* the university" in American public life.

c. The persisting task of education.—It may be time, then, for a new approach. We might begin by saying what education broadly construed means to achieve, offering a framework for the role of higher education. A good starting point is a brief essay by theologian of culture Paul Tillich titled "A Theology of Education" (reprinted in Tillich, 1959:146-58). Given the modest task of saying something helpful about church schools, Tillich, drawing on his broad knowledge of culture, made the most of the opportunity. Every effort at education must reflect three aims: There is the task of induction, or what we can more clearly call *initiation.* "The induction of children into their families," Tillich writes, "with the tradition, symbols, and demands of the family, is the basic form of inducting education." He explains that one of the best examples of such initiation is found in the Old Testament command that parents tell the story of the exodus from Egypt when their children ask what the rituals of the Passover festival mean (cf. Deut. 6:20-25). (University and college administrators display a glimmer of awareness of the need for such initiation in the 'orientation' activities they compulsively schedule for incoming students, though their typical orientation techniques fall well short of the subtlety and psychological soundness of the biblical injunction.) Certainly no culture can survive the failure to provide such initiation to oncoming generations. Second, there is the aim of technical education, teaching the *techniques or skills* required for participation in society. For medieval students, this entailed Latin grammar; perhaps moderns will think of computer literacy? Tillich points out, though, that from the Middle Ages onward this aspect was more than mere technical training: "It included many elements of the humanistic way: discipline, subjection to the demands of the object in knowing and handling it, participation in the community of work, subordination to and criticism of the demands of the expert and of the community" (1959:146). Clearly these skills shade over, then, into Tillich's third aim, imparting the *humanistic ideal,* which, as he understands Western culture, has been inseparable from the teaching of religion.

Since §3 of this chapter will offer a development of these three aims I will not add my own comments here. It is interesting, though, to note two Tillichian emphases. First, there is the tribute he pays to the early Renaissance, reminding us of the connection between Erasmus and those early Christian humanists (mis)labeled Anabaptists. The free, inquiring spirit of the Renaissance contrasts with the later, rigidly mechanized world of Descartes and Newton. Tillich says that "where questions are asked or provoked and the answers are interpreted in the light of the question, there the humanistic spirit is at work" (1959:154). In other words, our study, whether in first grade or in graduate school, must express the God-given human capacity to outthink machines and machine-like minds by welcoming the fuller reality that confronts it.

Again, Tillich notes that initiation (his first educational aim) is sure to fail when the symbolic equipment provided the student does not come to terms with the reality of the world in which the student is to live. In these unhappy circumstances, as Tillich puts it, the student "normally comes to a point at which he doubts, or turns away from, or attacks the reality and the symbols into which he has been inducted. Living in a world hardly touched by the traditions which have come to him, he inescapably becomes skeptical" (1959:153). Here the theologian confronts a central difficulty of contemporary evangelism: how can a church-trained youth come to terms with a world that is alien to the traditions and convictions of his or her initiation? Tillich at least is very sure of one thing: the smooth identification of church and national culture, so much a part of the Germanic education he had himself received, had been a failure: it had led to the totalitarian debacle with its Holocaust and its war without boundaries; it is doomed to fail in every case. He could recall behind this an early-twentieth-century culture in which "this double emptiness, the emptiness of adjustment to the demands of the industrial society, and the emptiness of cultural goods without ultimate seriousness, led to indifference, cynicism, despair, mental disturbances, early crimes, disgust of life" (1959:152). Shortly, it had led, as Tillich realized sooner than most, to Adolf Hitler.

§2. Theology Essential to the University

The foregoing section recalled the debate between those who do and those who do not find a central place for theology in American or Western-type universities. I claimed above that theology had been central to the work of the university at its origin, and remains central even now. Those who believe otherwise must hold that the very idea of a university has changed: once, they may say, the West needed the medieval institution, but (happily) it is not saddled with it today. What this neglects is that not only the university, but also theology has changed. The opening chapter of this three-volume book tried to make that point clear. Theology is not just "ideas (or words) about God"; it is not a set of changeless beliefs associated with religion; it is not, despite the jokes, erudite discussion of inaccessible nonentities (we theologians had better listen to the jokes, though, and be prepared to reform our practice as needed to make them irrelevant). There is a more satisfying notion of what theology is that makes sense to many people: on the one hand, "it represents something deeply self-involving for its adherents"; on the other, even mystical theologies (and certainly they are not the only kind) "are attempts systematically to connect mystical experience with what is and is not there in the world—or beyond it." (The quotations are from my initial chapter—*Volume I*, One §1*a*.) What begins to arise is that authentic theology represents something of deepest importance to people—and as people differ about what *is* of deepest importance, the content of theologies is bound to vary, reflecting those differences. Thus there are atheistic and polytheistic theologies, and theologies in which the concept of God does not even arise.

Volume I (and my prior and subsequent work with philosopher James M. Smith) found it helpful to approach theology by acknowledging that people (and collections of people, such as members of a university) are deeply shaped by beliefs they may not consciously have chosen but that they are certainly not prepared to give up—the beliefs that make them the people or groups of people they are. We called such beliefs *convictions.* Then it follows that one way to use the word "theology," I think the best way, is as the discipline or systematic study that investigates, interprets, and sometimes re-forms human convictions. So theology has a representative (or cognitive) dimension; it also has an affective dimension, insofar as the convictions it engages are deeply self-involving; and finally it has a practical or action dimension, since theologians are not mere sideline spectators of the human scene but engage some part of it and mean to change that part for the better. None of this, faithful reader, is new; I am simply repeating the point of view that has guided this work throughout. As *Ethics* (One §1) said, theology is by definition *the discovery, understanding, and transformation of the convictions of a convictional community, including the discovery and critical revision of their [i.e., the convictions'] relation to one another* **and to whatever else there is,** the last six words being emphasized to counteract modernity's tendency to set theology aside (along with religion, a main realm of its expression) as only glorified emotion.

It follows that there is not only Christian theology; there are other sorts. Moreover, there are not only explicitly religious theologies (as this one is) but also theologies that structure sets of convictions without a place for religion or its usual concerns. Smith and I acknowledged that some would balk at calling such secular versions of the study of convictions "theology"—they would not like the associations of that word. So we offered them an alternative word, *theoretics*—by which we meant the same thing (*CONV.*, chap. 7). (I strongly prefer gutsy, old-fashioned sounding "theology" in every case, since "theoretics" may suggest too airily mental a discipline, but others will have their own preferences. In any case, one misunderstands if one takes "theoretics" in a sense that brackets or omits the substance of theology.)

Now we can make more sense of the debate between those who say that theology is an essential part of a university and those who deny this. The question is *not* whether universities must always be dominated (Burtchaell?) or ensouled (Marsden?) by Christianity—who can say for sure when that is or is not the case? Christianity is, as W. B. Gallie warned us in the preceding chapter, an "essentially contested concept," one whose life and usefulness depend upon ongoing strife about its meaning. The question at issue is rather this: if a university is understood as a *studium generale,* a school from whose inquiries none of the higher studies is on principle excluded, will it be appropriate, or even fully possible, to exclude the disciplined, open-ended, but at the same time concrete and life-involving examination of the convictions that make human communities what they are? For theologies are often unconsciously embraced. The 'secular university' (that *other* oxymoron) has its theology (its theoretic); it cannot help doing so. All that remains is to determine whether its formative convictions are to be unconsciously possessed while contrary convictions are unconsciously expelled. To grant that such convictions must needs be brought to light, deserve to be examined, cannot in an atmosphere of free inquiry remain unconscious, is to grant theology (or theoretics) its rightful role in any university.

a. Newman's 'Idea.'—What we want, then, is not 'Christian' universities, or 'secular' universities, but real universities. John Henry Newman (1801–90), whose brilliant role as modern theologian appeared in Chapter Eight (§1*a*.ii), wanted that as well. By mid–nineteenth century Newman had advanced from his Oxford Anglican stage with its quest for a *via media* between Protestantism and Catholicism to become a Roman Catholic convert and shortly, the leading British theorist of education among Catholics. At the request of the Irish bishops, Newman gave in Dublin in 1852 a series of lectures that were published as *The Idea of a University* (1873). He took his stand on three principles that parallel the Christian concerns of earlier college and university founders: church sponsorship, character formation, and theological content in instruction. Each of these took distinctive shape in Newman's formulation. By his day, British authorities were attempting to establish national universities in which matriculation required no religious tests and from which theology as a discipline was excluded. Newman stoutly opposed this trend. So-called mixed education (Catholics and non-Catholics together) would defeat the 'idea' of a university. For a university was an institution whose characteristic feature was not research but *teaching*. (His old academic home at Oxford with its old college, Oriel, was Newman's paradigm here.) Newman regretted that no single English word signified the proper goal of such instruction (was he thinking here of Greek *paidea* or *gnōsis?*), but in default of a better he would call this goal "philosophy, philosophical knowledge, enlargement of mind, or illumination," an informed reasonableness that equipped students for full participation in the world (1873:94). To this end, all the 'sciences' or departments of knowledge must be taught, and here Newman issued a severe warning: The omission from the curriculum of any constituent part of human knowledge is not only wrong but in practice impossible, for "if you drop any science out of the circle of knowledge, you cannot keep its place vacant for it; that science [being] forgotten; the other sciences close up, or in other words, they excel their proper bounds, and intrude where they have no right" (Newman, 1873:55)—a theme already introduced above.

Now consider that Newman's understanding was that truly there was only one theology, revealed, timeless, and (as it happened) fully embraced only by Roman Catholics. This theology is simply "the Science of God, or the truths we know about God put into a system; just as we have a science of the stars, and call it astronomy" (1873:46). To be sure, theology in the university must not be quarantined. Newman said it must be in constant interaction with other disciplines, and they with it. For God is the ever-provident Creator, so that all earthly matters and especially all human affairs are from him.

> Man, with his motives and works, his languages, his propagation, his diffusion, is from Him. Agriculture, medicine, and the arts of life, are His gifts. Society, laws, government, He is their sanction. The pageant of earthly royalty has the semblance of the benediction of the Eternal King. Peace and civilization, commerce and adventure, wars when just, conquest when human and necessary [this was, after all, the Victorian heyday of Empire], have His co-operation, and His blessing upon them. The course of events, the revolution of empires, the rise and fall of states, the periods and eras, the progresses and the retrogressions of the world's history, not indeed the incidental sin, over-abundant as it is, but the great outlines and the results of human affairs, are from His disposition. (Newman, 1873:48f)

And the contrary is true also: the several 'sciences' all bear upon theology, which alas, they may misconstrue to the harm of their students.

> For example, it is a mere unwarranted assumption if the Antiquarian says, "Nothing has ever taken place but is to be found in historical documents"; or if the Philosophic Historian says, "There is nothing in Judaism different from other political institutions"; or if the Political Economist, "Easy circumstances make men virtuous." These are enunciations, not of Science, but of Private Judgment; and it is Private Judgment that infects every science which it touches with a hostility to Theology, a hostility which properly attaches to no science in itself whatever. (1873:73)

Yet in the well-formed university these matters are perpetually under adjustment, for in its selective choice of (Catholic) students and faculty, in its nurture of each individual student as by his own *alma mater,* and in the interdependence of inquiry in all the sciences including theology, the university imparts not mere knowledge, but true philosophy, its proper end or goal. So far, Newman's *University.*

We will see what is right in this plan, though, only by separating from it what is wrong. The central issue is the nature of theology itself, for in its long history theology has not been a partisan but a *dialogical* discipline; it has not been merely Newman's theology, or merely that of Westminster, or any other. This 'science' has made its headway by the meeting of strong currents of thought that together form new channels.

Theology is "a science of convictions" (*CONV.*, chap. 7), not in the flabby, subjective sense that it is only the opinion of this or that party (a reduction to which Newman's view of theology is more vulnerable than my own), but that it examines convictions, the deep assents constituting a people of conviction, connected (in theology's intent) *to whatever* else *there is.* Thus the theology that graces the real university will be as subject to checks and balances, as open to discovery and new theory, as alive to debate and dissent, as that of any science in the curriculum, perhaps more than any, since it will by nature be forever examining the deep assumptions as well as the little pieties of convention that silently shape us one and all. Had this not been true in the past, there would have been no Reformation at Wittenberg; had it not been true, Balthasar Hubmaier would never have become a Radical Reformer. Consequently there is no need for the university to remain subject to its founding tutelage or sponsorship, for that it is or becomes a real university guarantees that it will become or remain theological as well as artistic and scientific, while the fact, that theology is the dialogical, many-sided discipline that it is, guarantees that sooner or later any good theology (I say in optimism, surely the best theology) will rise high among the sorts examined and embraced. Newman's 'idea' was bigger than he knew.

b. How theology answers the university's need.—It remains now to point out the features of one kind of theology, evident in this and the two preceding volumes, that qualify it for this task. I mean to say here, more by instance and example than by summary abstraction from this trilogy, what such a theology can mean to the university.

i. Theology as ethics.—To speak of the university's morals seems a precarious undertaking, for the topic risks reduction to concerns about alcoholic excess at fraternity parties, or parietal regulations or their lack in student living quarters, or perhaps a discussion of the conflict between free speech on campus and the rights of minority ethnic or racial groups to be free of intimidation. Without dismissing these as of no consequence, the morality of the university must strike in at a deeper level. The very structure of its chapters suggests that *Ethics* is not primarily focused on morality as a matter of 'rights' and the (less-frequently mentioned) corresponding duties. Instead, among the several wedges of entry that *Ethics* provides into the moral sphere, I recall here the concept of morality as a kind of *beauty* (*Ethics,* 124f).

Here, too, there is a clue from Newman. Intellectual culture, he argues, is not first of all 'useful' knowledge, valuable for some external aim or end. Rather it has its use in itself; it is intrinsically worthwhile. He asks, rhetorically, "[I]f a College of Physicians is a useful institution, because it contemplates bodily health, why is not an Academical Body, though it were simply and solely engaged in imparting vigour and beauty and grasp to the intellectual portion of our nature?" (1873:122). He finds his answer in beauty as the measure of the university. For "[t]here is a physical beauty and a moral: there is a beauty of person, there is a beauty of our moral being, which is natural virtue; in like manner there is a beauty, a perfection, of the intellect" (1873:92).

There is a beauty, a moral beauty, that is the university's own. Once it caught that beauty from the church, and thereby from the church's holy Source. Beauty in this sense is a certain kind of wholeness, whether it be the beauty of a yellow rose or the beauty of a human life well-formed or the beauty of a great university fulfilling its goal. First of all, this is the beauty of its practices, their moral loveliness, lovelier than any Grecian urn, more lovely even than "she that looketh forth as the morning" (Song of Sol. 6:10 KJV). The university's patterns of thought, its sciences and letters, its shaping of young minds and its common good still correspond (like distant stars forever resonating with the physics of the big bang) to the holiness of redemption, the wholeness of creation, God's holy wholeness. Not just its societal debt but its true good, not only its duty but its true beauty: this is the moral theme confronting the university. Long ago this wholeness or beauty was the gift of the church to the university, whether to Bologna in the twelfth century or to Massachusetts in the seventeenth century or to Palo Alto or Chicago or Waco in the nineteenth century. In receiving it, the university received a gift that calls forth its artistry, summons it to realize its gifted beauty and share it with society, share it with students and with all the world.

If the university's beauty is the measure of its work, it is preeminently found not in the beauty of its architecture or the splendor of its museums (themselves not to be despised) or in the grandeur of its endowments or the luster of its alumni, but in the beauty of its *practices.* The university, Newman correctly saw, is nothing if it is not a teacher. In its practice of teaching, then, it realizes or fails to realize its gift. To teach is to form minds able to glimpse the beautiful in all its permutations, whether the beauty of a mathematical equation, a molecular structure, a Shakespearian play, or a political system. In each case a philosophical mind sees wholes, perceives patterns, undertakes analyses, divides, relates, comprehends. Hence the sciences, hence the arts. The purpose of the practice is to stretch the minds that come to it, to challenge their little complacencies, to open up difficulties, explore utopias, explode orthodoxies. The ancient name for this task is liberal (i.e., liberating) learning.

Still, teaching is not the university's only practice and thus not its only opportunity to realize its true beauty. The university recruits and admits students, it raises funds, it administers the corporate existence of a diverse and sometimes unruly academic community, it conducts research, sponsors sports, nurtures the arts. What has theology to say to all this? In answer, the central Part of *Ethics,* "The Sphere of the Communal," focused on 'powerful practices.' These are cooperative endeavors aimed at some human good or goal, requiring skill and progressive training for their right functioning, and capable, in every case, of doing great good or perversely of causing great harm (*Ethics,* Six §1). Following again a lead from John Yoder (1992), I mention five common and necessary university practices in order to show their relation to the theological ethics which stands behind them. This time around, though, instead of naming the Christian practice and proceeding to its worldly counterpart I will start with the latter as it appears in the university. (1) There is in the university the practice of *conflict resolution.* Every business manager, every dean, every department chairperson confronts demands for conflict resolution every day of his or her working life. These officials need not rest their judgments on instinct alone. An entire discipline of conflict resolution exists, providing psychological and sociological wisdom and offering guidelines for its practice. Yoder reminds us that this practice, so fraught with good or evil in any institution's life, is the counterpart of the gospel practice called *the rule of Christ,* which offers its own paradigms for conflict management including solo and group interventions, tactics of reproach and of reconciliation, all shaped by forgiveness and an underlying sense of belongingness that (in the theological case) is founded upon being "one body in Christ" (Matt. 18:15ff; Eph. 4:11-13).

(2) Often itself the source of conflict, a related university practice is (to give it a rather stuffy name) *interethnic inclusiveness,* the university's policy that guarantees, like its medieval prototype, that its students (and of course, faculty) come "from all parts," so that none is excluded on the basis of race or ethnicity or gender or other supposed default. This inclusion remains a great ongoing project as I write, and while some bars have been overcome (in my own lifetime Princeton University finally ended its long-standing quota system for admitting Jews, and state universities in the South ended their own black-white racial barriers), the task is problematic still. There is a historical reason, Yoder shows, for the difficulty: the secular practice of inclusion is not based directly on the scriptural precedent (cf. Gal. 3:27-29) but on the Enlightenment concept of "equality"—equal treatment for those of equal ability. Yet this puts the inclusiveness of the university constant-

ly at the mercy of those who find new ways to measure *in*equalities among various groups. If the inequality is there, is not the university justified in its discrimination? Equality, though, was not the basis of the great barrier-breaking *new peoplehood* that came with the gospel into the world. The message then was that non-Jews might be included in the Israel of God along with Jewish members. Yet this was not because Gentiles were discovered to be "just as good as Jews." How good were Jews? They themselves were God's people not because of their virtues but by God's grace, which had borne them "on eagle's wings" into their covenant standing (Exod. 19:4). This covenant was renewed and widened in Jesus Christ. Thus, as Yoder points out,

> The original Christian equality message, to sum up, was rooted in the work of Christ, not in creation or providence. It was integrally part of the very definition of the meaning of the cross [Eph. 2–3], not merely a derivative from or an implication of the Christian's change of heart or mind. It was visible in the concrete bodily form of people who changed their dietary patterns so that they could eat with each other. (Yoder, 1992:40)

More briefly I mention three other practices. (3) The university necessarily practices a kind of *economic leveling*. Not only does this entail pay grades that are equivalent for those of equal rank or responsibility, it also sets up tensions with the outside world, as it appears that law professors will not earn as much as they might in private practice, that scientists serve for a pittance measured by what they might earn in industry, and that even the chiefs of powerful universities are paid less than many of their trustees. Needless to say, this leveling is not without its own hitches and flaws, which is all the more reason to be reminded of the corresponding Christian practice. Yoder calls this "primal socialism," grounded, he says, in the original meaning of eucharist or Lord's Supper or (earliest name of all) the *breaking of bread,* a practice that looked as far back as the manna in the wilderness but had its immediate foundation in the itinerant life Jesus shared with his first disciples (Yoder, 1992:chap. 2). Eating at one table, all disciples give up the claim to exclusive ownership of the means of life.

(4) The university practices a division of labor based upon its *acknowledgment of vocation.* Not every professor can be department chair; not every chair is qualified to lead as president, and (lest it be forgotten) not every university president is competent to teach English 101. Behind this cooperative sharing of labor and authority stands Martin Luther's revision of the Christian doctrine of vocation: it was

not for priests and monks alone; every Christian had a vocation, to be lived out "in the same calling wherein he was called" (1 Cor. 7:20 KJV). But behind Luther stands a practice more radical still, which Yoder labels *the fullness of Christ*. By this practice, not only is there a distinctive place for each in the 'body,' that is, the Christian community; there is a distinctive understanding of what these cooperative relations are all about. As he puts it, "Every human being, Christian or not, is less than he or she could and ought to be if not part of a body in organic interdependence with many peers" (Yoder, 1992:50). The Christian emphasis is on the integrity (we might say, the beauty) of the corporate whole rather than upon extraordinary individuals or ideological control.

(5) This brings us to the fifth needed university practice, *a voice for all*. Sometimes against great resistance the university has struggled to gain, and has then lost and had to regain this practice. In the 1960s, for example, students in Europe and America found they collectively possessed a political voice the university had ignored. The orderly processes of faculty assemblies depend on this very rule. Here the root in Christian practice is easier to find than elsewhere: Guided by New Testament texts the seventeenth-century Puritan movement of Congregationalists, Quakers, Presbyterians, and Baptists hammered out a congregational style of church life that provided a fresh pattern for university and wider social polity alike. Yet as before, the biblical practice is more radical still. Some have called this practice *the rule of Paul*, basing the term on the Apostle's instructions to the Corinthian church (1 Cor. 14:26-33). Yoder sums it up in a motto: "God's will is known by the Spirit working in the meeting" (1992:67). Taken to its full, this practice seems to threaten anarchy. Yet a careful reading of 1 Corinthians 14 leads to a different sense: the practice has its intrinsic order as well as its startling liberty.

ii. Theology as doctrine.—The underlying theme of *Volume II*, considered as a whole, was a theological answer to the question, Who (or what) is God? Its successive Parts dealt with God's rule, God's (triune) unity, God's holy presence. As the contemporary university seeks its metaphysical footing, I suggest now, it finds available a presuppositional order, a set of deep and primary convictions, that correspond to this trinitarian format, even if the university has so neglected the theology it lives by as to be unable to recognize the match. The corollary of *the rule (or kingship) of God* is that the university cannot itself be God or even a god to itself or to others. This rule is violated when the powers that constitute the university arrogate all power to themselves, whether this is done by the fiat of trustees or by the power-lust of administrators or by the (feckless) vainglory of teaching staff. The antidote to these idolatrous pretensions, though, is forever at hand: it lies in the recall of the university's gifted nature; it was given to serve. If God alone is God, the university is precisely God's servant—servant of the God whom it may not know but whose place, nevertheless, it may not supplant if it is to remain itself. Visibly, the university is the servant of society and of its own students. Thereby, it serves its invisible and perhaps unrecognized Source.

The corollary of the *identity of God* (in Christian theology, an identity inseparable from the identity of Jesus Christ in whom it is known) is the coherence of inquiry. This may require a bit more explanation. If we seek to state the underlying assumption, in technical terminology the 'metaphysical conviction' that informs the work of the modern university, we can hardly improve upon Harvard's Lowell Lectures delivered in 1925 by mathematician and philosopher Alfred N. Whitehead (1861–1947). Asking what it was that had made the thought-patterns of the modern world possible, enabling them to displace medieval thought-patterns and launching a new scientific epoch of thought, Whitehead declared that the "new tinge to modern minds is a vehement and passionate interest in the relation of general principles to irreducible and stubborn facts." By way of supporting illustration he cites a sentence from a letter William James, who had just completed his landmark *Principles of Psychology,* wrote to his brother Henry James: "I have to forge every sentence in the teeth of irreducible and stubborn facts" (Whitehead, 1925:2f).

In the teeth of stubborn facts! Yet that concrete habit of mind, still relevant almost a century later, had been paradigmatically laid down in the epoch-straddling central doctrine of biblical religion, which said that in that knotty factual sequence of events that constituted the peoplehood called Israel, and in its blossoming in Jesus the Christ, the world had a graphic answer to its yearning for the identity of God. So, at least, goes the central argument of the central chapter (Six) of *Doctrine*. For all the doctrines of Christology (in *Doctrine,* Chapters Five through Seven) depend upon contingent yet true factual claims: that there was once a human being named Jesus of Nazareth who lived such and such a life, that he died a death whose time and place can be located in ancient history ("crucified under Pontius Pilate"), and supremely that New Testament faith was launched by the fact of his resurrection from the dead. Constantly alongside the factual dimension of Christian doctrine, though, stands its theoretical dimension, in Whitehead's term, the "general principles" that it deploys. From Origen of Alexandria (fl. 250), whose *De principiis* is perhaps the earliest systematic exposition of Christian theology after the New Testament itself, to the current crop of theologians around the globe, too numerous to name, Christian theology has been committed to a rationality inherited partly from Israel, partly from Greece. Without this scientific-metaphysical model in its Renaissance form, Whitehead implied, the science that arose then and still reigns today would not have begun.

Many will recall a still more familiar passage from Whitehead's first Lowell Lecture: "When we compare the tone of thought in Europe with the attitude of other civilizations when left to themselves, there seems but one source for its origin. It must come from the medieval insistence on the rationality of God, conceived as with the personal energy of Jehovah and with the rationality of a Greek philosopher" (1925:13). Yet this seems to challenge the discontinuity that Whitehead introduced when he drew so sharp a line of separation between Renaissance science and its medieval predecessor. In fact, more recent historians have indicated, that line is indeed blurred.

Here, as the citation of William James reminds us anew, we meet not merely the factuality of experimental science (a 'factuality' much modified, by the way, by more recent philosophy of science) but a tenor of mind that constitutes the modern intellectual world entire, however far back its roots extend. The university passed from its medieval to its modern existence by embracing more clearly and more fully this central methodological habit of its own native thought. If in its medieval form it was for a time too dazzled by metaphysics and logic to attend to factual investigation and had to be rescued by the new science, it has since William James's day perhaps been too preoccupied with the overwhelming flow of available facts to pay adequate attention to its own set of rational assumptions. If so, the still more recent postmodern acknowledgment that all facts come theory-laden is balanced by the recognition that the facts do nevertheless come. My present point is simply that such merging of fact and theory corresponds to the central Christian convictions as they appear in *Doctrine.*

The corollary of *the fellowship of the Spirit* is the university's existence as a community. The original meaning of Latin *universitas* was just that, a community or corporate body of students or masters. Christian theology has a watchword for this corporate entity. For it came out in Part III of *Doctrine* that Christian community was multi-ethnic on principle. While Jesus in his teaching ministry held firm to the priority of the Jews, the very passages that record this priority show his reach beyond it. Typically, such passages show Jesus' interaction with foreigners—and with women (e.g., Mark 7:24-30 and par.; John 4:8-20). In any case, in apostolic times this limit, fitting during gestation, was forever broken (Acts 8:26-40; 10; 11:20f; 13:43; 14:27; 15; etc.).

Here we must firmly note that a university is not a church, not a front for the church, not an intellectual church, not any kind of church. The university as such has no gospel, no sacred scripture, no sacraments or ordinances, no ordained ministers, no saving mysteries. It baptizes no candidates. It has, to be sure, an eternal Judge to whom it must give account with all the nations when judgment time shall come (Matthew 25), but as a university its full responsibility to that Judge is just to be itself, unfailingly true to its own mission. A high doctrine of the church (and I hold one) requires that we not confuse the mission of the church with the mission of the university. As such, the university need maintain no chapels, establish no worship, subscribe no dogmas, provide no spiritual care. To be sure, like hospitals and jails and other institutions of culture, the university may furnish some of these amenities to its members, yet they are no more essential to its gifted being than are athletic teams or faculty parking. Universities exceed their charter when they pose as churches.

An authentic church was one in which the barriers between peoples were breached by a *new humanity:* a people composed of all peoples was appearing. The earliest universities inherited this policy. From many political and ethnic bases, students converged upon Bologna to study law. There and at Paris they formed ethnic enclaves, 'nations' for political protection as foreigners and for mutual comfort in a strange city. These 'nations' were replicated at subsequent universities including Oxford, where the (two) nations were named *Boreales* and *Australes,* denoting students' origins north or south of the English river Trent. From earliest times, then, universities have dealt with what is now called ethnicity; without obscuring their diverse homelands, they have had to draw together a body from members already divided upon arrival. The theological guidance here can hardly be Newman's appeal to restrict enrollment (in his case, to Roman Catholics only). *Doctrine* (Chapter Ten) notes the various appeals to unity the world can make: unities based on religion, on political dominance (as by a 'super-power'), on economics and ideology (communist or capitalist). Recognizing the failure of each of these proposed bases for universal unity, it offered a model for syzygy, for yoking together the world's diversities, found in heaven's own unity, where the triune God's redemptive-creative intent is finally realized. However, Christians are taught to pray for the coming rule of God ("Thy kingdom come . . . on earth as it is in heaven") and the reality of Christian community lies in that (until now, partial) realization.

Yet for this ideal unity to be realized, it must enter and rule "the kingdom of matter and death" by rising *within* each individual

> human being. Syzygic unity is not externally achieved by self-serving Don Juans, or externally imposed by a Dictator God; it is not secured by any majority vote however clamorous: the mission of the Spirit achieves syzygic unity precisely by confronting each living human being with the reality of life in the risen Christ, displaying the way of his cross, accepting the uniqueness of each, and inviting from each a response that can be made only by the power of the Spirit of love. (*Doctrine,* p. 449)

If such an appeal seems fantastic to frustrated university officials facing fresh crises of division—black from white, rich from poor, ideologue from rival ideologue—they may wish to recall the very human acts of decency and fellowship that broke "every barrier down," as a gospel hymn reports it—apostolic missionaries sitting at table with those estranged from one another by rules of diet, sharing rich gifts with poor hearers, breaking existing rules in quest of their syzygic goal. The university, fixed in its cultural chrysalis, may not know how to voice this appeal to unity (may not recognize "the power of the Spirit of love"), but in the public acts of its members, especially its teachers, it may do some surprising barrier-breaking.

To review, *Doctrine* in each of its Parts suggests a cultural counterpart, and that counterpart, as accessible to unbelievers as to the faithful, stands among the necessary assumptions of the university's intellectual project.

***iii. Theology as* loggia.**—While *Ethics* asked how the church must live to be the church, and *Doctrine,* what it must teach to be the church, *Witness,* the present volume, has asked how in order to be itself the church must relate to the world outside the church. Two-thirds of this volume offered a survey of that world, first some of the phenomena of its culture, then a look at philosophy as an indicator of changing ways of thought, hinged on the life-work of Ludwig Wittgenstein. This volume's final third investigated a theology of culture that can interpret this changing order of things. Part III first provided a survey of current theologies, then in a 'constructive' chapter (Nine) provided a theology of witness. In it, Christian theology as understood here comes into its own. This achievement is not merely framing the internal logic of Christian faith (its grammar, in George Lindbeck's use of that term—1984) but is the correspondence, the intellectual e-mail, by which the thought that makes the church truly church reaches to engage the world in ongoing, two-sided conversation.

What has this to do with the university? Well, the teaching university, I have just said, stretches the minds that come to it, challenges their complacencies, opens up difficulties, explores utopias, explodes orthodoxies—including, of course, the orthodoxy of the world but also every orthodoxy of the church that closes it off from the legitimate hungers of the world. In consequence the university is likely to seem unsafe, and indeed it is a risky arena for closed minds as well as a threat to frivolous ones. Like church and gospel its original donors, the university is by nature a liberating force. What follows is that theology as understood here has a natural affinity for the university and thus a natural role within it.

Ralph Wood points out in an occasional piece that a 'Christian university' cannot silence the opposing voices. Such a university, he says, must have "sparring partners," advocates of views he like other Christians would likely rebut, in order that the education the university intends may prepare its students for the worldly reality they face. One might add that the so-called secular university must have a like duty: if it really means to prepare its students for successful secularity, will it not need to expose them to the alternatives to secularity? Not, of course, to caricatures of the alternative, but to the real thing? In the culture of the West, it seems to me, to do so requires faculty voices in the arts and sciences—and of course in theology also—that will give voice to the truth as it is in Christ Jesus and not merely to the truth as it would be in a godforsaken world.

I was for a time a member of a large religion department in a state-supported Eastern university that sought in its faculty to represent all the 'major' religious traditions of the world—Buddhist, Hindu, Muslim, of course, but also devil-worship, voodoo, and still others, as well as Judaism and Christianity. An acute colleague pointed out, though, that there was a profound inequality in the teaching these experts provided: The non-Christians without exception appeared unashamedly as advocates of their own traditions; the Christians' classroom treatment of Christianity was as its critics and censors. There is nothing wrong with criticizing Christianity—heaven knows it needs criticism, even if we mortals do not know it—but the net effect upon religion students was to enforce their suspicion that authentic religion could never be Christian.

The opening chapter of Volume I, "How Theology Matters," defended Christian theology against critics by arguing that, so far from being inturned or in the bad sense 'dogmatic,' this discipline provided an avenue of communication with those who did not embrace its convictions. It suggested the image of the gallery that in an earlier generation graced residences in any American town. In good weather, family members sat on the gallery, providing opportunity for many a friendly exchange between residents and passers-by. A similar function on a grander scale was served by the *loggia* or public arcade of Italian Renaissance cities, open to the street and thus to all comers. These city-states, whose existence depended so strongly on commerce but also upon common purposes shared by most citizens, fostered the loggia as a place where friends, even strangers, might meet and converse. My suggestion was that theology itself constitutes such a loggia. While the main point was that it enhanced the ability of baptists to talk with one another (!), the application did not end there. Our theological conversation is with every actual and every potential sharer of the good news. Since we cannot know how far those wide limits reach, theology must intend its conversation as an invitation to all to hear and respond. Yet this means that theology is a discipline uniquely suited to the university, which to be itself from medieval times on has been obliged to welcome scholars "from all parts," and which, as the following section argues, must be an institution not only artistic and scientific but also theological.

§3. Theology in the University Curriculum

> If on the other hand it turns out that something considerable *is* known about the Supreme Being, whether from Reason or Revelation, then the institution in question professes every science, and yet leaves out the foremost of them. In a word, strong as may appear the assertion, I do not see how I can avoid making it, and bear with me, Gentlemen, while I do so, viz., such an Institution cannot be what it professes, if there be a God. (Newman, 1873:18)

Having with these words thrown down the gauntlet to universities that would exclude theology, Newman went on in *The Idea of a University* (discourses III and IV) to demonstrate that "other branches of knowledge" had matters of substance to bring to theology, and it to them. Here it has been necessary to adjust Newman's notion of theology: it is a dialectical discipline not a single-voiced one; theology (theoretics) may be Christian—and Catholic as well—but that is not its only option. It follows that the place of theology in the curriculum must be rethought. How in its present maturity can theology take its place alongside the arts and sciences? If students are to become authentic bachelors (i.e., qualified novice scholars) of *arts* and true masters of *arts,* if advanced students are truly to be, by way of their several specialties, doctors of *philosophy* as their diplomas warrant them to be, what place has theology in their education? To answer, we need a clear idea of what 'philosophy' means here, and a clear idea of the preparatory role of arts (and sciences). Certainly the sort of philosophy intended by these time-honored degrees cannot strictly mean the program of today's philosophy departments—else to receive a "Ph.D. in philosophy" (a common enough locution) is a mere redundancy, and doctorates in chemistry or politics or psychology would claim for their bearers a familiarity with epistemology and ethics and metaphysics as these are taught in departmental philosophy—familiarity that in most cases they clearly lack.

In this matter I propose to follow Newman: the 'philosophy' an educated man or woman will have acquired must mean something more accessible than the *Principia* of Russell and Whitehead or the early Wittgenstein's *Tractatus*. Philosophy in this wider sense retains something of its classical aspect: for ethics, though, read knowing what to do; for epistemology read knowing how to find out; for metaphysics read knowing what's what. In a sentence Newman says that the graduate thus become a philosopher "may be right or wrong in his opinion, but he is too clear-headed to be unjust; he is as simple as he is forcible, and as brief as he is decisive"—on all counts a fair description of John Henry Newman himself (1873:160).

The longer paragraph in which this capsule description is found (Newman, 1873:160), if updated for gender usage, might reasonably be inscribed on today's university walls for all to read.

Is it possible, though, for education up to a bachelor of arts or sciences to produce such graduates? To answer, we need a clear idea of the aim of arts and sciences, including their necessary partnership with theology.

a. Arts and sciences theologically awake.—The 'seven liberal arts' that constituted the curricular base of the medieval university were divided into a training in 'communication' with others (the *trivium* of grammar, logic, and rhetoric) and further training (the *quadrivium* of music, arithmetic, geometry, and astronomy) meant to enable communication with, or better said, participation in, the natural order. We have seen, though, that this would be a reductive account of the liberal arts even in the Middle Ages. What of the present?

i. Arts and sciences.—Certainly arts today are more than ways to communicate, sciences more than participation in nature, else typing might count as a liberal art and sunbathing as a science. Characteristically, art has a double reference: it refers to the world that is but also to the world that might be; art's creativity makes for a new world which will often be a criticism of the existing order of things (Chapter Four, Intro.; Hartt, 1967:355). Moreover, art's communication is always three-dimensional: it employs existing conventions (symbols?) in creative *action* whose dual *reference* is *affectively* conveyed to its audience (Chapter Four, Intro.). Does this apply to education's liberal arts? It does, for whether the instructor's task is teaching French verbs or the history of architecture, whether the student is learning to understand *Hamlet* or to write differential equations, all these artistic dimensions are potentially present.

The message here can be made more pointed (and less welcome to some): Whatever training or instruction does not qualify as liberating art and science does not qualify a student—not even in part—for the bachelor's degree. Academic emphasis rightly varies from school to school (reflecting the gifts of its doctors and the contents of its library) and from student to student (reflecting the aptitude of each). Not every university will have a great faculty in classical literature; not every student is suited to the study of advanced mathematics. What cannot replace the bachelor's liberal arts education is (for examples) a degree in 'business management' or oenology, though of course the university may offer such training as well. A degree called "bachelor of arts in Christian education" (another sad example) is quite likely a sin against the liberal arts.

A like point can be made about the teaching of undergraduate science. The chapter on science (Chapter Three, written by Nancey Murphy) pointed out the intimate relation between science and Western culture, using the case of Darwinian evolution as an extended illustration. Consequently, in our educational triad (initiation, skills, ideals) firsthand acquaintance with scientific practice is an essential part of the initiation that admits newcomers to 'philosophy' as well as providing skills or techniques needed to negotiate the culture. (This was already the case in the medieval university, where 'liberal arts' included the science of the day.) Our science chapter shows that this intimate involvement of science with art is in no sense one-sided. While evolution has influenced our thinking about human history and natural history, vastly extending their time lines while tightening the link between them, Chapter Three shows that energy flows in the opposite direction as well: the culture of the day caused Darwinian evolution to adopt the shape that it did (§2). As everyone knows, evolution influenced theology, too, requiring a fresh and, I believe, more profound reading of the biblical creation narratives. Yet here, too, the impact has been bidirectional: a gospel-shaped theology permits a fresh reading of organic nature (§§3–4).

ii. ***Theology.***—This introduces the role of theology in teaching the arts and sciences. It is not necessary, or even best, for the theological dimension of artistic and scientific issues to be explored in separated theology courses. The approach to the arts and sciences in the classroom is already, and inevitably, theological in one way or another. Recall the nature of theology itself: it discovers, examines, and sometimes tries to revise the deep convictions that make us the people we are. Yet to read Shakespeare or to play jazz or any art music, to study departmental philosophy or today's physics, is to evoke such convictions—in the happy case, to confront them afresh and consider them anew. When this is not so, the classroom is unworthy of a place within the liberal arts. Every teacher of the liberal arts including the sciences necessarily meets in them his or her own convictions; good teachers are alert to their students' convictions as well. Since theology is the very 'science' of convictions, every classroom therefore has its theological dimension. It only remains to be seen, *what* theology, what sort of theology, arises there.

Yet if no trained theologians are at hand in the faculty, what opportunity have experts in other disciplines to consider and to refine their own theology? Here appears the inescapable place of academic theology in the faculty of arts and sciences—of theologians who do their research and make their public presentations, who engage students in theology classrooms, who meet experts in other disciplines in office corridors and faculty lounges, thus taking their full place in the university. Suppose, to imagine a ridiculous counterpart case, there were a university where the only place students met biology was in a theology classroom! That would not of necessity mislead students (as witness the biology presented in our Chapter Three), but it would be pitifully *inadequate.* And so it is with theology learned only as part of history or biology or some other art or science.

The third aim of education, intertwined with initiation and the acquisition of skills, is the evoking of ideals, and here theology comes fully into its own. Take as a first example Christian theology alone, and consider it now not in the confined sense of its treatment in this trilogy (ethics, doctrine, and theology of culture) but as Christian theology in all its natural breadth. This will embrace its roots in Hebrew Scripture and history, the knowledge of its radical Founder, its apostolic origin and early expansion, its classic encounter with Greco-Roman philosophy and culture, its role in the unfolding Christian mission to people around the globe, its entailed skills such as ancient languages and its associated practices or applications—consider Christian theology thus, not forgetting its constant and critical attention to its own flaws, and one will likely see the ideal it pursues. To study these exfoliations of Christian theology is to meet and be challenged by that ideal. Yet there is no reason for today's university, East or West, to limit theology's portfolio to Christianity, or to the biblical religions, alone. Every worldview, every serious examination of human convictions in light of one another *and in light of whatever else there is* (no reductionism is acceptable in this work)—all this has some claim upon the curriculum, the prominence of each claim being proportionate to its perceived value in the larger arts curriculum and in the wider culture. For the university's goal, lest we forget, is not to make Christians or any other sort of religious adherents of its students, but to make them in Newman's broad sense philosophers, men and women capable of taking a place in the world that God so loved (cf. John 3:16). That is the aim the university was given when it was first given to the world. That aim has not changed.

b. The 'real' university.—What, then, would such a University of Utopia be to its public, to its founders, and to its God? First, to the public it served, Utopia University (doubtless soon abbreviated UU) recognizes its obligation to provide education to all comers. It will have its 'higher' schools of law, medicine, perhaps ministry, and still other schools such as commerce, agriculture, and education, as well as a graduate school that presses further inquiry in the liberal arts and pure sciences themselves. These various schools have a common basis: they presume that teachers and students are alike liberal artists, initiated into the skills and ideals that make philosophers (in the sense explained above) of undergraduates. What of theology within these 'higher' schools? As before, theology will be inescapable, for the concerns that engage the graduate divisions are inseparable from those that constitute theology itself: namely, the convictions that make men and women what they are, convictions they cannot surrender without deep and lasting change in themselves.

Chairs in Christian theology, embracing as does the present trilogy the narrative shape of Christian convictions—the biblical story and its entailed lesser stories old and new—would be a first step in the right direction for many a present-day university. Consequently, awareness of such theology will be as much the possession of professors of law and medicine as it must be of professors of arts and sciences. For a University of Utopia in all its branches must be conscious of the culture it means to serve.

At both its European and its American beginnings, the university existed especially, though never exclusively, to educate church leaders—priests and pastors, missionaries and monks—and that remains one of the tasks at Utopia. Yet soon the cultural mission widened in each of these cases; as in Europe, in America, too, the student body came to include particularly those who would rule the young nation. That task remains, and certain American universities pride themselves exactly on educating future senators and presidents. Yet as the 'rule of Paul,' *a voice for all,* penetrates a culture, its political forms will often mutate toward democracy, a government whose 'rulers' are (at least nominally) everybody. Thus Utopia University recognizes a new task: it has a share in the education not only of clergy and princes, or artists and scientists (the rulers of technocracy), but of the ruling *dēmos,* that is, of *all.*

How likely, cynics and skeptics will ask, is the actuality of such a university as *Utopia*? Of course the skepticism is in order (though not the cynicism), for the goal, the real university here and now, is elusive. Yet even its partial realization depends mightily upon *Utopia University*'s understanding of another relation: What shall it be to its *founders and donors*? Here, too, the pattern was laid long ago: it was in obtaining its freedom from the local bishop in Bologna or Paris, or in America its freedom from the mothering Christian bodies, that the university began to discover its true identity. What is not so clearly perceived is that the government-begun university has an identical need for liberation. The true beauty of the University of Utopia is hardly discovered while it continues in servility to denominational watchdogs—*or* remains in servility to the demands of 'national security': Reserve Officer Training Corps, research leading to weapons manufacture, and their kin. Again, it little profits today's church-begun university to slip the cable anchoring it to a church body only to find that the funds it obtains from commercial firms commit it to research goals and ideology (which in every case entails theology) fostered by that new sponsor. The meaning of a university is found in being itself, true to its own goals, in pursuit of its own beauty.

What, then, of God and the university? If Utopia was established as a secular school, or alternatively if its religious awareness was that which George Marsden says was Stanford's founding aim: to be "nontheological, nonsectarian," but nonetheless "vaguely Christian" (Marsden, 1994:254), then it is entitled to a happy liberation from these versions of Egyptian bondage; if theology is not forbidden there, a university will come into its own by discovering its irrepressible theological being. God *can* be mentioned in the classroom! Yet this liberty, like every liberty, has its price—God can no more be carelessly mentioned, or airily dismissed, than can the atomic weight of elements or the laws of supply and demand or the emotional depths of good music. To speak of God in Utopia University will require discipline, training, and (if not the perpetual, hesitating silence regarding deity of old Simonides) at least the awareness that holiness has its own imperatives as surely as do nature and culture.

The skeptic's voice is indeed in order here. Utopia University is not easily built, not ready to hand. Its appearance and its vitality demand a radical recovery of some old hopes, and their mutation into some new dreams. They demand the service of a few brilliant leaders (today's equivalents of the University of Chicago's Robert Hutchins in the 1930s) and even more, the services of many women and men who love their college or university, who wish for it true beauty, and who invest their lives in it without hope of an equivalent reward. Utopia also demands of theology, my own discipline, a willingness to undergo radical reform (a phrase from which baptists, of all people, should not shrink) in pursuit of this one among theology's many duties: to help create the real university. Theology in doing so recalls that the university is the church's ancient gift, really God's gift, and will believe with Scripture that

> [e]very good and generous action and every perfect gift come from above, from the Father who created the lights of heaven. With him there is no variation, no play of passing shadows. Of his own choice, he brought us to [the new] birth by the word of truth to be a kind of firstfruits of his creation. (James 1:17f)

* * * * *

Groping for a single lively metaphor to capture what has been said in this volume, I discovered the following sentence:

> The whole history of the Christian movement exhibits an alternation between periods of what may be called diastole, when Christianity reaches out into culture to absorb elements which it may use for the enrichment of its own life and thought, and periods of systole when the church draws into itself in a contractive movement which tries to exclude cultural forces so as to recover its own uniqueness. (Aubrey, 1954:30)

And Aubrey goes on to say, succinctly, that this image "raises the whole problem" of the nature of the culture in which the church finds itself (1954:31).

Edwin Ewart Aubrey (1896–1956), a Baptist trained at the University of Chicago, came to teach in the University of Pennsylvania in the field of religious thought (which was rather like our 'theology'). When invited to give public lectures in the Colgate Rochester Theological Seminary, Aubrey took the opportunity to reject the scorn of culture he perceived in recent neo-orthodoxy. He went out of his way, though, to express admiration for Paul Tillich; he may belong, then, in the Tillich-Hartt-Yoder trajectory followed here. Aubrey called the book made from the lectures *Secularism a Myth* (1954).

The image of a rhythmic diastole and systole, an alternate relaxation of the heart followed by its expulsive contraction, represents for Aubrey a church which at one phase of its history draws from the culture needed resources but then in another phase discards it as do lungs discharging unwanted carbon dioxide. This suited what I had said in *Witness:* the church necessarily draws upon cultural resources: culture's religion and its science, its art and its wisdom, its humane learning and its deliberate, life-risking adventure—all these are elements that the church folds into its heart and adopts as its own, yet later filters and ejects (in part) as contaminating, counting these as the 'worldly' sins it too readily made its own. How clear an image! Then, however, I recalled that I had already adopted from Julian Hartt the metaphor of the rhythmic, pumping heart in a quite different way. Not having presented the relevant Hartt passage earlier, I quote it here:

> The fifth cardinal feature of the church's life is its rhythm of going-out and return. Inevitably the diastolic and systolic rhythm of the human heart comes to mind as the ordained metaphor with which to express this feature of the being of the church. . . . [W]hen the rhythm is broken up the church falls at once into severe illness; and if the rhythm were not restored the church would die. (Hartt, 1967:300f)

And Hartt goes on to flesh out the metaphor differently: "[T]he church goes out into the world with the ministry of prophecy, interpretation, exorcism, and healing . . . to make the Word of God fruitful in the world." But that going out alternates with a necessary and regular return. Here

> the church withdraws into the secret life of sacramental grace. Every Christian sacrament is a disclosure of the Kingdom of God.

> But there is a time when man's spirit must adore God in all of the beauty of His holiness; then the stress of campaigning is abated, the love of conflict is stilled, and the ministering company is attended to. (Hartt, 1967:301)

Going out in service, but service in which the church risks exhausting its power; returning to worship, and worship in which that power is restored. This prior commitment was still my own. Was the church, then, an organism with *two* circulatory systems, one Julian Hartt's system of alternating worship and service, the other Edwin Aubrey's more ponderous rhythm of cultural acquisition followed by its (partial) rejection? Both uses of the metaphor seemed true to reality, but how could they be combined? That was the implicit question on every page I had written, reduced for me now to a contested metaphor.

I had overlooked, though, a basic fact about human (and animal) circulation: both sorts of circulatory system are engaged in every heartbeat. The same systolic contraction of the heart that drives blood out to the body's members simultaneously pumps blood through another artery into the lungs, where its impurities are removed and fresh oxygen is acquired. The same diastolic relaxation and enlargement of the heart, thanks to its cleverly divided chambers, at once permits matter drawn through veins from all parts of the body to the heart *and* through another great vessel permits fresh, lung-purified blood to enter another of the heart's chambers. If *either* of these two processes ceases, or if they improperly leak together in its chambers, the heart fails. So it is, if you my reader will permit it, in our work here: Theology means struggle, and part of the struggle for Christians is to permit the dual rhythm of both circulatory cycles to form one bloodstream supporting one single church of Christ, one Israel of God. That is what I have struggled to represent here; if I have done so, albeit imperfectly, the outcome of my struggle is rightly termed theology.

Bibliography of Classical and Often-Cited Works

Bible versions:

KJV *King James Version* (1611)
NJB *New Jerusalem Bible* (1985)
NRSV *New Revised Standard Version* (1989)
REB *Revised English Bible* (1989)

Citations to Classic Writings:

Greek and Latin works:

Anselm of Canterbury
Cur Deus homo (Why a God-Man?).
Aquinas, Thomas
ST *Summa Theologiae* (I have quoted *Summa Theologiae: Latin Text and English Translation.* 1964–76. 60 vols. New York: Blackfriars, with McGraw-Hill). (example: ST 1.2.5)
Augustine of Hippo
Civ. dei *The City of God.* (I have used Marcus Dods's translation, New York: The Modern Library, 1950.)
Conf. Confessions. (I have quoted from Henry Chadwick, trans., Oxford: University Press, 1991.)

Modern works:

CD Karl Barth, *Church Dogmatics.* 1936–69. Trans. G. W. Bromiley et al. Edinburgh: T. & T. Clark. (example: CD I/2 §23.2; example: CD IV/3/2)

CF Friedrich Schleiermacher, *The Christian Faith.* 1830. Trans. and ed. H. R. Mackintosh and James S. Stewart. Edinburgh: T. & T. Clark, 1928. (example: CF §33)

CONV. James Wm. McClendon, Jr. and James M. Smith, *Convictions: Defusing Religious Relativism.* Valley Forge, Pa: Trinity Press International, 1994 (first edition: *Understanding Religious Convictions.* Notre Dame, Ind.: University of Notre Dame Press, 1975).

Inst. John Calvin, *Institutes of the Christian Religion.* (I have used the 2-volume translation by Ford Lewis Battles in Library of Christian Classics. Philadelphia: Westminster, 1960 (1559).

Speeches Friedrich Schleiermacher, *On Religion: Speeches to Its Cultured Despisers.* 1799. (I have used John Oman's translation, New York: Harper, 1958.)

Ludwig Wittgenstein:

AMB *Wittgenstein's Lectures: Cambridge, 1932–1935.* Ed. Alice Ambrose and Margaret Macdonald. Totowa, N.J.: Rowman and Littlefield, 1979.

BB. *The Blue and Brown Books.* Oxford: Basil Blackwell, 1960.

CV *Culture and Value.* Ed. G. H. Von Wright. Chicago: University of Chicago Press, 1980.

LC *Lectures and Conversations on Aesthetics, Psychology and Religious Belief.* Ed. Cyril Barrett. Berkeley: University of California Press, 1967.

LE "A Lecture on Ethics." *Philosophical Review* XXX (January 1965):3-12.

NB *Notebooks 1914 –1916.* Ed. G. E. M. Anscombe and G. H. von Wright. New York: Harper and Row, 1969.

OC *On Certainty.* Ed. G. E. M. Anscombe & G. H. von Wright. Trans. Denis Paul and G. E. M. Anscombe. New York: Harper & Row, 1972.

PI *Philosophical Investigations.* Trans. G. E. M. Anscombe. New York: Macmillan, 1953.

RFGB *Remarks on Frazer's Golden Bough. Bemerkung über Frazers Golden Bough.* 1979. Ed. Rush Rhees. Trans. A. C. Miles. Atlantic Highlands, N. J.: Brynmill Press, 1995.

TLP *Tractatus Logico-Philosophicus: The German Text of Ludwig Wittgenstein's Logisch-philosophische Abhandlung*. 1922. Trans. D. F. Pears and B. F. McGuiness. Intro. Bertrand Russell. London:

Routledge & Kegan Paul, 1961. First English ed., trans. Frank Ramsey, 1922.

Encyclopedias:

DCA *Dictionary of Christianity in America.* 1990. Ed. Daniel G. Reid. Downers Grove: InterVarsity Press.

DJG *Dictionary of Jesus and the Gospels.* 1992. Ed. J. Green et al. Downers Grove: InterVarsity.

Enc. Brit. Encyclopædia Britannica. 1992. 15th ed. Chicago: Encyclopædia Britannica Corp.

Enc. Phil. Encyclopedia of Philosophy. Ed. Paul Edwards. 8 vols. New York: Macmillan and Free Press, 1967.

EMCT *Encyclopedia of Modern Christian Thought.* Ed. Alister McGrath. Oxford: Blackwell, 1993.

ER *Encyclopedia of Religion.* Ed. Mircea Eliade. 16 vols. New York: Macmillan, 1987.

ME *Mennonite Encyclopedia.* Ed. H. S. Bender. Vols. 1–4, C. J. Dyck and D. D. Martin, vol. 5. Scottdale: Herald Press, 1955–90.

Bibliography of Other Works Cited

(See also preceding abbreviations of classic and frequently cited works.)

ABBOTT, E. S., et al.

1947 *Catholicity: A Study in the Conflict of Christian Traditions in the West.* Westminster: Dacre.

AHLSTROM, Sydney

1972 *A Religious History of the American People.* New Haven: Yale University Press.

ALBERTSON, Chris

1978 *Louis Armstrong.* Alexandria, Va.: Time-Life Books.

ALLEN, Diogenes

1968 *The Reasonableness of Faith: A Philosophical Essay on the Grounds for Religious Beliefs.* Washington and Cleveland: Corpus Books.

1985 *Philosophy for Understanding Theology.* Atlanta: John Knox.

1989 *Christian Belief in a Postmodern World: The Full Wealth of Conviction.* Louisville: Westminster-John Knox.

1994 "Manifestations of the Supernatural According to Simone Weil." *Cahiers Simone Weil* 17:3 (September): 290-307.

AMMERMAN, Nancy Tatom

1990 *Baptist Battles: Social Change and Religious Conflict in the Southern Baptist Convention.* New Brunswick, N.J., and London: Rutgers University Press.

ANDERSON, Robert Mapes

1979 *Vision of the Disinherited: The Making of American Pentecostalism.* New York: Oxford University Press.

ARMOUR, Rollin Stely

1966 *Anabaptist Baptism: A Representative Study.* Scottdale, Pa.: Herald Press.

ARMSTRONG, Louis

1986 (1954) *Satchmo: My Life in New Orleans.* New York: Da Capo.

ARNOLD, Matthew

1869 (1966) *Culture and Anarchy.* Cambridge: Cambridge University Press.

AUBREY, Edwin E.

1954 *Secularism a Myth: An Examination of the Current Attack on Secularism.* New York: Harper & Brothers.

AUSTIN, J. L.

1961 (1970) *Philosophical Papers.* 2nd ed. Ed. J. O. Urmson and G. J. Warnock. London: Oxford University Press.

1975 *How to Do Things with Words.* 2nd ed. Ed. J. O. Urmson and Marina Sbisà. Cambridge, Mass.: Harvard University Press.

BAGEHOT, Walter

1869 *Physics and Politics, or Thoughts on the Application of the Principles of "Natural Selection" and "Inheritance" to Political Society.* London: King.

BAILEY, Albert Edward

1950 *The Gospel in Hymns: Backgrounds and Interpretations.* New York: Scribner's.

BALDWIN, James

1965 *Going to Meet the Man.* New York: Dell.

BARTH, Karl

1922 (1933) *The Epistle to the Romans.* 2nd ed. Trans. Edwyn C. Hoskyns. Oxford: Oxford University Press.

1972 *Protestant Theology in the Nineteenth Century: Its Background and History.* London: S.C.M., digested edition, 1959.

BARTH, Markus

1974 *Ephesians.* The Anchor Bible, Vols. 34 and 34A. Garden City, N.Y.: Doubleday.

BARTLEY, William Warren, III

1973 *Wittgenstein.* Philadelphia and New York: J. B. Lippincott.

BAUER, Walter

1934 (1971) *Orthodoxy and Heresy in Earliest Christianity.* Ed. Robert A. Kraft and Gerhard Krodel. Philadelphia: Fortress.

BEER, Gillian
1983 *Darwin's Plots: Evolutionary Narrative in Darwin, George Eliot, and Nineteenth-Century Fiction*. London: Routledge & Kegan Paul.

BEGBIE, Jeremy S.
1991 *Voicing Creation's Praise: Towards a Theology of the Arts*. Edinburgh: T. & T. Clark.

BELLAH, Robert N.
1970 *Beyond Belief: Essays on Religion in a Post-Traditional World*. New York: Harper & Row.
1975 *The Broken Covenant: American Civil Religion in Time of Trial*. New York: Seabury Press.

BELLAH, Robert N., et al.
1985 *Habits of the Heart: Individualism and Commitment in American Life*. New York: Harper & Row.

BENDER, Harold S.
1950 *Conrad Grebel c. 1498–1526: The Founder of the Swiss Brethren Sometimes Called Anabaptists*. Scottdale, Pa.: Herald Press.

BERGER, Peter L.
1967 *The Sacred Canopy: Elements of a Sociological Theory of Religion*. Garden City, N.Y.: Doubleday.
1969 *A Rumor of Angels: Modern Society and the Rediscovery of the Supernatural*. Garden City, N.Y.: Doubleday.
1979 *The Heretical Imperative: Contemporary Possibilities of Religious Affirmation*. Garden City, N.Y.: Doubleday.
1992 *A Far Glory: The Quest for Faith in an Age of Credulity*. New York: Free.

BERGER, Peter L., and Thomas LUCKMANN
1966 *The Social Construction of Reality: A Treatise in the Sociology of Knowledge*. Garden City, N.Y.: Doubleday.

BERKHOF, Hendrik
1962 *Christ and the Powers*. Trans. John Howard Yoder. Scottdale, Pa.: Herald Press.

BLOCH, Ruth
1985 *Visionary Republic: Millennial Themes in American Thought, 1756–1800*. New York: Cambridge University Press.

BLOOM, Harold
1992 *The American Religion: The Emergence of the Post-Christian Nation*. New York: Simon & Schuster.

BLOOR, David

1976 (1991) *Knowledge and Social Imagery.* Chicago: University of Chicago Press.

BOLES, John

1985 "Evangelism in the Old South: From Religious Dissent to Cultural Dominance." *Religion in the Old South,* ed. Charles R. Wilson. Jackson: University of Mississippi Press, pp. 13-34.

1994 *The Irony of Southern Religion.* New York: Peter Lang.

1997 *Great Revival: Beginnings of the Bible Belt.* Lexington: University Press of Kentucky.

BONHOEFFER, Dietrich

1972 *Letters and Papers from Prison.* Ed. Eberhard Bethge. New York: Macmillan.

BONONI, Patricia U.

1986 *Under the Cope of Heaven: Religion, Society, and Politics in Colonial America.* New York: Oxford University Press.

BRAATEN, Carl E., and Robert W. JENSON, eds.

1995 *A Map of Twentieth-Century Theology: Readings from Karl Barth to Radical Pluralism.* Minneapolis: Fortress.

BRACKNEY, William H., ed.

1998 *The Believers Church: A Voluntary Church.* Kitchener, Ont.: Pandora Press.

BRADBURY, Malcolm

1987 *My Strange Quest for Mensonge.* London: Penguin.

BRAUER, Jerald C.

1976 *Religion and the American Revolution.* Minneapolis: Fortress.

BRAUER, Jerald C., ed.

1968 *The Impact of the Church Upon Its Culture.* Chicago: University of Chicago Press.

BRODERICK, Francis L.

1963 *Right Reverend New Dealer: John A. Ryan.* New York: Macmillan.

BROOKE, John Hedley

1991 *Science and Religion: Some Historical Perspectives.* Cambridge: Cambridge University Press.

BROWN, Peter

1969 *Augustine of Hippo: A Biography.* Berkeley: University of California Press.

BROWN, Warren S., Nancey MURPHY, and H. N. MALONY, eds.
1998 *Whatever Happened to the Soul? Scientific and Theological Portraits of Human Nature.* Minneapolis: Fortress.

BRUGGE, David
1994 *The Navajo-Hopi Land Dispute: An American Tragedy.* Albuquerque: University of New Mexico Press.

BRUGGE, David M., and Charlotte J. FRISBIE, eds.
1982 *Navajo Religion and Culture: Selected Views.* Santa Fe: Museum of New Mexico Press.

BUECHNER, Frederick
1982 *The Sacred Journey.* San Francisco: Harper & Row.

BULTMANN, Rudolf
1958 *Jesus Christ and Mythology.* New York: Scribner's.
1960 *Existence and Faith.* New York: World.

BURRIDGE, Kenelm
1978 "Introduction: Missionary Occasions." In *Mission, Church, and Sect in Oceania.* Ed. Daniel T. Hughes, James A. Boutilier, and Sharon W. Tiffany. Ann Arbor: University of Michigan Press, pp. 1-30.
1991 *In the Way: A Study of Christian Missionary Endeavors.* Vancouver: University of British Columbia Press.

BURTCHAELL, James Tunstead
1998 *The Dying of the Light: The Disengagement of Colleges and Universities from Their Christian Churches.* Grand Rapids: Eerdmans.

BUSHNELL, Horace
1965 *Horace Bushnell.* Ed. H. Shelton Smith. Library of Protestant Thought. New York: Oxford University Press.

CARTER, William
1991 *Preservation Hall.* New York: Norton.

CARTWRIGHT, Michael G.
1999 "Discipline in Black and White: Conflicting Legacies of Nineteenth-Century Euro-American Methodist and African American Methodist Disciplinary Practices." In *Doctrines and Discipline.* Ed. Dennis M. Campbell, William B. Lawrence, and Russell E. Richey. Nashville: Abingdon Press.

CASH, Sarah
1992 *American Art: Paintings from the Amon Carter Museum.* Fort Worth: Amon Carter Museum.

CHADWICK, Owen

1975 *The Secularization of the European Mind in the Nineteenth Century.* Cambridge: Cambridge University Press.

CHALMERS, Thomas

1833 *The Adaptation of External Nature to the Moral and Intellectual Constitution of Man.* 2 vols. Bridgewater Treatises. London: Pickering.

CHASE, Gilbert

1955 *America's Music: From the Pilgrims to the Present.* New York: McGraw-Hill.

CHRISTIAN, William

1972 *Oppositions of Religious Doctrines: A Study in the Logic of Dialog Among Religions.* New York: Herder & Herder.

CLEBSCH, William A.

1968 *From Sacred to Profane America: The Role of Religion in American History.* New York: Harper & Row.

COAKLEY, Sarah

1979 "Theology and Cultural Relativism: What Is the Problem?" *Neue Zeitschrift für Systematische Theologie und Religionsphilosophie* 21:223-43. Reprinted in *The Interpretation of Cultures; Selected Essays.* New York: Basic Books.

COLLINGWOOD, R. G.

1940 *An Essay on Metaphysics.* Oxford: Oxford University Press.

1946 (1956) *The Idea of History.* New York: Oxford University Press.

CONKIN, Paul Keith

1990 *Cane Ridge: America's Pentecost.* Madison: University of Wisconsin Press.

COOPER, James Fenimore

1985 *The Leatherstocking Tales.* New York: Library of America.

DAMASIO, Antonio R.

1994 *Descartes' Error: Emotion, Reason, and the Human Brain.* New York: G. P. Putnam's Sons.

DARWIN, Charles

1859 (1963) *The Origin of Species by Means of Natural Selection of the Preservation of Favoured Races in the Struggle for Life.* Ed. Hampton L. Carson. New York: Washington Square Press.

1871 (1981) *The Descent of Man and Selection in Relation to Sex.* London: J. Murray. Intro. John Tyler Bonner and Robert M. May. Princeton: Princeton University Press.

1872 *The Expression of the Emotions in Man and Animals.* London: Murray.

DAVIES, Paul

1992 *The Mind of God: The Scientific Basis for a Rational World.* New York: Simon & Schuster.

DESCARTES, René

1637 (1960) *Discourse on Method,* in *Discourse on Method and Meditations.* Trans. L. J. Lafleur. Indianapolis: Bobbs Merrill.

1641 (1960) *Meditations,* in *Discourse on Method and Meditations.*

DESMOND, Adrian

1989 *The Politics of Evolution: Morphology, Medicine, and Reform in Radical London.* Chicago and London: University of Chicago Press.

DE VAULX, Bernard

1961 *History of the Missions.* Trans. Reginald F. Trevett. New York: Hawthorn Books.

DE WAAL, Frans

1996 *Good Natured: The Origins of Right and Wrong in Humans and Other Animals.* Cambridge, Mass.: Harvard University Press.

DILLENBERGER, Jane, and John DILLENBERGER

1977 *Perceptions of the Spirit in Twentieth-Century American Art.* Indianapolis: Indianapolis Museum of Art.

DILLENBERGER, Jane, and Joshua C. TAYLOR

1972 *The Hand and the Spirit: Religious Art in America 1700–1900.* Berkeley: University Art Museum.

DILLENBERGER, John

1986 *A Theology of Artistic Sensibilities: The Visual Arts and the Church.* New York: Crossroad.

DiNOIA, Joseph

1981–82 "The Universality of Salvation and the Diversity of Religious Aims." *Worldmission* 32 (Winter): 4-15.

1992 *The Diversity of Religions: A Christian Perspective.* Washington, D.C.: Catholic University of America Press.

DOBZHANSKY, Theodosius, et al.

1977 *Evolution.* San Francisco: W. H. Freeman and Company.

DRAPER, John W.

1875 *History of the Conflict Between Religion and Science.* London: Henry S. King.

DRISKELL, David C.

1976 *Two Centuries of Black American Art.* Los Angeles County Museum of Art; New York: Knopf.

DuBOIS, W. E. B.
1903 (1986) *Souls of Black Folk*. In *Writings: The Suppression of the African Slave Trade; The Souls of Black Folk; Dusk of Dawn; Essays and Articles*. New York: Library of America.

DUNN, James D. G.
1990 *Unity and Diversity in the New Testament*. London: S.C.M.

DURKHEIM, Émile
1915 *The Elementary Forms of the Religious Life*. Trans. Joseph Ward Swain. New York: Free.

EDWARDS, James C.
1982 *Ethics Without Philosophy: Wittgenstein and the Moral Life*. Tampa: University Presses of Florida.

EDWARDS, Jonathan
1765 *Concerning the End for Which God Created the World*. In Edwards, 1989.
1989 *Ethical Writings*. Ed. Paul Ramsey. The Works of Jonathan Edwards, vol. 8. New Haven: Yale University Press.

ELLISON, Ralph Waldo
1952 *Invisible Man*. New York: Random House.
1999 *Juneteenth: A Novel*. Ed. John F. Callahan. New York: Random House.

ERASMUS, Desiderius
1509 (1942) *The Praise of Folly*. Trans. John Wilson. New York: Walter J. Black.

FARRER, Austin
1967 *Faith and Speculation: An Essay in Philosophical Theology*. London: Adam & Charles Black.

FEATHER, Leonard
1965 *The Book of Jazz from Then Till Now: A Guide to the Entire Field*. 2nd ed. New York: Horizon Press.

FEYERABEND, Paul K.
1975 *Against Method*. London: New Left Books.

FINNEY, Charles G.
1868 *Lectures on Revivals of Religion*. New York: Fleming H. Revell.
1876 *Memoirs of Rev. Charles G. Finney: Written by Himself*. New York: A. S. Barnes & Co.

FORD, Alice
1985 *Edward Hicks: His Life and Art*. New York: Abbeville.

FORD, David F., ed.
1997 *The Modern Theologians: An Introduction to Christian Theology in the Twentieth Century.* 2nd ed. Cambridge, Mass., and Oxford, U.K.: Blackwell.

FRAZER, Sir James George
1922 *The Golden Bough: A Study in Magic and Religion.* Abridged ed. New York: Macmillan.

FREEMAN, Curtis, James Wm. McCLENDON, Jr., and Rosalee VELLOSO DA SILVA
1999 *Baptist Roots: A Reader in the Theology of a Christian People.* Valley Forge, Pa.: Judson Press.

FREI, Hans W.
1974 *The Eclipse of Biblical Narrative: A Study in Eighteenth and Nineteenth Century Hermeneutics.* New Haven: Yale University Press.
1992 *Types of Christian Theology.* Ed. George Hunsinger and William C. Placher. New Haven: Yale University Press.

FREUD, Sigmund
1927 (1964) *The Future of an Illusion.* Ed. James Strachey. Trans. W. D. Robson-Scott. New York: Doubleday.

FRIESEN, Abraham
1998 *Erasmus, the Anabaptists, and the Great Commission.* Grand Rapids: Eerdmans.

GALLIE, W. B.
1964 *Philosophy and the Historical Understanding.* New York: Schocken.

GAMBONE, Robert L.
1989 *Art and Popular Religion in Evangelical America, 1915–1940.* Knoxville: University of Tennessee.

GAUSTAD, Edwin S.
1987 *Faith of Our Fathers: Religion and the New Nation.* San Francisco: Harper & Row.
1996*a* *Thomas Jefferson: A Religious Biography.* Grand Rapids: Eerdmans.
1996*b* "Disciples of Reason: What Did the Founding Fathers Really Believe?" *Christian History* 15:2 (50): 28-31.

GEERTZ, Clifford
1973 *The Interpretation of Cultures; Selected Essays.* New York: Basic Books.

GILLESPIE, Neal C.
1979 *Charles Darwin and the Problem of Creation.* Chicago: University of Chicago Press.

GLOCK, Hans-Johann
1996 *A Wittgenstein Dictionary.* Oxford, U.K., and Cambridge, Mass.: Blackwell.

GOLDBERG, Michael
1995 *Why Should Jews Survive? Looking Past the Holocaust Toward a Jewish Future.* New York: Oxford University Press.

GOMBRICH, E. H.
1969 (1961) *Art and Illusion: A Study in the Psychology of Pictorial Representation.* Bollingen Series, vol. 35. Princeton, N.J.: Princeton University Press.

GOODMAN, Stan
1993 *Melville's Protest Theism: The Hidden and Silent God in Clarel.* Dekalb: Northern Illinois University Press.

GREEN, Garrett
1995 "Challenging the Religious Studies Canon: Karl Barth's Theory of Religion." *The Journal of Religion* 75:4 (October): 473-86.

GREENE, John C.
1981 *Science, Ideology, and World View: Essays in the History of Evolutionary Ideas.* Berkeley: University of California Press.

GRENZ, Stanley
1983 *Isaac Backus—Puritan and Baptist.* Macon, Ga.: Mercer University Press.

GRIFFIN, David Ray, William A. BEARDSLEE, and Joe HOLLAND
1989 *Varieties of Postmodern Theology.* Albany: State University of New York Press.

GUNTON, Colin E.
1993 *The One, the Three, and the Many: God, Creation, and the Culture of Modernity.* Cambridge, U.K.: Cambridge University Press.

HACKER, P. M. S.
1996 *Wittgenstein's Place in Twentieth-century Analytic Philosophy.* Oxford, U.K.: Blackwell.

HANDY, Robert T., ed.
1966 *The Social Gospel in America: Gladden, Ely, Rauschenbusch.* A Library of Protestant Thought. New York: Oxford University Press.

HARNACK, Adolf
1896 (1961) *History of Dogma (7 Volumes in 4).* Trans. Neil Buchanan. New York: Dover.

HAROUTUNIAN, Joseph
1932 *Piety Versus Moralism: The Passing of the New England Theology.* New York: Henry Holt.
HARTT, Julian N.
1967 *A Christian Critique of American Culture.* New York: Harper & Row.
1977 *Theological Method and Imagination.* New York: Seabury.
HATCH, Nathan O.
1977 *The Sacred Cause of Liberty: Republican Thought and the Millennium in Revolutionary New England.* New Haven: Yale University Press.
1989 *The Democratization of American Christianity.* New Haven: Yale University Press.
HAUERWAS, Stanley
1974 *Vision and Virtue: Essays in Christian Ethical Reflection.* Notre Dame, Ind.: Fides Publishers.
1983 *The Peaceable Kingdom: A Primer in Christian Ethics.* Notre Dame, Ind.: University of Notre Dame Press.
1998 *Sanctify Them in the Truth: Holiness Exemplified.* Nashville: Abingdon Press.
HAUERWAS, Stanley, Chris K. HUEBNER, Harry J. HUEBNER, and Mark Thiessen NATION, eds.
1999 *The Wisdom of the Cross: Essays in Honor of John Howard Yoder.* Grand Rapids: Eerdmans.
HAUERWAS, Stanley, and L. Gregory JONES, eds.
1989 *Why Narrative? Readings in Narrative Theology.* Grand Rapids: Eerdmans.
HEGEL, G(eorg) W(ilhelm) F(riedrich)
1807 (1977) *Phenomenology of Spirit.* Trans. A. V. Miller, with a foreword by J. N. Findlay. Oxford: Oxford University Press.
1832–40 (1895) *Lectures on the Philosophy of Religion.* Trans. E. B. Spiers and J. B. Sanderson. 3 vols. London.
HEIM, S. Mark
1985 *Is Christ the Only Way?* Valley Forge, Pa.: Judson Press.
HEIMERT, Alan
1966 *Religion and the American Mind from the Great Awakening to the Revolution.* Cambridge, Mass.: Harvard University Press.
HENRY, Carl F.
1947 *The Uneasy Conscience of Modern Fundamentalism.* Grand Rapids: Eerdmans.

HERBERT, Christopher
1991 *Culture and Anomie: Ethnographic Imagination in the Nineteenth Century.* Chicago: University of Chicago Press.

HERTZ, Heinrich Rudolf
1894 (1956) *The Principles of Mechanics.* Trans. D. E. Jones and J. T. Walley. New York: Dover.

HEYER, Paul
1982 *Nature, Human Nature, and Society: Marx, Darwin, Biology, and the Human Sciences.* Westport, Conn.: Greenwood Press.

HEYRMAN, Christine Leigh
1997 *Southern Cross: The Beginnings of the Bible Belt.* New York: Knopf.

HICK, John
1989 *An Interpretation of Religion: Human Responses to the Transcendent.* New Haven: Yale University Press.

HIMMELFARB, Gertrude
1959 (1962) *Darwin and the Darwinian Revolution: A Biographical, Historical, and Philosophical Study of the Impact of Darwinism on the Intellectual Climate of the Nineteenth Century.* New York: W. W. Norton & Co.

HUGHES, Philip
1959 *A Popular History of the Reformation.* Garden City, N.Y.: Doubleday.

HUGHES, Robert
1997 *American Visions: The Epic History of Art in America.* New York: Knopf.

HUME, David
1777*a* (1975) *Enquiries: Concerning Human Understanding and Concerning the Principles of Morals.* 3rd ed. Ed. and introduced by L. A. Selby-Bigge. Revised by and notes by P. H. Nidditch. Oxford: Oxford University Press.
1777*b* (1956) *The Natural History of Religion.* Ed. H. E. Root. London: Adam & Charles Black.
1779 (1948) *Dialogues Concerning Natural Religion.* Ed. Henry D. Aiken. New York: Hafner.

JACOB, Margaret C.
1976 *The Newtonians and the English Revolution, 1689–1720.* Ithaca, N.Y.: Cornell University Press.

JAIMES, M. Annete, ed.
1992 *The State of Native America: Genocide, Colonization, and Resistance.* Boston: South End Press.

JAMES, William
1902 (1987) *The Varieties of Religious Experience: A Study in Human Nature*. In *Writings 1902–1910*. New York: Library of America.

JANIK, Allan, and Stephen TOULMIN
1973 *Wittgenstein's Vienna*. New York: Simon & Schuster.

JONES, Greta
1980 *Social Darwinism and English Thought: The Interaction Between Biological and Social Theory*. Sussex, England: Harvester Press.

KANT, Immanuel
1787 (1929) *Critique of Pure Reason*. Ed. Norman Kemp Smith. New York: St. Martin's Press.
1794 (1960) *Religion within the Limits of Reason Alone*. Trans. Theodore M. Greene and Hoyt H. Hudson. New York: Harper & Row.

KERR, Fergus
1997 *Theology After Wittgenstein*. 2nd ed. London: SPCK. (1st ed. Oxford: Blackwell, 1986).

KIERKEGAARD, Søren
1846 (1992) *Concluding Unscientific Postscript to Philosophical Fragments*. Kierkegaard's Writings Vol. XII.1. Princeton, N.J.: Princeton University Press.
1940 *The Present Age (with "Two Minor Ethico-Religious Treatises")*. Trans. Alexander Dru and Walter Lowrie. Oxford, U.K.: Oxford University Press.

KING, Martin Luther, Jr.
1986 *A Testament of Hope: The Essential Writings of Martin Luther King, Jr.* Ed. James M. Washington. San Francisco: Harper & Row.

KLUCKHOHN, Clyde, and Dorothea LEIGHTON
1962 *The Navaho*. Rev. ed. Garden City, N.Y: Doubleday.

KROEBER, A. L., and Clyde KLUCKHOHN
n.d. *Culture: A Critical Review of Concepts and Definitions*. New York: Vintage.

LARSON, Edward, and Larry WITHAM
1997 "Scientists Are Still Keeping the Faith." *Nature* 386 (April 3): 435-36.

LATOURETTE, Kenneth Scott
1953 *A History of Christianity*. New York: Harper & Brothers.

LAW, William
1728 (1966) *A Serious Call to a Devout and Holy Life*. Grand Rapids: Eerdmans.

LAZEROWITZ, Morris, and Alice AMBROSE
1984 *Essays in the Unknown Wittgenstein.* Buffalo, N.Y.: Prometheus Press.

LEWIS, R. W. B.
1955 *The American Adam: Tragedy and Tradition in the Nineteenth Century.* Chicago: University of Chicago Press.

LINCOLN, Andrew T.
1990 *Ephesians.* Word Biblical Commentary. Vol. 42. Dallas: Word.

LINDBECK, George A.
1984 *The Nature of Doctrine: Religion and Theology in a Postliberal Age.* Philadelphia: Westminster.

LINDBERG, David C., and Ronald L. NUMBERS, eds.
1986 *God and Nature: Historical Essays on the Encounter Between Christianity and Science.* Berkeley and Los Angeles: University of California Press.

LITTELL, Franklin H.
1952 (1964) *The Anabaptist View of the Church.* Boston: Starr King Press. Reissued as *The Origins of Sectarian Protestantism.* New York: Macmillan.

LOCKE, John
1689 (1961) *An Essay Concerning Human Understanding.* 2 vols. Ed. John W. Yolton. London: Dent.
1690 (1960) *Two Treatises of Government.* With an introduction and apparatus criticus by Peter Laslett. Cambridge: Cambridge University Press.

LOEWEN, Howard John
1985 *One Lord, One Church, One Hope, and One God: Mennonite Confessions of Faith in North America, An Introduction.* Elkhart, Ind.: Institute of Mennonite Studies.

LUMPKIN, William L.
1969 *Baptist Confessions of Faith.* Rev. ed. Philadelphia: Judson Press.

LUTHER, Martin
1943 *A Compend of Luther's Theology.* Ed. Hugh T. Kerr. Philadelphia: Westminster.

LYELL, Charles
1830–1833 *Principles of Geology.* 3 vols. London: Murray.

LYOTARD, Jean-François
1984 *The Postmodern Condition: A Report on Knowledge.* Trans. Geoff Bennington and Brian Massumi. Minneapolis: University of Minnesota Press.

McCLENDON, James Wm., Jr.

1953 *The Doctrine of Sin and the First Epistle of John: A Comparison of Calvinist, Wesleyan, and Biblical Thought.* Doctoral dissertation, Southwestern Baptist Theological Seminary, Fort Worth, Texas.

1990 *Biography as Theology: How Life Stories Can Remake Today's Theology.* Philadelphia: Trinity Press International (1st ed., Abingdon Press, 1974).

McCLENDON, James Wm., Jr. and John Howard YODER

1990 "Christian Identity in Ecumenical Perspective." *Journal of Ecumenical Studies* 27/3 (Summer: 561-80).

McGUINESS, Brian

1988 *Wittgenstein: A Life.* Volume 1: *Young Ludwig 1889–1921.* Berkeley: University of California Press.

MACKINTOSH, Hugh Ross

1937 *Types of Modern Theology: Schleiermacher to Barth.* London: Nisbet.

McLOUGHLIN, William G.

1967 *Isaac Backus and the American Pietistic Tradition.* Ed. Oscar Handlin. Boston: Little, Brown.

MALCOLM, Norman

1984 *Ludwig Wittgenstein: A Memoir.* (2nd ed.) New York: Oxford.

1994 *Wittgenstein: A Religious Point of View?* Ed. Peter Winch. Ithaca, N.Y.: Cornell University Press.

MALINOWSKI, Bronislaw

1921 *Argonauts of the Western Pacific: An Account of Native Enterprise and Adventure in the Archipelagoes of Melanesian New Guinea.* London: Lund Humphries.

1944 *A Scientific Theory of Culture and Other Essays.* Chapel Hill: University of North Carolina Press.

1967 *A Diary in the Strict Sense of the Term.* Trans., Norbert Guterman. New York: Harcourt, Brace and World.

MALRAUX, André

1974 *The Voices of Silence.* Trans. Stuart Gilbert. London: Paladin.

MALTHUS, Thomas Robert

1798, rev. 1803 (1970) *An Essay on the Principle of Population and a Summary View of the Principle of Population.* Ed. Antony Flew. Harmmondsworth, Middlesex: Penguin.

MARQUIS, Donald M.
1993 *In Search of Buddy Bolden: First Man of Jazz.* Baton Rouge, La.: L.S.U. Press.

MARSDEN, George M.
1994 *The Soul of the American University.* New York: Oxford University Press.

MASTON, Thomas B.
1962 *Isaac Backus: Pioneer of Religious Liberty.* Rochester: American Baptist Publication Society.

MASUZAWA, Tomoko
1998 "Culture." In *Critical Terms for Religious Studies.* Ed. Mark C. Taylor. Chicago: University of Chicago Press, pp. 70-93.

MATHEWS, Donald G.
1977 *Religion in the Old South.* Chicago History of American Religion. Chicago: University of Chicago Press.

MATSON, Wallace I.
1987 *A New History of Philosophy, Volume I, Ancient and Medieval, Volume II, Modern.* New York: Harcourt Brace Jovanovich.

MAY, Henry F.
1949 *Protestant Churches and Industrial America.* New York: Harper & Brothers.

MEAD, Sidney E.
1963 *The Lively Experiment: The Shaping of Christianity in America.* New York: Harper & Row.

MEGILL, David W., and Paul O. W. TANNER
1995 *Jazz Issues: A Critical History.* Madison, Wis.: Brown & Benchmark.

MEGILL, Donald D., and Richard S. DEMORY
1996 *Introduction to Jazz History.* 4th ed. Upper Saddle River, N.J.: Prentice-Hall.

MELVILLE, Herman
1851 (1983) *Moby-Dick.* In *Redburn, His First Voyage; White-Jacket, or The World in a Man-of-War; Moby-Dick, or, The Whale.* Ed. G. Thomas Tanselle. New York: Viking Press (Library of America).
1984 *Billy Budd, Sailor (an Inside Narrative).* In *Pierre, Israel Potter, the Piazza Tales, the Confidence-Man, Uncollected Prose, Billy Budd, Sailor.* New York: Library of America.

MERTON, Robert K.
1938 (1970) *Science, Technology, and Society in Seventeenth Century England.* New York: H. Fertig.

MEYER, Ben F.
1979 *The Aims of Jesus*. London: S.C.M.

MILBANK, John
1990 *Theology and Social Theory: Beyond Secular Reason*. Oxford: Basil Blackwell.
1997 *The Word Made Strange: Theology, Language, Culture*. Oxford, U.K., and Cambridge, Mass.: Blackwell.

MILLER, Perry
1961 "From Covenant to Revival." In Smith and Jamison.
1965 *The Life of the Mind in America: From the Revolution Through the Civil War*. Books One through Three. New York: Harcourt, Brace & World.

MINEAR, Paul Sevier
1946 *Eyes of Faith: A Study in the Biblical Point of View*. Philadelphia: Westminster Press.

MONK, Ray
1990 *Ludwig Wittgenstein: The Duty of Genius*. New York: Free.

MOORE, James R.
1979 *The Post-Darwinian Controversies: A Study of the Protestant Struggles to Come to Terms with Darwin in Great Britain and America 1870–1900*. Cambridge: Cambridge University Press.

MULLINS, Edgar Young
1908 *The Axioms of Religion*. Philadelphia: American Baptist Publication Society.

MURPHY, Nancey
1990 *Theology in the Age of Scientific Reasoning*. Ithaca, N.Y.: Cornell University Press.
1996 *Beyond Liberalism and Fundamentalism*. Valley Forge, Pa.: Trinity Press International.
1997 *Anglo-American Postmodernity: Philosophical Perspectives on Science, Religion, and Ethics*. Boulder, Colo.: Westview Press.

MURPHY, Nancey, and George F. R. ELLIS
1996 *On the Moral Nature of the Universe: Theology, Cosmology, and Ethics*. Minneapolis: Fortress.

MURPHY, Nancey, and James Wm. McCLENDON, Jr.
1989 "Distinguishing Modern and Postmodern Theologies." *Modern Theology* 5:3 (April): 145-68.

MYERS, Ched
1988. *Binding the Strong Man: A Political Reading of Mark's Story of Jesus*. Maryknoll, N.Y.: Orbis.

NEWMAN, John Henry
1845 *An Essay on the Development of Christian Doctrine.* London: James Toovey.
1873 (1960) *The Idea of a University.* Ed. and introduced by Martin J. Svaglic. New York: Holt, Rinehart and Winston.
1877 *The Via Media of the Anglican Church.* 2 vols. London: Longmans, Green (3rd ed., 1918).
1970 *Newman's University Sermons.* Ed. D. M. McKinnon and J. D. Holmes. London: S.P.C.K.

NEWTON, Sir Isaac
1687 (1946) *Philosophiae Naturalis Principia Mathematica (Mathematical Principles of Natural Philosophy).* Ed. F. Cajori, trans. S. Motte. Berkeley: University of California Press.

NIEBUHR, H. Richard
1951 *Christ and Culture.* New York: Harper.

NIEBUHR, Reinhold
1935 *An Interpretation of Christian Ethics.* New York: Harper.
1941–1943 *The Nature and Destiny of Man: A Christian Interpretation. Volume I, Human Nature; Volume II, Human Destiny.* Gifford Lectures. 2 vols. New York: Charles Scribner's Sons.

NIELSEN, Kai
1967 "Wittgensteinian Fideism." *Philosophy* 42:161 (July): 191-209.

NOLL, Mark A.
1977 *Christians in the American Revolution.* Grand Rapids: Eerdmans.

OAKES, Edward T.
1998 "Radical Naturalism." Paper presented at Templeton Course Workshop, Denver, Colorado, March 28.

OKHOLM, Dennis L., ed.
1997 *The Gospel in Black and White: Theological Resources for Racial Reconciliation.* Downers Grove, Ill.: InterVarsity Press.

OSPOVAT, Dov
1981 *The Development of Darwin's Theory: Natural History, Natural Theology, and Natural Selection, 1838–1859.* Cambridge: Cambridge University Press.

PALEY, William
1802 *Natural Theology.* London: Rivington.

PARSONS, Mikeal
1988 " 'Allegorizing Allegory': Narrative Analysis and

Parable Interpretation." *Perspectives in Religious Studies* 15:1 (Spring): 147-64.

PATTISON, George
1991 *Art, Modernity, and Faith.* New York: St. Martin's Press.

PERCY, Walker
1961 *The Moviegoer.* New York: Vintage Books (Random House).
1985 *Conversations with Walker Percy.* Ed. Lewis A. Lawson and Victor A. Kramer. Jackson: University Press of Mississippi.

PETER, John C.
1988 "Wittgenstein's Wonderful Life." *Journal of the History of Ideas* 49 (Jl-S): 495-510.

PHILLIPS, Dewi Z.
1965 *The Concept of Prayer.* London: Routledge & Kegan Paul.
1986 *Belief, Change, and Forms of Life.* Atlantic Highlands, N.J.: Humanities Press International.
1993 *Wittgenstein and Religion.* London: Macmillan.

PIPKIN, H. Wayne, ed.
1994 *Essays in Anabaptist Theology.* Elkhart, Ind.: Institute of Mennonite Studies.

PITCHER, George, ed.
1966 *Wittgenstein: The Philosophical Investigations: A Collection of Critical Essays.* Modern Studies in Philosophy. Garden City, N.Y.: Doubleday.

PLANTINGA, Alvin
1967 *God and Other Minds: A Study of the Rational Justification of Belief in God.* Ithaca: Cornell University Press.
1981 "Is Belief in God Properly Basic?" *Nous* 15:1 (March): 41-51.
1984 "Advice to Christian Philosophers." *Faith and Philosophy* 1(3) (July): 253-71.

PLANTINGA, Alvin, and Nicholas WOLTERSTORFF, eds.
1983 *Faith and Rationality: Reason and Belief in God.* Notre Dame, Ind.: University of Notre Dame Press.

PUTNAM, Hilary
1995 *Pragmatism: An Open Question.* Cambridge, Mass., and Oxford, U.K.: Blackwell.

RABOTEAU, Albert J.
1978 *Slave Religion: The "Invisible Institution" in the Antebellum South.* New York: Oxford University Press.

RAHNER, Karl, and H. VORGRIMLER

1965 *Theological Dictionary.* Ed. C. Ernst, trans. R. Strachan. New York: Herder & Herder.

RASHDALL, Hastings

1895 (1936) *The Universities of Europe in the Middle Ages.* 3 vols. Ed. F. M. Powicke and A. B. Emden. Oxford: Oxford University Press.

RAUSCHENBUSCH, Walter

1907 (1967) *Christianity and the Social Crisis.* Ed. Robert D. Cross. New York: Macmillan.

1912 *Christianizing the Social Order.* New York: Macmillan.

1916 *The Social Principles of Jesus.* New York & London: Association Press.

REYNOLDS, David S.

1995 *Walt Whitman's America: A Cultural Biography.* New York: Knopf.

RHEES, Rush, ed.

1981 *Ludwig Wittgenstein: Personal Recollections.* Totowa, N.J.: Rowman and Littlefield.

RHOADS, David, and Donald MICHIE

1982 *Mark as Story: An Introduction to the Narrative of a Gospel.* Philadelphia: Fortress.

ROLSTON, Holmes, III

1994 "Does Nature Need to Be Redeemed?" *Zygon* 29:2 (June): 205-29.

RORTY, Richard

1979 *Philosophy and the Mirror of Nature.* Princeton, N.J.: Princeton University Press.

RUDWICK, Martin

1981 "Senses of the Natural World and Senses of God: Another Look at the Historical Relation of Science and Religion." In *The Sciences and Theology in the Twentieth Century.* Ed. A. R. Peacocke. Notre Dame: University of Notre Dame Press, pp. 241-61.

RUSE, Michael

1979 *The Darwinian Revolution.* Chicago: University of Chicago Press.

RUSSELL, Robert J., Nancey MURPHY et al., eds.

1999 *Neuroscience and the Person: Scientific Perspectives on Divine Action.* Vatican City State and Berkeley: Vatican Observatory and Center for Theology and the Natural Sciences.

RUSSELL, Robert J., W. S. STOEGER, and F. J. AYALA, eds.
1998 *Evolutionary and Molecular Biology: Scientific Perspectives on Divine Action.* Vatican City State and Berkeley: Vatican Observatory and Center for Theology and the Natural Sciences.

RYAN, John Augustine
1906 *A Living Wage: Its Ethical and Economical Aspects.* New York: Macmillan.
1916 *Distributive Justice: The Right and Wrong of Our Present Distribution of Wealth.* New York: Macmillan.

SALES, Grover
1984 *Jazz, America's Classical Music.* Englewood Cliffs, N.J.: Prentice-Hall.

SCHAFF, Philip
1846 *What Is Church History? A Vindication of the Idea of Historical Development.* Philadelphia: J. B. Lippincott.

SCHLEIERMACHER, Friedrich
1799 (1958) *On Religion: Speeches to Its Cultured Despisers.* Trans. John Oman. New York: Harper & Row.

SCHOOF, Mark
1970 *A Survey of Catholic Theology 1800–1970.* Trans. N. D. Smith. Paramus, N.J.: Paulist Newman Press.

SCHWEITZER, Albert
1906 (1968) *The Quest of the Historical Jesus.* Trans. W. B. D. Montgomery; ed. James M. Robinson. New York: Macmillan.

SHELDON, Charles Monroe
1890? *In His Steps.* Chicago: Thompson & Thomas.
1914 *Jesus Is Here! Continuing the Narrative of In His Steps.* New York: Hodder & Stoughton, George H. Doran.

SHENK, Wilbert R.
1999 *Changing Frontiers of Mission.* Maryknoll, N.Y.: Orbis.

SHENK, Wilbert R., ed.
1983 *Exploring Church Growth.* Grand Rapids: Eerdmans.
1984 *Anabaptism and Mission.* Scottdale, Pa.: Herald Press.

SLOAN, Douglas
1994 *Faith and Knowledge: Mainline Protestantism and American Higher Education.* Louisville: Westminster-John Knox.

SMART, Ninian
1983 *Worldviews: Crosscultural Explorations of Human Beliefs.* New York: Scribner's.

SMITH, Adam
1776 (1966) *An Inquiry Into the Nature and Causes of the Wealth of Nations.* 2 vols. Oxford: Oxford University Press.

SMITH, James M.
1987 "Convictional Pluralism and the Aristotelian Project." Presented to the Pacific Coast Theological Society, Berkeley, California.

SMITH, James Ward, and A. Leland JAMISON
1961 *The Shaping of American Religion.* Religion in American Life, Volume I. Princeton, N.J.: Princeton University Press.

SMITH, Theophus
1994 *Conjuring Culture: Biblical Formations of Black America.* New York: Oxford University Press.

SMITH, Timothy L.
1957 (1976) *Revivalism and Social Reform: American Protestantism on the Eve of the Civil War.* Nashville/New York: Abingdon Press. (Reissued by Peter Smith, Gloucester, Mass.)

SMITH, Wilfred Cantwell
1963 *The Meaning and End of Religion.* New York: Macmillan.

SPICER, Edward H.
1962 *Cycles of Conquest: The Impact of Spain, Mexico, and the United States on the Indians of the Southwest, 1533–1969.* Tucson: University of Arizona Press.

STASSEN, Glen
1998*a* "Opening Menno Simon's *Foundation-Book* and Finding the Father of Baptist Origins Alongside the Mother of Calvinist Congregationalism." *Baptist History and Heritage* 33:2 (Spring): 34-44.

1998*b* "Revisioning Baptist Identity by Naming Our Origin and Character Rightly." *Baptist History and Heritage* 33:2 (Spring): 45-54.

STASSEN, Glen, D. M. YEAGER, and John Howard YODER
1996 *Authentic Transformation: A New Vision of Christ and Culture* with an Essay by H. Richard Niebuhr. Nashville: Abingdon.

STEUER, Axel D., and James Wm. McCLENDON, Jr., eds.
1981 *Is God GOD?* Nashville: Abingdon.

STOUT, Harry
1986 *The New England Soul: Preaching and Religious Culture in Colonial New England.* New York: Oxford University Press.

1996 "Preaching the Insurrection." *Christian History* 15:2 (50).

STRONG, Josiah
1885 *Our Country: Its Possible Future and Its Present Crisis.* New York: American Home Mission Society.

SUITS, Bernard
1978 *The Grasshopper: Games, Life, and Utopia.* Toronto, Canada: University of Toronto Press.

SYKES, Stephen
1984 *The Identity of Christianity: Theologians and the Essence of Christianity from Schleiermacher to Barth.* Philadelphia: Fortress.

TAGORE, Rabindranath
1916 *The King of the Dark Chamber.* New York: Macmillan.

TANNER, Paul O. W., David W. MEGILL, and Maurice GEROW
1997 *Jazz.* Eighth ed. Madison, Wis.: Brown & Benchmark.

TAYLOR, Charles
1975 *Hegel.* Cambridge: Cambridge University Press.

THOMPSON, Philip E.
1999 "A New Question in Baptist History: Seeking a Catholic Spirit Among Early Baptists." *Pro Ecclesia* 8/1 (Winter): 51-72.

THORNTON, John Wingate
1970 *The Pulpit of the American Revolution.* New York: Burt Franklin.

TILLEY, Maureen A.
1996 *Donatist Martyr Stories: The Church in Conflict in Roman North Africa.* Liverpool, U.K.: Liverpool University Press.

TILLICH, Paul
1919 (1987) "On the Idea of a Theology of Culture." In *Visionary Science: A Translation of Tillich's "On the Idea of a Theology of Culture" with an Interpretive Essay.* Translator and essayist Victor Nuovo. Detroit: Wayne State University Press.
1951–63 *Systematic Theology.* 3 vols. Chicago: University of Chicago Press.
1957 *The Protestant Era.* Abridged edition. Chicago: University of Chicago Press.
1959 (1978) *Theology of Culture.* Ed. Robert C. Kimball. New York: Oxford University Press.
1963 *Christianity and the Encounter of World Religions.* New York: Columbia University Press.

TOLSTOY, Leo
1881 (1892) *Kurze Darstellung des Evangelium.* Trans. from Russian by Paul Lauterbach. Leipzig: Philip Reclam.

1960 *Lift Up Your Eyes: the Religious Writings of Leo Tolstoy.* New York: Julian Press.

TOMBERLIN, James E., and Peter van INWAGEN, eds.

1985 *Alvin Plantinga.* Dordrecht/Boston/Lancaster: D. Reidel.

TOULMIN, Stephen

1990 *Cosmopolis: The Hidden Agenda of Modernity.* New York: Free.

TRACY, David

1975 *Blessed Rage for Order: The New Pluralism in Theology.* New York: Seabury.

TURNER, Frank M.

1978 "The Victorian Conflict Between Science and Religion: A Professional Dimension." *Isis* 69:356-76.

Von WRIGHT, George Henrik

1982 *Wittgenstein.* Minneapolis: University of Minnesota Press.

WALLS, Andrew F.

1990 "Conversion and Christian Continuity." *Mission Focus* 18/2 (June): 17-21.

WARNER, Michael J.

1970 "Protestant Missionary Activity Among the Navajo, 1890–1912." *New Mexico Historical Review* 45 (July): 209-32.

1977 *Protestant Missionary Work with the Navajo Indians from 1846–1912.* Ph.D. dissertation, University of New Mexico.

WARNER, R. Stephen

1993 "Work in Progress Toward a New Paradigm for the Sociological Study of Religion in the United States." *American Journal of Sociology* 98:5 (March): 1044-93.

WEIL, Simone

1973 *Waiting for God.* Trans. Emma Craufurd. New York: Harper & Row.

WEISBERGER, Bernard A.

1958 *They Gathered at the River.* Boston: Little, Brown.

WELCH, Claude

1972–85 *Protestant Thought in the Nineteenth Century, Volume I, 1799–1870, Volume II, 1870–1914.* New Haven: Yale University Press.

WESTPHAL, Merold

1999 "Taking Plantinga Seriously." *Faith and Philosophy* 16:2 (April): 173-81.

WHITE, Andrew Dickson
1896 (1960) *A History of the Warfare of Science with Theology in Christendom.* 2 vols. New York: Dover.

WHITE, Michael G.
1991 "Evolution of a Cultural Tradition." *Cultural Vistas, a Journal of the Louisiana Endowment for the Humanities* (Winter): 18-38.

WHITEHEAD, Alfred North
1925 (1967) *Science and the Modern World.* New York: Free Press.

WHITMAN, Walt
1982 *Walt Whitman: Complete Poetry and Collected Prose.* Includes *Leaves of Grass* (1855) and *Leaves of Grass* (1891–92). New York: Library of America.

WILLIAMS, Bernard
1972 *Morality: An Introduction to Ethics.* New York: Harper & Row.

WILLIAMS, Martin
1967 *Jazz Masters of New Orleans.* New York: Macmillan.

WILLIAMS, Raymond
1958 *Culture and Society 1780–1950.* New York: Columbia University Press (Penguin edition, 1993).

WILLIAMS, Roger
1644 *The Bloody Tenent, of Persecution, for Cause of Conscience, Discussed. . . .* in Williams, 1963: Vol. 3.
1963 *The Complete Writings of Roger Williams.* 7 vols. New York: Russell and Russell. (A reprint of the Narragansett edition, with a seventh volume added.)

WILSON, James L.
1990 *Clementine Hunter: American Folk Artist.* Gretna, La.: Pelican Publishing Co.

WILSON, Jonathan R.
1995 "From Theology of Culture to Theological Ethics: The Hartt-Hauerwas Connection." *Journal of Religious Ethics* 23:1 (Spring): 149-64.
1996 *Theology as Cultural Critique: The Achievement of Julian Hartt.* Macon, Ga.: Mercer University Press.

WINCH, Peter
1958 *The Idea of a Social Science and Its Relation to Philosophy.* London: Routledge and Kegan Paul.

WINK, Walter
1992 *Engaging the Powers.* Philadelphia: Fortress.

WOOD, Ralph C.
1988 *The Comedy of Redemption: Christian Faith and Comic Vision in Four American Novelists.* Notre Dame: University of Notre Dame Press.

YODER, John Howard
1964 *The Christian Witness to the State.* Newton, Kans.: Faith and Life Press.
1968 *The Pacifism of Karl Barth.* Scottdale, Pa.: The Church Peace Mission.
1971 (1992) *Nevertheless: The Varieties and Shortcomings of Religious Pacifism.* Revised edition. Christian Peace Shelf Series. Scottdale, Pa.: Herald Press.
1977 *The Original Revolution: Essays on Christian Pacifism.* Scottdale, Pa.: Herald Press (1st edition, 1971).
1979 "Stone and Morgan Lectures." Unpublished typescript.
1984 *The Priestly Kingdom: Social Ethics as Gospel.* Notre Dame, Ind.: University of Notre Dame Press.
1985 *He Came Preaching Peace.* Scottdale, Pa., and Kitchener, Ont.: Herald Press.
1987 *The Fullness of Christ.* Elgin, Ill.: Brethren Press.
1992 *Body Politics: The Practices of the Christian Community Before the Watching World.* Nashville: Discipleship Resources.
1994*a* *The Royal Priesthood: Essays Ecclesiological and Ecumenical.* Ed. Michael G. Cartwright. Grand Rapids: Eerdmans.
1994*b* *The Politics of Jesus: Vicit Agnus Noster.* 2nd ed. Grand Rapids: Eerdmans (1st ed. 1972).
1997 *For the Nations: Essays Public and Evangelical.* Grand Rapids: Eerdmans.

YOUNG, Robert M.
1985 *Darwin's Metaphor: Nature's Place in Victorian Culture.* Cambridge: Cambridge University Press.

Index of Names and Topics

Biblical Index